TRANSFORMATIONAL TRENDS IN GOVERNANCE AND DEMOCRACY

National Academy of Public Administration

Modernizing Democracy:
Innovations in Citizen Participation

Edited by Terry F. Buss, F. Stevens Redburn, and Kristina Guo

Meeting the Challenge of 9/11:
Blueprints for More Effective Government

Edited by Thomas H. Stanton

Foreign Aid and Foreign Policy:
Lessons for the Next Half-Century

Edited by Louis A. Picard, Robert Groelsema, and Terry F. Buss

About the Academy

The National Academy of Public Administration, like the National Academy of Sciences, is an independent, nonprofit organization chartered by Congress to identify emerging issues of governance and to help federal, state, and local governments improve their performance. The Academy's mission is to provide "trusted advice"—advice that is objective, timely, and actionable—on all issues of public service and management. The unique source of the Academy's expertise is its membership, including more than 650 current and former Cabinet officers, members of Congress, governors, mayors, legislators, jurists, business executives, public managers, and scholars who are elected as Fellows because of their distinguished contribution to the field of public administration through scholarship, civic activism, or government service. Participation in the Academy's work is a requisite of membership, and the Fellows offer their experience and knowledge voluntarily.

The Academy is proud to join with M.E. Sharpe, Inc., to bring readers this and other volumes in a series of edited works addressing major public management and public policy issues of the day.

The opinions expressed in these writings are those of the authors and do not necessarily reflect the views of the Academy as an institution.

Transforming Public Leadership for the 21st Century

Edited by Ricardo S. Morse
Terry F. Buss
C. Morgan Kinghorn

Foreword by David M. Walker

NATIONAL ACADEMY OF
PUBLIC ADMINISTRATION

TRANSFORMATIONAL TRENDS IN
GOVERNANCE AND DEMOCRACY

M.E.Sharpe
Armonk, New York
London, England

Library of Congress Cataloging-in-Publication Data

Transforming public leadership for the 21st century / edited by Ricardo S.
Morse, Terry F. Buss, and C. Morgan Kinghorn.
    p. cm. — (Transformational trends in governance & democracy)
  Includes bibliographical references and index.
  ISBN 978-0-7656-2041-5 (cloth : alk. paper)— ISBN 978-0-7656-2042-2 (pbk. : alk. paper)
  1. Public administration—United States. 2. Leadership—United States. 3. Organizational
change—United States. 4. Political leadership—United States. I. Morse, Ricardo S., 1971–
II. Buss, Terry F. III. Kinghorn, C. Morgan, 1946–

JK421.T86 2007
352.23'6—dc22   2007002132

Printed in the United States of America

We dedicate this book to the memory of

Larry Terry,

scholar, colleague, public servant.

Contents

Foreword
    The Honorable David M. Walker   ix
Preface and Acknowledgments
    Terry F. Buss   xiii

1. The Transformation of Public Leadership
    Ricardo S. Morse and Terry F. Buss   3

Part I. Politics, Administration, and Public Leadership

2. Transformational Leadership
    Newt Gingrich   23

3. Public Leadership as Gardening
    H. George Frederickson and David S.T. Matkin   34

4. Twenty-First-Century Career Leaders
    Dwight Ink   47

5. Leadership by Top Administrators in a Changing World:
New Challenges in Political-Administrative Relations
    James H. Svara   69

Part II. Leadership Frames

6. Trans-leadership: Linking Influential Theory and
Contemporary Research
    Matthew R. Fairholm   105

7. The Changing Leadership Landscape: A Military Perspective
    George Reed and Georgia Sorenson   125

8. Leading at the Edge of Chaos
   Nanette M. Blandin — 138

9. Transformational Stewardship: Leading Public-Sector Change
   James Edwin Kee, Kathryn Newcomer, and S. Mike Davis — 154

Part III. Leadership and Collaboration

10. Leadership for the Common Good: Creating Regimes of Mutual Gain
    John M. Bryson and Barbara C. Crosby — 185

11. Creating Public Value Using Managed Networks
    Edward DeSeve — 203

12. Consensus Building and Leadership
    John B. Stephens — 221

13. The Challenge of Leading through Networks: Institutional
    Analysis as a Way Forward
    Brent Never — 243

Part IV. Leading Change in Different Contexts

14. Leadership and Management in Local Government
    Karl Nollenberger — 263

15. Four-Frame Leadership in Authentic, Results-oriented Management
    Reform: Case Studies in Canada and the United States
    Brendan F. Burke and Bernadette C. Costello — 284

16. Leadership Strategies for Large-scale IT Implementations
    in Government
    Marilu Goodyear and Mark R. Nelson — 308

17. Government's New Breed of Change Agents:
    Leading the War on Terror
    Daniel P. Forrester — 324

18. Leadership and Ethics in Decision Making by Public Managers
    Christine Gibbs Springer — 344

About the Editors and Contributors — 357
Index — 365

Foreword

THE HONORABLE DAVID M. WALKER
COMPTROLLER GENERAL OF THE UNITED STATES

In the twenty-first century, our nation faces, both at home and overseas, a range of unprecedented challenges and opportunities that know no geopolitical boundaries. These challenges and opportunities include powerful demographic trends, such as an aging population and slowing workforce growth; terrorism and other security threats; impact of globalization on issues ranging from trade to public health; and rapid advances in science and technology. Due to the retirement of the baby boomers and the subsequent "baby bust," along with rising health care costs and relatively low federal revenues as a percentage of the economy, the United States also faces a growing fiscal imbalance that, absent meaningful reforms, threatens future generations with staggering debt levels and tax burdens.

To address these and other complex issues, our government must move beyond long-standing but often ineffective ways of doing business. Too much of today's government is based on economic, demographic, national security, workforce, and other conditions from the 1950s and 1960s. In addition, too many existing government spending and tax policies are on autopilot. This situation is neither prudent nor sustainable. What we need are more leaders who understand the urgent need to transform government to better position our country for the future.

It is time to ask a series of simple but profound questions: What is the proper role of the federal government in the twenty-first century? How should it be organized? Who should do the related work? How should we define and measure success? How much will government cost? How should we pay for government? In my view, we need nothing less than a top-to-bottom review of programs and policies to determine which of them remain priorities, which need to be overhauled or combined, and which have outlived their usefulness.

Overall government transformation may take a generation or more to complete. Success will take the combined and sustained efforts of elected, appointed, and career officials for a long period of time.

Today, however, leaders in both the public and private sectors tend to suffer from myopia and tunnel vision. Public officials often dwell on this year's budget submission and the next election cycle. In doing so, they tend to lose sight of the "big picture" and the challenges that lie ahead. All too often, an issue has to reach "crisis proportions" before government will act.

More than ever, we need leaders in government who think strategically, take a long-term and broader view, and are concerned with achieving positive results today while discharging their stewardship responsibility. An ability to innovate is also important. The government of tomorrow will be shaped by men and women who are unafraid to think outside the box and try out new approaches to solve current and emerging challenges.

My personal definition of an effective leader is someone who generates positive results and manages risk today while, at the same time, helps to create a more positive future with and through others. My favorite president, Theodore Roosevelt, summed up this leadership philosophy by saying, "The best executive is one who has sense enough to pick good men to do what he wants done, and self-restraint enough to keep from meddling with them while they do it." This quote needs to be updated to reflect the important contributions being made by women today, but otherwise it still rings true.

Since becoming Comptroller General of the United States in November 1998, I have made achieving a cultural transformation at the U.S. Government Accountability Office (GAO)—formerly the General Accounting Office—a priority. Today, GAO has adopted a more strategic, collaborative, integrated, and results-oriented approach to doing its work. We now use four interrelated institutional performance dimensions to gauge success: delivering measurable results, such as financial and nonfinancial benefits; meeting legitimate needs of our congressional clients; hiring, retaining, empowering, and rewarding a top-quality workforce; and partnering with other entities and institutions in government and in different sectors, both domestically and internationally, on issues of shared interest and concern.

Different individuals bring varied approaches and styles to leadership roles. In general, however, I believe that the following six principles are relevant to executives both inside and outside of government.

First, have a plan that focuses on results. If you fail to plan, you are likely to fail. As the Boy Scout motto states, "Be prepared." Early in my tenure at GAO, we established a strategic plan to guide our efforts to serve Congress and the American people. This document defines the agency's mission, lays out the key public policy themes that GAO plans to focus on, and lists specific objectives that GAO hopes to achieve. GAO issued its first strategic plan in the spring of 2000, and we have been updating it periodically to reflect changing national needs and priorities. All of GAO's budgeting and spending decisions are now linked to the strategic plan. People, dollars, and technology are deployed with an eye toward achieving immediate results as well as the agency's long-term goals.

Attitude and effort matter, but in the end it is results that count most. At GAO, a portion of employee compensation is now tied to achieving the goals of our strategic plan. Public reporting of results to key stakeholders is also important. GAO issues an annual report that informs Congress and the American people about the agency's accomplishments and its plans for the coming year.

Second, lead by example. Philosopher and missionary Albert Schweitzer said, "Example is leadership." Leadership provides an opportunity and obligation to show others the way forward and demonstrate how things can and should be done. Those at the top must set the professional and ethical tone for the rest of the organization. They should set high standards for others to follow, practice what they preach, and deliver on their promises. After all, leaders who are credible and trusted are more likely to motivate and inspire others.

Third, do what is right. Leaders today must be competent, and they need to bring energy and enthusiasm to the job. Equally important, they should have a well-developed sense of right and wrong and empathy for others. Recent scandals in both government and private industry underscore the fact that ethics and integrity are an indispensable element of true leadership. The law and professional standards prescribe only a minimally acceptable standard of conduct. We need leaders who set their sights higher and have the courage to do what is right for today and tomorrow. Life is full of difficult decisions, and the right choice is not always easy or popular. In my experience, however, principled choices based on sound facts and reasoned analyses are the surest way to a good reputation. And in the end, all any of us are left with is our reputation.

At GAO, we have adopted a set of core values—accountability, integrity, and reliability—that define the nature of our work, the character of our people, and the quality of our products. These core values supplement the law and applicable professional standards. Among other things, they help guide our dealings with our congressional clients and ensure that every congressional request is treated fairly and consistently.

Fourth, innovate and communicate. Many of the most basic processes and procedures at federal agencies are years out of date. From investing in new computer technology to modernizing job classification and compensation systems, to adopting best management practices from the private sector, federal agencies need to consider new approaches to help them do their jobs better within current and expected resource levels.

An ongoing, meaningful, and two-way dialogue with employees is likewise essential. Leading change depends on an ability to articulate a compelling vision and the need for action. At the same time, true leaders are unafraid to listen and learn from others at all levels of their organization. Government leaders must be willing to tap into the ideas of rank-and-file employees who, being on the front lines and in their jobs for the longer term, often have the best sense of what is working well, what needs to be fixed, and how problems can best be solved. A successful leader tries to gather the best available information from every corner of his or her organization before arriving at a decision.

At GAO, we have a twenty-two-member Employee Advisory Council that meets regularly with me and other top GAO executives to discuss issues of mutual interest and concern. GAO also regularly solicits employee input and feedback on all aspects of the agency's operations. For example, as comptroller general, I make it a point to talk to all GAO employees via live videocasts at least once a quarter to explain my thoughts on possible and pending policy changes and other key matters. During these sessions, I typically answer a number of questions from GAO employees.

In knowledge-based organizations such as GAO, employees are the most important asset, and they must be heard and, when appropriate, heeded. This is not to suggest that leadership requires acquiescence to popular sentiment. As Harry Truman once asked, "How far would Moses have gone if he had taken a poll in Egypt?"

Fifth, partner for progress. Maximizing value and managing risk requires partnering both internally and externally—especially in times of constrained resources. For example, GAO has used matrix management principles successfully to bring together experts from different parts of the agency to add value to and reduce risk on a wide range of challenging assignments. We also partner externally with accountability and other public interest organizations, domestically and internationally. After all, the more players who are working toward a common goal in an integrated and coordinated manner, the more likely you will be successful.

Sixth, be a steward. True leaders take seriously their stewardship responsibilities —not just to their organization but to society as a whole and to future generations. In my view, leaders have an inherent obligation to leave their organization, whether it is a federal agency or a corporation, not just better off when they leave than when they came but also better positioned for the future. Stewardship requires prudence today while preparing for tomorrow. Responsible leaders seek positive results, but not by putting their organization's or their nation's long-term future at risk.

In the case of the federal government, individual leadership by itself is unlikely to yield lasting results. A capable and motivated workforce is also essential. Yet most federal agencies have neglected human capital management for years. Too many agencies today lack enough people with the right skills. Unfortunately, despite the wave of federal retirements that is expected in the future, few agencies have succession plans in place. A growing human capital crisis now threatens the ability to carry out their missions. The situation is so serious that GAO put "strategic human capital management" on its list of the highest-risk areas in government. Government transformation will occur only when agency heads and other top officials begin to view federal employees as part of a team—their team—and treat them as an asset to be developed rather than a cost to be cut.

In the wake of recent scandals from Wall Street to Washington, the future direction of leadership in this country is a subject worthy of serious discussion. The National Academy of Public Administration should be congratulated for taking the time and effort to assemble so many contributions on public-sector leadership from such distinguished authors.

Preface and Acknowledgments

It is a privilege to present this collection of articles representing the latest thinking on public leadership to practitioners, scholars, and students of public administration, and to the public at large interested in why government and governance are the way they are, where they might be headed, and what should be done about them. I have long been interested in public leadership as the offspring of two parents who practiced it well, although quite differently. My father—a career Army infantry officer and war hero, who rose from the rank of private to lieutenant colonel in just twenty years—was widely acknowledged as a highly effective leader throughout his career. To this day, I still receive contact from men in their mid-eighties whose loyalty to my father has not diminished over more than half a century. My mother—a compassionate, tireless volunteer worker for those in need—continues to lead volunteers in numerous charities ranging from hospital auxiliary women's groups through assisting victims with debilitating diseases and injuries to operating food pantries for the poor. I cannot estimate the thousands of people she has helped over the past sixty years. I mention them in tribute, because their lives represent the very best in public leadership, demonstrating some fundamental truths about leadership, truths explored variously in the chapters in this book.

This work is part of a series of edited books, Transformational Trends in Governance and Democracy, that captures the latest thinking in public management. The books collectively represent what we believe are fundamental, transformational trends emerging in governance and democracy. Each book addresses the questions: How is governance or democracy being transformed? What impact will transformations have? Will forces arise to counter transformations? Where will transformations take governance and democracy in the future?

The National Academy of Public Administration sponsors the series in partnership with M.E. Sharpe, Inc. Many of the chapters in the series have been contributed by Academy Fellows and professional staff. We have also drawn on leaders in public management representing different ways of thinking about public management. I am editing the series overall, with well-known experts editing individual volumes. Initial books in the series include the following titles, available at www.mesharpe.com:

- *Meeting the Challenge of 9/11: Blueprints for More Effective Government*, edited by Thomas H. Stanton (2006).
- *Modernizing Democracy: Innovations in Citizen Participation*, edited by Terry F. Buss, F. Stevens Redburn, and Kristina Guo (2006).
- *Foreign Aid and Foreign Policy: Issues for the Next Half-Century*, edited by Louis Picard, Robert Groelsema, and Terry F. Buss (2007).

The next book in the series, *Innovations in Public Leadership Development,* edited by Ricardo Morse, Terry F. Buss, and C. Morgan Kinghorn (forthcoming 2008), is a companion to this work. Contributors offer insights into how to develop public leaders.

Acknowledgments

Rick Morse and Terry Buss would like to thank Scott Belcher, executive vice president, for marshalling Academy resources in developing this project; Morgan Kinghorn, then Academy president, not only for promoting the project widely across the institution but also for participating in the project as co-editor; and Academy President Howard Messner for his support and encouragement. Rick Morse would also like to thank his family for their patience and support and for the UNC Chapel Hill School of Government for supporting his work on this project.

The Academy would also like to thank M.E. Sharpe, especially Harry Briggs, Elizabeth Granda, and Angela Piliouras, for their assistance and encouragement in the preparation of this manuscript for publication.

Terry F. Buss
Columbus, Ohio

Transforming Public Leadership for the 21st Century

1

The Transformation of Public Leadership

RICARDO S. MORSE AND TERRY F. BUSS

Public leadership—the way it is practiced and how it is conceived—is undergoing a transformation, corresponding with changes in the public sector generally that some have termed *the new governance* (Salamon 2002). What exactly is public leadership? Is it *really* changing? If so, how? Further, how *should* public leadership change? What does this mean for the theory and practice of public administration? These are the questions taken up in this book.

Patricia Ingraham recently commented that "it is impossible to overlook the limited extent of systematic analysis of *public* leadership issues" (2006, 361). Larry Terry notes the "neglect," in terms of scholarly attention, of what he called "bureaucratic leadership" (2003, 4). Matthew Fairholm also observes that "in the face of technicism, strict policy implementation, and a fear of administrative discretion, it has often been a significant struggle to discuss the philosophy of leadership in public administration" (2004, 577).

We concur with these assessments, particularly when speaking of public leadership by non-politicians. For some reason, the body of literature on public leadership, that is, the study of leadership from a public-sector perspective, is very small, especially in comparison to the enormous offerings from business schools and management gurus.[1] And a great majority of what is called *public leadership* is focused on what might be better termed *political* leadership; that of presidents, governors, and other high-level government executives (elected and political appointments). We argue that public leadership is, more than anything, the domain of those in the public service; in other words, public administration. Certainly "political leadership" is part of the public leadership landscape, but we leave that discussion, for the most part, to others.

This book focuses on public leadership from an unabashed public administration point of view. The contributors to this volume, though representing a variety of perspectives, bring into focus the work of public servants in different venues. We believe that public leadership is distinctive and that generic treatments of leadership are not sufficient for the public leaders navigating the "transformation of governance" (Kettl 2002).

In this introduction, we first clarify what we mean by the terms *leadership, public leadership*, and *transformation* and otherwise define the scope of this book. We then outline some of the trends transforming governance and, by extension, public leadership, and we offer an overview of the main dimensions of the transformation. Finally, we provide an introduction and overview of the chapters in this book.

Public Leadership and Transformation

It is important that we clarify terms. First, we should speak about what we mean by *leadership*. Most scholarship on leadership defines it (in one way or another) as a process of influence where a person or group influences others to work toward a common goal (e.g., Northouse 2004, 2–4; Gardner 1990, 1). Thus a dynamic is set up with leaders influencing followers to do something. However, the leader-follower construct takes us only so far. In a "shared-power" world (Crosby and Bryson 2005) where "nobody [is] in charge" (Cleveland 2002), the leadership-as-motivating-followers notion often breaks down. Thus, Harlan Cleveland's more simple definition of leadership as "bringing people together to make something different happen" may be the more appropriate definition for today and into the future (2002, xv). The distinction is subtle yet important. The former, more conventional understanding assumes a leader-follower dynamic whereas the latter does not.

With that simple definition of leadership in place, we now turn to what *public* leadership means. It is difficult to characterize the public leadership literature, much less the leadership literature in general, in any definitive way. What is apparent to any analyst is that use of public leadership varies greatly. We find it useful to sort the literature into three perspectives.

First, policy elite, or *political leadership,* focuses on political leaders, either elected or high appointees. *Leader,* in this sense, refers to people in government with positional authority who are legislators or senior executives. Much of the so-called public leadership literature represents this perspective, examining the behavior of top government leaders (Kellerman and Webster 2001). More specifically, these studies examine what these powerful, very visible, leaders do to create and sustain change. Burns's *Leadership* (1978), for example, really focuses on political leadership. The many studies of U.S. presidents exemplify this branch of scholarship (e.g., Greenstein 2004).

Second, public *organizational leadership* focuses on formal leadership within public organizations: on "leadership" positions in public organizations—from line supervisor on up—and how those "leaders" lead organizational change and produce results. Van Wart's (2005) textbook, *Dynamics of Leadership in Public Service,* is an example of scholarship aimed squarely at organizational leaders in the public sector. Another example of public leadership research from this perspective is Behn's (1991) study of organizational leaders in the Massachusetts Department of Public Welfare.

Finally, what many generically call *public leadership*—and what others have labeled "collaborative leadership" (Chrislip 2002), "catalytic leadership" (Luke

1998), and "leadership for the common good" (Crosby and Bryson 2005)—focuses not on public "leaders" (people in formal leadership positions in government) so much as on *the process of creating public value* inside and outside government and at all levels of organization. Here we think of public leadership as a process that extends beyond public organizations and beyond formal leaders. It reflects the realities of a "shared power world" where governance is the product of many organizations—not just government. While formal leaders still play a prominent role, there is more of an emphasis on those—with and without formal leadership positions—that lead from "the middle" as opposed to "the top." Whereas public organizational leadership focuses squarely on *intra*organizational context, this broad notion of public leadership emphasizes *inter*organizational context. This broad, process-focused view of public leadership is captured by the Center for Public Leadership's interpretation of "acts, large and small, of individuals and groups as they tackle challenges facing a community or society" (Pittinsky et al. 2006, 17).

Certainly considerable overlap exists among these three variants of public leadership; it is really a matter of focus. One perspective looks at political success, another at organizational, and the other on solving public problems. Crosby and Bryson argue that public leadership as "leadership for the common good" includes political and organizational leadership (2005). It is not so important to draw hard distinctions as it is to understand that some treatments of public leadership look broadly at processes among a wide variety of actors, in and out of government, that produce public value, while others look more narrowly at the workings of political elites or organizational leaders. The majority of attention to "public leadership" tends to be of this latter variety. However, more attention ought to be paid to public leadership that is non–big-P politics. Effective leadership within and across public organizations is just as crucial to resolving America's "leadership crisis" (Pittinsky et al. 2006) as is reforming Congress.

The contributors to this volume, for the most part, bring into focus organizational and public (or collaborative) leadership, though important aspects of political leadership are touched upon in several of the chapters. We feel that the transformative forces on public administration lead to a greater emphasis on public—as in interorganizational—leadership, though steady intraorganizational leadership remains essential. While political leadership more often makes the headlines, it is the more pervasive, on-the-ground leadership that is changing communities and policy domains in exciting and innovative ways. And as Dwight Ink points out in this volume, more global, political success is highly dependent on alignment with the non-political leadership that is the public administration.

We also need to be very clear about what we mean in selecting this book's title. We are not referring to the specific idea of "transforming leadership" as articulated by James McGregor Burns (1978). Rather, we are thinking more broadly about how the public leadership landscape is changing or transforming. The context in which public leadership occurs is transforming. The practice of public leadership is transforming. And the way we think about public leadership is transforming.

Of course, these three transformations are intertwined and linked. The changing context leads to changes in practice. Changes in practice lead to changes in how we think about leadership. The changes in how we conceptualize leadership also shape practice, which in turn shapes or alters the context.

For at least a decade now, public administration scholars have been making the case that changing circumstances have altered the field from a study of government to one of "governance." In this sense, governance is more than what governments do; rather, it is collective actions taken to solve public problems. This "new governance" thus shifts emphasis away from the agency toward a broad array of "tools" that might include contracting out, interagency or intersectoral collaborations, and so on (Salamon 2002). The transformation toward the new governance coincides with a transformation of leadership in the public sector.

Oftentimes we speak of transformational change in the sense of something new that *replaces* something outmoded. This is perhaps the wrong connotation here. In saying that public leadership is being transformed, we do not mean to imply that it is being replaced by something entirely new. Rather, consider the biological synonym for transformation: metamorphosis. The change from a caterpillar to a butterfly is remarkable and dramatic, yet the organism itself has not been replaced; rather, it has changed from one state to another. The change we speak of is the result of significant changes in context (discussed in the next section). These environmental changes require leadership to evolve, to transform; to go through a metamorphosis of sorts. The change keeps (hopefully) the lessons from the past, the elements of good management and leadership, of high-performing organizations, and so on. Essential components of good public administration remain. Yet, radical changes in context mean we must go beyond these conceptions of leadership and reach for something more.

The title of the book can thus be interpreted in a variety of ways. On the one hand, we could argue that leadership is going through a transformation—it is being transformed—and this book reports on that transformation. On the other hand, we could argue that, given our circumstances in the dawn of the new millennium, we need to transform present conceptions of leadership. In other words, this book could be about how we should go about transforming leadership. We see this book as taking both positions simultaneously. In certain respects, leadership is already being transformed. Discussions of the "new governance" provide ample evidence that the practice of public leadership is changing. Further, conceptions of public leadership are beginning to include broader ideas going well beyond specifically leading public organizations (e.g., Crosby and Bryson 2005; Luke 1998).

Yet, there is too little scholarship, in our view, on the leadership dimensions of the new governance. We still find that there is much to do in transforming how public leadership is thought about, practiced, and taught. The language of leadership is still by and large dominated by a hierarchical, organizational, positional paradigm and has not caught up with new notions of governance, networks, and collaboration.

The chapters here fill some of these gaps. The entries in this volume present various perspectives on public leadership, offering insights into both how public leadership is changing and how it should be changed. Before discussing the chapters, we first highlight some of the trends transforming governance and outline the main themes of transforming public leadership.

Transformational Trends

What contextual changes are so significant as to require a transformation in how we think about and practice public leadership? In a word, globalization. Incredible advances in transportation, communication, and information technologies have shrunk the world, or rather, made it "flat" to use Thomas Friedman's analogy (2005). The major changes in the public sector we are seeing today are very much connected to the broader societal, economic, and political changes brought about by globalization.

As we have entered into a new millennium, we have also entered a new phase of globalization—what Friedman labels "Globalization 3.0"—that has profound social, economic, and political repercussions. Friedman explains that "Globalization 1.0" (1492–1800) was about nation-states "breaking down walls and knitting the world together, driving global integration" (2005, 9). The world shrunk from "large" to "medium" size. "Globalization 2.0" (1800–2000) was about the expansion of multinational corporations. Advances in "hardware" such as railroads in the early years and telecommunications in the latter years drove increased global integration, shrinking the world further to a size "small" (2005, 8–9). Around the time of the new millennium, Friedman argues, "Globalization 3.0" began to emerge with the convergence of several forces, most prominently advances in software and IT infrastructure. The world is now size "tiny" and the playing field for individuals is getting flatter and flatter (2005, 8–9).

The flattening described by Friedman is leading to a global capitalism that is not only turning China and India into economic superpowers but also making borders and other "boundaries" less meaningful. Globalization means that cities can no longer afford to think in terms of competing with their neighbors because now the competition is among regions on a global scale. Friedman argues that the emerging global market is "making some very new politics" (2005, 201). The world is moving from a "primarily vertical (command and control) value-creation model to an increasingly horizontal (connect and collaborate)" model that "affects everything" from how "communities and companies define themselves, where companies and communities stop and start, how individuals balance their different identities as consumers, employees, shareholders, and citizens, and what role government has to play." All of this, according to Friedman, requires a "sorting out" on a global scale (2005, 201–205).

The unanswered questions in Friedman's analysis—all of the "sorting out" that is to occur—is very much the domain of public leadership. How the redefinitions work out, who wins and who loses, and what it all means for communities, states, and nation-states will be determined in large measure by public leaders in the broadest sense, again, realizing that these leaders can come from all sectors. Our collective sense making of the "globalization" phenomena only underscores the idea of "nobody in charge" that Harlan Cleveland has been speaking about for three decades now.

Several branches off of the main trunk of globalization are directly applicable to public leadership. The first is the global wave of administrative reform, labeled by many as the New Public Management (NPM). At its core, NPM is about "running government like a business." Denhardt and Denhardt note that NPM has "literally swept the nation and the world" (2002, 13). "The common theme in the myriad of applications of these ideas has been the use of market mechanisms and terminology, in which the relationships between public agencies and their customers is understood as involving transactions similar to those that occur in the marketplace" (Denhardt and Denhardt 2002, 13). Public leadership, within the NPM paradigm, is often envisaged as the bold, risk-taking entrepreneur, much like private-sector heroes such as Jack Welch or Lee Iacocca.

However, in all fairness, the reality of NPM is not as one-sided as its critics suggest. Critics of NPM characterize it in stark terms, emphasizing the private-sector influence on the public sector and warning of the threat such ideas pose to democratic governance. While the philosophical arguments are important and not unrelated to practice, the reality is that NPM has reshaped the public sector in a variety of ways, including, perhaps paradoxically, a stronger emphasis on collaboration and citizen engagement.

A recent study by the IBM Center for the Business of Government identifies six trends that are "transforming government" that all connect to the broader "trend" of NPM. These trends, which can be seen as corresponding with NPM as well as the more general globalization phenomena, are:

1. "Changing the rules" of government so that managers have more flexibility to manage effectively. This includes administrative procedures, financial management, and even structural reform (e.g., the creation of the Department of Homeland Security).
2. "Using performance measurement." The public sector is clearly becoming more performance oriented, and the use and sophistication of performance measures by governments at all levels has greatly increased in recent decades.
3. "Providing competition, choice, and incentives." A wide range of market-based tools such as public-private partnerships, incentives, outsourcing, and vouchers are increasingly being used to create public value.
4. "Performing on demand." More and more, public organizations are expected to provide service 24/7 and be able to respond to non-routine events effectively. Information technology has been an important tool in transforming government to one that "performs on demand."

5. "Engaging citizens." Public agencies are becoming more innovative in their attempts to involve citizens, both as a result of increased demand for openness and transparency and as a realization that such involvement enhances the legitimacy of the enterprise.
6. "Using networks and partnerships." This is perhaps the most dramatic trend as it relates to public leadership. The idea of network governance is superseding the traditional image of government as the top-down bureaucracy. Public management today occurs in a network setting, across organizations within government as well as across sectors (Abramson, Breul, and Kamensky 2006).

These six trends capture very well the transformation of governance that, we argue, stems from the larger transformation that is globalization.

In addition to these broad trends, we also want to briefly note three contextual trends that are having and will increasingly have a major impact on public leadership in the coming years. The first is the twin demographic shifts that have been termed the "browning" and "graying" of America. The so-called browning of America refers to the fact that Asians and Hispanics are the fastest-growing groups in the United States and that population projections predict "nonwhite ethnic minority groups" will surpass non-Hispanic whites in the United States by the middle of this century (Johnson, Farrell, and Guinn 1997). The "graying" of society refers to the fact that "in the years ahead, the age structure of most advanced industrial societies will be unlike anything previously seen in human history, with both the average age of the population and the absolute number of old people increasing dramatically" (1997, 1055). The President's Council on Bioethics reports startling statistics (e.g., the fastest-growing age group in the United States is eighty-five-plus) to underscore the large impact of our aging society (2005). Clearly, the browning and graying of America are major drivers for social, economic, and political changes and challenges.

Like the browning of the U.S. population, the second major contextual factor we wish to point out is also connected in interesting ways with globalization. While there is no precise label for it, we will suffice to refer to it here as the increased presence of global threats. Global terrorism, border security, the avian flu, and natural disasters, to name a few, are all related in that they present major, discontinuous threats that place a huge burden on government and require a whole different level of public leadership. These global threats are all examples of major public problems that cross jurisdictions, time, and other "boundaries." These problems are not only "interconnected" (Luke 1998), they are also to a large extent unpredictable, as Hurricanes Katrina and Rita so painfully exposed. The increasing presence of these global threats dramatically highlights the need for effective public leaders.

It might be argued that the final contextual element is also connected to globalization. That is, we live in an age of low trust not just in government but in all large institutions generally (see Pittinsky et al. 2006). Public leaders operate in a climate of built-in suspicion of government and a general antitax sentiment. The leadership landscape is not a friendly one.

The trends discussed briefly here highlight the need for greater networking and collaboration—for a greater focus on interorganizational leadership. On the other hand, the same forces mentioned earlier may be making the ability to collaborate easier. As the world becomes "flatter," as the actors become more diverse, as the challenges are greater, and the faith in monolithic solutions wanes, the door is more open than ever for a transformation of public leadership along the lines of the transformation Friedman explains in his account of "Globalization 3.0." As "the world starts to move from a primarily vertical (command and control) value-creation model to an increasingly horizontal (connect and collaborate) creation model" (2005, 201), the transformation of public leadership must, in turn, move toward one of connecting and collaborating.

Overview of the Book

As mentioned earlier, in public administration an intellectual struggle over NPM has occurred. However, seen another way, the NPM is public management. Public administration, not just in the United States but across most developed countries, has become more businesslike, entrepreneurial, market driven, and performance based.[2] Alternative perspectives that emphasize democratic (as opposed to market-based) values, encapsulated so well in Denhardt and Denhardt's *The New Public Service* (2002), serve not so much as a true alternative to the NPM but as a needed corrective. In other words, in our day and age when governments are more market driven and more focused on results, it is important for leaders to remember that government is not just like business and that democratic values must be at the core of the public service.

We highlight some of these tensions in part I, "Politics, Administration, and Public Leadership," chapter 2, "Transformational Leadership" by former Speaker of the House, Newt Gingrich. Gingrich surveys the transformational changes in technology and communications, arguing that public management needs to catch up, not with small adjustments here and there but with a paradigm shift of how we view what we do. His main point is that rather than tweaking at the margins, we should ask "how would we do it today" rather than how should we modify what we have been doing. Gingrich's transformed public leadership echoes the terrain carved out by NPM over the last two decades. It is the image of the entrepreneur, getting things done and explaining later, focusing on results. Gingrich speaks of culture change, abandoning what most refer to pejoratively as the "bureaucratic culture" and creating organizations that meet the needs of today's flat world.

In chapter 3, George Frederickson and David Matkin's "Public Leadership as Gardening" offers a sharp contrast to Gingrich's essay and to the change-agent model of leadership generally. As opposed to the paradigm-shifting, revolutionary change agent Gingrich hopes for, Frederickson and Matkin ask us to think of leading organizations, and even transforming them, as a gentle, patient, subtle, adaptive process. This process is a lot like gardening. Though the connection is not made explicitly, the public leader as gardener metaphor echoes Larry Terry's theory of administrative conservatorship (2003), a pointed and deliberate contrast to NPM notions of public leadership.

Dwight Ink's "Twenty-First-Century Career Leaders" (chapter 4) also offers an important contrast to calls by some for more radical change. Ink, reflecting on his long and distinguished career in the federal bureaucracy, warns that if transforming means discarding the whole to invent something totally new, we are misguided. A transformation of public leadership should be informed not only by present needs but by lessons of the past. Ink highlights the critical role of federal career administrators, who he calls "operational leaders." He highlights many contemporary factors that limit the leadership effectiveness of these career public servants, among them a preoccupation with reinvention or always seeking new ways of doing things. Each new wave of reform, he argues, has failed to draw effectively on earlier lessons.

Ink further argues that presidential agendas often fail or are slow to succeed due in large part to the failure to utilize career leadership and the too-strong reliance on political leadership. He offers advice to career leaders working with new administrations as well as to new administrations that want to be truly effective in realizing their goals. Ink also makes an important distinction between adopting and adapting. NPM reforms seem too intent on adopting private-sector practices wholesale. But the public and private sector are not the same, so public leaders must rather seek to adapt (not adopt) practices in appropriate ways. Ink's discussion turns to crisis management as a prime example of the need to let career leaders lead. With direct application to contemporary issues such as Hurricane Katrina, Iraq, and presidential transitions, Ink's essay makes a strong case that now is the time to establish effective political-administrative connections and utilize career leadership.

Chapter 5, "Leadership by Top Administrators in a Changing World: New Challenges in Political-Administrative Relations" by Jim Svara expands upon some of the themes staked out by Ink. Svara's rich, sweeping essay surveys administrative leadership within the context of political-administrative relations in the West. Images of administrative leadership have evolved from the "aspiring" administrator of the nineteenth century to the "assured" administrator of the twentieth century, and now a new phase of the "adaptive" administrator is taking shape in the twenty-first century.

Svara finds that in recent years political officials are asserting more authority, scope of influence, or "leadership" on public organizations, and thus the capacity of administrators as policy leaders seems to be diminishing. A related issue for administrative leaders is the reality that more of the actors they must work with are not under their control. So while in some respects leadership influence may be diminishing within the organization due to more political influence, administrators are seen to have more influence in network or extraorganizational settings. Therefore, public (administrative) leaders need to be adaptive in this new climate of greater political influence and working across boundaries. Svara's answer is the notion of "complementarity" between administrators and elected officials. Administrative leaders must be more politically astute and political leaders must appreciate and utilize the work of what Ink calls "career leaders" in government.

In part II, "Leadership Frames," we offer four chapters that present leadership models that illustrate the richness and complexity of leadership theory and what it has to offer public leadership. In chapter 6, "Trans-leadership: Linking Influential Theory and Contemporary Research," Matthew Fairholm offers a philosophical discussion that examines three types of leadership all sharing the prefix *trans-*: transactional, transformational, and transforming. While transactional and transformational theories emphasize organizational change, Fairholm explains that a third—transforming—is about personal change. The first two are organizational and rely mostly on formal authority, whereas transforming leaders are everywhere. This notion of transforming leadership corresponds in interesting ways with the broad notion of public leadership discussed earlier in this chapter and featured in part III of this book.

George Reed and Georgia Sorenson in chapter 7, "The Changing Leadership Landscape: A Military Perspective," offer a fascinating study of the changing nature of leadership in the military that offers lessons for not just military but all public leadership. The authors demonstrate the strategic implication of "tactical" choices to underscore a broader argument that the different "levels" of leadership are no longer as distinct as we once thought. They present a model of leadership in practice where direct, organizational, and strategic leadership overlap one another, thus indicating a shift not only in practice but in the training needs of emerging leaders and in the way we study leadership in the public sector.

In chapter 8, "Leading at the Edge of Chaos," Nanette Blandin provides a sketch of what she and others see as a new leadership paradigm drawn from the "new sciences" of chaos and complexity. The interconnected nature of public problems, the shrinking of the world due to information, communications, and technology advances, and other contextual factors detailed throughout this book call not for a new or adapted skill set but rather a whole new paradigm, shifting our thinking away from hierarchy and command and control and toward relationships. Because predictability and control are oxymoronic in terms of "leading" complex systems, the public leader must come to think of herself as a facilitator, a catalyst, a collaborator in an ongoing process of change, as opposed to the traditional leader who directs from the top.

In chapter 9, "Transformational Stewardship: Leading Public-Sector Change," Jed Kee, Kathryn Newcomer, and Mike Davis bring together two disparate images of the public servant—the steward and the change agent—to introduce the idea of the transformational steward. Transformational stewards effectively bring about change in public organizations but are grounded by a deep commitment to the agency's mission and to the public interest in general. Transformational stewardship can be and is exercised by appointees, career civil servants in executive leadership roles, and other managers in public agencies; however, the manifestation of leadership will be different in each case. Each has particular strengths regarding different aspects of transformational stewardship; thus the authors conclude that "effective transformation requires the collective, complementary action of transformational stewards at all levels within the organization." The transformational stewardship model strikes a balance between the need to adapt and change with the need to be true and consistent with core public values, in a way addressing all of the concerns outlined in part I.

Part III, "Leadership and Collaboration," presents scholarship that speaks directly to the challenge of leading in a shared-power world or, put differently, leading in a network setting. John Bryson and Barbara Crosby's chapter 10, "Leadership for the Common Good: Creating Regimes of Mutual Gain," maps out the terrain of "regimes of mutual gain." The authors illustrate that the different "sectors" of government, nonprofit, market, media, and community are all building blocks for creating public value, each of them with particular strengths and weaknesses. The creation of networks across these sectors that produce public value do so in a way that takes advantage of each sector's strength while making up for weaknesses. The authors highlight the role of public leadership in the development of these regimes and suggest that a stakeholder analysis by sector is the key first step for public leaders seeking to build and develop regimes of mutual gain that create public value. An example is given to illustrate what this kind of analysis looks like in a real-world setting.

In chapter 11, "Creating Public Value Using Managed Networks," Ed DeSeve, similar to Gingrich, argues that today's context requires new forms of organizing. He too points out how the bureaucratic mind-set stifles the kind of innovation we need in the public sector today. The Public Value Network (PVN) is presented as a twenty-first-century tool to meet current challenges. DeSeve argues that public value should be the organizing principle of public agencies and that the role of leadership is critical in creating public value. In today's networked society, though, public value is often the product of work across organizations within government as well as across sectors. DeSeve views these purposefully created "Managed Networks" not as replacements for hierarchy but rather important tools for creating public value in our networked society. He offers a research tool to analyze PVN that includes a Typology of different kinds of networks and a series of Critical Elements of PVN. He demonstrates the research tool with three case studies.

Chapter 12, "Consensus Building and Leadership," by John Stephens, connects the ever-growing literature on consensus building with our discussion of public leadership. Public leaders in the network age need a broader skill set, including the ability to forge consensus among disparate stakeholders. As leadership happens more in the middle than from the top, the careful art of creating win-win solutions is more and more important. Stephens demonstrates the complexity of thought and practice that falls under the "consensus building" moniker and offers careful words of advice to public leaders seeking to better understand these processes. He further elaborates how the practitioners and analysts of consensus processes need to be more attentive to the role of leadership. Consensus processes often evoke a "leaderless" sensibility when in fact convening and facilitating collaborative processes are very much acts of leadership.

Chapter 13 also provides new insight on public leadership in the context of what some call "collaborative public management" (Agranoff and McGuire 2003). Brent Never's "The Challenge of Leading through Networks: Institutional Analysis as a Way Forward" provides a much needed institutional analysis of leading in networked settings. Institutions refer to the "rules of the game" that are contained in an organization's culture. Leading networks involves understanding that actors from different organizations have their own sets of rules from their organizations and their own mental models developed within their home organizational context. Effective network leadership, therefore, involves creating new rules of the game and understanding and shaping mental models in ways that help the different actors work together effectively. A careful explanation of mental models demonstrates why it is important for leaders to understand the social psychological basis of action. It is through these subjective considerations that leaders can be most effective. This is no easy task, but Never persuasively makes the case for a task of network leadership being the discernment of others' hierarchy of mental rules in order to know which can be altered and which cannot.

Part IV, "Leading Change in Different Contexts," concludes this volume with five chapters demonstrating why the study of public leadership is so important. Contributors examine public leadership in various contexts and from several perspectives. They all support Bob Behn's (1991) conclusion that leadership, indeed, "counts."

In chapter 14, "Leadership and Management in Local Government," Karl Nollenberger surveys the role of leadership in local government as exercised by professional managers and mayors. One of the important trends identified is the increasing leadership role managers take on in their communities. Another finding is a move toward stronger mayors in council-manager forms of government. However, Nollenberger argues that the search for stronger political leadership does not mean diminishing the importance of managerial leadership or the end of the council-manager form of government. The kind of mayoral leadership people are looking for is the facilitative leadership as articulated by Jim Svara, a form of leadership that is complementary to managerial leadership that emphasizes innovation and change within the organization and policy leadership in the community.

Nollenberger also highlights differences in the political aspect of leadership between mayors and managers. Mayors' political leadership is often connected to partisan politics and direct responsiveness to citizens whereas managers' political leadership is more about policy making, visioning, and general political astuteness in a non-partisan way. One is "big-P" political while the other is "little-p." Both, however, are community leaders, and both can complement the other in the quest for good government and governance.

Chapter 15 also looks at public leadership at the local level, however, this time focusing specifically on the implementation of management reforms. Brendan Burke and Bernadette Costello's "Four-Frame Leadership in Authentic, Results-oriented Management Reform: Case Studies in Canada and the United States" draws on rich empirical data of "reputation leaders" in "results-oriented management" to help us better understand the role of leadership in differentiating "authentic" results-oriented organizations from the more common organizations that are results oriented in name only. They use Bolman and Deal's "four frame" approach to examine eight model jurisdictions and unpack and carefully explain what authentic, or Holistic, reform looks like. Organizational culture is key to authentic, results-oriented reform, and leadership is about shaping culture.

Chapter 16, "Leadership Strategies for Large-scale IT Implementations in Government," by Marilu Goodyear and Mark Nelson offers practical advice for public leaders in the context of IT implementation. The authors demonstrate that IT transformation projects in the public sector are exceedingly complex and, like other forms of organizational change, require strong leadership to be successful. These changes have a major impact not only on the organizations that carry them out but on the general public. Reviewing several strands of relevant literature, the authors summarize the leadership requirements for successful large-scale IT implementation. It appears that the technical aspects of IT implementation are much more straightforward than the organizational aspects. Public leaders working with IT-related transformation must be cognizant of the "soft" leadership skills, including communication, trust building, and so forth.

The context shifts to the War on Terror in chapter 17, "Government's New Breed of Change Agents: Leading the War on Terror," by Daniel Forrester. An empirical study of "change agents" from the Departments of Defense and Homeland Security and the Central Intelligence Agency identifies practices of these key leaders in the War on Terror, develops a profile of these change agents, and seeks to understand how they measure success. Forrester argues that the "new breed of change agents" is doing things very differently than in the past.

However, as we try to emphasize with our notion of transformation, the management practices identified are not new; earlier "career leaders" such as Dwight Ink exemplify the profile Forrester identifies in today's dynamic leaders in the War on Terror. What has changed is the context, and with the War on Terror the change is dramatic and transformative. Good leadership practices are still good leadership practices, but they must be adapted to a new context.

Forrester's snapshot of today's leaders gives us a sense of how leadership is transforming or adapting to meet today's needs. Forrester's chapter is full of practical, on-the-ground advice from many contemporary leaders in one of the most complex and high-profile domains of public leadership, the War on Terror. In this chapter, we hear directly from these leaders. Speaking of public leaders, "These people see value in enterprise-wide thinking versus stove pipes," explained Keith Herrington of the Defense Intelligence Agency. This is critical. Distinguishing organizational versus enterprise thinking is perhaps one of the most salient themes in this book and is highlighted here by none other than leaders from the front on the War on Terror.

Chapter 18, "Leadership and Ethics in Decision Making by Public Managers" by Christine Gibbs Springer, concludes this volume. Here Springer utilizes survey and interview data of public managers to examine the ethical and decision-making aspects of public leadership. Springer's research identifies and articulates seven characteristics of effective public leaders and explains what ethical decision making by public leaders means. Springer also offers wisdom based on her distinguished career, explicating how to measure ethical performance and how to structure difficult decisions faced by public leaders.

The Challenges of Transformation

Our contributors approach the topic of public leadership from a variety of perspectives and contexts, yet certain themes stand out and cut across them all. These themes present to us several challenges as we move forward in the transformation of public leadership. Public leaders and those who study public leadership would do well to consider these challenges in the years ahead.

The first set of challenges follows the strong thread of what we might call inter-organizational, or network, leadership. It is quite clear that today's context demands high levels of coordination and collaboration. Hurricanes Katrina and Rita and the intelligence community's problems are but two recent examples of how far we have to go in this respect. As practitioners and students of public administration survey the public leadership landscape, the reality of "network governance" is clear.

Yet our structures, systems, and, for the most part, our conventional approaches to leadership are hierarchical. In many cases, there are not adequate incentives to collaborate, or rather, there are institutional disincentives that stem from being in a hierarchical system. It is foolish to think that hierarchy can be replaced, however. So the question becomes how to lead collaboratively, across organizations, within a hierarchical context. As several chapters in this volume demonstrate, public leaders are adapting and answering this question as they go along, thanks to their pragmatic sensibilities and tremendous commitment to the public good. Clearly though, more research is needed on how to lead networks within a hierarchical system.

A related issue has to do with maintaining the integrity of our public organizations in this age of network governance. As boundaries (jurisdictional, organizational, and so on) are becoming more and more blurry, what must public leaders do to simultaneously be conservators, to use Terry's term (2003), as well as innovators and change agents? "Creating public value" and "focusing on results" are guiding values that are hard to argue with. This outcome orientation, coupled with the environmental factors discussed earlier, leads naturally to governance by network. But as the forms change and as leadership changes, how can we ensure that our institutions are not eroded in the process? Is it possible to be a change agent, an innovator, a network leader, and still "protect and maintain administrative institutions in a manner that promotes or is consistent with constitutional processes, values, and beliefs" (Terry 2003, 24)? Does transforming public leadership mean abandoning the notion of public leadership including the conserving of public institutions?

Another set of issues raised here has to do with the increasing politicization of administration and the damaging effects this has on the ability of public servants to lead. To what extent are politicians exerting more partisan politics into administration? How are public managers dealing with this when it occurs? How does the increasing political influence affect organizational leadership and interorganizational leadership? One of the big take-aways for politicians from this book would be to value and respect the leadership role played by public administrators and to work in partnership with them. On the flip side, administrative leaders must become more politically savvy and adaptive in this time of increasing political influence on administrative operations.

On the other side of the political influence issue is the increasing leadership role public administrators are playing in their communities. We might call this the problem of little-p politics. The New Public Service model outlines a very active leadership role for public administrators that goes well outside their organization's boundaries (Denhardt and Denhardt 2002). Denhardt and Campbell's (2006) recent articulation of transformational leadership for the public sector similarly highlights a very public role for public administrators. This line of thought has been a strong undercurrent in the public administration literature for a long time. Some have even traced this strong democratic ethos back to the founding of the republic (McSwite 1997). In any case, there is ample evidence that administrators are, in fact, seeing themselves in a more public role (Nalbandian 1999). The questions this raises are similar to those previously mentioned regarding conflicting roles. What are the risks to becoming more "political" in this sense? What institutional constraints might disrupt such behavior? On the other hand, what is gained by "opening up" public organizations more in this way?

The "new paradigm" that Gingrich presciently calls for is already emerging. Perhaps we have just not settled on a name yet. Following the public administration literature, "the new governance" or perhaps just plain "governance" are prime candidates for an overarching name for this new paradigm. Public leadership practice is changing, and as the authors in this volume can attest, the way we are talking about public leadership is changing. At the root of this change is a radical shift, away from hierarchy and command-and-control leadership based on vertical relationships of power and authority and toward one of lateral relationships of shared power.

Mary Follett has been called the "prophet of management." Warren Bennis once said that "just about everything written today about leadership and organizations comes from Mary Parker Follett's writings and lectures" (Graham 2003, 178). Indeed, her notion of "power-with" (as opposed to "power-over") perfectly captures the essence of what public leadership means in the network age. The following passage, from an essay, "The Essentials of Leadership," is remarkably apt today for something written in a time of top-down leadership (1995, 172).

> Leader and followers are both following the invisible leader—the common purpose. The best executives put this common purpose clearly before their group. While leadership depends on depth of conviction and the power sharing coming there from, there must also be the ability to share that conviction with others, the ability to make purpose articulate. And then that common purpose becomes the leader.

This is good description of how public leadership might be accomplished across traditional organizational boundaries. Public leaders everywhere who are seeking to create public value recognize that this task requires collaborating across traditional boundaries (organizational, jurisdictional, and sectoral). Effective leadership in this context is less about motivating followers to work toward one's own vision than it is discovering or creating that common purpose, or common vision, that becomes the driving force for joint work and shared accountability. These new public leaders produce not just results but results that matter.

Notes

1. The huge leadership literature that emanates from management scholars is either explicitly private-sector focused or what might be termed "generic." The generic approach to leadership (and management) assumes applicability across sectors. Public sector examples may occasionally be used, but by and large the leaders in question are private-sector leaders. The implicit argument that management is management and leadership is leadership is flawed, however. Public leadership is different. While there are similarities across sectors, the context of leadership in the public sector is distinctive, a point articulated well in Rainey (2003; see chapter 3). Public leadership is about creating public value, which is not a goal shared by the private sector.

2. These issues are explored at length in *Performance-Based Management and Budgeting*, edited by Steve Redburn, Robert Shea, and Terry Buss, M.E. Sharpe, 2007.

References

Abramson, Mark A., Jonathan D. Breul, and John M. Kamensky. 2006. *Six Trends Transforming Government.* Washington, DC: IBM Center for the Business of Government.

Agranoff, Robert, and Michael McGuire. 2003. *Collaborative Public Management: New Strategies for Local Governments.* Washington, DC: Georgetown University Press.

Behn, Robert D. 1991. *Leadership Counts: Lessons for Public Managers from the Massachusetts Welfare, Training, and Employment Program.* Cambridge, MA: Harvard University Press.

Burns, James MacGregor. 1978. *Leadership.* New York: Harper & Row.

Chrislip, David D. 2002. *The Collaborative Leadership Fieldbook.* San Francisco: Jossey-Bass.

Cleveland, Harlan. 2002. *Nobody in Charge: Essays on the Future of Leadership.* San Francisco: Jossey-Bass.

Crosby, Barbara C., and John M. Bryson. 2005. *Leadership for the Common Good: Tackling Public Problems in a Shared-Power World.* 2nd ed. San Francisco: Jossey-Bass.

Denhardt, Janet V., and Kelly B. Campbell. 2006. "The Role of Democratic Values in Transformational Leadership." *Administration and Society* 38 (5): 556–72.

Denhardt, Janet V., and Robert B. Denhardt. 2002. *The New Public Service.* Armonk, NY: M.E. Sharpe.

Fairholm, Matthew R. 2004. "Different Perspectives on the Practice of Leadership." *Public Administration Review* 64 (5): 577–90.

Friedman, Thomas L. 2005. *The World Is Flat: A Brief History of the Twenty-First Century.* New York: Farrar, Straus and Giroux.

Gardner, John W. 1990. *On Leadership.* New York: Free Press.

Graham, Pauline, ed. 2003. *Mary Parker Follett—Prophet of Management: A Celebration of Writings from the 1920s.* Cambridge, MA: Harvard Business School Press.

Greenstein, Fred I. 2004. *The Presidential Difference: Leadership Style from FDR to George W. Bush.* 2nd ed. Princeton, NJ: Princeton University Press.

Ingraham, Patricia W. 2006. "Leadership: The Challenge and the Opportunity." *American Review of Public Administration* 36 (4): 361–2.

Johnson, James H., Jr., Walter C. Farrell, Jr., and Chandra Guinn. 1997. "Immigration Reform and the Browning of America: Tensions, Conflicts and Community Instability in Metropolitan Los Angeles." *International Migration Review* 31 (4): 1055–95.

Kellerman, Barbara, and Scott W. Webster. 2001. "The Recent Literature on Public Leadership Considered." *The Leadership Quarterly* 12: 485–518.

Kettl, Donald F. 2002. *The Transformation of Governance: Public Administration for Twenty-First Century America.* Baltimore: Johns Hopkins University Press.

Luke, Jeffrey S. 1998. *Catalytic Leadership: Strategies for an Interconnected World.* San Francisco: Jossey-Bass.

McSwite, O.C. 1997. *Legitimacy in Public Administration: A Discourse Analysis.* Thousand Oaks, CA: Sage.

Nalbandian, John. 1999. "Facilitating Community, Enabling Democracy: New Roles for Local Government Managers." *Public Administration Review* 59 (3): 187–96.

Northouse, Peter G. 2004. *Leadership: Theory and Practice.* 3rd ed. Thousand Oaks, CA: Sage.

Pittinsky, Todd L., Seth A. Rosenthal, Laura M. Bacon, R. Matthew Montoya, and Weichun Zhu. 2006. *National Leadership Index 2006: A National Study of Confidence in Leadership.* Cambridge, MA: Harvard University, Center for Public Leadership, John F. Kennedy School of Government.

Rainey, Hal G. 2003. *Understanding and Managing Public Organizations.* 3rd ed. San Francisco: Jossey-Bass.

Salamon, Lester M. 2002. "The New Governance and the Tools of Public Action: An Introduction." In *The Tools of Government: A Guide to the New Governance,* ed. Lester M. Salamon, 1–47. Oxford: Oxford University Press.

Taking Care: Ethical Caregiving in Our Aging Society. 2005. Report of the President's Council on Bioethics. Leon R. Kass, Chairman. Washington, DC, September.

Terry, Larry D. 2003. *Leadership of Public Bureaucracies: The Administrator as Conservator.* 2nd ed. Armonk, NY: M.E. Sharpe.

Van Wart, Montgomery. 2005. *Dynamics of Leadership in Public Service: Theory and Practice.* Armonk, NY: M.E. Sharpe.

Part I

Politics, Administration, and Public Leadership

2

Transformational Leadership

NEWT GINGRICH

I am delighted to join you this evening. I remember speaking with some of you in Atlanta several years ago. But I must say this is a more prestigious field tonight—being here at the Ronald Reagan Center and being this year's James E. Webb Lecturer.[1]

Paradigm Shift

I chose to focus my remarks tonight on improving governance overseas. I want to start by suggesting a couple reference points. One is an article in *Science Magazine* from October 1964 titled "Strong Inference" by John Platt. Platt made the argument for why microbiology and high-energy physics were making progress at a faster rate than many other aspects of science. His essential argument was that there had become areas in which the cost of the experiment was so expensive that you actually had to have thought through what you were trying to learn and that you had to force a strong inference that was testable. Therefore, you were simply getting a very rapid branching of information flow.

This trend is captured differently in Thomas Kuhn's *The Structure of Scientific Revolutions* (1996), which essentially argues that very large-scale change tends to be generational. If you go back and look at most of the physicists available in 1895, almost none of them believed in quantum mechanics or relativity. They died believing that Einstein and Planck were nuts. But the younger physicists actually looked at the evidence and overwhelmingly selected the ideas of Max Planck and Albert Einstein. *The Structure of Scientific Revolutions* is a very interesting and thoughtful book, but it is overdone to some extent. For example, when plate tectonics were proven by the research of the International Geophysical Year, virtually all of geology accepted the change in a year because the evidence was so overwhelming. This discovery was a profound change, because plate tectonics—the idea that the continents float on these plates—had been soundly repudiated when Wegener first proposed it in 1915 and was considered lunatic. Interestingly, paleontologists had always assumed plate tectonics were true, because they couldn't explain certain patterns of fossil distribution without assuming that the continents fit together. But standard geologists all thought it was nuts. Yet, once the decision was made, the migration was stunningly fast.

I should mention one example that is worth considering: the last chapter of Richard Dawkins's book *The Selfish Gene* (1989), in which he essentially argues that the purpose of genes is to reproduce themselves—and really successful genes have more descendants than unsuccessful ones. The last chapter makes the argument that humans have invented a cultural adaptation to biology. Then, Dawkins writes about the concept of a mean as a way of describing culture; for example, Mozart outcompeted all other cultural patterns of music in his generation. Therefore, you are likely to listen to Mozart in more places today than you are to listen to any of his contemporaries. That was an example of an exact parallel to genetic competition being done inside cultures.

From my vantage point, Jim Webb confronted the challenge that we do not have the same kind of structured pattern of information for human organizational behavior that we have for what we think of as science—partly because there's a lot more variability and partly because we don't spend nearly as much energy on it. If you think about the total number of people in America working on a theoretical model of how people organize compared to the total number of people working on traditional science, the number in the investment base is radically different. So, we get about what we pay for.

What I want to suggest tonight is what I think Kuhn would have called a *paradigm shift* or *scientific revolution*. To understand the best of the last century of management, you can start with Peter Drucker's *The Effective Executive* (1967), and then go to Alfred Sloan's works on how he redesigned General Motors (1963), and then study how George Catlett Marshall organized the Second World War.[2] Then, you have a core model of stunningly effective decision making and implementation that actually worked. I am a historian in the pragmatic sense: I like to study history because I think imitation is cheaper than invention. Anytime I face any kind of problem, I try to figure out who solved it previously and how.

Drivers of Change

My first assertion this evening is that the world will experience four times as much change in the next twenty-five years as it did in the last 100. I would argue that this is a literal—not hyperbolic—number. The number one driver of that rate of change is the sheer number of scientists. Take the following equation: number of scientists currently working times the rate of exchange of information. It's a duality. There are more scientists alive today than in all of previous human history combined. That's an actual number. And because of the Internet, the cell phone, and the jet airplane, they are swapping information at rates that far transcend what Darwin could have done. There is this double multiplier: more scientists working times more rapid information exchange. Therefore, it strikes me that the burden of proof should be on those who argue for less than this rate of change.

I think there are five primary drivers of the change in science and technology. They are information technology, communications, nanoscale science and technology, quantum mechanics, and biology. These drivers are to the next twenty-five years what physics was in 1935. By physics I include X rays, radar, radio, and all the different things that were so important to us in the Second World War.

The emerging genuine world market is a major driver. India and China today are the reserve margin of production on the planet. This has several fascinating implications, but let me suggest that it's really important to understand that if the United States is in the world market, many of our economic assumptions change. For example, if you have a consumption-led strategy to come out of a recession, a true world market in which India and China are the marginal producers means that a fair amount of your tax cut and spending increase are actually going offshore. New factories would be built—just not here.

On the other hand, you have dramatically lower prices and more choices. Being the most open market in the world, we routinely have lower prices than any place else because the lowest marginal producer will show up here. But, that's a different equation than a national model of how you manage this economy, and it requires rethinking what we mean by a competitive American economy.

The impact of science and technology, which is inherently deflationary, and the impact of a larger world market with low-priced marginal producers create very similar patterns to the period from 1873 to 1896 when the standard of living went up every year but price deflation was obvious. It's a very tough world for producers and a pretty good world for consumers, and I think that's the right analog. We don't currently have any problem with a 1929 kind of deflation. But I think we have a real challenge for an 1873 kind of deflation, because we are a real estate–leveraged debt society. And real deflation in the 1873 to 1896 model, if we tilt it over, would become really expensive socially as much as economically.

I also think you have to confront the reality of 24/7 communication worldwide. We now live in a global web, which is a combination of 24-hour television, cell phones, regular telephones, satellite phones, and Internet in such a pattern that the world never goes to sleep. The decision cycles of the past are totally obsolete, because information moves so much faster than they could cope with. In terms of the challenge to us worldwide, there is the spread of democracy, human rights, and a very profound notion that every person on the planet deserves good health and health care. The way I describe it, the American mission is to help everybody in the planet in the next half century achieve safety, health, prosperity, and freedom. That is an enormous challenge. But in the age of worldwide television, it is sort of the minimalist state—especially if you're going to accept Franklin Delano Roosevelt's model of being a good neighbor on a planetwide basis.

If you take the notion that we're going to have four times the rate of change in the next twenty-five years as we did in the last 100, you can take 1903 to 2003 and that's your analog. If you took that ruling literally—no commercial radio, no television, no microwave, no air-conditioning, no mass-produced car—we're still a month away from the Wright brothers flying for the first time. The first flight, by the way, was shorter than the wingspan of a Boeing 747 and averaged ten miles an hour. So, take that scale of change: Literally in the lifetime of most of the people in this room, that's what you're going to live through.

This may surprise some of you: I am a Theodore Roosevelt Republican. I believe in free markets within a regulatory environment. So I like having McDonald's and Wendy's compete, but I want the water to be drinkable and the hamburger to be beef. And I'm prepared to sanction the government to ensure that.

Information technology is another driver. I often discuss people getting cash out of ATMs, using self-service gas stations with credit cards, and using Travelocity to order airline tickets. My goal with audiences is to immerse people for about ten or fifteen minutes in the core idea that most of the changes that I advocate in health care represent the recent past. They are not futuristic. If I suggest to you, for example, that bar coding really works, this does not represent the future. One hospital, which belongs to our Center for Health Care Transformation, is going to a bar-coding system where patients have a bar code on their wrist. The nurse has a bar code on her badge, and there's a bar code on the medicine. They believe they will save $300 million a year in avoiding patient medication errors. That's just in forty-seven hospitals. Take that kind of a model, that is real change, and all it is doing is adapting health to systems that are somewhere between twenty and forty years old.

Transformational Change

I'm a disciple of Edwards Deming. I really believe in a culture and system of quality. I also believe in an individually centered system of knowledge, finance, and choice. In that sense, I very much believe in Adam Smith's *The Wealth of Nations,* in the context that it was written after *The Theory of Moral Sentiments.* Smith assumes a moral world within which there is capitalism. And it's a mistake to only read volume 2. Welfare reform in that sense worked. The core to welfare reform was a moral issue: Are you better off being passive and receiving money for doing nothing, or are you better off getting a job or an education? And the country made a cultural values decision, not an economic one. In fact, we've had better than a 60 percent reduction in welfare recipients as people moved off [welfare]. In general, their incomes have gone up and family stability has increased.

When you look seriously at weapons of mass murder, biological weapons are more dangerous to the twenty-first century than nuclear weapons. If American society really gets shattered, it will not be, I think, because of a nuclear attack. It will be because of a sophisticated expert system of biological [weapons]. In order for us to cope with the biological threat, we must profoundly transform our health system. And our model is Eisenhower's 1955 proposal for an interstate highway system. Originally, it was known as the National Defense Interstate Highway System, designed to evacuate cities in case of nuclear war. I think we need a similar substantial federal investment in information technology for health, recognizing the same challenge we are going to face with biologicals. All the things I'm describing are transformational, not managerial. These are not, "Fix a little of this, and fix a little of that, and it's going to work." These are really large changes.

There is a model I use, which is based on the mountains in Washington State. In this model, the clouds come in off of the Pacific, go up the mountains, and become rain. There is a temperate rain forest on the west. This creates a rain shadow on the other side of the mountain, where there are three to five inches of rain per year; it's a semidesert. The point is: Which side of the mountain you're on is a big deal, because they're not marginally different. That's what I mean by transformation. You actually have to manage in both situations, but getting across the mountains involves a kind of leadership that is profoundly different.

A traditional system contains a critical mass that is resistant to transformation and explains obstacles. One of the favorite phrases is either "no because" or "that's impossible because." When you cross over to a transformational system, people understand every day that if we're not transforming, we're losing ground. So, there's a perennial focus in favor of "yes," "how can we solve it," and "what will it take?" This is a totally different attitude. This attitude toward the future—this attitude toward stability versus change—is at the heart of whether you can build a transformational system or whether you're trapped in defending the past.

Chipmunks and Antelopes

When you deal with really large-scale change, there is a biological principle that often is overlooked. It is the biological principle that lions cannot afford to hunt chipmunks because even if they catch them, they starve to death. I've used this example for about a year, and my colleagues were shocked this week when *Science Magazine* referenced a study of very large dogs that lived in North America 30 million years ago. The study didn't use chipmunks—it used mice. Lions cannot afford to hunt mice because they literally will starve to death, even if they catch them. Lions and all large carnivores have to hunt game large enough to justify the investment, so they have to hunt antelope and zebra. Why is this important? Because most senior executives are really big on chipmunks.

The person who taught me this was George Schultz. I was at the Hoover Institution talking with him about what it was like to work for President Reagan. Schultz essentially said that Reagan had an amazing knack for focusing, and that people didn't get it. As his letters get published, it's increasingly obvious he was a very subtle, sophisticated man. He had a deliberate persona of being pleasant and simple in public, but, in fact, he was doing all sorts of things for a fifty-year period.

The way I characterize it is that Reagan would get up in the morning and say, "I'm leading the free world. I'm the president of the United States. What are the antelope I'm hunting?" He had three:

- Instill a new belief in American civic culture, so people would be proud to be American again.
- Cut taxes and regulation so the economy would grow.
- Defeat the Soviet empire.

Reagan would walk into the Oval Office and a chipmunk would run in. And you can be a $10 billion federal chipmunk. Reagan was very pleasant. He'd listen very carefully, he'd smile and say that you are a terrific chipmunk . . . "Have you met Jim Baker?" Baker became the largest collector of chipmunks in American history.

Schultz's point was that when Mikhail Gorbachev took over the U.S.S.R., Reagan studied almost every night for a year. When Reagan and Gorbachev had their first meeting, Schultz suggested to the senior staff only the president, Gorbachev, and a translator should attend the meeting. The staff were all horrified. Schultz said: First of all, he [Reagan] knows what he believes; second, he was a labor union negotiator who led a strike in the forties; and third, he's been studying Gorbachev for a year and he understands him better than the rest of the staff. And that's how he got through the very first meeting. It was just the two of them.

To show you Reagan's ability to focus on little things that add up to a big animal, some of you may remember this meeting. It's winter. Reagan arrives first and is the host. He's inside. There's a nice fire. Gorbachev is coming up in a motorcade. Reagan steps out to the door; it's a very brisk day in Geneva and he's wearing only a suit. He comes down the stairs to greet the Russian president. Gorbachev gets out in a Russian overcoat and cap. Reagan embraces him for a moment. The world picture is: lean, brisk, confident, suited American versus a clunky, wrapped-up, very unconfident Russian. Reagan took him by the arm and escorted him up the stairs, as though Gorbachev were the older guy and Reagan the younger guy. And then, having biologically established the appropriate relationship, they started talking.

That had been thought through by some people who were really clever at focusing on what mattered. It may not seem like a big deal, but starting out a relationship like that was enormously helpful for moving in the right direction.

Entrepreneurial Public Management

So, when you go back to your organization, it's simple. You walk around, have five ideas, and see how many times people say "no, because," or "that's impossible," or "we couldn't possibly do that." And see how many times they say "well, maybe there's a circumstance in which we can get this done," or "yes, we could do that if." You'll know which side of this you and your organization are on.

As an initial language thought, if we take everything from the rise of public administration—and here you can argue that we're talking about the Confucian system translated through Austria and Germany to the West and then codified in the nineteenth century, or you can argue that it is civil service from the 1880s on, or whatever—I am suggesting that we want to consciously think about a transformation to what I would call entrepreneurial public management. We want to be very self-aware and say that this is going to be different. So when it sounds different, feels different, looks different, it's because this is different. We're crossing the watershed. I think that is very important in language.

I've done this five or six times in my career, such as when I created a Republican party in Georgia and when I walked around the Congress before I was even sworn in as a freshman saying, "You know, we've got to think about being the majority," which all of the minority Republicans thought was crazy.

I am suggesting that unless you change the words, unless you're self-aware, unless you're explicit, you can't get people up over the mountain because they'll redefine what you're doing back to what they're already doing, and tell you, "You know, we've been doing that for years." All of you have been through this in your careers—whatever the newest slogan is, you cut and paste the old stuff, paste the new slogan on it, and reannounce it.

Rethinking Africa

I want to give you a couple more examples. Our policies towards sub-Saharan Africa make no sense at all—and by the way, it's no longer a lack of money. President Bush is actually standing up and saying that we should spend billions of dollars, for example, on HIV/AIDS. If you took the total amount of money that we're directly or indirectly shipping to sub-Saharan Africa, it's a significant program. But it's not a program, because it dribbles out from this bureaucracy and that bureaucracy, and it dribbles to this country and that country. There is no coherence for trying to design a strategy for sub-Saharan Africa.

Yet all the modern technologies are regional. For example, you could afford to put up an African satellite that gives you a footprint for every country in sub-Saharan African if you divided the cost among all the poor countries. The first thing you'd run into, such as when I went to the World Bank with this idea, is the fact that there are local "kleptocracies" in many of those countries that own the local phone system, and they are shocked at the idea you'd actually lower the price. They have an absolutely obsolete worldview that charging a lot for a little bit is better than charging a little bit for a lot. It is a pre-industrial worldview, and we're now in the Information Age.

You could design all sorts of patterns that are system-wide. If you're going to spend $3 billion a year on AIDS, you ought to do it in an information-rich, highly sophisticated mode. Cell phone tests in Korea and Japan involve 100 megabits of information. That is, you could run a full movie on your cell phone—a totally different model, which allows you to do totally different things. But it means you've got to think out here. You've got to be like Eisenhower who said we need to connect the entire continent with highways. In the secular world, we thought as big as the challenge, and then we grew to the size of our thought. So take Africa as an example of how you could rethink it.

How Would We Do It Today?

Another example is that I feel sorry for current ambassadors. This is a sixteenth-century written note, personal courier, sterling ship model. "I am the ambassador. I am the personal representative of the president, and I didn't know he called you this morning. Was it a good call? Did you enjoy the call? And what did he tell you?" How often would you guess that happens? Alternatively, "I'm right in the middle of writing my memo to the president, which, by the time it goes through the various levels of bureaucracy, should arrive at the White House no less than three days after CNN's live coverage." Guess how much that's going to get read? I'm suggesting to you that we actually have to rethink: What do we mean by real-time worldwide communication? What does that do to the nature of being an ambassador? What should an ambassador do in the modern world? How should we organize embassies in the modern world? It's a totally different model.

I recently looked at continuance of government, which is a major Defense Department program perfectly designed for a 1958 potential threat of a Soviet first strike. And you start talking about, "Well, what if we just bought really good satellite programs for everybody? What if we allowed all the combatant commanders to be alternative headquarters so that we'd actually have six or seven of them around the world?" If you think you're going to be in a war where you lose six or seven combatant commander headquarters at one time, you're in a nuclear spasm exchange with somebody. But instead we still spend a fair amount of money doing things like we did in the 1950s.

It is important to rethink "how would you do it today," not "how do I modify what we've been doing?" The minute you say, "Let me modify what we've been doing," I'll guarantee it's wrong. Given this level of information flow and pattern of human reaction, this will totally change education the morning we get it. We'll quit fighting over vouchers. We'll quit trying to reform an 1840s model of public school with an 1870s model industrial structure with an agricultural era schedule—that is what we currently have.

There is a reason that kids think education is a mess. At every high school I visit I ask, "How many of you know somebody who cheats?" Every hand goes up every time in every class. It's all a game. It's not about learning. It's about meeting the state curriculum, filling out the paperwork, making sure the teacher looks okay when the scores come in. So kids think, "Fine—this is a game. This is not about learning; this is about a game. I know how to do games." But if you asked, "How would you learn?" At eight fifty-five-minute units at the convenience of the professor? Not if you could possibly get out of it. If we simply took how the people in this room learned for three months and then said, "What would a system or even a society look like that organized its young to learn based on how you all learn," you'd have a stunningly different parallel system that would be 24/7.

Don't try to fix what we have. Try to figure out: "How would you do it today?" There are two different ways to think of it. One is a great Drucker rule, that once a quarter you should walk around for a day and ask yourself, "If I wasn't already doing this, would I start it?" If the answer is no, why are you still doing it? The other is, instead of trying to start where you are and fix the future, go out on a blank piece of paper and design 2015. Then come back and figure out the bridges. This is a totally different way of thinking about things.

Changing Mind-sets

We currently have foreign aid as a functional process in bureaucracy. One of the reasons I gave a speech in the spring at the American Enterprise Institute taking on the State Department publicly was because I had just learned that after a year and a half in Afghanistan we had managed to pour [zero] miles of road (Gingrich 2003). There had been a quote in *The Washington Post* where somebody said the Afghanis need to understand the American AID [U.S. Agency for International Development] application process. This was not a bad human being; this is someone immersed in his or her own world.

So we're saying, "We're in the middle of a war on terrorism; we're desperately trying to get enough resources to Afghanistan for President Karzai to survive; we're trying hard to create a broad-based governance in Afghanistan. And, by the way, the paperwork will take approximately ninety days to process, and then we'll have to decide whether or not we can actually have the committee meet in order to decide whether or not we can cut the check."

I went to the White House on a very major issue just before the Iraq war, and I had been told by some layers down in the system that there was a congressional problem. I went in to say, "What can I do to break this loose?" They just said, "No. We have people at the White House who get up every morning and call the appropriate agencies and say to them, 'Cut the check.'" In six weeks, they couldn't get the check cut. That is just mindless, but perfectly normal because there will be a Government Accountability Office (GAO) report; an Inspector General (IG) report; a congressional hearing; five articles in *The Washington Post*—all if you don't follow the process. And if you try to change the bureaucracy, at least three of the people who are opposing it will leak information on you. So, "Do you want me to cut the check and save a country or do you want me to avoid all that pain?" "My choice is simple. I want to survive here. I'm not in Kabul. It's not my problem." That is a major challenge.

A retired Air Force general made a great point the other day. He said we still talk in the military about stability operations, and that language is exactly wrong. We're not trying to stabilize Iraq—we're trying to change Iraq. We're not trying to stabilize Afghanistan—we're trying to change Afghanistan. Change operations are very different from stability operations. They require different levels of resources, different attitudes, different psyches. There is a great story that a man told: He's a merchant banker from Texas who is closing a deal. He gets a phone call from his boss who says one Friday, "I have just accepted a job for both of us helping the president organize the financial community for war. You will show up here Monday." The merchant banker walks in Monday morning. The guy says, "We're a dollar a year people. The paperwork won't be done for sixty days. This is our only desk. You have that side; I have this side. Go to work. Assume you actually already have the job. Use the president's name. Just get things. We'll work it out later."

That would be legally impossible to do today. But we won the Second World War because we got it done and then explained it. We didn't slow down long enough to figure out how we could explain it before we got it done. I'm arguing that is actually a better model on most days. In entrepreneurial public management, you want to hold people accountable for mistakes, and hold people accountable for theft and corruption who understand the context in which they're exercising power. Don't allow them to get so mired down in process that you can no longer remember what the product was.

Focus on Learning

A couple more examples: As I said earlier, I think you'll see a dramatic shift from traditional, on-site education to 24/7 learning—as needed, where needed, and when needed—which is how I think people are going to operate in the Information Age. You want to know, you need to know now. You don't want to know it a day early and you don't want to know it a day late. You'd like it organized in a way so that you can learn it now.

One of the things this does is to eliminate the term *remedial education*, which assumes a hierarchical structure: If you didn't get X when you should have gotten X, you now must be in remediation. If you think about it, if I went to you and said, "I hate to tell you this, but you need six hours of remediation." Most of you would say, "I don't think so." On the other hand, if this is the year you decide to learn about quantum mechanics, going through a basic course introducing quantum mechanics is perfectly reasonable. Going through the remedial quantum mechanics course will be very offensive. It may not seem like a giant distinction, but culturally it is very, very profound.

The number one thing the U.S. Commission on National Security/21st Century (known as the Hart-Rudman Commission), of which I was a member, said threatened America in March 2001 was a weapon of mass destruction going off in an American city, probably from a terrorist (USCNS/21 2001). And we called for a homeland security agency. It wasn't noticed much in March, but on September 12, 2001, we thought we were very pressing.

At the same time, the Commission found that the number two threat to the survival of the United States is the failure of math and science education. Seven Democrats and seven Republicans unanimously agreed to the following sentence: There is no conceivable conventional war in the next twenty-five years that is as big a threat as the collapse of math and science education.[3] That's how profound I think this issue is. I was very pessimistic about how to solve it before I began to realize that if we focus on learning, not on teaching, it will all work. Because if you get to be thirty-seven and you need to learn it, the truth is that Americans will learn it. We're a stunningly pragmatic people. We could then design 24/7 convenience systems that enable you to learn.

You see this if you look at how many people over the normal age are back in college and graduate school. So it's actually happening, but we haven't thought through the implication: In a system of lifetime learning, if the National Science Foundation organized brilliant online ways to learn math and science, people would take them. The "brilliant" in part means entertaining and interesting. So this is a way of thinking—a totally different model.

Also notice that in the twentieth century and earlier, when we talked about diplomacy, it was government to government. It was my state talking to your state. But in the twenty-first century, when you have worldwide television, you have worldwide non-governmental organizations, you have worldwide democracies—people to people gets to be really important. This is a much more complex model of relationships between nations than the one that just said, "My ambassador will talk to your foreign minister, and your ambassador will talk to my secretary of state, and that is what we mean by relations."

I think one of the greatest challenges of the next decade is to figure out, "What would entrepreneurial public management be like, and how do we redesign the government and congressional oversight in order to migrate to that kind of a system?"

Notes

1. A speech in honor of James E. Webb, a founder of the National Academy of Public Administration, delivered at the Academy's annual meeting on November 21, 2003, in Washington, D.C.

2. See the *Papers of George Catlett Marshall* published by the Johns Hopkins University Press.

3. The exact quotation reads: "In this Commission's view, the inadequacies of our systems of research and education pose a greater threat to U.S. national security over the next quarter century than any potential conventional war that we might imagine" (USCNS/21 2001, ix).

References

Dawkins, Richard. 1989. *The Selfish Gene*. Rev. ed. Oxford: Oxford University Press.

Drucker, Peter F. 1967. *The Effective Executive*. New York: Harper & Row.

Gingrich, Newt. 2003. "The Next Challenge for Bush: Transforming the State Department." *The Washington Times*, 24 April, A21.

Kuhn, Thomas S. 1996. *The Structure of Scientific Revolutions*. 3rd ed. Chicago: University of Chicago Press.

Platt, John R. 1964. "Strong Inference: Certain Systematic Methods of Scientific Thinking May Produce Much More Rapid Progress than Others." *Science* 16 (October): 347–53.

Sloan, Alfred P., Jr. 1963. *My Years with General Motors*. New York: Doubleday.

United States Commission on National Security/21st Century (USCNS/21). 2001. *Road Map for National Security: Imperative for Change*. Phase III report of the U.S. Commission on National Security/21st Century. 15 February. www.au.af.mil/au/awc/awcgate/nssg/. (Accessed 3 November 2006.)

3

Public Leadership as Gardening

H. George Frederickson and David S.T. Matkin

The modern literature of administration (particularly business administration) argues that leadership is one of the keys to organizational effectiveness. That literature is filled with descriptions of powerful, heroic leaders—risk takers, visionaries, entrepreneurs, agents of change. We agree that leadership is one of the keys to organizational effectiveness and to organizational change but suggest that the change-agent style of leadership is often incompatible with organizational effectiveness in the public sector. Durable change (change that lasts) and effective organizational management in the public sector can almost always be traced to leaders who work like gardeners. Understanding public jurisdictions and agencies as gardens and public leaders as gardeners facilitates an accurate and informative description of the multiple factors that contribute to building and improving those jurisdictions and agencies.

Why is the change-agent style of leadership inappropriate in the public sector? How does public leadership as gardening improve the effectiveness of public organizations? In this chapter, we explain why the change-agent leadership model fails to recognize core elements of public-sector institutions. In contrast to the change-agent leader, we present leadership as gardening and contend that such a view improves public leadership through increased attention to the ecology, history, culture, and values of public institutions. We conclude the chapter with a discussion of how change-agent and gardening approaches to leadership differ.

Why the Change-Agent Perspective Is Wrong for the Public Sector

The concept of the change-agent leader is based on an idealized and misplaced view of private-sector entrepreneurship, a view that glorifies risk taking and assumes that the primary responsibility of leaders is to change things. Such a perspective begins with the notion that things are broken and need to be fixed, usually quickly. This approach may ultimately prove unwise in the private sector, but it is especially problematic when applied in the public sector.

The study of public leadership from a change-agent perspective fails to recognize crucial elements of effective public-sector organizations, including the preservation of public order, the reliable and predictable provision of public services, and the practices of democratic self-government. Investments in our prevailing institutions—our cities, states, and nations and their established governments—are devalued, as are the accomplishments of those institutions. Order, stability, and predictability are likewise undervalued. However, the preservation of order, reliability, and predictability is a unique expectation of public leaders, an expectation that may matter less in the private sector.

The importance of stability in public institutions is one of the key findings in recent empirical studies of organizational effectiveness in Texas public schools. In summarizing the characteristics of effective schools, Kenneth J. Meier (2006) points to the importance of order, stability, and predictability. The characteristics of effective districts include long-term stable leadership. In these districts, superintendents stay in their positions for longer periods of time or are hired from within the school district. In effective school districts, leaders apply high academic standards to both teachers and students. Effective school districts remain committed to their curriculum and do not chase the latest education fads. Meier even finds that the stability of a curriculum is more important than its content. Effective school districts value hard work and avoid "magic bullet" solutions. What works for one school district, so-called best practices, may be the cause of failure in another; therefore, leaders must understand their unique environment and respond accordingly. Finally, effective districts are supported by high levels of parental involvement. Effective school administrators do not try to do it alone, a position that is glorified by the change-agent perspective; rather, effective leaders find ways to cultivate support from the environment.

The change-agent leader understands institutional values and traditions as important but views them as problems that need to be changed. However, institutional values in the public sector are often democratically derived by the will of the people. Leaders who seek to change institutional values and traditions are challenging the democratic foundations of the organization.

To equate organizational change with organizational improvement is to make a logical mistake. On the basis of simple probability, the likelihood that the results of a change will be negative is at least equal to the probability that it will be positive. These probabilities are improved when the leaders of organizations move carefully, taking incremental steps using the logic of trial and error. Because the modern language of leadership does not include the word *error,* it may be difficult for leaders to openly embrace the phrase *trial and error.* Change-agent leaders place too much emphasis on bold change, without recognizing the possibility of error, and increase the probability of negative, unintended consequences. We need leaders who increase the probability of success as they move in a step-by-step manner and always leave open the possibility of a step back or a step to the side, should the evidence indicate that the direction of change is negative. We are so bold as to formulate the Mertonian Law of Public Sector Leadership: *In the public sector, the probability that a proposed change will make things worse is at least 50 percent.*

The former secretary of the Navy, Richard Danzig, in a James Webb Lecture at the National Academy of Public Administration, gave the most informed and thoughtful speech on public-sector leadership and transformation that we have heard in years. Danzig (2000) identifies several of the reasons why the change-agent perspective is wrong for the public sector. A few highlights in Danzig's own words follow:

> [Popular ideas of leadership are] derived from the business community ... people like Henry Ford or [Edwin] Land and the Polaroid camera or Steve Jobs or Bill Gates, people who had some notion about what they were going to do, the creators of FedEx, the Waltons and Wal-Mart, and built from a different vision about an organization. . . . [T]he literature on these subjects is not by and large built from government service; it's built from the world of business. . . . I think this model is actually a little more evocative and taps into what Jung would have called a "universal archetype." . . . It is a Moses-like notion. Preach a new vision. Go up on the mountain and see it. Then lead the chosen people through forty years in the wilderness, to the Promised Land.
>
> That vision of leadership really underlies what we preach. My trouble with it is that I think it's wrong. I think it's misleading. I think in many situations it's dangerous. It has, I think, some virtues in some unusual situations, but they apply least to transformation of governmental organizations and to transitions, which bring in outsiders to this new organization.
>
> Let me note its faults. First of all it's remarkably arrogant. . . . It's okay for Moses. He, after all, presumably had access to God. . . . But, if you look at all of our visions, they are presumably not so divinely inspired. . . . [M]any visions are, in fact, fundamentally wrong. . . . [T]he premise of the business world . . . is that nine out of ten organizations can fail if the tenth one succeeds. [As a public official], I've got a fundamental problem if I start to bet the organization on some fundamental monotonic kind of conception of the future, because I can't play the odds for it to work out overall in good kinds of ways. I can't let nine out of ten navies fail while the tenth one succeeds because we don't have ten navies.
>
> This second problem, you'll notice . . . that it takes [Moses] forty years . . . The average government appointee will serve for two years. . . .
>
> [Third], who was it who Moses brought to the Promised Land? The answer is the chosen people, but not the Egyptians. As secretary of the Navy I've got to persuade the Egyptians to do something different. I can't go create a new navy, leading out the people who follow me, and leaving the rest behind to suffer ten plagues.

Public Leadership as Gardening

Understandings of public leadership as gardening appear to trace to a short paragraph in a little out-of-print book edited by Peter Szanton (1981). At the end of a very good study of patterns of federal government reorganization, he wrote: "So reorganization had best be viewed as a branch of gardening rather than of architecture or engineering. As in gardening, the possibilities are limited by soil and climate, and accomplishment is slow. Like gardening, reorganization is not an act but a process, a continuing job. And like gardening, reorganization is work whose benefits may largely accrue to one's successors" (24).

Public leadership and gardening begin with the wisdom of John Gaus (1947) who advised us to build, quite literally, from the ground up; from the elements of a place—soils, climate, location, for example—to the people who live there—their numbers and ages and knowledge, and the ways of physical and social technology by which from the place and in relationships with one another, they get their living. It is within this setting that their instruments and practices of public housekeeping should be studied so that they may better understand what they are doing and appraise reasonably how they are doing it.

Gardening, as an understanding of public leadership, following Gaus, makes demands upon our powers to observe, upon a sensitive awareness of changes and adjustment and upon our willingness to face the political—that is, the public housekeeping—basis of administration. Gardening, like the powers of observation and awareness in public leadership, requires time, patience, and experience. Seasons matter because planning done in the winter is often more important than hard work in the spring and summer. Experienced public leaders know seasons—the budget cycle, the legislative cycle, the unique rhythms, patterns, and routines of each organization. Our best gardeners know when to prune, to plan, to plant, and to cultivate.

Gardeners work with available resources—soil, water, seeds, climate. And so it is with public administration. In our better practices, public administration gardeners are shrewd managers of these resources, and among these resources none are more important than the plants—the people. A genuine caring for and knowledge of each plant and an understanding of each plant's potential marks the difference between the casual planter of seeds and the gardener. Being responsible for the whole garden, the gardener must also know how all plants and groups of plants can be harmoniously related to make a beautiful garden. Plants need nourishment, water, sunshine, and encouragement. And the good gardener knows the limits of resources and the capacities of each plant and works carefully within those limits. So it is with public administration.

Gardeners recognize the importance and strength of administrative culture and seek to improve organizational effectiveness through its influence. Administrative culture, "a pattern of beliefs, values, and behaviors in public agencies about the agency's role and relationship with the public" (Anechiarico 1998, 17), is influenced by historical trends, social attitudes, and political factors. Gardeners seek to understand their administrative culture and respect the sources of the culture before seeking to influence the culture.

Gardeners understand that changes to administrative culture may take a long time. Change agents seek to make immediate and dynamic changes and therefore view the administrative culture values of order, stability, and predictability as barriers to effective management. However, real change in organizational culture requires an understanding of the public organization as a garden, where plants and trees must grow and develop at their own pace.

Changes in the garden, as in public organizations, tend to be incremental. Present circumstances, the condition of the garden, in the words of Johan Olsen (2004), are usually the result of long historical processes, involving conflicts, victories, defeats, and compromises, as well as processes of interpretation, learning, and habituation. It is difficult to subject institutional evolution to tight control, and history becomes a meander. Working with what they have inherited, gardeners understand that change is experimental, step-by-step, and subject to the power of uncontrollable external forces. Nevertheless, patient gardeners know that a 5 percent annual change in the garden, compounded annually, will, in a few years, make a mighty change in the garden. It is not unusual, in the rhythms of gardening, for a particular plan or experiment to fail the first or second season. But persistence pays. Sometimes short-run failures turn into long-run successes, as old plans are reactivated under new and more favorable circumstances.

Understanding public organizations as gardens has been picked up and developed by the so-called institutionalists, led by James March and Johan Olsen. Institutionalists understand organizational actors to be shaped by the ecology and history of their organizations. These scholars apply institutional theory to the decision process of public officials, insisting that on the one side are those who see action as driven by the logic of anticipated consequences and prior preferences. On the other side are those who see action as driven by the logic of appropriateness and sense of identity.

> Within the tradition of logic of appropriateness, actions are seen as rule based. Human actors are imagined to follow rules that associate particular identities to particular situations, approaching individual opportunities for action by assessing similarities between current identities and choice dilemmas and more general concepts of self and situations. Action involves evoking an identity or role and matching the obligation of that identity or role to a specific situation. The pursuit of purpose is associated with identities more than with interests, and with the selection of rules more than with individual rational expectations (1998, 951; see also March and Olsen 1983, 1995; Olsen 2004; Frederickson and Smith 2003).

The perspective of the public leader as gardener works from the premise that it is not possible to describe organizational or interorganizational order in terms of the simple notion of rational intention and design. "History is created by a complicated ecology of local events and locally adaptive actions. As individuals, groups, organizations, and institutions seek to act intelligently and learn in a changing world involving others similarly trying to adapt, they create connections that subordinate individual intentions to their interactions. . . . They co-evolve with the actions they produce" (March and Olsen 1983, 293).

The one book on leadership that should be on every public administrator's bookshelf is *Leading Quietly: An Unorthodox Guide to Doing the Right Thing* by Joseph L. Badaracco, Jr. (2002). Because gardeners are quiet leaders who are in it for the long haul, they tend to be realists about themselves, about their organizations, and about the contingent nature of the environment in which they work. Gardeners as quiet leaders tend to move carefully, step-by-step, in a generally agreed-upon direction. They recognize the age-old wisdom of effective planning—that no war plan survives the first battle. Good planning is a deeply contingent process. Plans always change depending on shifting resources, technologies, dangers, and opportunities. Gardeners are also realistic about their power—acutely aware of the limits and subtleties of power, even for leaders with impressive titles. In short, quiet leaders don't kid themselves.

Conventional stories of great leadership—stories about Mother Teresa, for example—portray the leader as a person of pure motives, high aims, and noble causes. Not so. Gardeners as quiet leaders understand and even learn to trust mixed motives. Altruism, courage, self-sacrifice, and dedication to great causes are splendid motives; but so too are ambition, recognition, and personal success, not to mention survival. In decision circumstances involving complex motives (are there any other kind?) Badaracco (2002) indicates that the effective leader:

- has a bias for action and does not get bogged down in the morass of motives,
- does not disqualify him- or herself because of mixed motives,
- learns to trust competing motives and to recognize the trade-offs involved, and
- understands that organizational effectiveness and personal success are usually compatible outcomes (51–2). → *wouldn't want to be a change agent?*

Time is on the side of gardeners as leaders. Effective leaders avoid, whenever possible, rushing forward with the answer. Instead they buy time, appoint committees, do studies, and wait until turbulent waters calm and a plausible course of action is evident. Quick fixes are just that. Quiet leaders will practice tactical stalling until a strategic direction is more or less clear, then move the organization step-by-step in that direction. While quiet leaders have a bias for action, they recognize that time is almost always their friend.

Gardeners as quiet leaders think carefully about how they spend and invest their organizational capital. Because leadership always involves risk, the prudent assessment of risk is essential to any important decision. Gardeners as leaders will tackle tough situations but will not foolishly risk either the organization's capabilities or all of their own goodwill. In the literature, leaders are exhorted to "do the right thing." That is too simple because it calls for courage but says nothing about cost and risk.

The ordinary view of leadership has a generic, disembodied quality to it—as if to suggest that great leaders are able to lead effectively in any setting. Although most of us know this to be nonsense, it is nevertheless the formulaic description of leadership. Badaracco (2002) calls such a view of leadership what it is—nonsense—and argues correctly that there can be no great leadership, quiet or otherwise, without a deep substantive knowledge of the technological and bureaucratic characteristics of the specific setting in which leadership is expected. Context matters and the governmental context matters greatly, as any public administrator knows. The senior position in a government agency is no place for neophytes to get on-the-job leadership training. Quiet leaders, as Badaracco (2002) puts it, drill down to levels of complexity so they know what they are doing. Organizational matters, particularly in government, are never simple and seldom yield to simple answers.

Public administrators work in a world of constitutions, laws, appropriations, regulations, and rules. The common formula in the business literature is that responsible leaders break the rules selectively. Indeed there is a good bit of evidence that too many business executives have believed the nonsense about the efficacy of breaking the rules (e.g., Buckingham and Coffman 1999, McLean 2003). Now they will need to tell it to the judge. Taking rules seriously is the safe, smart, and responsible thing to do in most public administration cases. When the rules get in the way of acting responsibly or ethically, quiet leaders will patiently find the pathway between the rules.

In the end, what do gardeners as quiet leaders do? They compromise. Compromise is, of course, not in the vocabulary of those who subscribe to the heroic leader thesis. But to quiet leaders, compromises are challenges to their imagination and ingenuity and occasions for hard, serious work. They believe that crafting a compromise is often a valuable way to learn and exercise practical wisdom. In their minds, the best compromises have little to do with splitting the difference or sacrificing important values to pragmatic considerations. Instead, they are powerful ways of defending and expressing important values in enduring practical ways. Crafting responsible, workable compromises is not just something that quiet leaders do. It defines who they are.

In support of Badaracco's (2002) perspective on gardeners as quiet leaders, Richard Danzig contends that public leaders must be skilled at understanding their organization. In Danzig's (2000) words:

> My view is that there is something better than the Moses example. It's a much more mundane, yet productive model to think about: the monkey who has his eyes covered and his ears covered and gags his mouth. . . . We need to un-stopper our ears and listen. We need to look very closely. Then, in my view, we need to speak to the organization.
>
> [T]he single-most useful thing I think a new appointee can do is to listen to what the organization is telling him about what it cares about and what it values. . . . [S]ome of the most interesting and important things that the organization says about itself it says in the form of its clichés. . . . [T]hese propositions have the characteristic that they are right. They're phenomenally sound in their significance. . . . [T]hey're almost universally shared; everyone can recite them, everybody agrees on them.
>
> It was said of [poet and philosopher] Bronson Alcott in his reflectiveness that "he soared into the infinite and fathomed the unfathomable, but never paid cash." The problem for us [in our organizations is that we soar] into the infinite and fathom the unfathomable in these great propositions, but we [don't] pay cash. We [don't invest the resources necessary to] translate them into the day-

to-day life of the organization. . . . The banal cliché carries within it the seeds of revolution, the seeds of a dramatically different organization. Now, to get there you [have] to hear first what the organization [is] saying, look hard at [those] propositions and see where they [lead] you, and follow their logic relentlessly . . . and [then speak to them]. . . . [A]n opportunity to speak to the organization is an opportunity to say what it is that it ought to care about and to begin to push the propositions about where the radicalism in the institution leads, where it ought to be going . . . [to figure] out how to pay cash. . . . Personnel systems change. . . . Different kinds of people [get promoted]. . . . [T]his follows from premises that everybody accepts, and from premises that people have sworn they're going to live by. It leads, I think, to a quite different kind of result.

[T]he most critical variable for persuading any group of people is to start where they are, not where you are. It's to listen first to what they care about and what they're thinking and what they're organizing around and then if you want to move them . . . show them how the logic leads elsewhere than they may have thought it led. That seems to me to be a fundamental technique in government that is under-represented or underutilized.

[N]one of us is Moses. None of us is going to make it work that way. If we could, all we would do is recreate the business model, creating new companies . . . while leaving the old to die, and the effects on government would be disastrous. . . . We have a vastly harder job [than business management], a bigger challenge, and one that requires us truly to convert the Egyptians.

[T]here's a new world of opportunity nascent in all [our] organizations, and my suggestion to you is we don't get there by preaching our vision; we get there by opening our eyes to what's going on around us. . . .

Ronald Heifetz helps us understand the importance of public leadership as gardening. In his book, *Leadership without Easy Answers* (1994), Heifetz describes how the change-agent perspective results in misguided responses to understanding and addressing problems. In order to take swift action, the change agent simplifies complex problems. Only by overlooking the complexity of the garden can change agents make quick and decisive decisions, demonstrate strength, and lay out a clear vision of an idyllic future. However, because change agents oversimplify complex problems, their response is ineffective and often leads to harmful unintended consequences.

In contrast, public leaders as gardeners understand the complexity of public problems and understand that such problems do not have easy answers. Quick fixes fail because they do not sufficiently address the divergent attitudes, behavior, and values that underlie complex problems. Effective leaders view the adaptation of these institutional values as their primary challenge. "Adaptive work consists of the learning required to address conflicts in the values people hold, or to diminish the gap between the values people stand for and the reality they face. Adaptive work requires a change in values, beliefs, or behavior. The exposure and orchestration of conflict—internal contradictions—within individuals and constituencies provide the leverage for mobilizing people to learn new ways" (Heifetz 1994, 22).

Public leaders as gardeners understand that conflicts over values and objectives are frequent and inevitable. "[T]he clarification and integration of competing values itself becomes adaptive work" (Heifetz 1994, 3). The effective leader develops the adaptive capacity of his or her organization.

Gardening as Governance

Public leaders as gardeners are more responsive to the increasing need for public administrators to engage in cooperative relationships where the traditional command-and-control style of leadership is not possible. Much of the modern governance literature seeks to understand how public managers can improve organizational effectiveness and solve public problems in an environment where they do not have authority over all the important stakeholders. In order to have better governance, one must be a gardener.

Governance, like gardening, works with circumstances and conditions as they stand and assumes that leaders will use their skills to make organizations effective under present circumstances. In many modern situations, this means that a leader in one organization or garden can be effective only if he or she works carefully and regularly with leaders in nearby organizations or gardens. Gardening involves respect for the internal culture of the organization and for the context in which the organization is nested. Gardening is about both carefully guiding the processes of organizational change and cooperating with other organizations to work together to deal with problems that transcend organizational borders.

It was Harlan Cleveland (1972) who first used the word *governance* as an alternative to the phrase *public administration*. In the mid-1970s, one of the themes in Cleveland's particularly thoughtful and provocative speeches, papers, and books went something like this: "What the people want is less government and more governance." What he meant by governance was the following cluster of concepts, these concepts being suited to both *governance* and leadership as gardening. Although Cleveland doesn't use the term *gardener*, our reading of his words leads us to believe that to Cleveland good governance is gardening.

Gardeners recognize that power is diffused and shared. Cleveland states that

> [t]he organizations that get things done will no longer be hierarchical pyramids with most of the real control at the top. They will be systems—interlaced webs of tension in which control is loose, power diffused, and centers of decision plural. "Decision-making" will become an increasingly intricate process of multilateral brokerage both inside and outside the organization which thinks it has the responsibility for making, or at least announcing, the decision. Because organizations will be horizontal, the way they are governed is likely to be more collegial, consensual, and consultative. The bigger the problems to be tackled, the more real power is diffused and the larger the number of persons who can exercise it—if they work at it (1972, 13).

Like gardens with blurred boundaries of seasons, natural elements, and ecological forces, Cleveland saw a similar blurring of the distinctions between public and private organizations, and he associated this blurring with his conception of governance. He reasoned what it meant as follows: "These new style public-private horizontal systems will be led by a new breed of man and woman. I call them Public Executives, people who manage public responsibilities whether in 'public' or 'private' organizations" (1972, 14).

Cleveland clearly understood the challenges of individual accountability associated with horizontal multiorganizational systems. Who, exactly, do these modern public executives work for and to whom are they accountable? Consider this remarkably bold argument: "Public ethics are in the hearts and minds of individual Public Executives, and the ultimate court of appeals from their judgments is some surrogate for people-in-general" (Cleveland 1972, 117). Note, he does not argue that accountability is ultimately to the people or the elected officials of one's jurisdiction. Cleveland's idea of public responsibility is much bigger than that. The moral responsibility of public executives includes basic considerations of four fundamental principles, none of which are valued in the change-agent style of leadership: "a sense of welfare; a sense of equity; a sense of achievement; and a sense of participating" (1972, 126–27).

What would be the results of such a grand conception of the moral responsibility of the public administrator? "In a society characterized by bigness and complexity it is those individuals who learn to get things done in organizational systems who will have a rational basis for feeling free" (Cleveland 1972, 135).

Gardeners are not limited by the scope and complexity of nature; rather, they seek to develop skills that liberate them from perceptions of environmental chaos. "By the development of their administrative skills, and by coming squarely to terms with the moral requirements of executive leadership, individual men and women can preserve and extend their freedom. Freedom is the power to choose, and the future executive will be making the most choices—whom to bring together in which organizations, to make what happen, in whose interpretation of the public interest. Those who relish that role will have every reason to feel free, not in the interstices but right in the middle of things" (Cleveland 1972, 140).

Gardening as governance is an especially important word/concept because of the mismatch or disconnect between jurisdictions on one hand and social, technological, political, and economic problems on the other hand. Cleveland understood this, too: "One of the striking ironies of our time is that, just when we have to build bigger, more complicated "bundles of relations" to deal comprehensively with the human consequences of science and technology, many people are seized with the idea that large-scale organization is itself a Bad Thing. My thesis is the reverse . . ." (1972, 139–140). Big problems, Cleveland believes, require big responses and big gardens. In these situations, effective gardeners recognize that their gardens are not isolated from their neighborhood. Pests, weeds, pollination, and plant diseases easily travel across property boundaries. The best gardeners instinctively cooperate. They recognize that their gardens are affected by and affect their neighbors' gardens. These collaborative responses will be multiorganizational and will involve

Table 3.1

Comparison of Gardener and Change-Agent Leadership

	Change Agent	Gardener
Decision Basis	Applies "universal leadership principles"	Adapts to each unique organization and its environment
Primary Values	Emphasizes change	Understands stability, order, predictability, and reliability and carefully adapts them
Perceptions of Organizational Values and Traditions	Traditions and organizational culture inhibit innovation and need to be changed	Traditions and organizational culture hold the keys to motivation and organizational changes that last
Source of Innovation	The leader	The organization
Time Frames of Change	Uses rhetoric of long-term benefits, but energy is put toward short-term results; views timing as a strategic planning element	Applies patience, planning, and understanding to the organization's natural rhythms and seasons; knows when to plant, to prune, to harvest, or to wait
Politics of Public Organizations	Views politics as a threat to overcome or a resource to exploit	Recognizes the representative democratic basis of public administration and respects the importance of self-government
The Vision	Formulates and articulates the organizational vision	Cultivates the organizational vision and strives, along with all organizational members, to embody that vision

both public and private organizations. And, these responses will be led not by one but many leaders. In order to be successful, such leaders should be gardeners.

The Gardener's Harvest

The remainder of the chapter describes the qualities of public managers who are gardeners and compares these qualities with those of change agents. How do these two approaches to leadership differ with regard to their primary values, decision basis, perceptions of organizational values and traditions, source of innovation, time frames for change, politics of public organizations, and organizational vision? Table 3.1 summarizes and compares the two approaches as presented in this chapter.

Change-agent leadership is about the leader. Change agents base their decisions on "universal principles" that are applied regardless of the organizational environment. These leaders value and emphasize change, which they view as synonymous with innovation. Change agents consider organizational traditions and cultures as inhibiting change and therefore as barriers to innovation. Because organizations are the problem, the leader is considered the source of innovation. Energy is directed toward short-term results, which are justified with the rhetoric of long-term benefits and strategic planning. Change agents view political institutions and democratic representation as threats to be overcome or as resources to exploit. Democratic institutions are not considered to be a valuable source for the organizational vision. Rather, change agents view themselves as the organizational architects who formulate and articulate the vision.

Gardeners shift the focus of leadership from the leader to the organization. Instead of applying "universal principles," gardeners adapt their leadership to the unique environment of each organization. The source of innovation is not the leader but the organization. Innovation comes from adapting the organization with the recognition that institutional traditions and culture hold keys to motivation and organizational changes that last. Gardeners understand that stability, order, predictability, and reliability are important values of public-sector organizations. Gardeners understand that patience, planning, and understanding the organization's natural rhythms and seasons are necessary in order to achieve lasting change. Gardeners must know when to plant, to prune, to harvest, and to wait. Gardeners recognize that public administration is based on representative democracy. Their respect for the importance of self-government leads gardeners to cultivate and embody the organizational vision rather than attempt to design and control that vision.

To understand public leadership as gardening is to know that it is all about the garden, not the gardener. In the long run, the patient public administration gardener will, working with the resources at hand, plan, adapt, guide, and nurture processes of genuine and lasting institutional change. This spring the gardens of public leadership are especially in need of our best gardeners.

References

Anechiarico, Frank. 1998. "Administrative Culture and Civil Society: A Comparative Perspective." *Administration and Society* 30 (1): 13–34.

Badaracco, Joseph, Jr., 2002. *Leading Quietly: An Unorthodox Guide to Doing the Right Thing*. Boston: Harvard Business School Press.

Buckingham, Marcus, and Curt Coffman. 1999. *First, Break All the Rules: What the World's Greatest Managers Do Differently*. New York: Simon & Schuster.

Cleveland, Harland. 1972. *The Future Executive: A Guide for Tomorrow's Managers*. New York: Harper & Row.

Danzig, Richard. 2000. *James E. Webb Lecture, 17 November*. Washington, DC: National Academy of Public Administration. www.napawash.org/resources/lectures/lecture_ transcripts_web_2000.html. (Accessed 4 October 2006.)

Frederickson, H. George, and Kevin Smith. 2003. *The Public Administration Theory Primer*. Boulder, CO: Westview Press.

Gaus, John M. 1947. *Reflections on Public Administration*. University, AL: University of Alabama Press.

Heifetz, Ronald A. 1994. *Leadership Without Easy Answers*. Cambridge, MA: Belknap Press of Harvard University Press.

March, James G., and Johan P. Olsen. 1983. "Organizing Political Life: What Administrative Reorganization Tells Us about Government." *American Political Science Review* 77 (2): 281–97.

———. 1989. *Rediscovering Institutions*. New York: The Free Press.

———. 1995. *Democratic Governance*. New York: The Free Press.

———. 1998. "The Institutional Dynamics of International Political Orders." *International Organization* 52 (4): 943–69.

McLean, Bethany. 2003. *The Smartest Guys in the Room: The Amazing Rise and Scandalous Fall of Enron*. New York: Penguin Group.

Meier, Kenneth J. 2006. "The Role of Management and Diversity in Improving Performance of Disadvantaged Students: An Application of the Bum Phillips' Don Shula Rule." The Lent D. Upson Lecture in Public Administration, Wayne State University, Detroit, MI, 29 March.

Olsen, Johan P. 2004. "Citizens, Public Administration and the Search for Theoretical Foundations." *PS: Political Science and Politics* 37 (1): 69–79.

Szanton, Peter L. 1981. *Federal Reorganization: What Have We Learned?* Chatham, NJ: Chatham House.

4

Twenty-First-Century Career Leaders

Dwight Ink

Much has been written about desirable personal characteristics of public leaders, both political and career. These vary dramatically from person to person, from time to time, and from location to location; so much so that I leave to others the daunting task of finding the characteristics most often possessed by effective leaders. A smaller body of literature relates to external factors that have an impact on the effectiveness of leaders. In this chapter, I focus on external factors that limit the effectiveness of federal career leaders as we move into the twenty-first century. The potential impact of these limiting factors is not something of which the public is aware except in emergencies or times of scandal. Yet their day-to-day cost to the taxpayers, and the unnecessary loss of life and property during major crises they may cause, should be of great concern to our citizens.

There is general agreement that in the twenty-first century we will face complex circumstances that require far quicker government responses than before, more innovation, more coordination, and the capacity to address new challenges that may be so serious they threaten the very existence of our society. Since we seem to have had difficulty meeting a number of our twentieth-century challenges, it would appear that we need all the resources and talent we can muster to meet the more difficult problems of this new century. An important step will be utilizing our career leaders to the fullest in responding to future challenges. Especially critical will be their role in crises such as a possible nuclear detonation in New York City that is ten or a hundred times more powerful than the Hiroshima and Nagasaki bombs combined, an earthquake in Los Angeles of the magnitude that struck Alaska in 1964, or the economic disaster that a powerful, hostile Asia might trigger in another generation or two.

Today I believe we have a wonderful reservoir of talent within our Senior Executive Service (SES) and lower-level federal managers. But how well do circumstances permit this talent to be fully developed and utilized in meeting the formidable challenges of the future? It is my view that our ability to tap this enormous human resource is declining significantly.

In this chapter, I explore factors that increasingly limit the effectiveness of our career leadership that is so vital to our national well-being, and I conclude with a suggestion for beginning to reverse this course.

Preoccupation with Reinvention

One of the strengths of the United States is that throughout our history, we have looked with optimism to the future. We continuously strive to innovate and try new things in nearly every aspect of human endeavor. Our political process reinforces this behavior in government because each new mayor, governor, and president is eager to claim credit for his or her initiatives that are presumably much better than were those of a predecessor. But in the federal government, the downside to this admirable trait often restricts operational leaders when the need to explore various options is needed most. We unnecessarily limit our range of useful approaches to new problems with our preoccupation with the latest well-publicized idea that often contains more rhetoric than substance, and which frequently requires devoting enormous amounts of time and money striving to reinvent what has already been developed. We can easily recall the resources devoted to Planning Programming Budgeting System (PPBS), Zero-Based Budgeting (ZBB), Total Quality Management (TQM), and National Performance Review (NPR). Each of these had value, but I would argue that none drew effectively on earlier lessons, thereby detracting from their potential contribution.

In rejecting serious consideration of past lessons learned as too outdated to build upon or adapt to current challenges, we unintentionally limit the potential contribution of our career leaders. We are often told that the beginning of the twenty-first century is a period of unusual change, a period of transformation, which by definition requires entirely different concepts. New challenges are said to require abandoning old ideas and substituting new ones. It is argued that a new brand of leadership is required.

I would agree that this is a period of great change, and new ideas are needed. But we should not delude ourselves into thinking that transformation in the public sector is a new phenomenon, thereby requiring us to cast aside what we have learned from past successes and failures in our zeal to invent entirely new management strategies and approaches to leadership.

I would suggest, for example, that the period in which this nation was coping with the Depression and gearing up for the greatest war in history was also a period of great transformation in public administration development. There is much to learn from the leadership approaches used so effectively by that great civil servant, General George Marshall, who served so ably during World War II as the Army chief of staff and then became secretary of state and defense. Later, striving to address the poverty and civil rights issues of the mid-twentieth century, while engaged in a civilization-threatening cold war, we experienced another time of great change requiring management innovations, some of which may still have relevance today.

It would be interesting to catalog a few of the significant lessons a number of us have learned from earlier periods as we were developing ways to implement new presidential goals. For example, when President Reagan appointed me to handle our economic and technical assistance programs in the Western Hemisphere, I found my country mission directors complaining loudly that over the years far too many costly processes had evolved that compounded the time and cost of planning and delivering foreign assistance. Yet the previous political assistant administrators of U.S. Agency for International Development (USAID) had apparently provided no political support for their efforts to streamline the systems. As part of our response to this problem, we overcame a range of political concerns and adapted several streamlining approaches to delivering assistance that Don Stone had earlier incorporated in the design of the landmark Marshall Plan forty years earlier.[1]

A major reason President Nixon was so successful in his remarkably quick launching of the sweeping New Federalism grant reforms was that he had no hesitancy in building upon a series of Bureau of the Budget (BOB) pilot operations conducted during the Johnson administration (Ink 1996). The nationwide system of regional operations, for example, was built upon the field coordination arrangements instituted to address Alaska's recovery from its 1964 earthquake.

It is interesting to compare the speed with which our government moved into entirely uncharted territory during the Manhattan Project, and the skill with which the professional physicists and managers were utilized, with the problems we have today in mounting major initiatives of national importance. Placing a man on the moon was another impressive example. Both of these earlier programs relied heavily on a government-industry partnership in which accountability was clear and scandals were rare. Yet today we see case after case of poor contract administration and scandal. Both of these earlier successes also depended much more heavily on professional leadership from career personnel than we see today.

In stressing the value of looking at past lessons and adapting past approaches that have proven their value, as well as searching for new ideas, I recognize that there are those who are much too wedded to the past. Pockets of resistance to needed change have to be dealt with, but those can be addressed by effective leaders with surprising ease. In any event, their existence certainly does not justify a climate in which so many political appointees discourage career leaders from drawing upon earlier lessons as well as seeking new approaches in meeting operational challenges. In almost every case, permitting career leaders to utilize both the old and the new will enable a new president to move far more quickly with his or her agenda in carrying out campaign promises to the voters, an important feature of our political system. And in the process, the new political appointees will gain a better appreciation for the value of the career leaders and will be likely to use them more fully than if their experience is ignored during the launching of a new administration.

Expanding the Role and Number of Political Appointees

I share the view that the number and role of federal government political appointees is gradually weakening the opportunity of career men and women to provide the professional leadership this country needs to administer our laws effectively. Other advanced nations have not followed this unfortunate path.

Responding to concern about the steady conversion of senior management positions from career to political some years ago, and remembering the dramatic abuses of these and other steps toward politicizing the career service that had occurred in the Watergate period, we included in President Carter's 1978 Civil Service legislation a provision to halt this increase by limiting the number of political SES positions to the percentage of 10 percent of comparable positions that existed at that time. We would have liked to reduce the percentage below 10 percent, but we knew we would be very fortunate to simply halt the increase, and to push our luck further by proposing cuts would jeopardize both White House and congressional support for introducing any controls.

However, while the total number of federal employees has remained surprisingly stable for decades, most administrations have gradually added political appointees outside the civil service system, thereby nullifying the curb on future growth of political appointees that Carter's Civil Service Reform sought to achieve. Both Volcker commissions went further than Carter's reform by recommending a major cut in the number of political employees, but this significant recommendation has gone nowhere.

Several problems, discussed in the next sections, grow out of our excess of political appointees.

Obscuring of Presidential Vision

Career leadership is increasingly complaining that the proliferation of political appointees has eroded, rather than increased, the clarity with which they receive the president's vision of what the new administration is to accomplish.[2] Low-level political appointees tend to aggrandize their importance by implying a familiarity with the president's intentions well beyond their degree of knowledge, thereby introducing a filtering process that obscures depth of knowledge about the presidential concepts needed for effective agency implementation. Misguided political signals from lower-level appointees may totally miss nuances that make a large difference in what the president has intended and may undermine political strategies for gaining public or congressional support. When that occurs, it is generally the career person, not the political appointee, who is held responsible by the White House for the resulting problem.

Numbers Overwhelm Screening Capacity

Several of the most experienced former directors of White House personnel, regardless of how they feel about the number of appointees needed, have complained that they have not had the capacity to screen the lower-level appointees sufficiently from the standpoint of relevant experience. I stress *relevance*, because we have seen so many people eminently qualified in other fields who have struggled mightily in government leadership roles for which their prior skills had little or no relevance.

Further, many appointees have been told that the key to better government is to run it more like a business, but they do not realize until too late that there are some fundamental differences between running a corporation and a government agency.

Questionable Operational Qualifications

This problem is compounded by the misuse of appointees after hiring. Most political appointees are supposed to fill policy-level positions in which they help the president translate his or her campaign promises into realistic policies and legislative proposals. Unfortunately, lower-level political appointees are used increasingly for other purposes that are more operational, roles for which many are unqualified. Writing campaign speeches or contributing to a presidential campaign will not prepare one to help run an agency with thousands of employees and a multibillion-dollar budget. Operating an agency for a new president is no place for on-the-job training, especially when one realizes that the first few months of a presidency is the time in which a new president has the most political capital and is in the best position to implement the campaign promises made to the voters.

The role of political appointees should be more clearly understood to be that of policy development, advocacy, and agency oversight, not hands-on operations, a role for which career men and women are better qualified in most cases. I believe this clarification of roles would reduce agency costs and improve effectiveness of operations. This change could also pave the way to follow the Volcker Commission recommendations of sharply reducing the excessive number of lower-level political appointees (2003).

This does not mean that career people do not have an important role in policy development, or that political appointees should isolate themselves from operations. Far from it. However, while recognizing there are always gray areas, I believe accountability for policy should lie with the political appointees, and the political leadership should hold career leaders accountable for effective implementation of those policies, that is, the management of operations. More than some, I stress the difference between the desirability of involving both political and career leaders as a team in making any agency function effectively and the need to avoid blurring policy and operational accountability for which I believe the two have different roles.

Layering Decreases Effectiveness

Although the percentage of federal employees who are political appointees is small, the operational problem presented by their growth is disproportionately large. For example, adding political positions, such as associate deputy assistant secretaries and chiefs of staff to assistant secretaries, generally have the practical effect of further layering a department that likely already has too many layers at the top. These layers generate additional levels of approval and an increased number of required concurrences. Longer processing and decision-making time results. Accountability tends to become more diffused. This layering clearly decreases the effectiveness of career leaders.[3]

Mixed Loyalties

Many former cabinet members and agency heads have complained that they are pressured to accept low-level appointees whose loyalty is more to their political sponsor, such as an important mayor or large donor, than to them or the president. On critical issues, this can be a serious problem when the sponsor has different interests and priorities than the president. At times, such appointees use backdoor channels to advance their own role by secretly undermining the cabinet member through leaks and secret communications. Because this problem may not be apparent during the early stages of a cabinet member's tenure, considerable damage can occur before it can be dealt with.

Reduction in Contribution of Career Service

As mentioned earlier, the proliferation of low-level political appointees has inevitably led some increasingly away from their policy roles into operational roles. This has tended to push down the level of operational responsibilities available to career leaders, and taken them totally out of certain positions they are best equipped to handle, especially in the field. In addition to the frequent drop in operational skill from this substitution of political appointees, there is a widespread view that, in general, career leaders receive less political pressures to influence program management, resulting in fewer allegations of abuse and favoritism in the issuance of grants and contracts.[4]

Centralization

During the Johnson administration, we saw highly centralized federal approaches to administering many of the Great Society programs because of lack of confidence in either the capacity or the will of state and local governments to ensure that the objectives of these programs were met. The established power structures were regarded as not having much sensitivity or understanding with respect to the disadvantaged who had lost patience with their local leadership. Cities were burning, and Johnson had to deal with a growing urban crisis. The result was that field career leadership in most federal agencies had only a limited role in planning these new programs and in decisions regarding their implementation. Washington micromanagement of plans, approvals, and oversight was the result.

Most notable among the important exceptions to this general move toward centralizing controls in Washington was the formation of a heavily decentralized Department of Housing and Urban Development (HUD), soon to be followed by the Department of Transportation (DOT), both of which established strong field offices but retained effective Washington monitoring capabilities. The original design of HUD blanketed the country with a series of regions headed by strong GS-17 and GS-18 career regional administrators who were delegated department-wide responsibility for program implementation with several Federal Housing Administration (FHA) exceptions. Not very popular with most political assistant secretaries in Washington, they were nevertheless well received by local government and community leaders, especially those administrators buttressed by metropolitan expediters.[5] We tend to forget that HUD was regarded by many at the time as a highly effective domestic department, and was chosen by the Nixon administration as the best model on which to advance its ambitious reorganization of the domestic departments and agencies. The career assistant secretaries for administration in HUD and DOT were assigned the lead task of monitoring decentralization and helping secretaries see that departments as a whole functioned as intended.

President Nixon quickly reversed the Great Society centralized approach. Forgotten by many is the fact that during his very successful first years in office, Nixon drew heavily on Washington career leaders to design and manage his New Federalism, the centerpiece of his domestic initiatives. Especially significant is the fact that this broad-based initiative to move decision making out of Washington relied heavily on agency field offices headed largely by career leaders.[6] This was in sharp contrast to his later disastrous strategies in which he layered the career service in Washington and the field with political appointees and increasingly isolated himself from both the career service and much of his own political leadership.

The decline in the role of field offices after the 1972 election, the loss of coordination among these offices, the replacement of agency career field leaders with political appointees, combined with the 1973 loss of the Office of Management and Budget (OMB) intergovernmental management staff led to a large number of operational responsibilities gravitating back to Washington. As a result, the career role in program delivery has been downgraded significantly to the detriment of our citizens.

In addition, the move toward federal government centralization occurred during the same period that the role and number of White House staff increased greatly, weakening the role of most departments and distancing career leaders even more from detailed information about presidential initiatives useful for effective implementation.

Career-Political Partnership

The career service represents the primary resource upon which any incoming president must rely to carry out the promises he or she made to the people during the campaign. It is a resource without which a president cannot develop and launch successful new program initiatives of any magnitude. The career service is the only vehicle through which a president can govern. Yet we continue to see instance after instance of White House staff and agency leaders not only failing to reach out to the men and women on whom their political success will largely rest but also quickly alienating them through distrust and marginalizing their roles. Our slowness in developing political-career teamwork in a new presidency has reduced the contribution of career leaders during the critical initial period when a president generally has the greatest freedom to act.

These issues are well known within the public administration community where many books and articles on the subject have been written. Not so in the world of politics where this partnership notion is viewed as heresy. I agree with those who believe that, in general, the career-political relationship has eroded in recent years, limiting the effectiveness of both career and political leadership.[7] What is the practical effect of this change?

First, limiting the level of participation of career managers in the design of new program initiatives reduces the odds of their being workable, as we saw in Hillary Clinton's ambitious health care initiative. Career leaders best understand what will work and what will not, and they often best understand what can be guided through Congress. Their knowledge needs to be meshed with the political considerations of the new president.

Those who argue that the heavy involvement of career men and women will delay or even jeopardize an initiative by generating a list of objections, or that they will use their ties to the Hill to undermine needed legislation,[8] either fail to understand how to provide policy leadership or lack management skills to lead the career service. In the 1960s, 1970s, and 1980s, it was often career personnel who provided key leadership in designing the more successful programs a new president needed to implement his policies. Career-political partnerships during those years certainly enabled a president to move far more quickly than more recent instances in which the career men and women have played lesser roles.[9]

Limiting the career role in moving ahead with new presidential initiatives also reduces the sense of ownership and incentives to help the initiative succeed that would have been gained by the career service if they were permitted to participate fully in the planning phase. And because of their limited role, more time is needed for the career leaders to understand the intent of the president sufficiently well to engage each level of the department in successful implementation, generally causing months of delay in moving forward.[10]

Problems in forging an effective working relationship between new political appointees and career leaders are long standing. Most presidential appointees enter government having campaigned on the need for change, and to them the career service represents the status quo that needs to be controlled and their mind-set needs to be changed. Career people are viewed as supporters of the prior president and his or her agenda, and thus are assumed to oppose changes initiated by the new administration. Few presidential appointees see a distinction between the obligation of career people to support the constitutional office of the president as an institution, regardless of their political affiliation, and personal support of the person of the president within a political framework. Yet from the standpoint of effective government, the difference is fundamental.

The challenge of developing political-career teamwork does not lie solely with the political appointees. Not many career people are skilled at communicating with incoming politicians. Most dislike the amount of simplistic and extreme rhetoric that was part of the campaign that brought most of their new bosses into the government. Especially distasteful is the political rhetoric that blames the bureaucracy (that is, the career men and women) for the government waste, perceived as a major obstacle to government action or balancing the budget. This negative response from the targeted careerists is understandable. But career leaders must try very hard to place themselves in the shoes of the appointees and strive to understand what is important to them and what they believe the new administration hopes to achieve. No small amount of effort may be required to present their ideas and values in language that a politician without prior government experience can understand. Demonstrating how good management is also good politics for the new administration is not readily apparent to most appointees, and skill in explaining how good management will assist their presidency is an art that can be of great help in developing a political-career partnership. Doing so also strengthens the voice of the career man or woman who may later find it necessary to protest political interference in operations that might lead to inequities or favoritism in contracts, grants, and delivery of services.

One word of caution: In developing an effective partnership between political appointees and career leaders, it is important to keep in mind the need for the appointees to retain policy accountability and for career men and women to be held accountable to those appointees for agency operations.

Remaking Government as a Business

Over the past two decades, we have seen a continuing effort to make government function more like the private sector. This movement should be distinguished from the more modest concept of selecting certain private-sector practices that can be usefully adapted to government. The two ideas are fundamentally different. This emerging concept of running government like a business dilutes attention to those values of public service most important to effective functioning of democratic institutions. A private-sector vision of government also reduces its appeal to young people who have a strong motivation to serve the nation and its citizens, a loss that deprives us of an unknown number of future dedicated leaders.

As Ronald Moe (2004) often reminds us, this movement ignores how fundamental the differences are between the basis for government service and business employment. They grow largely out of the fact that government employees are empowered to do only those things that are authorized by law developed within the framework of our Constitution, whereas private-sector organizations are empowered to act in all areas not prohibited by law. In dealing with the public, government employees must observe due process of law. Their role is to serve the public with equity, transparency, and responsiveness, whereas the basic role of business is, and has to be, that of making sure the bottom line reflects a profit.[11]

However, this distinction does not lead to management in the two sectors being totally different. There are certain management techniques given heavy emphasis in most well-run corporations that can, and should, be adapted to government. Similarly, one can argue that just as public agencies are concerned about how citizens are treated, sound businesses also need to be concerned about their clients. But the latter concern grows largely out of the fact that failure to exhibit concern loses customers rather than out of a fundamental responsibility to serve them effectively. This difference in roles is illustrated by the fact that, unlike government, a business has no responsibility to serve those for whom such service would be unprofitable.

Considerable judgment needs to be exercised in determining what private-sector practices should be adapted to government needs and to what extent. In the General Services Administration (GSA) some years ago, for example, we realized that our warehousing practices were outdated, and we had much to learn from adapting private-sector practices. Yet when we essentially adopted a successful Sears, Roebuck system for our office furniture revolving fund, we came close to violating the antideficiency act at the highest level in our history. Because this approach to a revolving fund worked so well in the private sector, we tried to use it without paying attention to the fact that government is fundamentally different from a private business. We adopted when we should have adapted.

Other activities present much greater potential problems than do revolving funds when we press career leaders too far toward the private sector. This private-sector emphasis encourages career leaders to focus too heavily on business practices based primarily on dollars and cents as compared with designing a process that is responsive to the needs of those to be served. It gives priority to efficiency over the overarching goal of public service: effectiveness. Insufficient attention is given to some of the most important characteristics of public service such as transparency and equity. Public accountability becomes blurred. Application of market principles may be useful with respect to GSA supply schedules, but in other circumstances it will undermine an agency's responsibility for equity in pursuing its mission and may give undue influence to wealthy special interest groups.

We have seen case after case in which the more restrictive public service ethic continuously lands highly talented people from the private sector in trouble after they enter government, but the public rightly continues to oppose efforts to relax public ethics standards to be more like those in business.[12]

Numerous government observers have also become uncomfortable with the extent to which the private-sector emphasis is contributing to the denigration of the value of a public-service career. When the objective of entering public service is simply that of government being just one among a number of jobs during a varied career, we shortchange our citizens. Managers who concentrate on the short-term view of their government experience tend to focus undue attention on their own welfare and less on the success of their agency in achieving its mission and serving the public.

Viewing federal service as simply another job of limited duration has also reduced mobility opportunities that help qualify career people for important leadership roles. A career in the public service provides more opportunities to meet the original objectives of the SES whereby a potential leader could serve in different assignments with increasing responsibility over time among a variety of agencies.[13] Many complain about a loss of mobility among top career leaders in recent years. To the extent this is true, this trend will contribute to a further drop in the number of broadly experienced career men and women equipped to handle high-level management assignments. We see too many persons without benefit of varied agency experiences approaching high-level SES assignments with the limited vision of only their prior organization. Lacking experience in different agencies with a variety of cultures and objectives that require different management strategies, they are not well equipped to tailor their management strategies to different circumstances or take risks.

The mobility concept has been damaged by the occasional use of the SES mobility provisions for partisan political purposes by transferring a talented SES member to "Siberia" or to a desk with no duties, in the hopes of forcing the member out of government, despite provisions in the Civil Service Reform designed to prevent such abuse. In contrast to our limited opportunities to broaden one's federal leadership experience, most advanced countries, and our own military, require a variety of assignments for those with the talent to progress to top career levels. This was an important objective of the SES that remains largely unfulfilled.

The private-sector model does not fit public leadership roles in other ways essential to a democratic system such as ours. The degree of transparency in agency management is very different from that of private enterprise. The extent to which public managers must be in a position to defend and explain their every action to the press, to citizens, and to various oversight bodies has almost no counterpoint in the private sector. In fact, private-sector experience does not prepare one for most of the checks and balances that constitute the foundation of our constitutional system, yet these limits have a major impact on agency management. This public/private sector difference also requires a very different concept of accountability.

Some of our most dedicated public servants, political and career, believe that the requirement for government employees to take the oath of office deepens one's sense of obligation to carry out their public duties in an honorable way. Especially for those interested in a public-service career rather than simply a job, it serves as a lifelong pledge of integrity that helps strengthen one's resistance to improper work behavior. Many of us regard public service as a calling and believe it is a privilege to serve the public—a somewhat different mind-set than the principal factors motivating people to succeed in the private sector.

Because of the foregoing factors, I believe the overemphasis on making government more like the private sector is handicapping the development of effective career leaders and needs to be replaced with the more modest objective of looking at specific private-sector practices that can be usefully adapted for agency use. To the extent to which we strive to remake government like a business, we run the risk of weakening the awareness of public-service leaders to basic public-service concepts, and the understanding of how to function in our constitutional framework of checks and balances.

The Missing Presidential Management Arm

Over much of the last fifty years there has been justifiable criticism that, except for short periods, both the BOB and OMB have relied much too heavily on the budget as the primary means of advancing the management agenda of presidents and implementing congressional legislation. The problem is not the continuing emphasis on effective budgeting; this is a fundamental requirement of good government. Further, although presidential budget policies may be highly controversial at times, the professional skill of those handling the budget in OMB continues to be impressive, and their work is of invaluable importance to a president. Instead, the problem is that the strong budget activity is not balanced by a central management arm of the president that addresses those elements of effective government that are difficult to address through the numbers-oriented focus of the budget. As one result of this imbalance, we are limiting the broad management strategies needed for effective career leadership.

The budget can play a constructive role in management decisions and improving agency operations on some occasions. But the use of the OMB budget leverage has an enforcement aura that, in my view, is not nearly as effective for most purposes as a broader OMB leadership approach that emphasizes assistance to agencies in enhancing their managerial effectiveness. This is a very different environment that directs the attention of career leaders to values not easily reflected in budget numbers. For example, it gives greater emphasis to such values as equity in program delivery systems, safeguards against favoritism in contract administration, and the politicizing of grant award processes. It encourages greater emphasis on effective internal and external field-level coordination and intergovernmental cooperation. This approach provides greater help to agencies needing to increase their management capabilities than does a budget-dominated strategy. Budget processes are rarely useful—and are often counterproductive—in reorganization issues, especially in establishing new agencies.

In part, this overreliance on the budget for management purposes may have resulted from focusing on efficiency rather than effectiveness as the principal objective of government operations, but OMB has recently begun to rectify this problem to some extent.[14] I believe it has more to do with a failure to recognize what can be accomplished through means other than the budget, many of which have proven themselves to be effective in improving government. In addition to their intrinsic value, these approaches also have the advantage of not becoming as entangled with volatile partisan issues as major budget issues do, making it easier to deal with Congress on a bipartisan basis.

The earlier Organization and Executive Management (OEM) division in the

BOB worked closely with budget examiners in exchanging information, but seldom looked to the budget process in achieving the president's management goals. Instead, it relied on its drafting of presidential executive orders; participation in developing policy initiatives and legislation from a management perspective; issuance of government-wide circulars; assistance in strengthening the management capacity of troubled agencies; establishment and monitoring of interagency and intergovernmental coordinating arrangements; handling of presidential reorganization proposals; monitoring of agency program delivery operational outcomes; establishment of government-wide productivity programs; modernizing financial, information, and procurement systems; simplification and integration of administrative and program management systems; handling of reorganizations; and design of crosscutting presidential initiatives. This OEM leadership was provided exclusively by career men and women. Career managers participated in the daily meetings of the top White House staff and occasionally presented management issues to the president and the cabinet. It had an excellent track record with Congress.

These activities used to provide exciting opportunities for the finest career leaders to help the president and cabinet members improve government. This approach cultivated greater genuine agency support for presidential management initiatives, support that extended much further down within the departments. Sadly, OMB no longer has either the positions or the degree of interest with which to provide most of these leadership roles.[15]

In addition, for some years the OMB career leaders have been layered in by the political program assistant directors (PADs), and the president-appointed and Senate-confirmed OMB heads of the Office of Procurement Policy, the Office of Financial Management, and the Office of Information and Regulatory Affairs, who reduce the opportunity for the career staff to interact directly with the White House and cabinet members.[16] This change has diluted the influence of professional, nonpartisan advice that used to be available to the president and his aides in addition to the political advice that came from his political appointees.

We need to revisit the issue of what management needs could be best met today by strategies in addition to, or in lieu of, the current budget-focused approaches. What type of institutional structure would need to be established to provide leadership for these strategies? Should it be established within an OMB as originally contemplated, perhaps through a modernized OEM, or do we now need a separate structure in the Executive Office of the President?

However it is structured, a person with considerable prior government operating experience should head it. Similarly, departments should have either assistant secretaries for administration or undersecretaries for management, headed by individuals with extensive prior government experience, to provide cabinet members with effective leadership within the department for both administrative and program management. Ideally, these should be filled with SES members with high levels of success in several different agencies, having demonstrated skill in both leading career personnel and working effectively with agency political leaders. The next best arrangement would be for these posts to be filled with political appointees with prior government experience, combined with SES deputies. Filling the top two positions in the offices of either an undersecretary for management or an assistant secretary for administration with political appointees new to government would be an irresponsible act. The unusual amount of secrecy surrounding the operation of the Department of Homeland Security (DHS) undersecretary has made a full assessment of its operation virtually impossible thus far, but its apparent ineffectiveness resulted from questionable initial leadership and failure of either OMB or DHS to understand the role of the office.

Crisis Management

Special attention must be given to how well we utilize our career leadership in dealing with crises of this new century because they may be of devastating magnitude. The limited extent to which career leaders were in a position to quickly meet the challenge of Hurricane Katrina is disheartening. So are stories coming from Iraq concerning the constraints placed on career leaders in important operational decision-making positions, especially with respect to the extremely difficult task of so-called nation building. Underutilization of professional career people in times of crisis can cost many millions of dollars and contribute unnecessarily to suffering and loss of life. Conceivably, it could make the difference between success and failure. Because of the high visibility of how we respond in times of crisis, failure to utilize career leaders undermines the confidence of the American people in their government, as Katrina demonstrated.

Two basic approaches to management of recovery from natural disasters have been used. First has been the traditional approach in which the president relies on a permanent agency for leadership such as the Federal Emergency Management Agency (FEMA), now located within the current DHS. When well managed, this approach has worked in most natural disaster recoveries. However, in a few highly complex recoveries requiring extensive utilization of resources from other departments and interdepartmental decision making, it has been difficult for such an agency to secure the degree of rapid and wholehearted cooperation needed from sister agencies, especially after the initial response phase.

A second approach has been the less-well-known action of a president creating a temporary, overarching coordinating mechanism led by an experienced government manager reporting directly to the president and empowered to draw upon the total resources of the federal government without time-consuming negotiations or clearances. Although capable of extremely fast action and streamlined interagency and intergovernmental arrangements, this second approach places a premium on visible presidential commitment and professional leadership having extensive knowledge of federal agencies and Congress.

Utilizing the first approach effectively, James Witt is justifiably credited for remaking FEMA into a far more effective agency than had existed before. One of the reasons for his success most often advanced was the care with which he developed and motivated career leaders, giving them major responsibilities and then equipping them to move quickly and effectively in those positions. Among other things, he demonstrated the value of political-career teamwork and mutual trust in dealing with disaster recoveries. Very important, the president had confidence in Witt, giving him leverage with other agencies.

President Johnson gave even greater emphasis to the use of career leadership by appointing a career person, the author, to head the Alaskan earthquake recovery operations after the devastating 1964 earthquake, using the second approach of a temporary overarching arrangement to direct the recovery.[17] While directly impacting only about 200,000 people, between the 1906 San Francisco earthquake and Hurricane Katrina, it was the most complex natural disaster recovery we had experienced in the United States, and also the most urgent because of the short Alaskan construction season. Nixon followed a similar path to straighten out the recovery problems of the Harrisburg flood from Hurricane Agnes by appointing Frank Carlucci, deputy director of OMB, who had been for many years a career foreign service officer.[18] In the case of both Alaska and Harrisburg, no political appointee was given direct operating responsibilities, although they played essential roles in policy making and in supporting the career staff directing operations.

I stress that had I been required to work through political appointees in directing the operational aspects of the rebuilding of Alaska, or struggle with an unwieldy organization such as DHS, we would have failed, and tens of thousands of families would have been forced to abandon the state for the Lower Forty-eight. Yet we now expect the much weaker, more complicated DHS arrangement to provide successful leadership for future crises that are likely to be much larger than the Alaskan earthquake and even more urgent. One thing is very clear: Regardless of whether we organize along the Witt lines or use the Johnson-Nixon approach, we must remove the current limitations on the role of career leaders in times of crisis. Operational decisions must be made by experienced career leaders as was done in Alaska and Harrisburg. These leaders need to have firsthand knowledge of the role of various agencies and how they work. They need to understand agency headquarters/field relationships as well as intergovernmental relationships. They should understand how to work with Congress, hopefully having established close relationships with key members before taking on their disaster-related assignments. These leaders must understand how to arrange immediate collaboration with the many agencies on whose human and dollar resources a successful recovery will depend.

In times of crisis, every hour counts in responding to disasters or terrorist attacks. Even the longer-term major rebuilding and economic development decisions cannot wait for the usual administrative processes to work their way through the system. Many of these processes have to be dramatically simplified within the first several weeks, requiring greater reliance on the knowledge and expertise of those directing the recovery. It is the career men and women who best understand how to operate in the absence of the customary slow-moving processes that cannot be tolerated in times of crisis.

We all agree that military operations should be led by professional career officers within the policies determined by civilian leadership. Likewise, I believe that defending our homeland requires our recovery operations to be led by professional men and women. Why should we be satisfied with less skilled protection from attacks at home than we demand in the case of overseas warfare?

Presidential Transition

One seldom finds career people in the transition headquarters of the president-elect. It is exceedingly difficult for the winning candidate and his or her campaign team to make the mental transition from campaigning to governing during the few weeks of the presidential transition. This leads to the failure to recognize the need for involving career leaders during this critical period. In fact, many transition leaders view career people as slow, unimaginative creatures they take care to exclude from their plans to change government and remake Washington. Contrary to this conventional political wisdom, I suggest that effective use of career SES men and women in planning how to translate campaign promises into presidential actions and proposed legislation would make a huge difference in the quality of transition planning, the speed with which a new president could advance the agenda, and the effectiveness with which initiatives could be implemented.

Further, the presidential transition is the ideal time to begin reversing the trends discussed in the previous sections that are unduly limiting the effectiveness of career leaders. Helping the transition team lay the foundation for effective relations with Congress, for example, is an area where the career experience and their long-standing relationships with the Hill could be invaluable. Utilizing career leaders to help guide the design of new initiatives along lines that reduce unnecessary congressional objections, and are workable in application, would have helped past presidents avoid a variety of early embarrassments and delays. Any thoughts the president-elect might have concerning government-wide improvement in operations, a favorite topic of most incoming presidents,[19] must involve career men and women in leadership roles to be truly successful. Yet too often they are brought in as an afterthought and at too low a level to have much impact.

This early involvement of career leaders should also lay the groundwork for improved political appointee–career relationships as the new presidency moves forward, helping a new president throughout his or her term.

Revitalizing Career Leadership

The trends discussed earlier that limit effectiveness of career leaders are so deeply ingrained in federal government that not many believe it is realistic to reverse them. Difficult, yes, but not impossible. Iraq, Katrina, and other recent events have given greater visibility to the unfortunate consequences of failing to fully utilize the potential role of career leaders. I believe there are enough nonprofit organizations interested in effective government that the foregoing issues could attract serious consideration from several of them. These groups developed several very significant proposals for the 2000 presidential transition.[20]

I suggest that in their planning for the next transition, these organizations include consideration of ways in which career men and women can recover a stronger leadership role in government operations, relating the topic to the need for effective implementation of presidential initiatives.

Groundwork for this effort should begin as soon as the respective campaigns for 2008 begin to get organized and well before the election. Otherwise, the subject of policy implementation, including the need for involving career leadership, has almost no chance of garnering attention during the hectic days between the election and inauguration, a period when the development of presidential initiatives critically needs career input. Ideally, a person in each campaign headquarters with past government experience can be persuaded to help ensure an awareness of the relationship of the career service to successful implementation of the president-elect's policy agenda. This person will not be one who is handling the fast-moving tactics of the campaign, but he or she should be one of the few members of the candidate's team concerned about governing after election day. Two transition suggestions are offered: developing a transition management unit, and review of the role of political appointees.

Transition Management Unit

Each campaign should be urging to plan, in the event of winning, the establishment of a small management unit in the transition offices of the president-elect, as was done by President-elect Reagan in 1980 at the suggestion of Ed Harper and approved by Ed Meese. That three-person team of experienced career government managers focused much of its attention on reorganization issues such as proposing the elimination of the antipoverty agency, the Community Services Administration (CSA), and reorganization of the Department of Energy.[21]

It might be wise for the new management unit to be charged with focusing on managing policy implementation, rather than the more general term of *management* used in 1980. The subject matter would be much the same, but this linkage to policy would be easier to relate to the political instincts of most transition figures and would have a greater chance of surviving the pressures and near-chaotic conditions of a transition environment. It is also a sufficiently broad concept to include both program and administrative management in developing and implementing new presidential initiatives. It would be the ideal place to begin integrating career leaders and political leadership in the early stages of a presidential transition, rather than waiting until after inauguration.

Each of the areas discussed in this chapter should be on the agenda of this policy management unit. This will be the best time for prospective political leaders of the new administration to learn the value of the career service and how to work with career professionals.

This management group should also facilitate the difficulties faced by a new president in shifting from campaigning to governing. There is widespread recognition of the importance of a new president moving his or her agenda quickly after inauguration, but few do. And when they try to act quickly, the efforts often fail for lack of sufficient planning and/or failure to lay the groundwork with the Congress. On the other hand, we recall Nixon's New Federalism in which he drew heavily on career leaders, enabling him to move forward with sweeping implementation of executive orders within two months after inauguration. And by July, his director of the Bureau of the Budget was already asking the agencies for status reports on outcomes they had achieved. By contrast, with most career leaders used only in lower leadership roles, Clinton's Reinventing Government took much of the first two or three years just planning what was to be done, and similarly the Bush Presidential Management Agenda had little departmental action the first two years of his presidency.

Political Appointee Review

One especially important management suggestion for key nonprofit groups and, if established, also the transition management unit to consider for the next presidential transition is a long-overdue bipartisan review of the role of political appointees. For too long, we have failed to address the enormous impact, positive and negative, that political appointees have on the extent to which the career service is utilized effectively, especially with respect to the career leaders. Although I argue that it is the career service that should be held accountable to political leadership for implementation of policies, the political leaders have much to do with the environment within which career leaders operate and the extent to which career personnel are equipped to carry out their operational role.

Think for a moment about the extent to which outstanding political leaders such as Elliot Richardson, Jim Webb of the National Aeronautics and Space Administration, and James Witt each provided such effective leadership for the career service and relied heavily on professional career leadership in accomplishing great things that brought credit to their organizations. We complain a good deal about political appointees who fail to provide good leadership but seldom give them credit when they do. We almost never examine carefully what might be done to improve the general effectiveness of political appointees. We think of these appointees almost entirely from the standpoint of their policy roles and not at all with respect to their impact on the effective functioning of government agencies. There are numerous reviews of various aspects of the career service, so why is it not appropriate to occasionally review the other portion of government service, that of political appointees?

The aforementioned nonprofit groups and the recommended transition management organization should include in their agendas the desirability of establishing a statutory bipartisan commission to review the roles of political appointees in federal departments and agencies. It would undertake a broad study of the political appointees' portion of the federal government public service somewhat similar to the extensive study of the career service on which the Civil Service Reform of 1978 was based, including (1) the roles that political appointees can best play in the government agencies, (2) roughly what percentage of the workforce is needed to fulfill that role, and (3) what White House Personnel Office capacity is required to handle that many appointees.

The scope of this review should include ways in which effective political appointees have been able to energize and motivate career men and women over the years in advancing the agenda of a new president. Steven Kelman's recent book, *Unleashing Change* (2005), describes in some depth how effective one appointee found the career service was in bringing about change when "unleashed" from undue constraints and encouraged to innovate.

Conclusion

In this chapter, I have identified some of the ways in which career leaders are unduly limited in providing the leadership that could help new presidents and department heads advance new initiatives quickly. Simply preaching the value of good government to the newcomers, including generic comments about the virtues of career men and women, will have little or no impact on a new administration. In order to demonstrate the potential contribution of the career service to a presidential team and to make headway in reducing the current limitations on what the career leadership can accomplish, the next transition agenda has to link the career service and operational success of the policy initiatives advanced by the new president. This linkage has to be portrayed in plain language with concrete examples, something we do not do well. The transition team should gather a few concisely written case studies of past experiences in which both Republicans and Democrats have benefited from career leaders helping to advance presidential agendas when free of constraints that typically limit their effectiveness.

We need to give visibility to the price we pay for the declining role of federal career leaders and to its negative impact on federal government effectiveness. Our failure to fully utilize our impressive career talent has enormous potential consequences, and it must be corrected if we are to serve our citizens well and meet the global competitiveness of the twenty-first century.

Notes

1. The distinction between *adopt* and *adapt* is key to this discussion. Latin America and postwar Europe were very different in many respects, but the need to eliminate unnecessary internal red tape in our economic assistance programs, especially Washington micromanag-

ing, was common to both situations. It turned out not to be difficult to discern which Marshall Plan processes could be adapted, while recognizing that none could be fully adopted.

2. Some cabinet members have expressed similar concerns to the author.

3. In *Thickening Government,* Paul Light (1995) points out that between 1960 and 1992, the number of "top jobs" in the Department of Agriculture increased from 81 to 242; in the Department of Commerce the increase was from 29 to 217; in Interior from 50 to 160; in HEW from 27 to 339, despite the loss of Education. Most of these are filled by political appointees. Lower-level appointees do not show up on charts as layers, yet even a modest Schedule "C" title such as "special assistant" to an assistant secretary (that is not even on the chart) can decrease the role and operational flexibility of a top member of the SES accountable for a project or program.

4. In assuming leadership of the independent agency, the Community Services Administration, I found that no career person was permitted to even make a recommendation on the awarding of a grant or significant contract—this role was reserved for political appointees. There was no concept of non-partisan administration of laws or agency programs.

5. Several big-city mayors, such as Mayor Daley of Chicago, who were accustomed to direct access to cabinet members and felt it demeaning to work through a regional administrator did not share this popularity. However, Secretary Weaver backed career leaders to the hilt, telling the White House he would resign rather than compromise on politicizing these positions. Johnson was not close to Weaver, but he did not want to lose the first black cabinet member in our history, and the regional administrators remained career until the Nixon administration.

6. There were notable exceptions. One was the strong effort to remove a career assistant secretary of administration in DOT, Alan Dean, because of his earlier Democratic activities in local government. The DOT secretary, John Volpe, who regarded him as extremely able, vigorously opposed this pressure. Ironically, a key member of the White House staff, Fred Malek, knew of Dean's ability and arranged for him to be transferred to the management staff of the new OMB, much to the consternation of other White House staff. Dean's outstanding performance in OMB quickly earned him high marks where he quickly became highly valued by the Nixon leadership. He was an outstanding example of the career perspective of dedicated service to the presidency rather than to the president as a person, in this case a man for whom Dean never would have voted. After the elimination of the intergovernmental staff in OMB, and before Nixon left office, the top field office positions began to revert back to political appointments as a matter of policy, a trend that continued under President Carter.

7. One of the more comprehensive discussions of political appointee–career leaders' relationships is found in Heclo's *A Government of Strangers* (1977).

8. Political-career teamwork will nearly always improve agency relations with Congress and strengthen the ability of a president to gain congressional approval of the principal portions of his agenda.

9. Nixon's New Federalism, as well as Johnson's response to the Alaskan earthquake disaster and Carter's broad-based Civil Service Reform are examples of presidential initiatives that moved very quickly and also very successfully, at least from the presidential perspective. Each was designed primarily by career leaders working closely as a team with supportive political leadership and pursuant to a presidential policy.

10. In a review the author conducted for President Nixon in late 1970 of ten bills last enacted, it was found that most cabinet members counted implementation as having occurred when the secretary issued an implementing document, generally within a month or less. In fact, the median time elapsing from the president's executive order until the frontline career employee in the field received his or her operating instructions, a more meaningful measure of implementation, was about eighteen months. Disconnects between political leaders and

career implementers were a major reason for the delays. As a result of the survey, OMB and cabinet members began monitoring the whole implementation cycle, not just headquarter's initial steps in the process.

11. See Yong Lee's *A Reasonable Public Servant* (2005) for an exploration of the constitutional basis for public service, which is fundamentally different than private-sector employment.

12. This distinction does not necessarily place government ethics at a higher level than those in private business. Some features are, but others simply grow out of the different nature of government and business. In this era of global competition, it would make no sense to require corporations to follow federal government–type regulations to assure checks and balances embedded in our Constitution or require open competition for supplying the company with goods and services or the competitive merit-based employee systems we require for public service.

13. The trend toward disaggregation of the SES, resulting from different agencies being given greater flexibility in their personnel systems, will also likely work against career mobility.

14. The Bush Presidential Management Agenda has included some useful efforts to lessen this emphasis on efficiency rather than effectiveness. For example, it has linked the budget with program outcomes, actions for which OMB deserves considerable credit. The A-76 outsourcing circular, as another example, no longer contains cost as the only measure for decision making, though it gives more attention than effectiveness in how most agencies apply the circular.

15. The Department of Homeland Security (DHS) presents a painful example of this failure. At the time DHS was launched, the OMB no longer had any expertise to provide it with experienced advice. There was no one, for example, to explain to the new department the critical role of the undersecretary for management, because the one person responsible for its inclusion in the legislation had left OMB by the time the department was organized. Consequently, the undersecretary role has never been developed. No assistance was provided the new DHS regarding the critical need for interagency and intergovernmental coordination mechanisms and the need for experienced career personnel in operational positions. The tragic price paid for this serious OMB deficiency was all too visible in the Hurricane Katrina debacle.

16. Despite concern about this added layer, and its filtering role, on the average the PAD appointees have been of high quality and have deflected some political flack from the career OMB personnel.

17. Also critical to the Alaskan success, Johnson reconstituted most of his cabinet as the Federal Reconstruction and Development Planning Commission for Alaska, chaired by a powerful senator, Clinton Anderson from New Mexico. This Commission developed policy within which the operating official worked, having a dual reporting responsibility to both President Johnson and to Senator Anderson in his second role as executive director of the Commission.

18. Nixon did not establish a policy body comparable to the cabinet commission established by President Johnson, but a highly respected OMB deputy director, Frank Carlucci, was in a position to easily call on agencies for prompt assistance.

19. The most recent such efforts have been Gore's National Performance Review and the Bush Presidential Management Agenda.

20. These organizations might include the Brookings Institution, the Council for Excellence in Government, the American Enterprise Institute, the National Academy of Public Administration, the American Society for Public Administration, and the Heritage Foundation, as well as others.

21. The CSA was closed as of September 30, 1981.

References

Heclo, Hugh. 1977. *A Government of Strangers: Executive Politics in Washington.* Washington, DC: Brookings Institution.

Ink, Dwight. 1996. "Nixon's Version of Reinventing Government." *Presidential Studies Quarterly* 26 (1): 57–70.

Kelman, Steven. 2005. *Unleashing Change: A Study of Organizational Renewal in Government.* Washington, DC: Brookings Institution.

Lee, Yong S., with David H. Rosenbloom. 2005. *A Reasonable Public Servant.* Armonk, NY: M.E. Sharpe.

Light, Paul C. 1995. *Thickening Government.* Washington, DC: Brookings Institution.

Moe, Ronald C. 2004. "Governance Principles: The Neglected Basis of Federal Management." In *Making Government Manageable,* eds. Thomas H. Stanton and Benjamin Ginsberg, 21–39. Baltimore: Johns Hopkins University Press.

Volcker, Paul A., et al. 2003. *Urgent Business for America: Revitalizing the Federal Government for the 21st Century.* Report of the National Commission on the Public Service. Washington, DC: Brookings Institution.

5

Leadership by Top Administrators in a Changing World

New Challenges in Political-Administrative Relations

JAMES H. SVARA

It has become hackneyed to refer to the challenges of the new century. Many phenomena will not be distinctly different just because a new century has begun. Administrative leadership, however, is in the midst of a transition, and the time boundaries for this transition and an earlier one roughly correspond to the beginning and end of the twentieth century. In the first period of political-administrative relations during the second half of the nineteenth century, administrators aspired to make a larger contribution based on professionalism. In the second period that covered most of the twentieth century, they occupied a prominent and assured position in the government-centered process of governance. Starting in the late 1970s and now well established are a number of changes that will at least challenge and in some respects threaten the role of public administrators. In the twenty-first century, administrators must become adapters who continuously adjust in the fluid context in which they work in order to fill their leadership responsibilities. It is important to realistically grasp the status of administrators during each of these periods to better understand how their circumstances are changing now. The future role will be different, but there are positive aspects of the change as well as negative ones.

The focus here is on top career administrators—local government CEOs and permanent secretaries in Europe and city/county managers and senior executives in the United States—who relate closely with top politicians (both top elected officials and political appointees) on the one hand, and the organization they more or less direct on the other. Although there has been substantial continuity in the values of top administrators, changes are occurring in the basic relationship with politicians as well as shifts in the way that top administrators relate to their organizations and to the community. They will continue to make substantial leadership contributions to the process of governance but will have to be more deft and flexible in the way they do it. Although administrators have always needed the capability to change, adaptiveness now becomes their constant condition. The overriding challenge is finding ways to provide high-level leadership and maintain commitment to core values in an uncertain environment.

Transformation of the Status of Administrators

The suggestion that there are three distinct periods in the development of the status and role of administrators does not mean that there are sharp divides between the periods or that all top administrators uniformly demonstrate the same characteristics starting at the same time. Some experience new conditions earlier, and many lag behind as conditions change. Still, one can argue that the shifts in conditions and characteristics were well under way around the start of the twentieth and twenty-first centuries.

The Aspiring Administrator

The nineteenth century witnessed the emergence of public administration distinguishable from other centers of organized political power and able to function with some autonomy. Administrators during this period aspired to take on a larger role. In Europe, administrators who were already well organized in an administrative state separated themselves from the monarch and began to have direct interaction with politicians and the public as democratic institutions developed (Stillman 1997). In the United States, administrative organization gradually became more formalized. Administrators were distinguished from politicians and given some protections and began to develop independent status. There were also the initial efforts to figure out the relationship administrators should have with politicians.

The respect for and self-confidence of British civil servants with legitimacy derived from their service to the monarch (Price 1985) is remarkable for the time. Northcote and Trevelyan, whose report provided the basis for the modern civil service, advocated having permanent officers subordinate to ministers "yet possessing sufficient independence, character, ability and experience to be able to advise, assist, and, to some extent, influence, those who are from time to time set above them" (1853, 2). In the United States, there was a more tentative and timid beginning in the early decades of civil service reform with an emphasis on protection and loyalty. Wilson (1887) was more assertive in his famous rationale for a respected and active public administration that combined differentiation, insulation, deference, and subordination on the one hand, and discretion and independence on the other (Svara 1999a). Approximating the British view, Wilson argued that "the ideal for us is a civil service cultured and self-sufficient enough to act with sense and vigor" and "intimately connected with the popular thought, by means of elections and constant public counsel" (1887, 217). The foundation was being established for the consolidation of the position of administrators.

The Assured Administrator

The twentieth was the century of the increasingly "assured" administrator. Goodnow (1900) conveyed a sense of certainty about the functions of administrators, although he was still unsure about how to specify the relationship between administrators and elected executives that spanned the political and the administrative spheres. In local government, there was the risk that with an elected executive mayor, politics would impact administration, as Goodnow put it, "not only in its action but also its organization, with the result that qualifications of even clerical and technical positions in the public service soon become political in character" (1904, 153). Broadening civil service protection removed some of the risk of interference in the national government and occurred at a slower pace in state and local governments with elected executives, although separation of powers would continue to confound political-administrative relations in these governments. In the council-manager form of government endorsed by the National Municipal League in 1916, the executive is appointed by the city council from the ranks of professional civil servants nationally (and usually from outside the city), and separation of powers is removed. This form would come to be used by a majority of cities except the smallest and the very largest by the middle of the century.

Weber examined the accumulated power of administrative organizations and provided the rationale for a new model of administrative organization that increased the competence, capacity, and independence of bureaucracy (Gerth and Mills 1946). Indeed, Weber feared that administrators would overwhelm politicians with their power. He sought ways to keep administrators out of policy to allay this danger (Overeem 2005). The differing perspectives of Goodnow and Weber set the tone for enduring divergent perspectives in the United States and Europe. In the United States, there is a lingering concern among professional administrators and some academics that public administration is a fragile institution at risk of corruption or marginalization by political forces, and this concern is periodically confirmed by experience. In Europe, there is deep-seated concern about the danger of *Beamten-herrschaft*, or civil service rule (Overeem 2006, 144), which is reinforced by the pervasive power exercised by agents of the nation-state or now the supranational state.

In both Europe and the United States, there was shared support for administrative differentiation and independence from politics, but these conditions did not represent the exclusion of administrators from making important contributions to policy or exerting political power. In the name of preventing political interference, the involvement of elected officials in the administrative sphere was challenged in the orthodox period in public administration of late twenties and thirties in the United States (Henry 1975). Although this approach increased the separation of politicians from administrators, it also expanded the power of administrators, and in neither Europe nor the United States did separation produce the clear subordination implied by the politics-administration dichotomy. The orthodox model overreached in its claims for administrative autonomy (Waldo 1948) but supported the consolidation of the administrative state in the United States, bringing it more closely in line with conditions already established in Europe.

Changes within the Era of Assurance

In the second half of the century, the governmental process was opened up without diminishing the position of the top administrator. One should not overstate the discontinuity between the pre–World War II period and changes that would come later (Lynn 2001). Professional values rooted in advancing the public interest were well established before the rethinking that occurred in the turbulent sixties and the New Public Administration (Svara 2001). The changes that emerged around this time were the more widespread acknowledgment of the long-standing policy contributions of administrators, more visible interplay between politicians and administrators, and a more forthright assertion of distinctive administrative values as administrators' long-standing support for equity and high standards of conduct became an explicit commitment to social equity and administrative ethics (Frederickson 1980; Cooper 1994). When Page (1985) summarized the relationship between politicians (non-permanent officials) and administrators (officials) in Europe and the United States, he presented as established knowledge the fact that permanent officials have political power: "the answer to the question of whether officials or politicians rule is easy enough: both officials *and* politicians rule" (130). Indeed the resources and influence of administrators were so well established that his study was "concerned with assessing the scope for political action by non-officials within a system in which officials have power" (Page 1985, 8).[1]

It is important not to demonize these influential "bureaucrats" of the twentieth century, particularly in the middle years, nor to romanticize the period as a golden era (Newland 1988) when administrators were listened to, free to interact with external groups, protected from partisan interference, and hired and promoted solely on the basis of merit. Conditions changed continuously and substantially over the century. A "sovereign state model" with total control by government of all aspects of societal governance did not persist until the appearance of "new governance" (Sorensen 2006, 100). There was not a leap directly from the bureaucratic model to New Public Management (NPM; Stoker 2006). Administrators became more open and democratic in their interactions with the public and more participative in their organizational management, but top administrators operated within an administrative state framework that was fairly constant internally and externally (Kathi and Cooper 2005). Building on the strong position in their relationship with politicians, top administrators were moving toward a redefinition of other key relationships with new emphasis on democratic citizenship, models of community, and organizational humanism (Denhardt and Denhardt 2000).

By no means were administrators free from the risk of preemptory removal, political intervention, instability, and challenge, but they were clearly well established during most of the twentieth century.[2] Existing organizational and communication technology reinforced centralized provision of services and state monopoly. Administrators were guided by elected executives and/or elected representatives, and they influenced their "masters" as well. They were part of the "core executive"—a term that seems natural in Great Britain (Smith 2003), the Netherlands (Hart and Wille 2006, 133), and other European countries. Most western European countries and Canada have top administrators with titles such as permanent secretary, undersecretary, and deputy minister at the central level who interact directly with ministers; and they have well-established appointed top administrators in local government who are often referred to as the chief executive officer (Mouritzen and Svara 2002). Although Americans do not use the term and would probably be somewhat uncomfortable with the concept of a core executive who spans the political-professional divide, top civil servants have in the past been at least grudgingly accepted as partners in the federal government (Aberbach and Rockman 2000).[3]

In local governments with the council-manager form, city managers have always made a substantial contribution to policy, and by the 1990s elected officials considered city managers to be more involved than they in mission and goal setting (Svara 1999b). In Europe, Australia, and the United States, most top city administrators viewed themselves as having the same influence as or more influence than mayors and council members (Mouritzen and Svara 2002), and this is probably true in other countries that have well-established municipal administrative cadres. The picture in American cities with mayor-council governments is mixed. There is still no chief administrative officer (CAO) in half of the mayor-council cities over 10,000 in population. When there is a CAO, mayors can and sometimes do turn the position into an extension of their political operation. Typically the top administrators who work with elected executives rate their own influence as lower than the mayors, but still they consider their influence to be substantial (Svara 1999c); they view themselves as professionals, and they commonly have professional but not necessarily prior local government experience (Nelson 2002).[4]

The key conditions of these assured administrators in the twentieth century have been relatively high security, respect, and power vis-à-vis politicians. Within the organization, administrators have enjoyed fairly high levels of authority and deference from subordinates. Starting in the sixties—at times with a push by elected officials—they started extending a formal role to citizens to participate in the administrative process. Administrators were starting to display more openness in their dealings with politicians, more empowerment of citizens, and more managerial inclusiveness at the same time that new external forces would challenge their assured position.

Models of Political-Administrative Relations

To provide a frame of reference for examining recent and current changes, it is useful to examine the prevailing models of political-administrative relations during the twentieth century found in the academic literature and in practice. Four models represent differing combinations of choices on two dimensions that can be used to analyze interactions: the nature of the hierarchical relationship on the one hand, and the differentiation of roles, distance between spheres, and choice of norms on the other.

The nature of the hierarchical relationship refers to the extent to which the administrator is subordinate to the elected official. Public administrators may be either "instrumental or usurpative" (Heady 1984, 408), agents or trustees (Hood 2002), servant or master, tool or independent body (Barker and Wilson 1997), or they can be both. It is possible that the two sets of officials are both influential and that they interact in a reciprocal way (Farazmand 1997; Meier and O'Toole 2006). Administrators' policy advice can be accepted because they are perceived to be neutral between parties (Dunn 1997). There can be, as Krause (1999) puts it, a "two-way street" between elected officials and administrators. Hart and Wille conclude that the relationship in the Netherlands "is a set of negotiated orders rather than classical hierarchies" (2006, 133).

The degree of separateness depends on the distinctness of roles and norms for behavior. When roles are separate, key functions are performed by a different set of officials, and the spheres in which they operate are closed. When roles overlap, both sets of officials share in performing functions. Administrative norms stress general values such as fairness, impartiality, consistency, and objectivity; the values of particular professional groups or technical experts; and impersonal rules based in the law as bases for decisions. Administrators may act on norms that are political when they are too "responsive" and adopt the rationale and logic of politicians.

The characteristics of the four models based on the extent of a hierarchical relationship and the relative distinctness of officials can be specified as follows (Svara 2006a):

- *Separate Roles*: Clear subordination of administrators to politicians and separate roles and norms. There is clear direction to and broad oversight of administrators by politicians but little politician/party/ideological politics in administration. Politicians stay out of the details of administrative decisions, whereas administrators have limited involvement in policy making and their discretion is narrowly conscribed.[5]
- *Autonomous Administrator*: Equal or greater influence for administrators that extends to the policy sphere. Administrators follow their own norms, prevent politicians from entering the administrative sphere, advance their administrative interests, and constrain the choices that politicians can make. Politicians have only limited control over administrators with greater capacity to block administrative initiatives than to secure full administrative compliance.
- *Responsive Administrator*: Subordination of administrators to politicians and dominance of political norms over administrative norms. There may be political incursion into administrative decision making and/or administrators may adopt political norms in making decisions.

- *Overlapping Roles*: Reciprocal influence between elected officials and administrators and shared roles with elected officials. Separate norms are maintained, and there is explicit but not necessarily contentious competition between political and administrative values.

Beyond the four standard models, it is possible to identify instances in which the dimensions have more extreme characteristics (Svara 2006a). Political officials may not only control administrators but also substantially diminish the consideration of independent professional contributions when making policy decisions. When strictly separated, the administrators may be "ignored" and their advice or analysis excluded from decisions. When elected officials and political appointees penetrate the administrative realm to alter the nature of administrative advice, the impacted administrators are not just responsive, they are "manipulated." At the other end of the spectrum, very great bureaucratic strength could be manifested by bureaucrats who are aloof from politicians and control elected officials in a bureaucratic regime. The combination of very low political control and very low differentiation would be a condition of politicized administrators who are openly and actively involved in a political exchange with elected officials who are themselves highly organized administratively, for example, Aberbach, Putman, and Rockman's "Image IV" (1981).

The bulk of the research over time has supported the existence of the overlapping roles model (Mouritzen and Svara 2002). The widespread occurrence of overlapping roles, however, does not mean that some aspects of the other models are not commonly found as well. Thus, rather than viewing the models as complete competitors, a different approach is to accept the possibility that political-administrative relations draw some characteristics from each of the models.

The assured administrator manifests a distinctive and well-established set of characteristics—eight interactions and values—that reflects the complementarity of politicians and administrators (Svara and Brunet 2003). Empirically, the interactions of politicians and administrators have these characteristics that have been observed in previous studies (adapted from Svara 2006b):

1. Politicians and administrators maintain distinct perspectives based on their unique values and the differences in their formal position.
2. Politicians and administrators are primarily involved in distinct functions: politicians in policy making and constituent relations; administrators in implementation, service delivery, and management. There are partially overlapping functions as politicians provide political oversight of administration, examining both particular cases as well as general patterns of performance, and administrators are involved in the formulation of public policy and shape policy through the exercise of discretion in the implementation of policy.
3. There is interdependency and reciprocal influence between politicians and

administrators. These characteristics are based on the resources that each set of officials possesses, which prevent one from completely controlling the other. This balance of resources is necessary to offset the inherent asymmetry in political-administrative relations in favor of politicians (Dunsire 1973, 160).[6]

Value commitments blend control and delegation on the part of politicians and blend independence and deference on the part of administrators. These norms include the following:

4. Administrators support the law, respect political supremacy, maintain political neutrality, and acknowledge the need for accountability.
5. Administrators are responsible for serving the public and supporting the democratic process.
6. Administrators are independent with a commitment to professional values and competence, and they are loyal to the mission of their agency.
7. Administrators are honest in their dealings with politicians, seek to promote the broadest conception of the public interest, and act in an ethically grounded way.
8. Politicians respect the contribution of professional administrators and the integrity of the administrative process. Administrators encourage politicians to fulfill their responsibilities.

Richards and Smith express a similar view when they observe that, although officials and ministers in Great Britain "have different interpretations of the world, these on the whole are complementary because what they do is reinforce, rather than challenge, each other's position" (2004, 787).

Complementarity can be seen as drawing from each of the major models even though it most heavily reflects the overlapping roles model. For two elements to complement each other, they must be distinct, and, therefore, aspects of the separate roles model are found in complementarity. Top administrators are influential and extensively involved in policy innovation, and elected officials are somewhat active in administrative matters—indeed, at times more than administrators would prefer. The boundary between politics and administration is often breached, but it continues to be important. Complementarity also entails responsiveness and the obligation to implement the policies of elected officials. Administrators should make it clear that they expect politicians to set clear policy and not take advantage of vague or inconsistent goals to establish their own priorities (Burke 1986). Finally, top administrators have varying degrees of influence over policy and the process of implementation, in part because of partially shared views[7] and extensive interaction with politicians but also because they control resources that support their independence, as the autonomous administrator model suggests.

Top administrators seek to maintain sufficient autonomy to act on the basis of their professional perspective and values. They have their own view of the public interest and are expected to advocate it in making recommendations. Without power resources, administrators would be ineffective at performing their core tasks and subject to greater and potentially harmful political incursion. It is more likely that they would be ignored in policy formulation. Some autonomy is presumably needed to check "rash politicians" (Wilson and Barker 2003, 370) and is a condition for constraining democratic controls that would undermine efficiency (Miller 2000). Administrators help politicians express their goals, but they do not feel an obligation to totally "harmonize" the recommendations they make with the political priorities of current holders of elected office. In contrast to the autonomous administrator model, however, under the norms of complementarity, influence is not exerted unilaterally nor primarily to advance administrators' or the agency's own interests. In this approach, the core political-administrative relationship is a reflection of reciprocity between the two sets of officials. The essential interdependence is limited to some extent by separation and independence and tempered by some degree of responsiveness. In the complex relationship that evolved during the twentieth century, there has been a blending and balancing of the competing values of politicians and administrators reflecting the more or less even division of power resources between the actors.

Defining the role of top administrators in terms of the relationship to politicians alone leaves out other key relationships, and the omissions are significant. Top administrators certainly have had important interactions with the "public," but one can argue that the relationship was secondary to the linkage with politicians in the core executive during most of the twentieth century. They also had a strong link to their organizations, and this relationship was more secure and structured than the others. Less and less did top administrators sit at the top of a Weberian hierarchy as the century wore on, but top administrators have been executives of organizations with internal lines of control and clear boundaries. Assured administrators were able to focus on the relatively stable but highly sensitive core political-administrative relationship, they could choose how much to develop the administrative-citizen relationship, and they could set the terms for relationships within the organization.

New Conditions in a New Century

In the twenty-first century, the old values continue, but there are shifts in roles and in relationships. The change is relative to the original base point in a country, but most countries are moving in the same direction. For example, one might see Great Britain today as having a more constructive relationship between politicians and administrators than that found in American national government, but in Britain a "shift from the continuities and certainties of the stable institution" in Whitehall "to a more threatened and fluid situation" has been observed (Wilson and Barker 2003, 370). The political-administrative relationship is changing with new conditions in the political arena, and citizen and organizational relationships require explicit attention and new approaches. Top administrators have expanded influence in some respects as they operate more actively in the community sphere, but they experience new constraints and constricting forces as well. Administrators continue to have a high level of activity, recognition, ability to initiate, and capacity to shape the terms of relationships, but none of these characteristics is assured. This is the new era of the adaptive administrator.

Assertion of Political Power at the National Level

The last quarter of the twentieth century was a period of transition when signs of the new conditions began to appear. The Thatcher revolution, beginning in 1979 in Britain, and the Carter and Reagan administrations in the United States reflected a questioning of administrative prerogatives on the part of elected officials. There is increasing evidence of expanded political control over administrators. The old tradition of ministerial responsibility under which the minister would take responsibility for problems and then hold the permanent secretary and subordinates responsible for bad advice or performance outside public view is breaking down (Hart and Wille 2006; Christensen 2006). Now it is common for blame to be shifted to subordinates, which is part of a broader assertion of political power and a reduction in the security of administrators. Denmark has examined the increased use of "special advisers" to ministers, and a study commission has examined the number of these advisers (still small compared to other countries) and their potential interference in internal communication within ministries (Danish Ministry of Finance 2004). According to Christensen (2006, 1009), political leaders in Denmark in the past decade have exerted increasing control over administrative selection through removing top administrators from their positions and picking successors from the civil service who are more closely aligned with their goals and who are "collaborators with whom they have close rapport." In addition, ministers have demanded and received more political support from their ministerial staffs. Similar changes have occurred in other countries in western Europe. In all cases Christensen examines—Denmark, France, Germany, Great Britain, Holland, and Sweden—"the merit civil service is intact, but subject to adaptation and modification as the political executive has confronted it with new demands" (2006, 1016).

In Great Britain, traditional relationships are weakening. Graham Allen, a Labor M.P., has argued that Britain has had its *last prime minister*, as the governmental process becomes ever more organized around the top politician who has assumed presidential-like power without the checks and balances of the American system (2003). Administrators in Britain have supported the concentration of power. The problem, in Allen's view, is not that Blair, like Thatcher, reasserted "the fundamental principle that politics should be in control," but rather it is "unchecked and monopolistic political power being concentrated in the Presidency and served by the Civil Service" (2003, 18). Senior civil servants "felt unappreciated, threatened, and disparaged by Conservative ministers" and "the tensions that existed under the Conservatives have continued" under Labour (Wilson and Barker 2003, 368). Appointing "more ideological, policy-oriented ministers" and expanding use of special advisers potentially weaken the "over-riding tradition of the Westminster model" (Richards and Smith 2004, 798). These developments lead some to conclude that the civil service is "too obedient, not too recalcitrant" (Barker and Wilson 1997, 244).

In the United States, the Bush administration has intensified trends already in place since the late 1970s. During the Carter administration, a number of forces coalesced to add an emphasis on flexibility in personnel administration to the traditional concern for protection and independence. The argument was commonly made in the Carter White House that "many executives were not responsive and that economic incentives were needed to motivate some while adverse actions were needed against others" (Newland 1988, 637). The Civil Service Reform Act of 1979 and the creation of the Senior Executive Service (SES) reflected this shift. According to Moynihan,

> Whereas the concept of political responsiveness had once been associated with the incompetence of the spoils system, it now appeared consistent with arguments for better performance and the success of the private-sector organizations. Responsiveness now found renewed justification and legitimacy in the context of an administrative doctrine that promised performance, a more socially acceptable goal than simply political control . . . . (2004, 10).

Linked to the emphasis on flexibility and performance was a new orientation to the issue of loyalty. For the first time in the history of civil service in the United States, Newland argues, the issue of "first loyalty" arose initially in the Nixon administration and then was resolved during the Reagan administration (1988, 627). Rather than expecting civil servants to be loyal to the law and agency mission, "responsiveness to the President and his appointees had become the principal standard of performance evaluation and success or non-retention in the SES" (640).[8] Reassignment of senior executives to promote ideological consistency (Moynihan 2004, 23) along with the appointment of more ideologically committed political appointees and exclusion of career staff from policy deliberations were hallmarks of the Reagan administration (Newland 1988, 641). Although there were pockets of resistance—both exit and voice—most administrators viewed it as their duty to support political initiatives (Golden 2000).

Presidents of both parties have challenged the desirability of neutral competence with Republicans tending to question the loyalty of administrators and Democrats questioning their responsiveness to new ideas (Rourke 1992). Increased distrust and criticism of administrators by elected officials has contributed to "overzealous politicization of supervision" (Garrett et al. 2006, 234). The Clinton administration witnessed more use of consultants as key assignments were given to outsiders (Moe 1994), and the same practice has been used extensively in the U.K. (Allen 2003,

15.) The National Performance Review of Clinton and Gore incorporated the idea of flexibility, although this administration did not eliminate civil service protections that were backed by the Democratic Party's union constituency (Moynihan 2004). The presidency of George W. Bush has been characterized by clearer differentiation of roles with career staff limited to providing information that may be used by political appointees in developing policy as well as instances of ignoring (environmental policy) and manipulating (foreign and security policy) administrators and imposing political criteria to determine the relevance and appropriateness of evidence (science policy).[9] The passage of the Homeland Security Act reduced civil service protections to promote greater flexibility (Moynihan 2004). These changes have not undermined the merit civil service, but they have weakened the security of administrators and reduced their resources relative to politicians.[10]

Changes at the Local Level

At the local level, there is also evidence of changing terms in the relationship between politicians and administrators. The logic of British local government reforms has been to improve accountability by vesting strong political leadership in a mayor, cabinet, or ruling group (John and Gains 2005, 5). Formerly, citizens did not know "who to hold accountable when things go wrong and who to complain to when problems arise" (Rao 2005, 44.) Generally, new elected officials expect to have an impact and pursue specific policy interests, not simply to preside over the ongoing implementation of long-standing policies. SOLACE, the organization of local chief executives in the U.K., recently completed a self-study that finds a "significant rise in the last few years in the number of Chief Executives who were finding themselves in difficulties either with their leader or with their Councils more generally" (2005, 8). The introduction of direct election of the mayor in England has been adopted in eleven cities, and the logic of linking top administrators more closely to the chief elected official appears to be generally accepted. "Officers in mayoral authorities have a joint commitment both to serve the mayor and the rest of the councilor group," Stoker observes, "but in most cases there is little doubt that the mayor exercises a considerable focus for their work programmes and sense of direction. Delivering the mayor's manifest is considered a highly legitimate objective alongside the broader responsibilities and concerns of the local authority" (2004, 13). The cabinet-leader form adopted in most of the rest of English cities also presumes a closer alignment of the chief executive to the political leader.

In the nineties in the United States, a new breed of mayors appeared on the scene that focused on changing the way their governments operate. In mayor-council cities, these mayors expected to battle the bureaucracy over changes in administrative performance and management practices (Flanagan 2004). In a number of large council-manager cities, mayors—or groups committed to change the structure of government—have sought to expand their powers or to change the form of government. The efforts have been promoted as a way to make city government more efficient and accountable. Mullin, Peele, and Cain argue that the change represents a "shift in emphasis from the Progressive ideal of professional management to contemporary demands for electoral accountability" (2004, 26). Mayors have increasingly become media-based leaders who rely on mass communication and information technology to connect with citizens rather than using intermediary organizations such as parties. These top elected officials want to have attention, good press, a consistent message, and clear alignment of administrative performance and practices with political goals. Beyond mayors, it appears that local elected officials in general are more aggressive, more activist, and more engaged in ombudsman activities for constituents (Svara 2003). Changes do not necessarily create conflict with administrators, but they represent more assertiveness on the part of local elected officials and can produce tensions.

City managers in the United States typically devote their careers to professional positions in public management, but they are not careerists in the sense of having civil service job protection. They have always had "flexible" appointments, that is, they serve at the pleasure of the city council. Empirical studies since the 1920s have documented that city managers are influential leaders who make substantial contributions including policy initiation in the communities they serve (Svara 1989). From the 1960s through the 1980s, city management moved away from doctrines that stressed separation from the council and the importance of the city manager's executive authority (Newland 1989), affirmed the democratic values of the profession, and recognized the integral role of the council and the contributions—formal and informal—of elected officials to functions once viewed as reserved exclusively for the manager (Svara 1998).[11] A task force in the nineties reaffirmed the importance of viewing the council-manager form as an approach to governance and management that combines the efforts of elected officials and professional administrators. The manager's responsibilities to direct the organization, appoint staff, and prepare the budget are considered to be important for assuring the accountability of the manager and the effectiveness of organizational performance, not as grants of authority to be exercised in isolation by the manager. In the strategic plan adopted in 2000, ICMA members distinguished between professional management and the exact institutional relationship with elected officials when they asserted their belief in the value of professionalism as an "integral component of effective local government" and in the council-manager form as the preferred form of government (ICMA 2000).

Two studies of elected officials capture shifts occurring in large council-manager cities in the past two decades. In the mid nineties in cities with population over 200,000, city managers played an even larger role in shaping goals and strategies than they had a decade earlier (Svara 1999b). Indeed, council members reported that they were less involved in broad steering activities than they had been previously and acknowledged that the city manager was more involved than they were in these decisions. At the same time, council members were focusing more attention on mid-level policy decisions than previously. It appeared that council members were reacting to the recommendation of administrators and providing tentative approval while intervening in specific decisions to fine-tune the way goals were carried out. They were also much more heavily involved in constituency complaints about service delivery reflecting a new (or more focused) concern with performance.

In contrast, a 2001 survey of council members showed that respondents from cities over 200,000 in population were less likely to view the city manager as a very important contributor to policy initiation than they had been twelve years earlier (Svara 2003). Whereas 68 percent and 43 percent considered the city manager and administrative staff, respectively, to be a very important source of policy initiation in 1989, the comparable figures were 32 percent for the city manager and 6 percent for administrative staff in 2001. There was more stability in ratings of the city manager's contribution in smaller cities, but in the largest ones, elected officials viewed themselves and not the city manager as a major policy initiator whereas earlier they considered both themselves and the city manager as very important. Only 6 percent viewed the city manager as the most important source of policy initiation in the largest cities compared to 31 percent in 1989. From these findings, it appears that city managers in large cities are not able to provide as much input or have as much influence as they had previously.

Pressures for Change

Underlying the changing relationship across countries and levels of government has been the emergence of a "counter" model of bureaucracy. The assured public administration was based on the long-standing self-perception that it is accountable and advances the public interest (Bailey 1962). This view has been challenged by the specific claim that administrators are ideologically liberal and biased in favor of the use of governmental power (Butler, Sanera, and Weinrod 1984), and the public choice perspective that administrators are self-interested, like all other political actors. It became common to question whether public administrators are public servants (Eggers and O'Leary 1995, 123). From this point of view, market forces, competition, and revenue reduction are needed to offset the self-interested tendencies of public administrators and agencies, and constructive change is produced by putting "outsiders" in charge of public administrators. Basic improvement, in the view of Eggers and O'Leary, can come only "by shifting activities from the public sector to the private" (1995, 40). The practice of "bureaucracy bashing" that has been particularly common in the United States promotes a negative image of administrators and increases the distance between political appointees and senior civil servants (Garrett et al. 2006).

As politicians are more resistant to advice from administrators, they are more receptive to advice from other sources. A number of "outsider" groups—including think tanks, advocacy groups, consultants, business leaders, and academic researchers—have been important sources of pressure for change and key participants in the reform process (Pollitt and Bouckaert 2000, 20). For example, conservative policy institutes such as the Adam Smith Institute in Britain and the Heritage Foundation in the United States have provided specific proposals for reorganizing and reorienting government. To illustrate the change, Pollitt and Bouckaert point out that in the U.K., "the civil service reforms of the 1960s were carried out largely as an internal matter, whereas almost every reform in the 1980s and 1990s included participation by one or more of the big management consultancies" (2000, 20). This has been true in other countries as well.

The Reinventing/NPM movement also reflected shifting attitudes about the political-administrative relationship. The steering versus rowing distinction asserts a new and artificial distinction between politicians and administrators. In a sense, it "re"-creates the separate roles model or a politics-administration dichotomy that has never actually been well established previously. Although the approach can be seen as diminishing the contribution of politicians by assigning them to a broad but thin governance role and removing them from direct involvement in constituency service (Hood 2002; Larsen 2005), it also implies that elected officials focus on setting goals and defining the preferred policy outputs that administrators are supposed to meet (Sorensen 2006). If politicians use the steering rationale to assert themselves, administrators may be removed from their traditional role as policy adviser. The steering-rowing distinction reinforces a heightened focus on elected officials.[12]

These changes have produced greater political control—or at least the opportunity and rationale for it—in the core political-administrative relationship and reduced the power resources of administrators, both absolutely and also in comparison to other actors. Shared "disdain for the bureaucracy" has unified political appointees and increased their power vis-à-vis administrators (Garrett et al. 2006, 236). The few politicians need to pick their shots carefully in dealing with the many administrators, but it appears that politicians often relying on external sources of expertise have become better able to influence administrators or undertake policy initiatives without the support of administrators or over their objections. In some instances, the impact of these changes has been overt conflict between politicians and administrators. Just as important, however, is a shift from "reciprocity and mutual understanding" to "mutual risk avoidance and hence less productive collaboration," as Hart and Wille observe in the Netherlands (2006, 144).

Changes in Management and External Relations

Management reforms usually with strong support from politicians (Pollitt and Bouckaert 2000) have altered the conditions of administrators. NPM reforms have impacted relationships within the organization and the boundaries of the organization itself, particularly outsourcing of service delivery, reducing individual and organizational permanence, and decentralizing organizations (Peters 2001). For individual managers, the focus on performance gives the top executive both new opportunities and places new demands on them. Combining new managerial flexibility to let managers manage and clear performance targets to make managers manage puts the spotlight on the top executive to improve organizational performance (Abramson, Bruel, and Kamensky 2003, 3). Whereas the internal management of public organizations was once the province of top administrators who presided over established administrative systems, politicians have demonstrated the capacity to reach into the public organization to change personnel and budgeting processes, create new measurement tools, and alter methods of delivering services.

Top administrators themselves may be supportive of reform, even if it causes tension within their organizations (Pollitt and Bouckaert 2000, 19). They may have different incentive structures than lower-level staff. As Dunleavy (1991) suggests, the CEO is not likely to pursue private interests through budget expansion and focuses instead on the benefits that come from "bureau-shaping." Administrators at the departmental level, on the other hand, may seek to protect and expand their resources and protect their programs, the traditional public choice view of administrators as budget maximizers. In Dunleavy's view, "rational officials want to work in small, elite, collegial bureaus close to the political power centres," and this is what top administrators do (1991, 202). Although this revised definition of self-interest partially explains the behavior of top administrators, there is just as much evidence that they strive as leaders of their organizations to advance public-service norms (Mouritzen and Svara 2002, ch. 10).

Occurring simultaneously has been the reexamination of the relationship with citizens and other external actors. New efforts to promote citizen participation and foster community leadership broaden and decentralize the connections between agency staff and citizens (Kathi and Cooper 2005). New information technology and mechanisms for e-government and e-democracy provide new kinds of access but also bypass traditional linkage channels. For top administrators, the inherently difficult task of supervising frontline and street-level bureaucrats becomes ever more difficult when interactions multiply and become digitalized. The electronic lines of communication between local elected officials, citizens, and staff members remake the organization chart and impact political-administrative relations, organizational management, and relationships with citizens. The focus on services may promote closer relationships between lower-ranking administrators and citizens (or may not, depending on the source of service delivery), but it replaces policy and rule-based guidelines for service delivery with an emphasis on serving the public (Denhardt and Denhardt 2000).

In external relations, there is increased reliance on networks and partnerships and the expansion of the "new governance" phenomenon in general (Goldsmith and Eggers 2004; Kettl 2002). The challenges of coordination and accountability are extensive when a range of public and private organizations and/or multiple governments are contributing to goal setting, developing "policy" responses, and delivering services. Whereas these major functions in the process of governing formerly occurred largely within governments and single jurisdictions (as well as across levels of government) and within national boundaries, they are increasingly occurring in shifting alignments of governmental and nongovernmental organizations (NGOs) and across jurisdictional boundaries at the same level of government as well as across levels both domestically and globally. Even without accepting the view that government officials have become "meta-governors" who largely attempt to coordinate the efforts of self-governing groups (Sorensen 2006), the number of actors in policy and administration directly controlled by top administrators is declining. Even when top administrators maintain the capacity to coordinate the efforts of their own staff, the networked organizational lines are unclear and unstable. Many of the relationships are dotted lines to peers or nongovernmental organizations rather than solid lines. The network members can change over time and vary with each policy and service area, and consequently the boundaries of organizations are open and shifting. SOLACE notes the new responsibilities that arise in networking: "Where no leading politicians serve on partnerships, Chief Executives will often be the most senior figure—and the most accountable—in partnerships and the most in touch (local politicians apart) with the whole local population because of the scope of the council's activities" (2005, 6).

Taking all the changes together, top administrators have seen their key relationships expand and become more intense and less predictable. In the political-administrative relationship, the boundary between politicians and top administrators is blurred and can shift when new politicians take office. When politicians assert control, top executives may find that they can no longer engage in customary activities or have the access and influence to which they are accustomed. SOLACE identifies the increasing need to clarify the "rules of engagement" between the leader and chief executive: "if the rules of engagement are not clear, if there is no shared understanding of roles and objectives, it is more likely that trust will break down" (2005, 5). Similarly, a self-study by top Danish administrators concludes that in their dealings with elected officials, top executives may struggle for "management space" with top politicians (Forum for Top Executive Management 2005, 16). The same kind of struggle may occur with many of the other participants in governance as well. More of the actors with whom top administrators interact are not under their direct control—not only elected officials but also NGOs, citizens groups and individual citizens, other governments, contractors, and even some of the employees in their own organization.

In many respects, the authority and independent influence of top administrators has been reduced compared to the prevailing conditions during the twentieth century. On the other hand, administrators may gain influence from their greater knowledge of networks, how they work, and what they are doing. Top administrators have distinct advantages in partnerships and networks. They may have a greater strategic sense of how to achieve a goal than other actors, and as the SOLACE report observes, they are more likely to be able to relate the goal of one partnership with other goals. The looseness of arrangements can give the top administrators unprecedented discretion in shaping the governing process in particular areas but at the same time limits their ability to direct it. The resources of the network manager are illusory, and the opportunities for direct control are limited, but the top administrators have the opportunity to shape direction. SOLACE highlights this potential when it refers to its members in British local government as "senior strategic managers."

How do top administrators respond to continuous change and disappearing boundaries? The simple answer is that top administrators must be capable of adapting to an extent not found previously as they fulfill their essential responsibilities and seek to advance the public interest.

The Adaptive Administrator: Challenges and Response in a New Era

The changes in progress will require top administrators to have more fluid, flexible, and less predictably bounded dealings with politicians while at the same time expanding their interactions with citizens and leaders outside the organization. Their responsibility for internal direction will also change along with the transformation of public "organizations." Drawing on all these elements, top administrators will provide guidance and facilitation to support new approaches to governance.

Changes in Political-Administrative Relationship

The combined effect of current changes will alter some characteristics of the complementary relationship of politicians and administrators even though the basic interactions and values persist. An abbreviated version of each of feature of complementarity follows along with an identification of how it will be impacted in the new era of adaptability. The feature that is most impacted by change is the sharing of functions in policy making and oversight, but all the characteristics of complementarity are affected to some extent.

1. *Elected officials and administrators maintain distinct perspectives based on their unique values and the differences in their formal position.*

The distinctness is sharpening, and the interplay of values is becoming more contentious. Elected officials are less likely to see the usefulness of administrative values. They are more likely to interpret arguments or reservations expressed by administrators as if they were objections that amount to putting obstacles in the path of elected officials. Administrators, on the other hand, are more likely to interpret expectations to support political initiatives as interference. Top administrators need to be more attuned to relating to the value concerns of elected officials and "translating" between the political and professional spheres (Nalbandian 1994.)

2. *Officials have partially overlapping functions as elected officials provide political oversight of administration and administrators are involved in policy making.*

The roles in policy making and oversight have been altered by changes in values and attitudes. Increased focus on the top elected official and the difference between politicians and administrators stressed in NPM have given more prominence to the contribution of elected officials while slighting the traditional contribution of administrators. In this view, elected officials maintain control through setting goals and objectives and measuring performance in meeting objectives. There may be some increased anxiety among top administrators as they fill the policy advisory role, since this appears to contradict the principle of steering by elected officials, but it is likely that they will continue to make a substantial contribution to policy making. Elected officials will give increased emphasis to assessing performance in politically sensitive areas, although systematic oversight is likely to be slighted in the future as it has been in the past. Indeed, administrators will need to continue to support the design of sound assessment processes as well as provide information about performance.

The greatest problem for administrators in filling the policy advisory role is how to advise politicians who do not want advice. It is sometimes true that politicians do not want input from administrators, that is, when administrators are excluded from deliberations or their recommendations are either ignored or preemptively rejected. In some instances, administrators are manipulated to provide public support for positions politicians have independently adopted. Still, it is probably most common for top administrators to be actively engaged in policy advice but for the interaction to be characterized by more give and take. More policy initiatives will be pursued without administrator input or in spite of their input, and elected officials will increasingly draw on sources of information outside the administration.[13] Top administrators need to be more sensitive to balancing advice with awareness of political priorities, but they must avoid allowing the range of alternatives that they recommend be restricted by excessive sensitivity to political goals or fear of negative reactions. When administrators internalize negative images fostered by bureaucrat bashing (Garrett et al. 2006) or accusations of disloyalty, they may pull their punches—not speak all the truth to power—in order to avoid reinforcing the public attacks (Pillar 2006).[14]

Administrators should also expect more give-and-take with politicians. In the past, top administrators commonly presented alternatives to which elected officials reacted. Increasingly, administrators are called upon to help advance the agendas of activist-elected officials who are committed to pursuing their own projects. In these situations, top administrators are increasingly called upon to react to the proposals that elected officials are promoting rather than the reverse. Administrators can help elected officials understand the implications, costs, and administrative arrangements needed to carry out their initiatives and understand how the specific project or policy relates to the overall work of the agency or the jurisdiction.

Administrators are likely to continue having a broader, more comprehensive, and longer-term view of the agency or jurisdiction than elected officials, and they are able to clarify the steering role of elected officials and the strategic choices they must make. To suggest that politicians create vision and administrators execute it (O'Neill 2005) leaves out an important part of the way that elected officials and top administrators have worked together in the past. Top administrators have helped to shape the vision and ground it in past and current goals for the government, and they can continue to do so. Top administrators as strategic leaders can assist elected officials in steering through volatile and uncertain conditions. They should expect that politicians will not always be happy getting their analysis of future trends and recommendations for goals and policies, but they should persist in offering them nonetheless.

3. There is interdependency and reciprocal influence between elected officials and administrators.

Interdependency is still the reality despite the rhetoric of political control, but there has been a shift in relative influence in the direction of politicians. They are more inclined to distance themselves from administrators, thereby reducing the opportunity for influence, or to reduce the scope of administrative input, and they are more inclined to assert their power. Assessing changes over the past quarter-century, Aberbach and Rockman (2006) conclude that there has been a

> retreat from what looked originally like a steady progression of bureaucratic influence in policymaking from Image I (politicians making decisions and bureaucrats implementing them) to Image IV (a deepening overlap of roles) back to Image II (with civil servants bringing facts and knowledge to the policy process and politicians defining values and representing interests).[15]

This conclusion appears to fit the constrained circumstances of American federal civil servants in particular and separation of powers-settings in general. It is likely that the contribution and influence of top administrators in unity-of-powers forms of governments nationally and locally is greater, but the direction of change is the same in these settings as well.

Administrators will continue to help shape the values of the governing process with variation related to their normative commitments, internal coherence, and resources. The relative resource position of administrators vis-à-vis politicians has surely declined, as the power of politicians and their willingness to use it have increased and top administrative control over information, service delivery, and organizational direction has declined.[16] On the other hand, administrators still have great resources on which to draw. Furthermore, in the complex world of new governance, administrators are much more widely dispersed in networks and alliances than politicians can be, have much greater knowledge of what is happening, and have a greater opportunity to shape and guide activities. They may increasingly be in a position to broker agreements between politicians and network participants.

The value commitments of complementarity blend control and delegation on the part of elected officials and blend independence and deference on the part of administrators. In the new conditions of the twenty-first century, control and deference have increased, and delegation and independence have declined, although all four characteristics will continue to be present. These trends are reflected in shifts in specific norms.

4. Administrators support the law, respect political supremacy, maintain political neutrality, and acknowledge the need for accountability.

Politicians often demand political responsiveness, and administrators are more attuned to the need for it. The heightened attention of the media and increased concern for media management has created the characteristics of a "permanent campaign" (Hart and Wille 2006, 142) in which consistency of messages from the political through the administrative spheres is stressed. Maintaining political neutrality—treating all superiors equally as opposed to pervasive value neutrality—is strained when administrators are expected to support the political message as well as the policy goals of politicians. In its 2005 report, SOLACE observes that "central to understanding political leadership is understanding the process by which political leaders achieve the position they hold and how they build and maintain their authority and legitimacy within their leading group or coalition" (5). Chief executives must be sensitive to the challenges that leaders face and the motivations and interests that are behind them. "While it is not the Chief Executive's job to intervene in the workings of the group," the report concludes, "the Leader will rightly expect the Chief Executive to understand the context in which the Leader operates and to advise accordingly" (SOLACE 2005, 5).

The demand for responsiveness often forces administrators to confront the tension between professionalism and politicization. A permanent secretary in Denmark summarized what politicians expect of top administrators in this way: "When the minister has a new tune, the permanent secretary should develop it into a melody and eventually into a symphony" (Kettl, Pollitt, and Svara 2004, 52.) The expectation is a democratically appropriate one on the part of the elected official assuming that the goal has been approved through the legislative process before the symphony is performed. Such a complete elaboration of a political goal by the top administrator is professionally appropriate if it is done in a way that is consistent with professional standards. The focus on the ombudsman role by elected officials and more incursive methods of oversight require that administrators maintain balance between policy, procedure, consistency, and fairness,on the one hand with the desirability of giving special but not partial attention to some specific cases on the other.

5. Administrators are responsible for serving the public and supporting the democratic process.

These responsibilities are expanding as administrators become more service-oriented and both develop and accept new ways of involving citizens in the governing process. Greater community leadership could produce more tension with politicians. It is possible that there will be resistance to the idea that administrators relate directly to citizens in other than a service-delivery role. Still, new governance requires that administrators participate in and foster links outside government and beyond their jurisdictional borders. The compelling drive to expand the use of IT will inevitably spread from e-government to e-democracy.

6. *Administrators are independent, with a commitment to professional values and competence, and they are loyal to the mission of their agency.*

This value is still important, and administrators must deal with pressures to shift their loyalty to the program of political superiors rather than the agency or the larger representative body. The "agency perspective" (Wamsley et al. 1990) is subject to substantial revision if elected officials change the mission and fundamentally alter how it is carried out. Independent behavior increases the likelihood of removal as politicians more actively monitor and intervene in the personnel selection process. Politicians look for loyalty to the incumbent rather than support for universal values and the established goals of the agency, but administrators must fulfill their duty to maintain professional independence if they are to uphold their part of the relationship with politicians and their responsibilities to the public.

7. *Administrators are honest in their dealings with elected officials, seek to promote the broadest conception of the public interest, and act in an ethically grounded way.*

Changing conditions probably mean that public administrators experience more situations that challenge them ethically. The pressure to be politically responsive makes it harder to assert views that are not in favor and make administrators more inclined to make recommendations that conform to the preferences of politicians or to remain silent. Politicians supported by party, interest groups, and ideologically congenial think tanks provide information to administrators to shape their thinking and make clear which alternatives they prefer. Administrators must have greater courage to stand up to political pressures[17] and at the same time exercise self-restraint when tempted to use administrative resources to undercut political goals.

8. *Elected officials respect the contribution of professional administrators and the integrity of the administrative process. Administrators encourage politicians to fulfill their responsibilities.*

There have been dramatic instances in recent years when respect for administrators has been absent, and it seems likely that the general level of respect for administrators has declined to some extent over the past quarter century. Administrators face the challenge of overcoming negative expectations in their dealings with each new wave of elected officials or political appointees (Garrett et al. 2006), and the increased appointment of fervent critics of agencies to top positions increases the likelihood of distrust (Newland 1988).[18] Still, it appears that often the contribution of administrators is acknowledged by political appointees and elected officials over time (Garrett et al. 2006, 234), and this is a resource on which administrators can build. Politicians and administrators should respect and understand each other, and Ferrara and Ross (2005) conclude that they often do.

Overall, a close working relationship—even a partnership under the right circumstances—between elected officials and top administrators is still possible, but it is not as easy to create or maintain as it once was. From the perspective of a top administrator accustomed to the assured position of the previous era, the changes required to maintain the relationship can be unsettling and even seem illegitimate. From a normative perspective that stresses a strong political voice and the active interchange between elected officials and administrators, the new conditions are a positive development because they reflect the strengthening of political influences and the opening up of the public organization to the community.[19]

There are needs for adjustment on the political side of the relationship as well. Elected officials and political appointees need to be more consistently competent and have goals that are broader than their own political future or the elected executive's narrow electoral interests. In settings where there is high mistrust of "bureaucrats," it would be useful for elected officials and political appointees to see the relationship in potentially positive terms. Administrators can help politicians develop and accomplish their goals if they are allowed to do so. Following the recommendations of Ferrara and Ross (2005), both sets of officials should start with the assumption that the relationship will be constructive and resort to aggressive or defensive measures only if that expectation is not met. Top politicians in separation-of-powers settings may be able to achieve a higher level of effectiveness by stressing a facilitative approach in their dealings with the legislature and the career civil service rather than relying on a power-based approach to leadership.[20]

For top elected officials in a unity-of-powers setting, developing a positive relationship is more natural. Without the divided-loyalty issues created by separation of powers, a cooperative approach is less likely to be undermined by conflicts over the interests of office and relative power. Politicians and administrators see "the virtues of complementarity and teamwork," and the benefits to both sides are evident when these characteristics are present (Hart and Wille 2006, 138). Elected leaders with no or limited separate formal powers, like mayors in council-manager cities in the United States, can choose to adopt a facilitative model of leadership (Svara and Associates 1994). They do not need to rely on power resources to reward supporters and punish opponents. Rather, they can be visionary leaders making use of the policy advice and the responsive and efficacious organizational direction that the city manager can provide.

In either formal setting, politicians and administrators would do well to devote time early on to "proactive meta-communication" about how the political leader wants to be advised (Hart and Wille 2006, 136) and how to interact effectively with the career staff without disrupting internal lines of control.

In terms of the models of political-administrative relationships presented earlier, the new political context probably causes top administrators to draw relatively more from the characteristics of the separate roles and responsive administrator models than they did in the twentieth century. They are likely, however, to still be operating primarily in the overlapping roles model and guided by the modified norms of complementarity.

Qualities of the Adaptive Top Administrator

In the new conditions, top administrators cannot define their role exclusively in terms of their relationship to politicians or the function of providing policy advice, and they must develop new capabilities to deal with the change and uncertainty in their context. Their circumstances will require "constant learning and adaptation," as Abramson, Bruel, and Kamensky indicate (2003, 6). To develop a proper orientation, they suggest going to an amusement park to experience a roller coaster: "Enjoy the ride! Your life in government in the years ahead might very well resemble that ride" (2003, 6). Some additional recommendations can be offered with brief commentary.

All Relationships Critical for Success

Each of the relationships—with politicians, citizens, and the organization—is important, and they are more intertwined with developments in one potentially impacting others. For example, politicians have altered the working relationship with administrators by changing the methods for delivering services to citizens. The adaptive administrator must develop each of these relationships, constantly monitor and adjust them, and perceive how conditions and changes in one sphere affect the others.

Capability to Make Shifts within Roles

Administrators need to make frequent shifts within their more dynamic relationships. The old, more established roles will persist, but administrators must shift back and forth from presenting an analysis of trends and options to responding to the initiatives of politicians, from being in charge to being an equal partner with others in a network, and from being responsible for meeting citizen needs and delivering services to being responsive to citizens in determining needs and co-delivering services.

Management Reform and Improved Performance

A major impetus to politicians pushing governmental change in the past quarter century has been a concern about governmental accountability and performance.

The same theme has been pursued by organizational managers themselves (for example, Forum for Top Executive Management) and academic researchers. Performance management is one of the major trends transforming public administration (Abramson, Bruel, and Kamensky 2003, 6). To stabilize the relationship with politicians and to meet responsibilities to citizens, administrators must demonstrate that they achieve results. Improving performance will require new methods of defining goals and measuring outcomes.

Improvisation

Administrators need to be more comfortable with and capable at improvisation. This refers to the general capacity to relate to a particular audience in a particular situation in a way that is perfectly suited for that moment, as Denhardt and Denhardt (2006) indicate. As is true of the adaptive condition generally, improvisation involves "creativity within structure" (115). It is behavior that draws on established knowledge, experience, and skills but moves into unknown, unscripted areas. An important additional element of improvisation is its affective dimension. Improvisation is "essential to the process of emotionally connecting with and energizing others" (109). With more spontaneous interactions and fewer established authority relationships, leadership is more difficult in all the administrators' key relationships. "Skilled improvisation on the part of a leader," the Denhardts conclude, "provides an important source of inspiration, guidance and connection with others" (110).

Innovation and Willingness to Advocate Change

Administrators also need to be capable of innovation. Responsible innovation requires inventiveness and creativity, the ability to build support within and outside the organization, and integrity as evidenced by incorporating the views of stakeholders and objectively evaluating how well the innovation is working (Borins 2000). Administrators must be self-critical regarding their personal traits and their programs and methods and willing to make changes. Loyalty to the mission of the organization and commitment to enduring values does not mean preservation of the status quo (Terry 1990). Creating and sustaining a culture of innovation involves transforming the organization to respond to new conditions that are changing the public sector. Top administrators must build trust and empower staff, serve citizens and foster their participation, encourage looking ahead and taking risks, and promote core values and sustained commitment that provide stability (Denhardt and Denhardt 2001). They should encourage subordinates to take on new responsibilities and develop new organization-wide perspectives.

Teamwork

The changing conditions mean that top administrators cannot be capable of handling all the responsibilities or possessing all the competencies that are required to meet their expanding roles. They must be capable of putting together teams with the balance of competencies needed to address their major challenges, and they must clearly communicate with team members what their contribution will be to decision making. Are they advising the top administrator and expanding his or her scope of knowledge and judgment, or are they jointly responsible for making the decision? As a study team to the Forum for Top Executive Management in Denmark recommended, "leadership by top executives consists of developing skills, responsibilities and motivations in others as well as achieving excellence in their own direct performance" (Kettl, Pollitt, and Svara 2004, 29). It is not easy, however, for top administrators to move from being at the apex of the organization and the primary source of communication with the top politician to being part of a shared leadership approach, and they must develop new competencies to accomplish the shift.

More Coordination by Communication

Direction can be given with memos, orders, and manuals of procedure, but increasingly there is a need for communication that is based on shared understanding, symbols, and information. This kind of communication is commonly disseminated through open media rather than relying on closed, internal channels. Top administrators need to have an appreciation of new forms of communication and greater capability in using them. They need to develop their own communication links with the public and other key actors, and they need to be better able to use the mass media. In addition, they must be part of the broader efforts in their governments to develop clear and coherent messages to a wide range of audiences.

Conclusion: Ethics and Power

For top administrators, a solid value base is even more important in their unstable circumstances than it was in a more stable time. As in the past, they must be guided by a strong sense of duty and thorough grounding in universal values to keep their bearings and to help assure that the means they employ to achieve their expanding and shifting responsibilities are ethically sound (Svara 2007). They face new ethical issues, and there are pitfalls they should avoid: slanting the issues raised to get attention from political superiors, allowing responsiveness to undermine professional standards, and exploiting loose accountability controls for self-advantage. Top administrators face the perennial ethical issue of how they use their power and resources. Maintaining administrative independence is ethically appropriate when it supports integrity, the capacity to articulate professional standards, and pursuit of the public interest. The values of complementarity support the positive purposes of public administration—its internal goods (Cooper 1987)—while the characteristics of complementarity describe the conditions needed to be able to pursue them. The application of the values may need to modified, as the earlier discussion indicates, but they continue to provide guidance even in changing times.

How does one assess the current status of top administrators and the future prospects for their involvement in governance? An effective and responsive governmental process requires contributions from politicians and administrators, both of whom have linkages to citizens and groups. Top administrators provide strategic guidance and help link the actors in the governance process. Generalist administrators, like permanent secretaries, and local chief administrators operate at higher levels with a wider range of issues than specialist senior executives and have greater potential for influence, but both continue to be more or less connected with top politicians in the core executive. The status of top administrators is not the same as it has been, but the future is not bleak despite the changes that are occurring.

Compared to the era of assurance, the status of top administrators appears to be diminished, and there is no reason to expect that the conditions that prevailed in the twentieth century will be restored. It is a distortion to look at this period as one in which top administrators presided over monolithic bureaucracies and set the terms of engagement with politicians. Still, there were large, competent, and centralized organizations that normally had the power to resist being manipulated to promote the political advantage of a particular political regime. These conditions were part of a necessary stage in the development of the administrative state, but this stage does not have to be restored or repeated. The late twentieth century witnessed an assertion of political control and citizen activism that altered the way that governmental organizations operate, and these changes contributed to and were influenced by a broader transformation in the way that societies are governed.

The nature of government and the roles of politicians and administrators are different when governance combines governmental and private actions, is cross-jurisdictional, and is global. The terms of engagement are altered in ways that at times reduce the capacity of administrators to shape and influence decisions, but top administrators must keep advising and informing and attempting to shape strategic direction. The contributions of top administrators formerly were to provide general and specialized advice to politicians on the one hand, and transmit policy goals to the administrative organization, monitor and adjust the process of accomplishing them, and report back to top politicians on the other. These tasks continue, but top administrators are not the only source of advice, and they now often react to the initiatives generated by politicians as well as get the reaction of politicians to alternatives they propose. They are much more focused on performance, and they have and are subjected to a wider array of measurement tools and technologies. At times, they only loosely preside over an expanding range of actors, many of whom they do not "control," but they are still responsible for accountability and have distinctive expertise in fashioning approaches to achieve it. They are increasingly called upon to empower citizens and encourage self-governance rather than being only the agents of governance. Their environmental and work context is uncertain and unpredictable, and they must be constantly adaptive in their outlook and behavior.

Despite all these changes, there is still a critical role to play and important contributions to be made by top administrators. The position can still be attractive, and the prospects for filling it "successfully" are still substantial for administrators who accept change and are able to be adaptive. The position may be more attractive than the earlier assured version to young staff members in organizations who have grown up in the new environment. They are likely to move into these positions in the future with more appropriate expectations than the current occupants. They will expect extensive give-and-take with politicians who themselves have a stronger activist orientation. They will expect to be managers as well as advisers. They will expect to work in networks and be facilitators of citizen participation, and many will have experience doing so based on movement between sectors in their careers. Presumably, they will not expect or want to be part of stable, well-bounded organizations.

Furthermore, top administrators will still have important resource advantages vis-à-vis politicians, and these will increase as government agencies enter into larger numbers of networks and partnerships. As in the past, resources help to ensure that administrators are able to block blatant forms of political incursion and able to bring professional standards and values into the governmental process. Despite politicians' ability to impose policy choices or exert pressure to secure compliance in specific matters, they will continue to depend on the loyalty and compliance of administrators in the full spectrum of policy advising and implementation. Top administrators will not be oriented to having control. They will find that they are part of a complex game of shaping messages to internal and external audiences that is shared with politicians and their agents, and they are likely to be more comfortable doing so than are present-day top administrators.

In the future, top administrators are less likely to be highly elevated above other administrators and less likely to be the only link between the political and administrative spheres. They will have to be nimble and adaptive in an uncertain world. But they will have a broader and more challenging job description as a key actor who connects many arenas and serves as adviser and strategizer with politicians, facilitator of networking and democratic action, and organizer of action, innovation, and accountability. All things considered, this is a different but attractive job description for top administrators.

Notes

1. The widespread acceptance of the idea that the politics-administration dichotomy is the founding concept of public administration has led American scholars and observers of public affairs to repeatedly present the policy role of administrators as if it were a break with established thinking. For example, a report on improving interaction between political appointees and career staff in 1987 recommended "that the notion that appointees craft policy while civil servants implement it be relinquished once and for all. Senior career people must be at the center of policy formation" (quoted in Newland 1988, 641).

2. There is evidence of varying but in some cases high levels of turnover related to political accountability. When the factors that contributed to the removal of the chief administrator in the United States in the mid nineties were compared to thirteen other western countries,

almost half the city managers left because of problems with politicians. In contrast, the average in all other countries was 18 percent (Svara 1999c).

3. Abramson (2005) argues that they should be accepted more fully at the present time. He views as the "biggest 'secret' in Washington" that "political appointees and career executives need one another; neither group can succeed without the other." In council-manager governments, there is reluctance to acknowledge that the mayor is part of the executive function because mayors typically lack any separate executive authority, and there is a desire to keep the council out of administrative activities. In contrast, a number of European countries that use quasi-parliamentary forms recognize the executive authority of the mayor and use an executive committee or cabinet form of government that brings a number of council members into the ongoing work of the executive.

4. According to Nelson (2002), the CAOs in mayor-council cities among the forty largest cities have extensive professional training and organizational experience, although typically it is not in city government. When all cities 20,000 and more in population are compared, 59 percent of city managers compared to 15 percent of city administrators previously were the top administrators or assistants in another city. In larger cities, city administrators are more likely to be drawn from the locality whereas city managers are likely to have had a career working in a number of cities (Svara 1999c).

5. These conditions would correspond to Lowi's (1993) ideal world.

6. In complementarity, as Richards and Smith observe, the "conceptualization of power" that applies to the relationship "does not involve the element of dominance" (2004, 783). Although political-administrative relations can break down into a zero-sum power relationship, this condition is not typical. The asymmetry in formal position means that political control can be imposed. For example, some ministers accept the part of the Westminster model "that portrays the minister as master who is able to direct the department as he pleases" but not the part that indicates that he should listen to top civil servants (797). The bureaucracy is not defenseless if relations break down into a zero-sum battle. It can quietly rebel and seek to ensure that a minister is a failure (Page 1985, 1).

7. Waterman and Meier (1998) note that principals and agents often share goals.

8. It is presumably still the case in Britain that civil servants have a "wider loyalty to the constitution and the public interest," which can be used to justify disobedience "in terms of the tradition of the Westminster model" (Richards and Smith 2004, 787).

9. For critical accounts, see Specter (2006) and Pillar (2006).

10. Some states in the United States have eliminated or are questioning civil service (Walters 2002).

11. Key developments were new recognition criteria in 1969, the report *New Worlds of Service* in 1979, the Declaration of Ideals published in 1984, and the report of the Task Force on the Council-Manager Plan in 1994 (Svara 1998).

12. To Osborne and Gaebler (1992), "steering" focuses on providing guidance and direction and should be done by government, whereas "rowing," or producing goods and services, is best provided by the private or nonprofit sectors. In some NPM discussions, on the other hand, steering is associated with elected officials and rowing with administrators (Pollitt and Bouckaert 2000; Larsen 2005).

13. Richards and Smith (2004, 797) identify bypassing career staff and drawing information from outside sources as a source of conflict between British ministers and officials.

14. Former national intelligence officer for the Near East and South Asia Paul Pillar (2006) argues that the "poisonous atmosphere" created by charges from administration supporters that intelligence officers (including him) sought to sabotage the president's policies on Iraq "reinforced the disinclination within the intelligence community to challenge the consensus view about Iraqi WMD programs; any such challenge would have served merely to reaffirm the presumptions of the accusers."

15. Wilson and Barker see the shift as a reversion all the way to Image I, or the separate roles model (2003, 370).

16. The change in the relative resource position of politicians and administrators is presumably related to the level of government and the size of the jurisdiction with a greater resource advantage for administrators at the local level and in smaller jurisdictions.

17. An example is the process of "suasion" by Defense Secretary Rumsfeld, who did not give orders to key military staff but "planted ideas and sent papers" that supported his agenda. Getting rid of top executives and political appointees who support career staff also sends a clear signal that loyalty is expected (Gordon 2006).

18. Ferrara and Ross summarize the results of interviews conducted during the Bush administration. Political appointees often come to their new positions in Washington with these perceptions of career staff: "careerists are loyal to the previous administration; careerists are not passionate about their work and don't work that hard; careerists are mostly interested in job security; careerists always say no to new policy ideas; and careerists don't want their political bosses to succeed" (2005, 5). Although careerists also have negative perceptions of political appointees, the authors say that the careerists have experienced persons who have the negative traits. For careerists, therefore, it may be more appropriate to conclude that they sometimes expect the worst rather than that they believe in myths with no basis in fact.

19. As M.P. Graham Allen puts it, to assert "the primacy of politics and to make it crystal clear that the civil service was there to serve" would in itself be welcome because it reestablishes "the fundamental principle that politics should be in control" (2003, 18).

20. This premise is being examined in case studies of several mayor-council cities being prepared by scholars for a symposium on facilitative leadership to be held in 2007.

References

Aberbach, Joel B., Robert D. Putnam, and Bert A. Rockman. 1981. *Bureaucrats and Politicians in Western Democracies*. Cambridge, MA: Harvard University Press.

Aberbach, Joel D., and Bert A. Rockman. 2000. *In the Web of Politics: Three Decades of the U.S. Federal Executive*. Washington, DC: Brookings Institution Press.

———. 2006. "The Past and Future of Political-Administrative Relations: Research from *Bureaucrats and Politicians* to *In the Web of Politics*—and Beyond." *International Journal of Public Administration* 29: 977–96.

Abramson, Mark A. 2005. "Get Along to Go Along." *Government Leader* (June): 9.

Abramson, Mark A., Jonathan D. Bruel, and John M. Kamensky. 2003. *Six Trends Transforming Government*. Washington, DC: IBM Center for the Business of Government.

Allen, Graham. 2003. *The Last Prime Minister: Being Honest about the UK Presidency*. Rev. ed. London: Societas.

Bailey, Stephen K. 1962. "The Public Interest: Some Operational Dilemmas." In *Nomos V: The Public Interest,* ed. C.J. Friedrich, 96–106. New York: Atherton Press.

Barker, Anthony, and Graham K. Wilson. 1997. "Whitehall's Disobedient Servants? Senior Officials' Potential Resistance to Ministers in British Government Departments." *British Journal of Political Science* 27: 223–46.

Borins, Sandford. 2000. "Loose Cannons and Rule Breakers, or Enterprising Leaders? Some Evidence About Innovative Public Managers." *Public Administration Review* 60: 498–507.

Burke, John. 1986. *Bureaucratic Responsibility.* Baltimore: Johns Hopkins University Press.

Butler, Stuart M., Michael Sanera, and W.B. Weinrod. 1984. *Mandate for Leadership II: Continuing the Conservative Revolution*. Washington, DC: Heritage Foundation.

Christensen, Jorgen Gronnegard. 2006. "Ministers and Mandarins under Danish Parliamentarism." *International Journal of Public Administration* 29: 997–1020.

Cooper, Terry L. 1987. "Hierarchy, Virtue, and the Practice of Public Administration: A Perspective for Normative Ethics." *Public Administration Review* 47: 320–28.

———. 1994. "The Emergence of Administrative Ethics as a Field of Study in the United States." In *Handbook of Administrative Ethics*, ed. Terry Cooper, 1–36. New York: Marcel Dekker.

Danish Ministry of Finance. 2004. *Civil Service Advice and Assistance.* English Summary. Report no. 1443. Copenhagen: Expert Committee on Civil Service Advice and Assistance to the Government and Its Ministers. June. www.fm.dk/db/filarkiv/9421/English_Summary.pdf. (Accessed 12 October 2006.)

Denhardt, Janet Vinzant, and Robert B. Denhardt. 2001. *Creating a Culture of Innovation: 10 Lessons from America's Best Run City.* Washington, DC: IBM Center for the Business of Government.

Denhardt, Robert B., and Janet Vinzant Denhardt. 2000. "The New Public Service: Serving Rather than Steering." *Public Administration Review* 60: 549–59.

———. 2006. *The Dance of Leadership: The Art of Leading in Business, Government, and Society.* Armonk, NY: M.E. Sharpe.

Dunleavy, Patrick. 1991. *Democracy, Bureaucracy and Public Choice. Economic Explanations in Political Science.* London: Harvester Wheatsheafs.

Dunn, Delmer. 1997. *Politics and Administration at the Top: Lessons from Down Under.* Pittsburgh: University of Pittsburgh Press.

Dunsire, Andrew. 1973. *Administration: The Word and the Science.* New York: John Wiley and Sons.

Eggers, William D., and John O'Leary. 1995. *Revolution at the Roots: Making Our Government Smaller, Better, and Closer to Home.* New York: Free Press.

Farazmand, Ali. 1997. "Introduction." In *Modern Systems of Government Exploring the Role of Bureaucrats and Politicians*, ed. Ali Farazmand. Thousand Oaks, CA: Sage.

Ferrara, Joseph A., and Lynn C. Ross. 2005. *Getting to Know You: Rules of Engagement for Political Appointees and Career Executives.* Washington, DC: IBM Center for the Business of Government.

Flanagan , Richard M. 2004. *Mayors and the Challenge of Urban Leadership.* Lanham, MD: University Press of America.

Forum for Top Executive Management. 2005. *Public Governance: Code for Chief Executive Excellence.* Copenhagen: Forum for Top Executive Management.

Frederickson, H. George. 1980. *The New Public Administration.* University, AL.: University of Alabama Press.

Garrett, R. Sam, James A. Thurber, A. Lee Fritschler and David H. Rosenbloom. 2006. "Assessing the Impact of Bureaucracy Bashing by Electoral Campaigns." *Public Administration Review* 66: 228–40.

Gerth, H.H., and C. Wright Mills, trans. 1946. *From Max Weber: Essays in Sociology.* New York: Oxford University Press.

Golden, Marissa Martino. 2000. *What Motivates Bureaucrats? Politics and Administration During the Reagan Years.* New York: Columbia University Press.

Goldsmith, Stephen, and William D. Eggers. 2004. *Governing by Network: The New Shape of the Public Sector.* Washington, DC: Brookings Institution Press.

Goodnow, Frank J. 1900. *Politics and Administration.* New York: Macmillan.

———. 1904. *City Government in the United States.* New York: The Century Co., 1910 [copyright, 1904]. Reprinted by Arno Press, 1974.

Gordon, Michael R. 2006. "Rumsfeld, the 'Agent of Change' Who Wouldn't Adapt to Changes." *International Herald Tribune* (April 22–23): 5.

Hart, Paul 't., and Anchit Wille. 2006. "Ministers and Top Officials in the Dutch Core Executive: Living Together, Growing Apart?" *Public Administration* 84: 121–46.

Heady, Ferrel. 1984. *Public Administration: A Comparative Perspective*. New York: Marcel Dekker.

Henry, Nicholas. 1975. "Paradigms of Public Administration." *Public Administration Review* 35: 376–86.

Hood, Christopher. 2002. "Control, Bargains, and Cheating: The Politics of Public-Service Reform." *Journal of Public Administration Research and Theory* 12: 309–22.

ICMA. 2000. *ICMA's Strategic Plan 2000*. Washington, DC: International City/County Management Association.

John, Peter, and Francesca Gains. 2005. *Political Leadership under the New Political Management Structures*. London: Office of Deputy Prime Minister, Evaluating Local Governance.

Kathi, Pradeep Chandra, and Terry L. Cooper. 2005. "Democratizing the Administrative State: Connecting Neighborhood Council and City Agencies." *Public Administration Review* 65: 559–67.

Kettl, Donald F. 2002. *The Transformation of Governance: Public Administration for Twenty-First Century America*. Baltimore: Johns Hopkins University Press.

Kettl, Donald F., Christopher Pollitt, and James H. Svara. 2004. *Towards a Danish Concept of Public Governance: An International Perspective*. Report to the Danish Forum for Top Executive Management. www.publicgovernance.dk/docs/0408260903.pdf. (Accessed 12 October 2006.)

Krause, George A. 1999. *A Two-Way Street: The Institutional Dynamics of the Modern Administrative State*. Pittsburgh: University of Pittsburgh Press.

Larsen, Helge O. 2005. "Transforming Political Leadership: Models, Trends, and Reforms." In *Transforming Political Leadership in Local Government*, eds. Rikke Berg and Nirmala Rao, 195–211. London: Palgrave Macmillan.

Lowi, Theodore. 1993. "Legitimizing Public Administration: A Disturbed Dissent." *Public Administration Review* 53: 261–64.

Lynn, Laurence E., Jr. 2001. "The Myth of the Bureaucratic Paradigm: What Traditional Public Administration Really Stood For." *Public Administration Review* 61: 144–60.

Meier, Kenneth J., and Laurence J. O'Toole, Jr. 2006. "Political Control Versus Bureaucratic Values: Reframing the Debate." *Public Administration Review* 66: 177–92.

Miller, Gary. 2000. "Above Politics: Credible Commitment and Efficiency in the Design of Public Agencies." *Journal of Public Administration Research and Theory* 10: 289–327.

Moe, Ronald C. 1994. "The 'Reinventing Government' Exercise: Misinterpreting the Problem, Misjudging the Consequences." *Public Administration Review* 54: 111–22.

Mouritzen, Poul Erik, and James H. Svara. 2002. *Leadership at the Apex: Politicians and Administrators in Western Local Governments*. Pittsburgh: University of Pittsburgh Press.

Moynihan, Donald P. 2004. "Protection versus Flexibility: The Civil Service Reform Act, Competing Administrative Doctrines, and the Roots of the Contemporary Public Management Debate." *Journal of Policy History* 16: 1–33.

Mullin, Megan, Gillian Peele, and Bruce E. Cain. 2004. "City Caesars? Institutional Structure and Mayoral Success in Three California Cities." *Urban Affairs Quarterly* 40: 19–43.

Nalbandian, John. 1994. "Reflections of a 'Pracademic' on the Logic of Politics and Administration." *Public Administration Review* 54: 531–36.

Nelson, Kimberly L. 2002. "Assessing the CAO Position in Strong-Mayor Government." *National Civic Review* 91: 41–54.

Newland, Chester A. 1988. "The American Senior Executive Service: Old Ideals and New Realities." *International Review of Administrative Sciences* 54: 625–60.

———. 1989. "The Future of Council-Manager Government." In *Ideal and Practice in City Management,* ed. H. George Frederickson, 257–71. Washington, DC: International City Management Association.

Northcote, Stafford H., and C.E. Trevelyan. 1853. *Report on the Organization of the Permanent Civil Service*. London: House of Commons. www.civilservant.org.uk/northcotetrevelyan.pdf. (Accessed 12 October 2006.)

O'Neill, Robert J., Jr. 2005. The Mayor-Manager Conundrum that Wasn't. Washington, DC: International City/County Management Association. www.icma.org/main/ns_search.asp?nsid=1543. (Accessed 12 March 2007.)

Osborne, David, and Ted Gaebler. 1992. *Reinventing Government: How the Entrepreneurial Spirit Is Transforming the Public Sector*. Reading, MA: Addison-Wesley.

Overeem, Patrick. 2005. "The Value of the Dichotomy: Politics, Administration, and the Political Neutrality of Administrators." *Administrative Theory and Praxis* 27: 311–19.

———. 2006. "In Defense of the Dichotomy: A Response to James H. Svara." *Administrative Theory and Praxis* 28: 140–47.

Page, Edward C. 1985. *Political Authority and Bureaucratic Power: A Comparative Analysis*. London: Wheatsheaf Books.

Peters, B. Guy. 2001. *The Future of Governing: Four Emerging Models*. 2nd ed. Lawrence: University Press of Kansas.

Pillar, Paul R. 2006. "Intelligence, Policy, and the War in Iraq." *Foreign Affairs* 85: 15–27.

Pollitt, Christopher, and Geert Bouckaert. 2000. *Public Management Reform: A Comparative Analysis*. Oxford: Oxford University Press.

Price, Don K. 1985. *America's Unwritten Constitution*. Cambridge, MA: Harvard University Press.

Rao, Nirmala, 2005. "From Committees to Leaders and Cabinets: The British Experience." In *Transforming Political Leadership in Local Government*, eds. Rikke Berg and Nirmala Rao, 42–58. London: Palgrave Macmillan.

Richards, David, and Martin J. Smith. 2004. "Interpreting the World of Political Elites." *Public Administration* 82: 777–800.

Rourke, Francis E. 1992. "Responsiveness and Neutral Competence in American Bureaucracy." *Public Administration Review* 52: 539–46.

Smith, Martin J. 2003. "The Core Executive and the Modernization of Central Government." In *Developments in British Politics*, eds. Patrick Dunleavy, Andrew Gamble, Richard Heffernan and Gillian Peele, chap. 4. London: Palgrave Macmillan.

SOLACE. 2005. *Leadership United: Executive Summary*. London: Society of Local Authority Chief Executives and Senior Managers.

Sorensen, Eva. 2006. "Metagovernance: The Change Role of Politicians in Processes of Democratic Governance." *American Review of Public Administration* 36: 98–114.

Specter, Michael. 2006. "Political Science: The Bush Administration's War on the Laboratory." *The New Yorker* (March 13): 58–69.

Stillman, Richard J., II. 1997. "American vs. European Public Administration: Does Public Administration Make the Modern State, or Does the State Make Public Administration?" *Public Administration Review* 57: 332–38.

Stoker, Gerry. 2004. *How Are Mayors Measuring Up?* London: Office of Deputy Prime Minister, Evaluating Local Governance.

———. 2006. "Public Value Management: A New Narrative for Networked Governance?" *American Review of Public Administration* 36: 41–57.

Svara, James H. 1989. "Policy and Administration: City Managers as Comprehensive Professional Leaders." In *Ideal and Practice in City Management*, ed. H. George Frederickson, 70–93. Washington, DC: International City Management Association.

———. 1998. "The Politics-Administration Dichotomy Model as Aberration." *Public Administration Review* 58: 51–58.

———. 1999a. "Complementarity of Politics and Administration as a Legitimate Alternative to the Dichotomy Model." *Administration and Society* 30: 676–705.

————. 1999b. "The Shifting Boundary Between Elected Officials and City Managers in Large Council-Manager Cities." *Public Administration Review* 59: 44–53.

————. 1999c. "U.S. City Managers and Administrators in a Global Perspective." *The Municipal Year Book 1999*. Washington, DC: International City Management Association, 25–33.

————. 2001. "The Myth of the Dichotomy: Complementarity of Politics and Administration in the Past and Future of Public Administration." *Public Administration Review* 61: 176–83.

————. 2003. *Two Decades of Continuity and Change In American City Councils*. Washington, DC: National League of Cities. www.nlc.org/content/Files/RMPcitycouncilrpt.pdf. (Accessed 12 October 2006.)

————. 2006a. "Politicians and Administrators in the Political Process: A Review of Themes and Issues in the Literature." *International Journal of Public Administration* 29: 953–76.

————. 2006b. "The Search for Meaning in Political-Administrative Relations in Local Government." *International Journal of Public Administration* 29: 1065–90.

————. 2007. *The Ethics Primer for Public Administrators in Government and Nonprofit Organizations*. Boston: Jones and Bartlett.

Svara, James H., and James R. Brunet. 2003. "Finding and Refining Complementarity in Recent Conceptual Models of Politics and Administration." In *Retracing Public Administration, Research in Public Administration,* Vol. 7, ed. Mark R. Rutgers, 185–208. Amsterdam: Elsevier Science.

Svara, James H., and Associates. 1994. *Facilitative Leadership in Local Government: Lessons from Successful Mayors and Chairpersons in the Council-Manager Form*. San Francisco: Jossey-Bass.

Terry, Larry D. 1990. "Leadership in the Administrative State: The Concept of Administrative Conservatorship." *Administration and Society* 21: 395–412.

Waldo, Dwight. 1948. *The Administrative State*. New York: Ronald Press Company.

Walters, Jonathan. 2002. *Life after Civil Service Reform: The Texas, Georgia, and Florida Experiences*. Washington, DC: IBM Center for the Business of Government.

Wamsley, Gary L., et al. 1990. *Refounding Public Administration*. Newbury Park, CA: Sage.

Waterman, Richard W., and Kenneth J. Meier. 1998. "Principle-Agent Models: An Expansion?" *Journal of Public Administration Research and Theory* 8: 173–202.

Wilson, Graham K., and Anthony Barker. 2003. "Bureaucrats and Politicians in Britain." *Governance* 16: 349–72.

Wilson, Woodrow. 1887. "The Study of Administration." *Political Science Quarterly* 2: 197–222.

Part II

Leadership Frames

6

Trans-leadership

Linking Influential Theory and Contemporary Research

Matthew R. Fairholm

Leadership is about change; but it is more useful to understand that change in three distinct ways, even three distinct opportunities, if we want to "do leadership" in any meaningful way. In so understanding change, we gain a better appreciation for leadership as something more than mere headship, and we understand better that not all change, like leadership itself, is the same. The implications for public administration are apparent as theorists and practitioners try to legitimatize different organizational stances that can be taken by public administrators.

Exploring Burns's (1978) work on transactional and transforming leadership and linking it with the rise of transformational theory, this chapter will use the prefix *trans-* to help us understand the different techniques, skills, or philosophies involved in leading change. The prefix *trans-* means "across," "through," or "beyond." Attaching that prefix to words like *action, formation*, and *forming* and then linking the newly formed words to leadership suggest a potential valuable course of examination. Hence, this chapter will pursue that course by looking at leadership in three ways: leadership through actions; leadership through formations, and leadership through forming. By reminding ourselves of seminal work on leadership philosophy, we are able to better understand the inherent focus on change that is so central to most of the practical and theoretical work done on leadership.

Leadership as Change

The work on change is a critical and vibrant branch of leadership studies. Change is a consistent theme in organizational and leadership theory and practice. With so much written on the topic of change and change leadership, finding common threads—threads that weave the fabric of leadership—should be easy. Like a lot of leadership research, though, consistency and commonality in the change literature is by no means taken for granted.

Kotter's (1990) work, though not the first on the topic, captures nicely the essence of change and leadership in his work distinguishing leadership from management. To him, management is about coping with complexity and leadership is about coping with change. Central to coping with complexity are skills that make routine or procedural organizational activities and functions like Command, Control, Compartmentalization, and Coping (see Abramson 1996). But leadership rings differently and must deal with the notion that we live in an age of uncertainty, where change is the only absolute. Bennis and Nanus (1985) say society is at a historic turning point where a new era is being born, marked with rapid and spastic change; where the problems of organizations are increasingly complex; where leaders are being scrutinized as never before; and where credibility is at a premium. Whether leadership is a historical creation or a notion for the ages, the idea is that leadership requires skills and functions like Communicating, Collaborating, Coaching, and Catalyzing—four actions that Abramson (1996) suggests are especially powerful when exercised together and convey a style of leadership not common (parenthetically) to the government in days gone by.

Leadership and change literature is not limited to organizational discussions. Leadership and change in terms of politics is common (Cronin 1987; Neustadt 1990; Post and George 2004). Links to communication (Garvin and Roberto 2005; Hackman and Johnson 1991) and conflict resolution (see Brett, Goldberg, and Ury 1990; Ready 2004) are also common. More personally, issues of self-deception (Arbinger Institute 2000), integrity (Covey 1992; Kouzes and Posner 1993), and spirituality (Bolman and Deal 1995; Fairholm 1997; Vaill 1989) are also relevant in the leadership and change literature. Much of what is found in the positive psychology movement (Cameron, Dutton, and Quinn 2003; Giacalone, Jurkiewicz, and Dunn 2005; Quinn 2005) and the authentic leadership research (Luthans and Avolio 2003; George 2003; Terry 1993) also has much bearing on (and foundation in) the change literature surrounding leadership studies.

Transactional, Transformational, and Transforming Leadership

Emerging from within this change literature are terms like *transition* and *transformation* for obvious definitional reasons. However, these terms have proven to be powerful shorthand for the kind of leadership meant by those who think leadership is something beyond or distinct from management and that leadership has to do with challenging the status quo, the culture, and/or changing people's lives at their core. For instance, Bridges (1991) added useful insight to the term *transition* when he described a human transition model distinct from an organizational change perspective.

However, the term *transformation* has certainly been the catchall term. It has nestled itself nicely in between Burns's discussion of transactional and transforming leadership and Bass's discussion of transformational leadership. Indeed, leadership is about change, about transformation. It might be useful, though, to look at the three common *trans-* leaderships—transactional, transformational, and transforming—to see if by understanding both their similarities and their differences we can learn something of the practice of leadership in general and public administration in particular. First, then, we will discuss the definitions and origins of each.

Although much of the current literature on leadership focuses on the biographical or historical approaches to understanding leadership through the study of leaders, James MacGregor Burns was one of the first authors to embark on a more philosophical approach to understanding and describing leadership. He first distinguishes between leaders and mere "power-wielders," noting that leaders satisfy the motives and tap into the values of their followers, whereas power wielders are intent only on realizing their own purposes. Power wielding is not leadership, though it certainly can induce change in others. That change is likely to be temporary, forced, and superficial. The difference is that power wielding is not about a concern for a relationship based on values of mutual importance to leader and led. It is rather about serving the interests and ego of the wielder himself or herself, without a real commitment to recognizing the object of power as anything other than power itself. Such reliance on coercive power, which while useful in the short run, is inevitably temporary and divisive (see Covey 1992). Whether the people over whom they exert their power share the purposes, motives, and values is inconsequential to the power wielder. To the leader, however, this sense of unity and shared values is his or her raison d'être and the source of his or her transforming influence.

With that foundation of values and relationship within the umbrella of power, Burns's distinction between transforming and transactional leadership emerged. Transforming leadership, as opposed to transactional leadership, forms the foundation of recent study on leadership. It focuses on the more personal side of organizational interactions. Words such as *vision, culture, values, development, teamwork,* and *service* make sense in the world of transforming leadership. Burns describes transforming leadership this way:

> Such leadership occurs when one or more persons *engage* with others in such a way that leaders and followers raise one another to higher levels of motivation and morality. Their purposes, which might have started out as separate but related, as in the case of transactional leadership, become fused. Power bases are linked not as counterweights but as mutual support for common purpose. . . . The relationship can be moralistic, of course. But transforming leadership ultimately becomes moral in that it raises the level of human conduct and ethical aspiration of both leader and led, and thus it has transforming effect on both (1978, 20).

Transforming leaders not only inform people's values, purposes, needs, and wants but also bring the people closer to achieving them.

On the other hand, transactional leadership focuses mainly on rewards or even punishments in exchange for performance. This in many ways defines the essence of management. Burns defines it this way:

Such leadership occurs when one person takes the initiative in making contact with others for the purpose of an exchange of valued things. The exchange could be economic or political or psychological in nature: a swap of goods or of one good for money; a trading of votes between candidate and citizen or between legislators; hospitality to another person in exchange for willingness to listen to one's troubles. Each party to the bargain recognizes the other as a *person.* Their purposes are related, at least to the extent that the purposes stand within the bargaining process and can be advanced by maintaining that process. But beyond this, the relationship does not go. The bargainers have no enduring purpose that holds them together; hence, they may go their separate ways. A leadership act took place, but it was not one that binds leader and follower together in a mutual and continuing pursuit of a higher purpose (1978, 19–20).

Burns begins to differentiate the practice of using external uses of power and incentives and internal fountains of commitment and development. In many ways, he is differentiating the science of management from the art of leadership, and he makes a compelling argument that the two are not the same. Despite one's point of view on the distinction between management and leadership, Burns presents a reasonable foundation to suggest that leadership is a phenomenon of change and fulfillment, either at a transactional, collective level or at a higher transforming, moral, individual level.

It was Bass (1985) and his fellow researchers (see Bass and Avolio 1994), however, who popularized transformational leadership theory and along the way almost overshadowed Burns's work on transforming leadership. Couto (1993) describes the transformation of transforming leadership. He suggests that Bass's transformational leadership downplays the two-way change process Burns envisioned with a one-way process where (1) a leader changes the follower and (2) the follower is found only in organizational contexts. Couto suggests that the "test for transformational leadership, for Bass, comes from management goals" and that change is likely to come "from inside formal organizations and institutions, to entail voluntary changes of organization, and to depend on causal factors and conditions that transformational leaders create and control" (1993, 106). As Bass himself puts it,

transformational leadership does not detract from transactional, rather it builds on it, broadening the effects of the leader on effort and performance. . . . Instead of responding to the immediate self-interest of followers with either a carrot or a stick, transformational leaders arouse in the individual a heightened awareness to key issues, to the group and organization, while increasing the confidence of followers, and gradually moving them from concerns for existence to concerns for achievement, growth, and development (1985, 22).

In essence, transformational leadership takes the more intimate, personal, and individual notions of transforming leadership and adapts them to aggregate issues of the organization writ large, essentially creating a bridge from transactional to transforming, though it may be a bridge few people see a need to cross.

Researchers and theorists have given us a vocabulary of trans-leadership. While the vocabulary is commonly accepted, the meanings of each term are often confused and misused. Transactional and transformational leadership are dependent upon positional authority and power that flows from it; transactional leadership depends much more on position than transformational, but both rely on it to do the substantial work of leadership. Transforming leadership relies not at all on position within an organization, but rather depends upon the forming of relationships and even an understanding of oneself and one's core values.

This may be why so many cry out for more leadership in the world. They simply may be looking further up an organizational chart at the positions that offer plans for change, when what they really want is to have their core values and beliefs refined, enhanced, and ennobled by people who inspire them, serve them, help them see themselves in new and better ways, and point to the aspirations that give meaning to life and to the relationships we have. They cry out for transforming leadership but receive only the techniques and results of transactional and transformational leadership. They seek to be changed for the better and affirmed in their moral progress, but look only at organizational hierarchy and command and control techniques. Leaders are all around us, but they are doing a quiet leadership beyond the scope of mere collectives. These leaders so many seek are changing people, their values, even their view of themselves one by one, little by little, in selfless, inspiring, and ennobling ways.

Implications of Trans-leadership

Each trans-leadership—transactional, transformational, and transforming—has implications for the practice of leadership that are worth noting. The implications of the trans-leadership theories may be most easily seen by separating the terms into their constitutive parts.

Trans-: *Across or Through*

First, the prefix *trans-* comes from Latin and signifies across or through. From this we can interpret transactional leadership as leadership through or across action or behavior or activity. Transformational leadership is leadership through formations of organizations and followers within them. Transforming leadership is leadership through the forming of self and others.

Leadership through Actions

Transactional leadership is that leadership that induces action based on values of mutual though temporary importance to leader and led. Relying mainly on utility power derived from an exchange of valued things (Covey 1992), the object of change in this leadership activity is focused on action, behavior, or the activity itself.

It is easy to see, therefore, that this leadership is often associated with traditional management theories. The object is to use transactions of valued things to cause another to behave or act, to do something that is in accordance to the leader's wishes and demands.

Public Administration Practice: This view of leadership is highly relevant to the work of public administration. In fact, much of the traditional theories of leadership have focused on this type of managerial activity (Gulick and Urwick 1937; Taylor 1915). Hence, one can see the source of much of the confusion about leadership and management. The object of this particular effort is change (hence, it must be about leadership), but the methods and focus of the change are concerned only with a modification of action or behavior to satisfy individual goals. The paramount goals are those of the leader, such as achievement of organizational ends, orderly worker compliance, and efficient processes. However, as an exchange is occurring, the goals of the led are also in play, such as financial rewards and a sense of accomplishment. These goals of leader and led are much more focused on transaction for controllable results and are, therefore, akin to traditional management ideas.

Transactional leadership forms the backbone of the traditional view of this field where efficiency and effectiveness rules supreme. Even more than that, though, it reflects the general notion that administration is about planning, controlling, decision making, and so on, to ensure productive workplaces, productive outputs, and productive employees.

Leadership through Formations

Transformational leadership focuses on changing formations and structures and the actors within those structures. As mentioned earlier, transformational leadership is not the terminology used by Burns, but rather is an adaptation of the ideas of transactional and transforming leadership by others (Bass 1985; Bass and Avolio 1994). Simply put, transformational leadership has to do with change at an organizational level. This is where "the leadership" of an organization exercises leadership that envisions certain structures, designs, and associated performance levels for an organization. Such leadership expends energy on things like reorganizing to efficiently line up the functions and hierarchy of the collective with the intended business or mission, realigning with agreed-upon collective values and visions of a future state, and steering the organization to specific measures of performance. This leadership understands the role of culture and performance and the need for the organization to have clear values, goals, and objectives (Collins and Porras 1997; Schein 1996). In many ways, this leadership is the ideal taught in most business schools as a way of maximizing performance through transactional leadership aligned with and grounded by a useful culture (Nirenberg 1998).

Indeed, this leadership is about change but change focused on altering organizational missions, vision, values, performance, and the like to achieve maximum efficiency and quality in product and service delivery. It also intends a change

Change in org → change in its people

in people as they agree to live by those organizational formations; they become "company men and women," committed to the organization and what it stands for. In other words, this leadership changes the formations of an organization hoping to establish the formation or structure or culture or performance levels and measures that will motivate employees to adopt the organization's stance in society and perform in the best possible way as defined by agreed-upon goals and objectives.

Public Administration Practice: Kiel (1994) describes the need to manage chaos and complexity in government through change, innovation, and organizational renewal. This fits nicely into the mode of public administration that transformational leadership develops. One expression of this leadership is the adoption of Total Quality Management ideals from Deming (1986), Juran (1989), and others. The notion is that transformation of any organization will take place under a leader who has a step-by-step plan to alter the former culture of the organization into one of high quality and continuous improvement. To institutionalize such change, everything from stated values, to vision statements, to job descriptions, to work flow, to organizational design is at the leader's disposal. The goal is transformation, not just incremental change, of the culture and organizational environment.

Such leadership recognizes, according to Beckhard and Pritchard (1992), that the pace and complexity of change to new forms and new ways of living and new values are of an order of magnitude never before experienced and, hence, require a fundamental change strategy that encompasses how business decisions are made, what external forces impact the organization, and what consequences emerge from the organization's activities. Such fundamental change is transformational and comes almost predictably from seasoned public administrators who understand the need for reinvention (Ingraham, Sanders, and Thompson 1998), communication strategies (Garvin and Roberto 2005), and planned change events (Kotter 1996). This is not an endeavor devoid of ethical considerations (Grundstein-Amado 1999). In fact, in today's climate such serious, dedicated transformational leadership is almost in itself considered to be *the* ethical leadership stance public managers should take (Behn 1998; Terry 1995).

As Malmberg (1999) argues, today's federal practitioner's ability to synthesize a variety of inputs—electronic, interpersonal, and intuitive—and to anticipate a pattern of consequences will drive his or her accomplishments on the job. For that practitioner wishing to excel, constructing the job, making sense of the trappings of government, and developing rational responses to change based on knowledge and organizational learning are essential to the practice of leading. Valle (1999) suggests that the changing nature of public service requires new leadership that has as its primary goal the development of—as the organization's primary core competence—an adaptive organizational culture. It is the modern public manager's job as he or she engages in transformational leadership to create and maintain such change, organizational learning, and cultural transformation. As managers master these skills, they transcend the limitations of mechanistic, deterministic, and reductionistic thinking and become authentic change masters (Shelton and Darling 2001), changing themselves to some degree and their organizations in depth.

Leadership through Forming — less authoritarian

Day (2000) quotes Peter Drucker as saying, "in the traditional organization—the organization of the last one hundred years—the skeleton or internal structure was a combination of rank and power. In the emerging organization, it has to be mutual understanding and responsibility" (581). While this may require a transformation of an organization's formations, mutual understanding and responsibility will also require a change in the way some people see themselves, others, and their mutual interactions. In sum, people may have to change the way they "form" themselves.

Transforming leadership is the ultimate leadership philosophy identified by Burns (1978). Rather than a specific focus on organizational performance and change, this leadership is at its heart a moral endeavor and is, therefore, ultimately intimate and personal in the relationships created between leader and led. The intimacy is centered on the mutual values that the leader and led agree or come to agree on through the interactions of leadership and the mutually ennobling results that such leadership delivers. This leadership is at its heart inspirational because it deals with the spirit of the people involved; it is moral because values at play are central to living life in relation to others in the hopes of raising each other to higher levels of morality.

This leadership is about change in that it focuses on changing the way people form themselves. This means that leadership endeavors to alter the way people view themselves independently and in relation to others and, hence, influence their values, wants, aspirations, and needs. This leadership also envisions changing the leader as much as the led, thus effectively distinguishing this leadership from other more authoritarian or positionally based leadership described earlier. This leadership is about identifying higher levels of values, showing by examples what those values may mean in the living of life, creating a sense of good versus ineffective behavior, and ultimately serving others with a sense of stewardship rather than authority to help them achieve their own higher potential, their ultimate form. This leadership takes place within and outside formal organizations.

This activity may require some sacrifice on the part of the leader, which in itself reinforces the values that have caused such selfless service in the first place. The change is focused on the leader and led better understanding themselves as individuals and as social beings in line with mutually agreed-upon values that make up their core selves—the values that form who they really are. Such leadership involves change, but it is very different from changing actions and behaviors, culture, and mission. This leadership is intimate and is about changing who we are. It is about changing us for the better so that we will necessarily act and behave and perform

change people → change org

in the ways that are valued because we value them ourselves; they are not forced, induced, incentivized, motivated, or trained. Rather, they are inculcated through inspiration, reason, and freedom of choice.

Public Administration Practice: For public administrators, transforming leadership takes place mostly at the personal, intimate level of their work—the people side of the work, the so-called soft stuff. Much focus is given to the work of getting things done (transactional) and providing the right service in the right way (transformational). But public managers also work with people and have an opportunity to impact employees, citizens, elected officials, and colleagues for good. Such impact can translate into better government, better governance, and better governors broadly defined. We dismiss this element of leadership in public administration at the risk of dismissing the underlying purpose for the field itself: the professional running of constitutions created by people who are trying to get along and maintain certain values, beliefs, and rights.

This transforming leadership harks back to the servant-leadership work of Green-leaf (1977) as it requires people to focus on serving even the developmental needs of others, and it points to recent work by Quinn (2004) on the more intimate and personal elements of what he calls the fundamental state of leadership. All of this seems to converge on what Frost and Egri (1990) believe is a need for perspectives large enough to embrace the fact that we are living, valuing beings—and to place that value-centric fact at the core of studying leadership questions.

Arthur et al. (2002) discuss how managers form reality for people in organizations. More specifically, constellations of values play such a crucial role in organizational thought that managers need to see the full process of social reality formation and their catalytic role within such formation. They suggest leadership is about recognizing "emerging patterns of relationships, and the deep tacit level—the blind spot—the place from which a system of people operates" (13) and using that understanding to help shape not only organizations but the people within them who then shape the organizations in which they participate.

Transforming leadership theory is the kind of theory that Graen and Uhl-Bien (1995) say helps move the discussion of leadership beyond a levels or formations perspective toward a thought process of leadership in broad relational contexts—contexts that help form people themselves and their interactions. This transforming leadership flows naturally from Wheatley's (1997) view of organizations as occurring from "inside out, as people see what needs to happen, apply their experience and perceptions to the issue, find those who can help them, and use their own creativity to invent solutions" (22–23). She continues by saying,

> [M]ost of us were raised in a culture that told us that the way to manage for excellence was to tell people exactly what they had to do and then make sure they did it. We learned to play master designer, assuming we could engineer people into perfect performance. But you can't direct people into perfection; you can only engage them enough so that they want to do perfect work (25).

Figure 6.1   **Summary of Approaches in the Three Trans-leadership Notions**

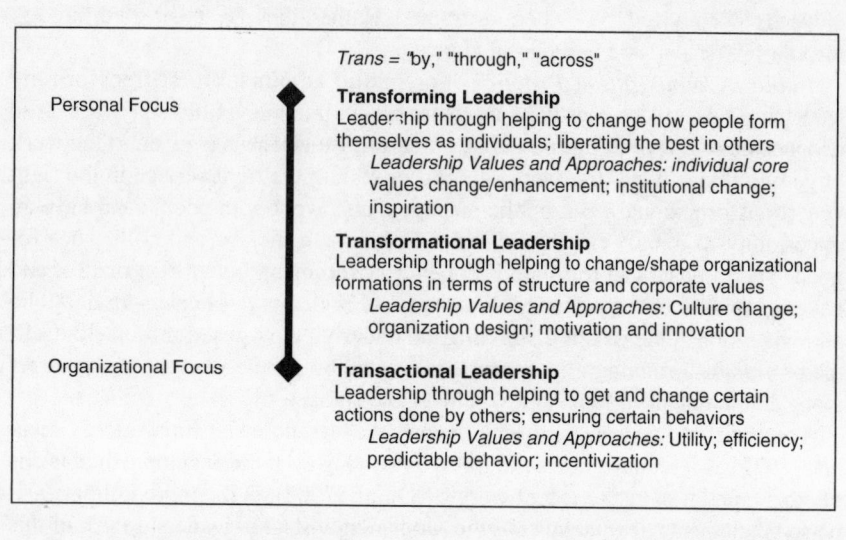

Trans = "by," "through," "across"

Personal Focus

Transforming Leadership
Leadership through helping to change how people form
themselves as individuals; liberating the best in others
Leadership Values and Approaches: individual core
values change/enhancement; institutional change;
inspiration

Transformational Leadership
Leadership through helping to change/shape organizational
formations in terms of structure and corporate values
Leadership Values and Approaches: Culture change;
organization design; motivation and innovation

Organizational Focus

Transactional Leadership
Leadership through helping to get and change certain
actions done by others; ensuring certain behaviors
Leadership Values and Approaches: Utility; efficiency;
predictable behavior; incentivization

Such is a view of transforming leadership that public administrators may use
to play a vital role in developing not only the people who serve the public but the
very public organizations themselves, and perhaps the broader set of institutions
and organizations of governance to which the public organizations find themselves
linked. That really is the key: As public administrators focus on those they serve
with, those public servants grow and enhance the very institutions within which
they operate, hence growing, developing, and forming the on-the-ground governance structures needed for and adapted to the missions at hand. This is what
Fairholm (1991) alludes to when he suggests we focus on the social interactions
within organizations and a reliance on values that allows the leader to not only
evoke excellent results from the organization but also, more important, develop
individual followers into leaders in their own right.

Implications for Public Administration Practice

Understanding these notions of leadership from transactional to transforming
provides the opportunity for public administration (PA) to understand its practice
in more specific ways. The implications for practice were briefly described earlier. However, a more detailed understanding of the work is possible as we apply
the three notions of leadership to different approaches to public administration
practice. While the field is complex, at least four categories of approaching the
field help us make sense of our practice. By fleshing out these perspectives and
then relating these to trans-leadership ideas, we achieve a matrix of practice that
offers more detailed identities that can explain what it is that public administrators do (or could do).

The first is the Public Law or Traditional approach. In this approach, public administrators execute the will of the people as determined by the political and legal process. Administrative discretion is severely limited and viewed as inappropriate, and issues of political accountability are paramount. Basically, bureaucrats are unelected and therefore unaccountable, hence, public decisions should be left to politicians and the processes in which they engage. Because of these defining notions, efficiency, effectiveness, and economy should be the battle cry and foundational values of public administration practice. Moe (1997) amplifies this approach in his defense of the administrative management paradigm as critical to the maintenance of a democratically accountable political system. His argument, in very simplistic terms, is that if we want better public administration we should make better public law. In defense of public law, he suggests that it is not an impediment to good governance and government management practices, but rather the clay from which new governmental institutions and management practices are molded.

The second perspective is New Public Administration. In the early 1970s, following the Minnowbrook Conference, an effort to redefine (or reclaim) the field emerged (Frederickson 1971/1992, 1980, 1997; Marini 1971). This approach viewed the politics/administration dichotomy as suspect and urged an understanding of the important role of administrative discretion in the work of public administrators. This approach embraces the idea that bureaucrats are in a wonderful position to influence and facilitate community activity. Because of that position, public administrators should embrace the key values of equity, representation, and active citizenship as equal to or even preferred to the traditional values of efficiency and effectiveness (Cooper 1991; Lipsky 1971). This approach opens the nonprofit sector and broader governance issues to the theory and practice of public administration, stretching the neutral civil servant ethos to its maximum. In this sense, if one wants better governance, one needs more active and more relevant bureaucrats.

The third perspective is New Public Management. In this idea of public administration practice, public administrators should effectively run government by breaking the grip of bureaucracy through the application of business approaches. Administrative discretion, then, is not only acceptable but required to adopt entrepreneurial models of governing. Disagreeing somewhat with Allison (1980) regarding the differences between the two sectors, this approach is grounded in the notion that government and business are not all that different organizationally and functionally and that innovation and economic efficiency are paramount concerns. Within this category of practice fall such terms as *new managerialism* and *reinventing government* (Terry 1998). Kamensky (1996) explains many aspects of this approach as he fleshes out the reinventing government movement of the 1990s. He suggests some key ideas include the notion that incentives shape behavior, the economic model based on quality and responsiveness is useful, customer focus and customer-driven behavior is essential, and technology enhancements are central. Above all, this view argues that a better system of measuring process and performance must be a major function of the public administrator. These ideas summarize much of the

Figure 6.2   **Four Public Administration (PA) Approaches**

Public	Law/Traditional PA	New PA	New Public Management	New Public Service
Approach to Practice	Legalistic	Representational	Managerial	Service-oriented
Primary PA Foundation	Politics/administrative dichotomy	Equity-oriented	Business practices	Community/citizenship concerns
Assumed Organizational Structure	Hierarchical and bureaucratic	Decentralized and interest-based	Decentralized and market driven	Collaborative and service driven
Administrative Discretion	Limited discretion	Expanded discretion for social equity goals	Expanded discretion for entrepreneurial goals	Constrained and accountable discretion
Primary Theoretical Foundation	Political theory	Theories of justice and representation	Economic theory	Democratic theory

Note: This figure modifies and adds to ideas in a table found in Denhardt, R.B., & Denhardt, J.V. (2000). "The New Public Service: Service Rather Than Steering." *Public Administration Review*, 60 (6): 549–59.

New Public Management approach and suggest that if one wants better governance, one must ensure that bureaucrats are innovative and entrepreneurial.

The fourth perspective is what is now being called "New Public Service." This approach is explained by Denhardt and Denhardt (2000) as they react to and critique the New Public Management movement described previously. They claim that New Public Management ignores key notions of the field (present in the early days of the profession) that need to be reinvigorated, especially because New Public Management advocates usually defend that approach in comparison only to a Traditional or Public Law approach. New Public Service claims that a return to the public administrator's responsibility to serve and empower citizens is essential. The ultimate work of public administration, then, is to "build public institutions marked by integrity and responsiveness" (2000, 549) through service to citizens who, along with notions of citizenship and public interest, are in the forefront of the very work being done.

The Denhardts (2000) summarize the New Public Service approach in seven key ideas: serve rather than steer; the public interest is the aim, not the by-product; think strategically, act democratically; serve citizens, not customers; accountability isn't simple; value people, not just productivity; and value citizenship and public service above entrepreneurship. If one hopes for better governance, then one needs bureaucrats who understand democratic values and citizenship, service, and the value of people within and without public organizations.

Placing the ideas of trans-leadership (Figure 6.1) and the different approaches of public administration (Figure 6.2) in a summary table provides a matrix that reveals significant details of and differentiations in the practice of public administration in terms of leadership theory. The matrix (see Figure 6.3) allows us to answer at least three questions within each cell that shed light on what we do in public organizations. The first question that emerges is what the public administration purposes within each cell are. The second question that emerges within a cell is what are the leadership values and approaches that ground the practice. The third question is not so easily seen in the matrix but emerges from the interplay between public administration approach and trans-leadership perspective. It revolves around the tools and behaviors that naturally flow from and are congruent with the interplay found within each cell.

Conclusion and Future Issues for Thought and Practice

Pioneers in leadership studies have given us a useful way to view leadership as a phenomenon of change that can influence the way public administrators both view and practice their work. Burns and Bass create a vocabulary and theoretical foundation for a triad of trans-leaderships that help us view the work of leadership in three distinct but important ways. Transactional leadership endeavors to change people's behaviors and actions by incentives grounded in individual wants and needs but focused on the fulfillment of "management's" goals and plans. Transformational

Figure 6.3 Trans-leadership and Public Administration (PA) Approach Matrix

	Public Law/Traditional PA	New PA	New Public Management	New Public Service
Transactional Leadership				
PA Approach:	*The Whip* Legalistic; politics/administration dichotomy; hierarchical and bureaucratic	*The Community Manager* Representational; equity-oriented; decentralized and interest-based	*The Line Manager* Managerial; business practices; decentralized and market driven	*The Conflicted Manager* Service-oriented; community/citizenship concerns; collaborative and service driven
Leadership Values and Approaches:	Utility; efficiency; predictable behavior; incentivization	Utility; efficiency; predictable behavior; incentivization	Utility; efficiency; predictable behavior; incentivization	Utility; efficiency; predictable behavior; incentivization
Transformational Leadership				
PA Approach:	*The (Re)Organizer* Legalistic; politics/administration dichotomy; hierarchical and bureaucratic	*The Streetwise Decision Maker* Representational; equity-oriented; decentralized and interest-based	*The General Manager* Managerial; business practices; decentralized and market driven	*The Steward* Service-oriented; community/citizenship concerns; collaborative and service driven
Leadership Values and Approaches:	Culture change; organization design; motivation and innovation	Culture change; organization design; motivation and innovation	Culture change; organization design; motivation and innovation	Culture change; organization design; motivation and innovation
Transforming Leadership				
PA Approach:	*The Hypocrite* Legalistic; politics/administration dichotomy; hierarchical and bureaucratic	*The Societal Activist* Representational; equity-oriented; decentralized and interest-based	*The Inspirational Executive* Managerial; business practices; decentralized and market driven	*The Servant* Service-oriented; community/citizenship concerns; collaborative and service driven
Leadership Values and Approaches:	Change/enhance individual core values; change institutions; inspiration	Change/enhance individual core values; change institutions; inspiration	Change/enhance individual core values; change institutions; inspiration	Change/enhance individual core values; change institutions; inspiration

leadership focuses on organizational formations, systems, and culture. By influencing those elements of work, transformational leaders implement change in service design, development, and delivery, and the people working in such organizations find themselves also changing in ways that reinforce and support the organizational goals. A transition from transformational to transforming leadership emerges as people begin to realize that organizational change occurs as people within the organizations change who they are, how they view things, and what they care about. Transforming leadership changes people, and then those changed people are able to change the things of the organization. It creates a cadre of self-led leaders who constantly strive to re-form themselves to achieve their highest potential.

These ways of looking at leadership help us see how individual perspective does certainly influence how we discuss and define leadership activities and leadership success (see Fairholm 2004). Public administrators who see the value in all three trans-leadership ideals will be able to not only get things done well (transactional leadership) and structure the systems of public organizations properly (transformational leadership) but will also be able to shape the public servants and the public governance structures themselves (transforming leadership) as they ply the craft. Such results of our practice may help us understand how a focus on leadership principles can indeed influence the work—in fact, even shape the work—we do in public organizations. It leads us to one area of future thought that encourages a broader view of leadership in the field.

Leadership across the Field

The work herein deals with leadership issues within certain approaches to public administration. To accommodate this discussion, it was necessary to divide the topic of leadership into three notions and also divide the field into four different approaches. While this dissection makes sense and gives us insight into what we do, one may be tempted to ask if there is one leadership notion that cuts across any approach to public administration. Perhaps the answer to this is too restrictive or, conversely, too broad to be helpful. However, the answer may also tell us much about a commonality across the government and nonprofit sectors in terms of leadership study.

The commonality is that no matter whether governmental or nonprofit, people doing public administration are doing it inside and around public (not private) organizations. The questions of public leadership may best be studied and broadly understood only in the context of public organizational life. Beyond outlining different approaches to the field, some have also identified images of public administration, and public administrators, generally (see Kass and Catron 1990). But these attempts generally give us a macro view of public administration. The micro view, what goes on inside any public organization, may give us much more insight into what public administrators do every day, on the ground. The assumption is that leadership is taking place inside the organizations in ways we can really never quite understand if we take only a macro look. Hence, a future area of studies that may enhance the day-to-day practice is to develop understanding of leadership across the field generally and within public organizations specifically. It is that notion of leadership found in the field generally that leads us to another area of future exploration.

Another New Dichotomy

What may be needed to inform both the theory and practice of the field is to recognize the growing dichotomy in leadership studies in terms of leadership and management. Such a dichotomy may inform or even supplant the politics/administration dichotomy. The orthodoxy of the politics/administration dichotomy is characterized by a reliance on the separation of decision and execution of government policies by a neutral administrator, the agreement that the methods of science are relevant to administration, and an emphasis on efficiency and economy (Goodnow 1900; Gulick and Urwick 1937; White 1926; Willoughby 1927). This approach defined the administration side of the field.

Others suggested that this emphasis was untenable. These thinkers held a much broader view of their role in society and found the separation of politics and administration unsound (Appleby 1949; Long 1949; Redford 1958; Sayre 1958; Selznick 1949; Waldo 1948 /1965). In fact, many believed that if there was such a thing as the dichotomy, the political (normative, values-based) context of the dichotomy should be emphasized over the administrative. This consistent back and forth of the dichotomy debate is a hallmark of the field. But, it highlights the confusion and awkwardness of the field more than it has exemplified the best of what we have to offer society. It has muddied the waters more than clarified our position and our roles.

The debate about leadership and management sheds important light on the practice of public administration. It is often based on dichotomous arguments, in much the same way politics and administration are and have been. There is much similarity between what is argued about normative activities, politics, and leadership and between administration roles, functions, and management. What we see is growing consensus between two different types of technologies at work in organizations: leadership technologies and management technologies. Each has separate foci and foundations, and yet both are important for organizational (and personal) success. Each can be found in the organization and management theory of the social sciences and in public administration particularly. Leadership technology emphasizes the "hows" and "whys" of organizations and the meaning and uses of individual relationships, culture, values, growth, and progress. Management technology focuses on the "what to dos" in organizations and the expertise, technical skills, and structural schemas to do them.

In many ways, the leadership and management debate is the same as the politics/administration dichotomy. Just as there is agreement that leadership and management technologies, though different, do and should exist in organizational

Figure 6.4   **Sample of Comparisons between the Leadership/Management and Politics/Administration Dichotomies**

Public Administration Organizational Technologies (Hows and Whys)	Public Administration Roles (What to Dos)
Leadership	**Politics**
• Relationships	• Representative of specific and group norms
• Values-focus/culture-orientation	• Policy maker/direction setter
• Vision/direction/goals	• Individual and societal mediator/facilitator
• Personal/organizational development, growth, progress	• Organizer of voluntary and involuntary mechanisms
Management	**Administration**
• Position and structural schemas	• Position holder
• Technical skills and expertise	• Technical expert
• POSDCORB	• POSDCORB implementer
• Efficiency and effectiveness	• Efficient and effective problem solver
• Organizational survival/efficiency	• Resources allocator

dynamics, the same may be said for the politics/administration dichotomy in that within all organized societies, people grapple with political (individual and collective interests) and administrative concerns. The politics/administration dichotomy focuses on *roles* public administrators might play. The leadership/management debate focuses on *technologies* public administrators must choose to engage. The difference is significant. Focusing on roles requires the field to continually defend itself as a legitimate actor in academia and society. Focusing on the technologies of public administration allows the field to define itself clearly as a practical contributor to organizational and societal life.

Figure 6.4 summarizes key ideas (similarities and contrasts) on the roles and organizational technologies of interest to the public administrator. It also shows how a discussion of leadership and management technologies would offer a useful way to examine the field while maintaining a link to the theoretical and practical underpinnings of the public administration field.

Understanding what administrators do in a way that explicitly reveals assumptions about that work is a major project for public administration. The emerging focus on distinct leadership and management technologies moves public administration away from focusing purely on roles to be played toward an explicit adoption of philosophies of social influence. It reframes the question of public administration toward a focus on more philosophical *and* practical concerns of getting things done (management) and enhancing relationships through individual and organizational health and growth (leadership). Public administration is at the nexus of people, organizations, institutions, and ideas. As such, describing public administration as a field that does both management and leadership marries the concerns of relationship and individual context while preserving the approaches of efficiently accomplishing group goals.

Certainly, then, including leadership studies and its literature has very real implications on how we view the work of public administration, both theoretically and practically. In fact, leadership studies may indeed be the most practical of theories with which public administrators can engage to really understand what it is they do generally in the field and how it impacts society, but also, more specifically, what they should be doing within their public organizations to help themselves and other public servants do and be the best of what public administration has to offer.

References

Abramson, Mark A. 1996. "In Search of the New Leadership." *Government Executive* 28 (9): 9–13.

Allison, Graham T. 1980. "Public and Private Management: Are They Fundamentally alike in all Unimportant Aspects?" Paper read at Proceedings of the Public Management Research Conference, Washington, DC, November 19–20.

Appleby, Paul Henson. 1949. *Policy and Administration.* University, AL: University of Alabama Press.

Arbinger Institute. 2000. *Leadership and Self-deception: Getting out of the Box.* 1st ed. San Francisco: Berrett-Koehler.

Arthur, Brian, Jonathan Day, Joseph Jaworski, Michael Jung, Ikujiro Nonaka, Claus Otto Scharmer, and Peter Senge. 2002. "Illuminating the Blind Spot." *Leader to Leader* 24: 11–14.

Bass, Bernard M. 1985. *Leadership and Performance beyond Expectations.* New York: Free Press.

Bass, Bernard M., and Bruce J. Avolio. 1994. *Improving Organizational Effectiveness through Transformational Leadership.* Thousand Oaks, CA: Sage.

Beckhard, Richard, and Wendy Pritchard. 1992. *Changing the Essence: The Art of Creating and Leading Fundamental Change in Organizations.* San Francisco: Jossey-Bass.

Behn, Robert D. 1998. "What Right Do Public Managers Have to Lead?" *Public Administration Review* 58 (3): 209–25.

Bennis, Warren, and Burt Nanus. 1985. *Leaders: The Strategies for Taking Charge.* New York: Harper Collins.

Bolman, Lee G., and Terrence E. Deal. 1995. *Leading with Soul: An Uncommon Journey of the Spirit.* San Francisco: Jossey-Bass.

Brett, Jeanne M., Stephen B. Goldberg, and William L. Ury. 1990. "Designing Systems for Resolving Disputes in Organizations." *American Psychologist* 45 (2): 162–70.

Bridges, William. 1991. *Managing Transitions: Making the Most of Change.* New York: Addison Wesley Longman.

Burns, James MacGregor. 1978. *Leadership.* New York: Harper & Row.

Cameron, Kim S., Jane E. Dutton, and Robert E. Quinn. 2003. *Positive Organizational Scholarship.* 1st ed. San Francisco: Berrett-Koehler.

Collins, James C., and Jerry I. Porras. 1997. *Built to Last: Successful Habits of Visionary Companies.* New York: Harper Business.

Cooper, Terry L. 1991. *An Ethic of Citizenship for Public Administration.* Englewood Cliffs, NJ: Prentice Hall.

Couto, Richard A. 1993. "The Transformation of Transforming Leadership." In *The Leader's Companion,* ed. Thomas J. Wren. New York: Free Press.

Covey, Stephen R. 1992. *Principle-centered Leadership.* New York: Simon & Schuster.

Cronin, Thomas E. 1987. "Leadership and Democracy." *Liberal Education* 73 (2): 35–38.

Day, David V. 2000. "Leadership Development: A Review in Context." *Leadership Quarterly* 11 (4): 581–611.

Deming, W. Edwards. 1986. *Out of the Crisis.* Cambridge, MA: Massachusetts Institute of Technology, Center for Advanced Engineering Study.

Denhardt, Janet V., and Robert B. Denhardt. 2003. *The New Public Service.* Armonk, New York: M.E. Sharpe.

Denhardt, Robert B., and Janet V. Denhardt. 2000. "The New Public Service: Service Rather than Steering." *Public Administration Review* 60 (6): 549–59.

Fairholm, Gilbert W. 1991. *Values Leadership: Toward a New Philosophy of Leadership.* New York: Praeger.

———. 1997. *Capturing the Heart of Leadership.* Westport, CT: Praeger.

Fairholm, Matthew R. 2004. "Different Perspectives on the Practice of Leadership." *Public Administration Review* 64 (5): 577–90.

Frederickson, H. George. 1971/1992. "Towards a New Public Administration." In *Classics of Public Administration,* ed. J.M. Shafritz and A.C. Hyde. Pacific Grove, CA: Brooks/Cole.

———. 1980. *New Public Administration.* University, AL: University of Alabama Press.

———. 1997. *The Spirit of Public Administration.* San Francisco: Jossey-Bass.

Frost, Peter J., and Carolyn J. Egri. 1990. "Appreciating Executive Action." In *Appreciative Management and Leadership,* ed. S. Srivastva and D.L. Cooperrider. San Francisco: Jossey-Bass.

Garvin, David A., and Michael A. Roberto. 2005. "Change through Persuasion." *Harvard Business Review* 83 (2): 104–12.

George, Bill. 2003. *Authentic Leadership: Rediscovering the Secrets to Creating Lasting Value.* 1st ed. San Francisco: Jossey-Bass.

Giacalone, Robert A., Carole L. Jurkiewicz, and Craig Dunn. 2005. *Positive Psychology in Business Ethics and Corporate Responsibility.* Greenwich, CT: Information Age Publishers.

Goodnow, Frank J. 1900. *Politics and Administration: A Study in Government.* New York: Russell and Russell.

Graen, George. A., and Mary Uhl-Bien. 1995. "Relationship-based Approach to Leadership." *Leadership Quarterly* 6 (2): 219–47.

Greenleaf, Robert K. 1977. *Servant Leadership.* New York: Paulist Press.

Grundstein-Amado, Rivka. 1999. "Bilateral Transformational Leadership." *Administration and Society* 31 (2): 247–60.

Gulick, Luther Halsey, and Lydal Urwick. 1937. *Papers on the Science of Administration.* 2nd ed. New York: Institute of Public Administration.

Hackman, Michael Z., and Craig E. Johnson. 1991. *Leadership: A Communication Perspective.* Prospect Heights, IL: Waveland Press.

Ingraham, Patricia, Ronald P. Sanders, and James Thompson, eds. 1998. *Transforming Government.* San Francisco: Jossey-Bass.

Juran, Joseph M. 1989. *Juran on Leadership for Quality.* New York: Free Press.

Kamensky, John M. 1996. "Role of the 'Reinventing Government' Movement in Federal Management Reform." *Public Administration Review* 56 (3): 247–55.

Kass, Henry D., and Bayard L. Catron. 1990. *Images and Identities in Public Administration.* Newbury Park, CA: Sage.

Kiel, L. Douglas. 1994. *Managing Chaos and Complexity in Government.* 1st ed. San Francisco: Jossey-Bass.

Kotter, John P. 1990. "What Leaders Really Do." *Harvard Business Review* 68 (3): 103–11.

———. 1996. *Leading Change.* Boston: Harvard Business School Press.

Kouzes, James M., and Barry Z. Posner. 1993. *Credibility: How Leaders Gain and Lose It, Why People Demand It.* San Francisco: Jossey-Bass.

Lipsky, Michael. 1971. "Street-level Bureaucracy and the Analysis of Urban Reform." *Urban Affairs Quarterly* 6: 391–409.

Long, Norton. 1949. "Power and Administration." *Public Administration Review* 9 (4): 257–64.

Luthans, Fred, and Bruce J. Avolio. 2003. "Authentic Leadership Development." In *Positive Organizational Scholarship: Foundations of a New Discipline,* ed. K.S. Cameron, J.E. Dutton, and R.E. Quinn, 241–261. San Francisco: Berrett-Koehler.

Malmberg, Kenneth B. 1999. "A Vision for the Future: The Practice of Leading in the Federal Workplace." Paper read at American Society for Public Administration, Orlando, FL.

Marini, Frank. 1971. *Toward a New Public Administration: The Minnowbrook Perspective.* Scranton, PA: Chandler.

Moe, Ronald C. 1997. "The Importance of Public Law." In *Handbook of Public Law and Administration,* ed. P.J. Cooper and C.A. Newland, 265–84. San Francisco: Jossey-Bass.

Neustadt, Richard E. 1990. *Presidential Power and the Modern Presidents: The Politics of Leadership from Roosevelt to Reagan.* 3rd ed. New York: Free Press.

Nirenberg, John. 1998. "Myths We Teach, Realities We Ignore: Leadership Education in Business Schools." *The Journal of Leadership Studies* 5 (1): 82–99.

Post, Jerrold M., and Alexander George. 2004. *Leaders and Their Followers in a Dangerous World.* 1st ed. Ithaca, NY: Cornell University Press.

Quinn, Robert E. 2004. *Building the Bridge as You Walk on It: A Guide of Leading Change.* San Francisco: Jossey-Bass.

———. 2005. "Moments of Greatness: Entering the Fundamental State of Leadership." *Harvard Business Review* 83 (7): 74–83.

Ready, Douglas A. 2004. "How to Grow Great Leaders." *Harvard Business Review* 82 (12): 20–25.

Redford, Emmette. 1958. *Ideal and Practice in Public Administration.* University, AL: University of Alabama Press.

Sayre, Wallace S. 1958. "Premises of Public Administration: Past and Emerging." *Public Administration Review* 18 (2): 102–105.

Schein, Edgar H. 1996. *Organizational Culture and Leadership.* 2nd ed. San Francisco: Jossey-Bass.

Selznick, Philip. 1949. *TVA and the Grass Roots.* Berkeley: University of California Press.

Shelton, Charlotte K., and John R. Darling. 2001. "The Quantum Skills Model in Management." *Leadership and Organizational Development Journal* 22 (6): 264–73.

Taylor, Frederick W. 1915. *The Principles of Scientific Management.* New York: Harper & Row.

Terry, Larry D. 1995. *Leadership of Public Bureaucracies: The Administrator as Conservator, Advances in Public Administration.* Thousand Oaks, CA: Sage.

———. 1998. "Administrative Leadership, Neo-managerialism, and the Public Management Movement." *Public Administration Review* 58 (3): 194–201.

Terry, Robert. 1993. *Authentic Leadership: Courage in Action.* San Francisco: Jossey-Bass.

Vaill, Peter. 1989. "Spirituality in the Age of the Leveraged Buyout." Paper read at Spirituality in Life and Work, Washington, DC., July 21.

Valle, Matthew. 1999. "Crisis, Culture and Charisma: The New Leader's Work in Public Organizations." *Public Personnel Management* 28 (2): 245–57.

Waldo, Dwight. 1948/1965. *The Administrative State.* New York: Ronald Press.

Wheatley, Margaret. 1997. "Goodbye, Command and Control." *Leader to Leader* 5 (3): 21–28.

White, Leonard D. 1926. *Introduction to the Study of Public Administration.* New York: MacMillan.

Willoughby, William F. 1927. *Principles of Public Administration.* Baltimore: Johns Hopkins University Press.

7

The Changing Leadership Landscape

A Military Perspective

GEORGE REED AND GEORGIA SORENSON

Military leadership may be distinctive in that military leaders ask subordinates to risk their lives and, in some instances, take lives, to achieve organizational goals (Prince and Tumlin 2004). These goals are never inconsequential, as General of the Army Douglas MacArthur reminded West Point cadets some forty years ago: "All through this welter of change and development, your mission remains fixed, determined and inviolable—it is to win our wars. [Yours] is the profession of arms—the will to win, the sure knowledge that in war there is no substitute for victory: that if you lose, the nation will be destroyed" (MacArthur 1962).

While attention on military leadership has focused on what Thomas Kolditz of the U.S. Military Academy terms "in extremis leadership"—dangerous situations literally at the point of death (2005)—it should also be noted that the Department of Defense as a public agency shares similar problems of large and complex public-sector organizations. And while distinct differences arise from its uncommon mandate and expanded mission, military leaders confront institutional challenges administrators of large agencies would find familiar.

This chapter focuses on one of these challenges: the emergence of the direct-level strategic leader and the concomitant reordering of the Army's traditional domains of leadership. We employ an abbreviated military case study, the Steel Tigers at Brcko Bridge, to illustrate the necessity for this reconfiguration and to make the case for strategic leadership at all levels of the modern organization.

Broadening Mission

General MacArthur's words in their poignant clarity established war fighting as the sine qua non of Army service, but today war fighting is only one of many missions that the military is called upon to execute. In the first part of the twenty-first century, complex contingency operations—hurricane relief in the United States, humanitarian operations in Pakistan and Southeast Asia, and peacekeeping in the Balkans—were in force simultaneously with combat operations in Iraq and Afghanistan. As of March 2006, there were 241,000 soldiers serving in 120 countries, putting our armed forces' deployment on par with the most robust of multinational corporate giants.[1]

Leadership and Management

Because of its singular mandate, the U.S. Army has always valued extraordinary leadership. Indeed, a strong case can be made that the Army—through funding of research efforts in World War II and after—incubated the formal study of leadership (Sorenson 1992) and strengthened modern management.[2] In his foreword to *Hope Is Not a Method,* the dean of the Boston University School of Management asserted, "Much of the way American management works was learned from the World War II practices of the U.S. military" (Sullivan and Harper 1996).

This influence continues to be prevalent in today's business environment. Witness new articles in *Harvard Business Review* on "After Action Reports" (Darling, Parry, and Moore 2005) and a study on leadership by Korn/Ferry International and Columbia Business School advising CEOs to "formulate a strategy for surmounting threats that have not yet materialized . . . identify enemies before they themselves realize they are adversaries, anticipate weapons before they are invented and attack before anyone else realizes there is a battle to fight (Hambrick 1989, 55).

C2 to L2

This year, Army Chief of Staff Peter Schoomaker reaffirmed the Army's historical commitment to leadership development: "The Army provides the Nation, the President, the Secretary of Defense and the Combatant Commanders a unique set of core competencies and capabilities. We train and equip Soldiers and grow leaders" (Schoomaker 2003).

The military's C2 environment—Command and Control—has always been undergirded by its L2—Learn to Lead—commitment. There is no greater indication of the military's commitment to "grow great leaders" than the investment made in the system of professional military education. A vast array of schools and programs exist to prepare service members for leadership at every level of responsibility. Army officers can expect to spend about four years in military schools that focus on preparation for leadership out of a twenty-year career. Many officers will pursue advanced degrees at civilian colleges and universities, a virtual prerequisite for senior leadership positions. Based on records compiled by the Army War College registrar, the class of 2006 arrived for the ten-month course of intensive study that emphasizes strategic-level leadership with 78 percent already holding advanced degrees. When they graduate from the War College, the pinnacle of the officer professional military education system, most will have earned a second master's degree in strategic studies.

Indeed, one could argue that nothing is more important to the Army than the education and development of its leaders (Reichard 2006). In its 100-year history, the Army War College closed only once—during World War II, due to a pressing need for officers in the field—a decision later subjected to criticism (Ball 1994). Few endeavors in the public or private sector make a similar commitment to leadership development.

In light of such a significant investment of resources in leadership development, one might reasonably ask if there is a sufficient return. Quantifying the benefits of a leader-centric culture is tricky business. One could argue that most evaluation efforts focus on individuals—*leader* development rather than *leadership* development. Even fewer have empirical evidence of a link between a particular leadership development program and leader development (Day 2001). In the Army, it is almost an article of faith that leader development provides the bedrock for an effective military force. While there may be scant empirical evidence for a direct correlation between leader development and organizational effectiveness, corporate America annually spends millions of dollars to recruit military officers to its ranks (Herron 2004).

Another measure of success might be public trust, and in this area military leadership ranks high. The military has earned considerable respect from the American public, especially in recent years. A May 2005 Gallup Poll measuring confidence in major institutions found that Americans had significantly more confidence in the military than in any other sector, including the church, the presidency, the media, public schools, labor, and business.[3] A February 2006 *Harris Poll* confirmed the public ranked the military above all other sectors.[4] Additionally, a qualitative study utilizing 1,374 interviews conducted by the Kennedy School at Harvard University found that in every measure studied—competence, professional character, personal character, and charisma—the American public has more confidence in the U.S. military than in any other segment of society (Pittinsky et al.).

While emphasis on leadership in the military remains strong, global changes are driving an internal reexamination of leadership concepts. The terrorist attacks of September 11, 2001, accelerated transformation efforts within the U.S. Army. Efforts to enhance joint war-fighting capabilities through organizational transformation and network-centric processes have led some to reconsider traditional Army leadership doctrine. Few would argue against the assertion that the Army is inherently a bureaucratic hierarchy; so are most federal agencies. Still, the Army places a high priority on discipline and the inviolability of leadership by chain of command. It also places accountability on commanders considered responsible for everything that their unit does or fails to do. In military parlance, this is referred to as *total* or *unlimited accountability*.

Within this traditional framework, it should be no surprise that the Army has long viewed leadership as having three levels: direct, organizational, and strategic. This perspective corresponds to three levels of war: tactical, operational, and strategic. It relies, in part, on a simplification of the organizational theories of Elliot

Figure 7.1 **Army Leadership Levels**

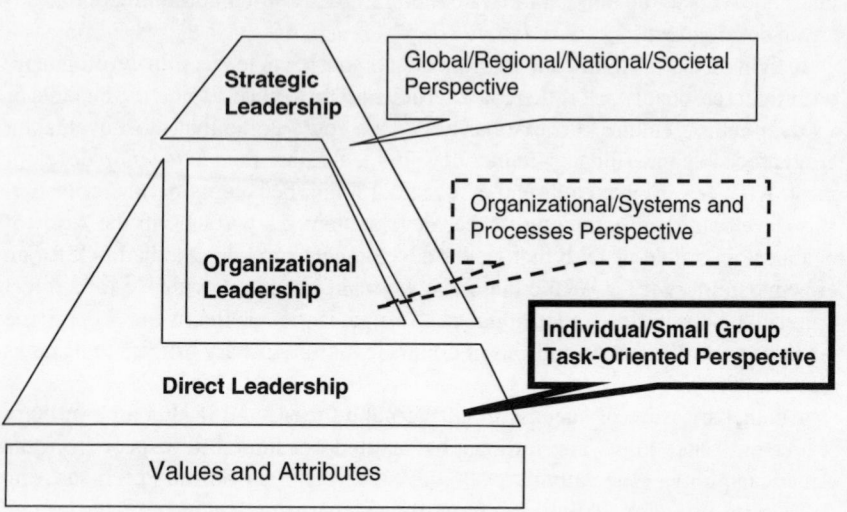

LEVELS OF LEADERSHIP

Source: Adapted from *Field Manual 22-100* (Department of the Army 1999, 1–10).

Jaques who hypothesized that there is an underlying stratification to work levels in bureaucracies (Jaques 1996). The three levels correspond with civilian notions of frontline, middle, and senior executive management. It is predictable then that the Army leadership field manual depicts leadership levels in the form of a pyramid.

The traditional Army view of leadership is captured in Department of the Army, *Field Manual 22-100 Army Leadership: Be, Know, Do* (1999), a document that serves as the capstone reference for all Army leaders. The field manual includes compelling historical vignettes that demonstrate timeless military virtues. As an example, it relates General George Washington's vigorous and public rejection of suggestions that the Army march on the seat of government in Philadelphia when the new government failed to supply the Army or pay its soldiers, thereby emphasizing the importance of civil control of the military.

Direct-level Leadership

The field manual also clearly delineates the three levels of leadership. Leadership at the direct level is associated with units ranging in size from a few to several hundred people. It is a frontline hands-on approach to leadership conducted eye to eye and with a relatively short time horizon. Leadership at this level emphasizes influencing others by setting an example that can be observed and emulated. Referent power, in which followers admire or identify with a leader, can be a source of considerable influence (French and Raven 1959). Interpersonal actions, such as mentoring, counseling, and team building, are key tasks at this level.

The effect of direct-level leadership on the organization is observable almost immediately. Quick and decisive decision making with limited information and technical competence are valued traits as are personal attributes of courage and ethical conduct. Leaders at the direct level operate within a fairly extensive set of doctrine, rules, tactics, techniques, and procedures that provide some sense of certainty and predictability.

Organizational Leadership

Organizational leadership is usually associated with military units from brigade through corps. For civilian leadership, this equates to civilians at the level of assistant secretary through undersecretary. In the military, the time horizon of interest for organizational planning focuses on the next two to ten years. For civilians at this level who are political appointees, the horizon is often the next midterm or presidential election. Political appointees do not have clear doctrine or policy guidance but rather a broad political mandate from above. In the military, middle-level leaders operate in a more indirect manner; they typically work through others, such as staffs, to exert influence. They rely on policies and procedures to influence others, and focus on implementing and maintaining organizational capabilities. There is often a time delay between actions and results, making it more difficult to determine the impact of actions by organizational leaders. At this level, organizational resource management is a central concern. Organizational leaders are characteristically responsible for administering infrastructure systems and processes that are essential to maintaining long-term capabilities.

Strategic Leadership

Strategic leadership is typically exercised at the senior executive level, at the head of large organizations of thousands to hundreds of thousand of people. In this sense, strategic leaders hold major commands in the military and serve in the public arena at the secretarial level and above. Strategic leadership has a longer-range focus, although in non-military organizations the horizon of the next election is always of central concern. Strategic leaders are responsible for developing and communicating a compelling vision for the organization. They represent the organization to outside constituencies, and their decisions have great consequence in terms of resource allocation and organizational priorities. The strategic environment, by definition, is inherently volatile, uncertain, complex, and ambiguous. The difference in leadership at the strategic level is evident in a quote by then Army Chief of Staff George C. Marshall that hangs in every classroom at the Army War College (U.S. Army War College 2004).

> It became clear to me that at the age of 58 I would have to learn new tricks that were not taught in the military manuals or on the battlefield. In this position I am a political soldier and will have to put my training in rapping-out orders and making snap decisions on the back burner, and have to learn the arts of persuasion and guile. I must become an expert in a whole new set of skills.

Marshall was prescient about the new terrain of strategic military leaders, though he would undoubtedly be surprised at the extent and scale of the required new skills.

The Army War College defines the strategic art as "the skillful formulation, coordination, and application of ends (objectives), ways (courses of action) and means (supporting resources) to promote and defend the national interests" (U.S. Army War College 2004, 1–2). Military leaders at the strategic level are expected to consider all elements of national power including diplomatic, informational, and economic elements and must increasingly expand their repertoire beyond the application of military force alone. Strategic artists who can do this effectively may require an entire career to develop.

The tiered model of Army leadership has much to commend it. While there are attributes, skills, and behaviors evident in an effective leader at all three levels, the fact that there are qualitative differences between them is apparent to all who attempt to make the difficult transition from one level to another. It seems self-evident that as leaders gain experience and a track record of success, they should also be entrusted with increased authority. Thus we expect that those who make decisions with the greatest impact will be those at the corresponding level of positional authority. Those with a lifetime of experience and proven ability should naturally make strategic-level decisions that impact ends, ways, and means, while direct-level leaders make day-to-day tactical decisions related to implementation of established policy. The realities of the today's post–9/11 environment, including a highly decentralized networked enemy, suggest that previously distinct levels of leadership are becoming less so.

Actions by low-ranking officials and soldiers increasingly have strategic implications, due in part to the rise of the nearly instantaneous reporting of events from the international communications grid and interdependence resulting from globalization. Leaders at increasingly lower levels of the organizational hierarchy are finding themselves in situations where they must make decisions previously reserved for more senior levels.

This observation prompted then Commandant of the Marine Corps General Charles Krulak to coin the term *strategic corporal* (1999). In "The Strategic Corporal: Leadership in the Three Block War," he spun a story about a small unit led by a fictional corporal who must make a direct-leadership decision that could determine the outcome of the mission and have strategic implications (1999). Soon his fictional concept of the "strategic soldier" was finding traction in real-life combat, perhaps most notably in the Steel Tigers at Brcko Bridge.

The Case of the Steel Tigers

In 1992, over 99 percent of Bosnians voted in a referendum to secede from Yugoslavia (Power 2002, 248). Shortly after the referendum, forces of the brutal Slobodan Milosevic regime teamed with local Serbs and began a process now known as "ethnic cleansing." They sought to rid the Srpska Republika of non-Serbs, including Muslims and Croats. Over the next three years, "200,000 Bosnians were killed, more than 2 million were displaced, and the territory of a multiethnic European republic was sliced into three ethnically pure statelets" (Power 2002, 251). In 1997, the United States had a sizable military contingent in place as part of the Stabilization Force (SFOR) to enforce a tenuous peace including about 1,000 soldiers near Brcko in Bosnia and Herzegovina. Strategic leaders understood that public support for the intervention was not guaranteed and national will could evaporate in the face of American casualties. Fresh in the minds of many was the experience of Somalia, a successful humanitarian operation that later unraveled with the deaths of eighteen U.S. soldiers in Mogadishu in 1993, their bodies dragged through the streets and broadcast on every news channel, leading to an ignominious withdrawal.

The city of Brcko was on key terrain where the currents of hate and history ran strong. A lone American infantry company guarded an important bridge across the Sava River at Brcko. One side led to Croatian-controlled territory, and the other was on Serbian turf. If the bridge were controlled by one faction, it would cut one of only two major lines of communication between Bosnia and the rest of Europe. The bridge simply had to remain under the control of SFOR.

Troops on the bridge, although well armed with heavy weapons and supported by helicopters, tanks, and armored fighting vehicles, were vastly outnumbered by a mob of over 800 rioters who overran local police stations. The mob included women and children, thugs, and some who were just paid to protest. Emboldened by their success in forcing the withdrawal of the international police force in Brcko, Serb-hardliners focused their rage on troops at the bridge. For over twelve hours, the Americans faced rocks, bricks, and Molotov cocktails.

The officer in charge of the forces on the bridge was Captain Kevin Hendricks. Captains normally have between four and ten years of Army experience. In response to the onslaught, Captain Hendricks directed a variety of carefully controlled measures to deter the crowd's actions that eventually included tear gas and warning shots from an automatic weapon. Many of his soldiers were injured by the mob, and the fighting was sometimes hand to hand, yet the level of discipline and restraint the American forces exercised was remarkable. Despite being undermanned, Hendricks prepared for a long-term engagement and rotated his solders out of the line so they could rest, eat, and recharge. The soldiers outlasted the mob, which eventually dispersed leaving the bridge under SFOR control.

In this desperate tactical situation, the young commander had more bad options before him than good ones, and the wrong choice would surely have strategic implications. If the Serbs provoked use of the heavy U.S. weaponry on the crowd that

Figure 7.2   **Levels of War**

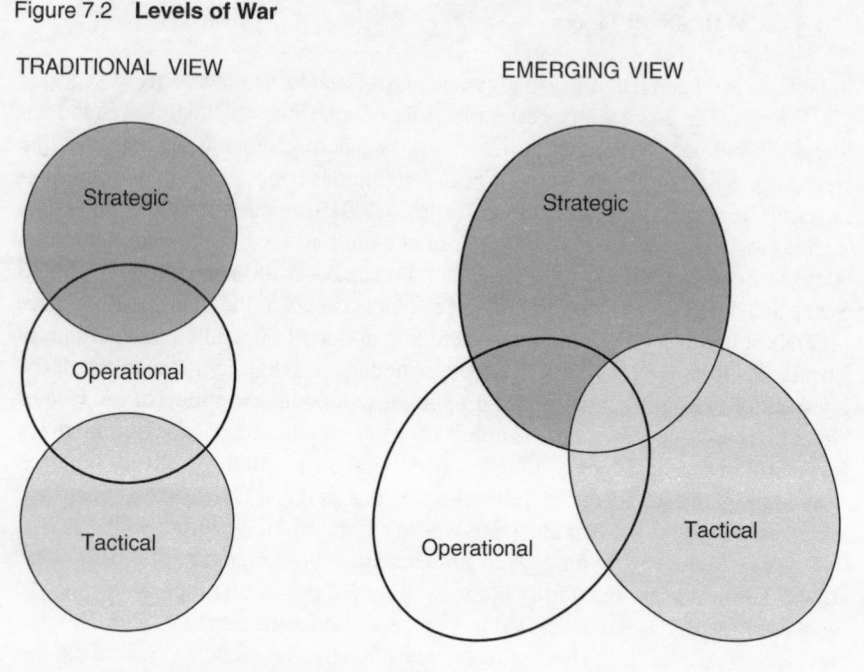

Note: Previously distinct levels of war are blurring since actions at the tactical level increasingly are having strategic impact.

included women and children, the resulting massacre would have played into the hands of Serb propagandists. If American soldiers were killed, it would certainly weaken American public support for the entire intervention in Bosnia. The results of either worst-case scenario would most assuredly be beamed worldwide by the international media in a matter of minutes. If the rioters provoked abandonment of the bridge, it might not result in as much press coverage, but it would further embolden attacks on stabilization forces and make restoration of order in Brcko extremely difficult. The Steel Tigers held true to their namesake despite extreme provocation, and it may well be that the fate of Bosnia depended on the judgment of an Army captain and the discipline of any number of soldiers who had fingers on triggers. This is not a responsibility that one would intentionally place on junior soldiers, yet this scenario plays out with increasing regularity in complex contingency operations.

The Steel Tiger case demonstrates a fundamental flaw with a stratified model of leadership relying on a hierarchical notion of leadership. Even those at the lowest levels of an organization can operate at the strategic level, at least in terms of impact. Of course that impact may not always be favorable, as the Dubai Port debacle in March 2006 demonstrates.[5]

The mirror side of this dilemma is perhaps just as problematic: the observation that

Figure 7.3   **The Three Domains of Leadership**

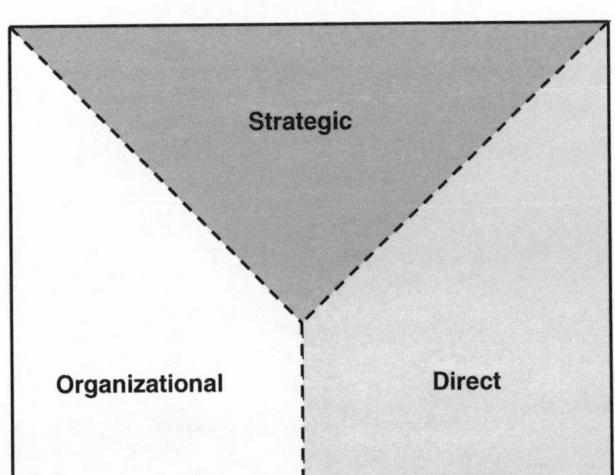

some senior-level leaders choose to delve into tactical details to the extent that they abdicate their influence at the strategic level. In fact, there is strong incentive to do so. Senior leaders usually rise to their station by mastering lower-level skills. They have been rewarded for being perceived as "in charge" and having a command of details of their organizations. In a high-stakes endeavor, it would take a supreme act of restraint to give a less-experienced subordinate latitude to act without some helpful attention. Yet we might ask, "Who is attending to strategic issues while the senior leaders' attention is focused at the lower level?" On the other hand, even the most senior leader has a number of direct reports. Those subordinates look to the strategic leader for direct-level leadership. And woe to the executive who focuses solely on the long term to the exclusion of operational priorities and who neglects immediate subordinates.

It is apparent then that leaders at all levels must operate in multiple domains, that while the organization may notionally function best when senior leaders operate at the strategic level and junior leaders focus on technical mastery, reality intervenes. In fact, it may be even more complex, as Hal Leavitt of Stanford Business School suggested to us recently: "At least in the private sector, strategic decisions may be pushed down to lower levels, but at the same time the expanded nature of sophisticated technology means the corporate "strategic soldier" is monitored constantly by higher-ups."[6] Such an environment is hardly a recipe for success. We need a conceptual model that recognizes the stratified requirements of leadership while accepting the need for leaders to operate across levels, especially in a decentralized environment.

We suggest that we begin by depicting the possible universe of leadership options as existing within the three recognized levels (direct, organizational, and strategic), recast as domains of leadership as in Figure 7.3.

Figure 7.4   **Three Ideal Types of Leaders**

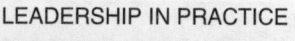

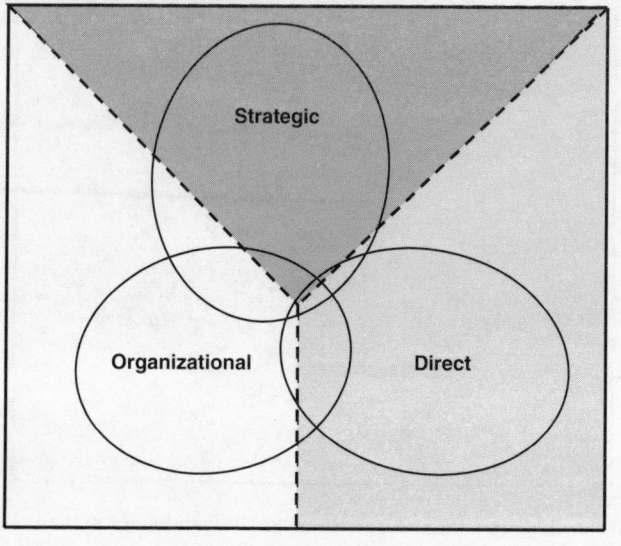

We eliminate the pyramid that suggests someone is operating in a domain by virtue of his rank or position. The boundaries between the three domains are difficult to establish with precision so we avoided the inclination to depict them as having discernable boundaries. This is consistent with new organizational research, acutely aware of the highly networked forms of commerce and business, which focus on "boundary regions" instead of distinct boundaries.

All leaders, we suggest, should operate to some degree in all three domains. Thus we see that while a junior leader such as the captain on the Brcko Bridge may appropriately operate at the direct level of leadership most of the time, some attention must be paid to the organizational infrastructure and in some circumstances the strategic level as well. To depict this in an ideal form, we illustrate the leader as operating within an ellipse superimposed on the appropriate domain as shown in Figure 7.4. The ellipse of the strategic leader similarly occupies a large portion of the strategic domain, while reaching into organizational and occasionally into direct leadership.

If a leader is operating in a domain inappropriate to his or her experience and responsibilities, then a personal or organizational adjustment may be in order. If an executive with a strategic portfolio is spending time focused on the short-term technical details to the exclusion of the big picture, the organization may well be strategically adrift. In the Army, some have been known to refer to such leaders as "Four-Star Squad Leaders." Junior-level leaders who devote too much energy to grand strategic-level debates of ends, ways, and means ("Second Lieutenant MacArthurs") run the risk of neglecting subordinates and the mission.

Implications

If we accept the notion that leaders must operate in all three domains, then it is insufficient to focus junior leaders solely on tasks related to technical proficiency.

Agility requires not only changing thoughts but, as management consultant John Thompson suggests, changing the operating system of the mind (1992). At the very least, they must recognize the strategic implications of their actions. Yet there is a limited and finite amount of time one can devote to leader development. Direct-level leader competence obviously depends on the mastery of certain technical skills. One of the more interesting debates under way in the Army relates to the perceived need to increase the strategic competence of midgrade and even junior officers and noncommissioned officers. In the current operating environment, such leaders are operating across widely dispersed areas with extraordinary responsibilities. In Iraq and Afghanistan, not only are they defeating an enemy that is hard enough in its own right but they are also building national capabilities for self-government. In the words of the Army chief of staff, "We must build a bench of leaders who think strategically and innovatively at all levels of war; leaders who are self aware and adaptive and who operate seamlessly in joint, interagency, and multinational environments" (Schoomaker 2003). Don Kettl describes this as a "center edge" strategy, working collaborative and in an informed integrated matrix from edge to center and vice versa (2005).

There are certainly important differences between leadership in the military context and other forms. Few agencies of the federal government may be able to task and compel their employees to the extent that is inherent in the armed services. Service members have at their disposal weapons of frightening destructive potential. The armed forces also have access to vast resources far in excess of other sectors of the government. But the differences may be more of scale than substance. Service to the nation is a value that is evident in all corners of the public sector. Agencies of the federal government are increasingly engaged overseas, and many are serving alongside soldiers in the world's hot spots. The faith and confidence of the American public as a bottom line is certainly a metric to which all agencies must attend. The challenges of globalization, an accelerating pace of change, networked and dynamic organizations, and the demand for ethical and accountable leadership extend to all organizations.

A recent study by the American Management Association (2005) posited four assumptions about future leadership across all sectors:

1. The huge impact of technology advancement on societies, businesses, and governments.
2. Global trends that include free-trade initiatives and demographic shifts leading to greater competition and regional conflict.
3. Growing interconnectedness requiring an "agile mind-set."

4. Changes in the global talent pool that vary by region but include an aging workforce in developed countries and social and political disorders from inequities in developing countries.

This means we are in an era of accelerating change and conflict that places new demands on leaders at all levels. The demands of this environment require leaders and organizations in the public and private sectors that can adapt quickly to unforeseen contingencies.

While the tragic events of September 11, 2001, lent a sense of urgency to our reexamination of cold war paradigms, much of the foundation for conceptual change was already under way. If great leaders are born in crisis as leadership scholar James MacGregor Burns contends, and the study of leadership has been enhanced by war as Sorenson asserts, there may be much to learn in these dark and troubling times. It is certainly appropriate that we reexamine our models and frameworks as well as our thinking about leadership in light of the exigencies of current events and search for applications that extend across various contexts of leadership.

Notes

1. Data accessed on www.us.army.mil/operations.
2. For example, in 1947 General Dwight D. Eisenhower, then the chief of staff of the Army, directed the U.S. Military Academy at West Point to design a formal program of leadership instruction and urged the creation of a department of leadership study. Later, as president, he would substantially fund leadership research through the Army Research Institute and other governmental laboratories.
3. *Gallup Poll*, May 23–26, 2005. N = 1,004 adults nationwide, margin of error ± 3.
4. *Harris Poll* #22, March 2, 2006. Conducted February 7–14, 2006. N = 1,016 adults nationwide, margin or error ± 3.
5. A commission approved the sale of port authorities in six major U.S. cities to a state-owned company in Dubai without consulting top leadership in the Bush administration.
6. Conversation with Hal Leavitt, February 23, 2006, Claremont, California.

References

American Management Association. 2005. *Leading into the Future: A Global Study of Leadership—2005–2015.* New York: American Management Association.

Ball, Harry. 1994. *Of Responsible Command: A History of the U.S. Army War College: The School that Shaped the Military Leaders of the Free World.* Carlisle, PA: Alumni Association of the U.S. Army War College.

Darling, Marilyn, Charles Parry, and Joseph Moore. 2005. "Learning in the Thick of It." *Harvard Business Review* 83 (7/8): 84–92.

Day, David. 2001. "Leadership Development: A Review in Context." *Leadership Quarterly* 11: 581–614.

Department of the Army. 1999. *Field Manual 22-100 Army Leadership: Be, Know, Do.* Washington, DC: Department of the Army.

French, John, and Bertram Raven. 1959. "The Basis of Social Power." In *Studies in Social Power,* ed. D. Cartwright, 150–67. Ann Arbor: University of Michigan, Institute for Social Research.

Hambrick, Donald. 1989. *Reinventing the CEO: 21st Century Report.* Korn/Ferry International/Columbia Business School.

Herron, Sean. 2004. "The Army Profession: Ostrich or Phoenix?" *Military Review* 84 (1): 61–66.

Jaques, Elliot. 1996. *Requisite Organization: A Total System for Effective Managerial Organization and Managerial Leadership for the 21st Century.* Green Cove Springs, FL: Cason Hall.

Kettl, Don. 2005. *The Next Government of the United States: Challenges for Performance in the 21st Century.* Washington, DC: IBM Center for the Business of Government.

Kolditz, Thomas. 2005. "The In Extremis Leader. Leadership Breakthroughs from West Point." *Leader to Leader* (Special Supplement, May): 6–18.

Krulak, Charles. 1999. "The Strategic Corporal: Leadership in the Three Block War." *Marines Magazine* 28 (1): 26–32.

MacArthur, Douglas. 1962. Speech delivered West Point, NY, 12 May. www.americanrhetoric. com/speeches/douglasmacarthurthayeraward.html. (Accessed 14 March 2006.)

Pittinsky, Todd L., Seth A. Rosenthal, Brian Welle, and R. Matthew Montoya. 2005. *National Leadership Index 2005: A National Study of Confidence in Leadership.* Cambridge, MA: Harvard University, Center for Public Leadership, John F. Kennedy School of Government.

Power, Samantha. 2002. *A Problem from Hell: America and the Age of Genocide.* New York: Harper Collins.

Prince, Howard, and Geoffrey Tumlin. 2004. "Military." In *The Encyclopedia of Leadership*, ed. George Goethals, Georgia Sorenson, and James MacGregor Burns, 1000–10. Thousand Oaks, CA: Sage.

Reichard, Rebecca. 2006. "Toward a Grounded Theory of Female Leader Development in the Military." *Leadership Review* 6 (Winter): 3–28.

Schoomaker, Peter. 2003. "CSA Remarks As Prepared." Presented at the Association of the United States Army Eisenhower Luncheon Speech, Washington, DC. www.army. mil/leaders/leaders/csa/speeches/20031007.html. (Accessed 28 November 2005.)

Sorenson, Georgia. 1992. "An Intellectual History of Leadership Studies: The Role of James MacGregor Burns." Paper presented at the Annual Conference of the American Political Science Association, Washington, DC.

———. 2005. "On Beyond Bion, Organizational & Social Dynamics." *Journal of Organizational Dynamics* 5 (2): 298–312.

Sullivan, Gordon, and Michael Harper. 1996. *Hope Is Not a Method: What Business Leaders Can Learn from America's Army.* New York: Broadway Books.

Thompson, John W. 1992. "Corporate Leadership in the 21st Century." In *New Traditions in Business*, ed. John Renesch, 209–24. San Francisco: Berrett-Koehler.

U.S. Army War College. 2004. *Strategic Leadership Primer.* 2nd ed. Carlisle Barracks, PA: U.S. Army War College.

8

Leading at the Edge of Chaos

NANETTE M. BLANDIN

To say that public managers operate in a time of change is a cliché. To say that they operate in a time of unrelenting turbulence, mind-boggling complexity, and unnerving uncertainty is more provocative, yet probably closer to the truth. I believe that practitioners know this intuitively. However, our theory base and many of our management and leadership practices assume otherwise. They, for the large part, are rooted in an old paradigm. The field of public management needs to come to terms with the new organizational reality and adopt new organizational, management, and leadership perspectives.

One surprising, but useful, place to look for these new perspectives is outside of our own field. All fields and disciplines have a tendency to become insular and to discourage boundary scanning. This is important in promoting stability and consistency within professional disciplines. However, it can also limit the accessibility of alternative perspectives and delay the acceptance of new paradigms.

I believe the field of public management would benefit enormously from looking outside of the field for new perspectives, outlooks, and ideas. One of the goals of this chapter is to introduce public managers to the field of complexity science and to offer some new perspectives about organizations and leadership.

The first section of this chapter discusses the context of leadership and leadership theory and the nature of the disconnect between theory and reality. In the second section, I will explore the contribution of complexity theory to creating new organizational metaphors and new perspectives about leadership. The third section offers some preliminary thoughts about what a new leadership paradigm might encompass in terms of philosophy, behaviors, and attributes. The concluding section examines issues, implications, and recommendations for further research.

Need for a New Paradigm

The disconnect between the reality of today's social systems and conventional organizational, change, leadership, and management theories and models has been discussed by a wide variety of scholars (Wheatley 1992; Stumpf 1995; Stacey 1996;

Eoyang 1997; Kelly and Allison 1999; Marion 1999; Fulmer 2000; Osborn, Hunt, and Jauch 2002; Knowles 2001; Marion and Uhl-Bien 2001; Olson and Eoyang 2001; Falconer 2002; Kettl 2002; Gronn 2003; Jackson 2003). According to these scholars, conventional theories assume a rational organizational environment of relative stability based on a mechanistic and scientific model. This organizational model emphasizes equilibrium, hierarchy, control, planned change, certainty, limited variance, and selective interaction with the environment.

These scholars argue that because today's organizational environment is markedly different, new theoretical models are needed to understand the nature of leading in highly complex and dynamic organizational environments where so many of the conventional elements of leadership are either nonexistent or substantially reframed. They contend that the implicit assumptions underlying conventional leadership theory need to be challenged. This is true across sectors. Kettl (2002) writes that one of the most significant challenges facing the field of public administration is that it possesses a theoretical tradition that no longer fits reality.

My view is that organizational and leadership theory has not kept pace with the changing context. Many of our current leadership models are based upon transformational leadership theory, which was developed by James MacGregor Burns in his 1978 book *Leadership*. This theory was developed as a way of promoting a deeper connection between leaders and followers, so that followers were positively motivated to help achieve the organization's mission. This idea was in stark contrast to transactional leadership, which viewed the relationship as an exchange—a job and salary in return for an employee's work.

While subsequent leadership models have been advanced by scholars, none has replaced transformational leadership as the dominant leadership paradigm. Osborn, Hunt, and Jauch (2002) argue that current scholarship in the field of leadership is "not invalid, but incomplete" because the "world of the leader has fundamentally changed."

In a provocative article titled "Leadership: Who Needs It?" Gronn (2003) outlines a series of issues with conventional leadership assumptions including the relationship between leadership and management, the connection between leadership and power, the leader-follower "binary," and the cult of the leader "exceptionality." He concludes that "[i]f leadership is to retain its conceptual and practical utility, then it has to be reconstituted . . ." (267).

Contribution of Complexity Science to Leadership

In this section, I define the term *complexity*, outline the evolution of the field of complexity science, and then discuss how it can contribute to thinking about complex social systems.

Field of Complexity Science

Complexity science is a new frontier of knowledge that is having a "transforming influence" on the study of society and social systems (Pagels 1988, 52). *Complexity* does not simply mean "many moving parts." Derived from the Latin root meaning "to entwine," it refers to the dynamic behavior of systems whose parts continually interact and reorganize themselves into more adaptive patterns over time (Pascale, Millemann, and Gioja 2000). It is "a systemic state on the cusp between chaos and order, a condition where uncertainty, variety, dependency, and interconnectedness are high" (Falconer 2002, 28) and "a grand compromise between structure and surprise" (Kauffman 1995, 15). As noted by Nicolis and Prigogine (1989), "Complexity is an idea that is part of our everyday experience" (6). Examples of complexity include a thermostat, an ant colony, the weather, traffic patterns, the rain forest, and the economy.

Complexity theory offers a new prism through which to examine and understand social systems. This shift could have a profound effect on all elements of an organizational system, including planning, mission, and leadership. Pagels suggests that "the nations and people who master the new science of complexity will become the economic, cultural and political superpowers of the next century" (1988, 10).

The field of complexity science is relatively new. It began to take shape in the late 1970s and coalesced as a discrete science during the 1980s and 1990s. Until fairly recently, the field had been heavily dominated by an elite group of scientists, mainly in universities and research organizations such as the Santa Fe Institute.

Even though it is a young science, complexity theory has made important contributions to many scientific fields. The opening passage in *Thinking in Complexity* (Mainzer 1997, 1) expands on the nature of these contributions:

> The theory of nonlinear complex systems has become a successful problem solving approach in the natural sciences—from laser physics, quantum chaos, and meteorology to molecular modeling in chemistry and computer-assisted simulations of cellular growth in biology. On the other hand, the social sciences are recognizing that the main problems of mankind are global, complex and nonlinear, too.

The application of complexity principles to leadership is a relatively recent endeavor. I would trace it to the 1992 publication of *Leadership and the New Science* by Margaret Wheatley. Since then, a number of scholars, mostly in Europe and the United States, have published a variety of books and articles that lay the groundwork for a new leadership paradigm based on complexity principles. According to Wheatley, complexity science addresses those issues that trouble organizations the most: "chaos, order, control, autonomy, structure, information, participation, planning and prediction" (1992, ix). More recently, Eisenhardt and Bhatia (2002) stress the value of complexity science in dealing with today's organizational context: "Ultimately, the most significant value of complexity theory within organizational thinking is in providing an explanation of how organizations adapt and grow, especially in high-velocity environments where pace, ambiguity, and uncertainty reign" (462).

Complexity theory contributes to a new understanding of organizations and

Table 8.1

A Comparison of Organizational Paradigms

As a Machine	As a Living System
Knowledge is structured in pieces	Knowledge is seamless
Organizations are structured in functions	Organizations are a whole system
Work is structured as roles	Work is flexible and without boundaries
People are narrowly skilled	People are multiskilled and continuously learning
Motivation is based on external forces	Motivation is based on links to the whole
Change is a troubling exception	Change is always present
Information is shared on a need-to-know basis	Information flows openly and freely; people decide what they need
Information flows up and down the organization	Information flows up, down, across, and around the organization
People work in prescribed roles	People work beyond their roles
Information from the outside world is often ignored	Information from the outside world is valued and used
Organizational barriers inhibit cross-functional interactions	Interactions across roles and functions are extensive
People see only their part of the work	People see their work in relation to the whole, knowing and doing what needs to be done

Source: R.N. Knowles, *The Leadership Dance* (2002, 105).

leadership by assuming that organizations exist as complex systems. Complexity theory provides a new organizational metaphor and thus a new language for understanding the role and nature of leadership.

Living System Metaphor

One exceedingly valuable contribution of complexity science is that it provides a new organizational metaphor, that of a living system, to replace the dominant machine metaphor. These two radically different paradigms are contrasted by Knowles in Table 8.1.

A visual representation of these two contrasting organizational models is offered by Gryskiewicz (1999, 14–15) in Figure 8.1. In these figures, the small circles represent individuals, the circles are teams, the small squares are designated leaders, and

Figure 8.1 **Contrasting Models of Organization**

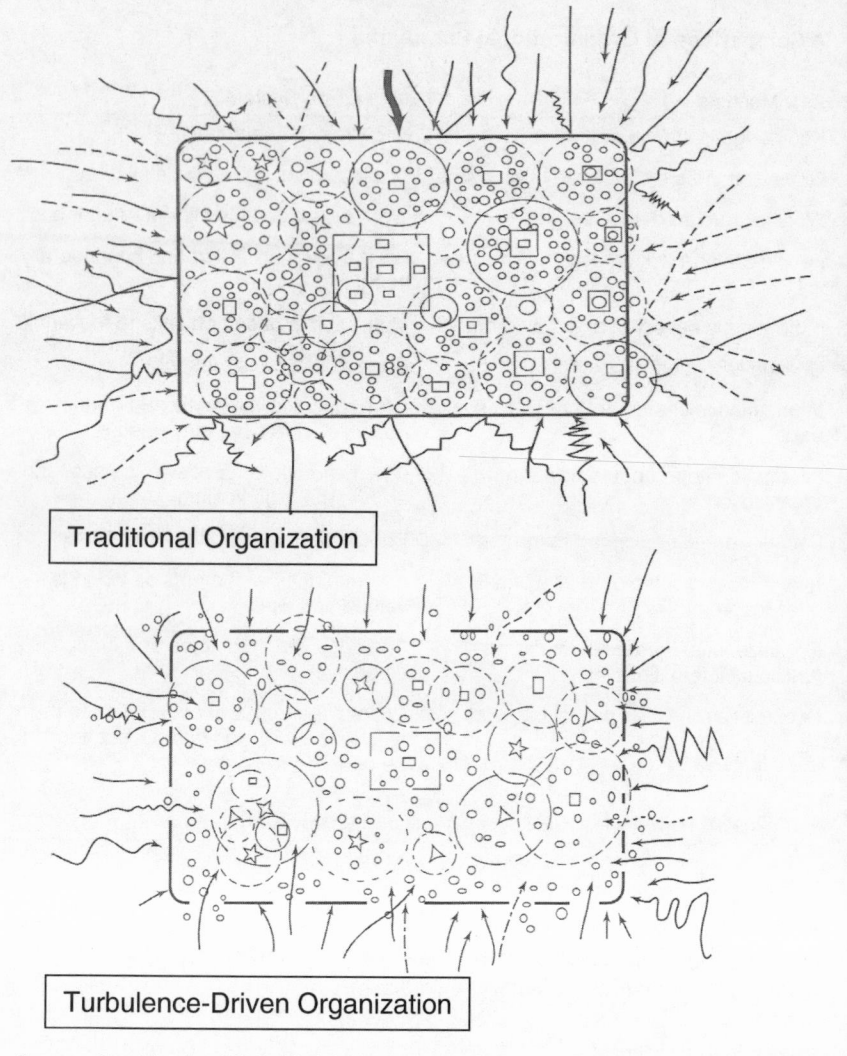

Traditional Organization

Turbulence-Driven Organization

Source: Gryskiewicz 1999, 14–15. Used by permission.

the stars are informal leaders. The arrows represent information from the external environment; the dotted arrows are more subtle signals than the solid lines. The two figures differ dramatically in terms of the extent to which the system accepts information from the outside and how boundaries are defined.

Both of these frameworks suggest that the organizational paradigm is shifting in significant ways. The implications for leadership are profound.

New Concepts/New Language

Complexity theory also offers a set of powerful concepts that can be useful as we think about organizations as dynamic, complex, and highly uncertain systems. The following key concepts drawn from complexity theory have particular relevance for the study of leadership. These concepts help to convey a different kind of leadership role and provide a common language to describe the evolving organizational climate.

Complex Adaptive Systems

Complex adaptive systems are systems that embody the principles of complexity theory discussed earlier. They are systems characterized by a large number of independent agents who are in dynamic interaction with each other and the environment, who through self-organization create emergent properties so that they can adapt, survive, and become increasingly fit over time (Stacey 1996; Pascale, Millemann, and Gioja 2000; Axelrod and Cohen 1999).

Complex adaptive systems operating at the edge of chaos are extremely flexible, can adapt rapidly to change, and are highly innovative and adaptable (Kauffman 1995). Complexity affords these systems a zone of adaptability, learning, innovation, and possibility (McMaster 1996; Sanders 1998). Important features of complex adaptive systems are their diversity, double-loop learning, continuous feedback, cultivation of conflict, existence of paradox, and sensitivity to small changes.

According to Knowles (2001), an emergency room of a hospital often functions as a complex adaptive system. It is characterized by a high level of uncertainty and adaptability to changing circumstances. Additional characteristics of complex systems that can be seen in an emergency room are connectivity, technology, sharing, transparency, fluidity, interdependency, accountability, teamwork, trust, respect, dynamism, and responsiveness. A high degree of learning occurs in complex systems, both through feedback and other means. Everyone has a role, and each role is understood and respected. Finally, communication and energy levels are usually robust.

Another example of a complex adaptive system is a jazz quintet (Sherman and Schultz 1998). In jazz, all of the musicians have agreed on the program and the instruments each will play. No formal leader is necessary. "[A]ll of the players work together to shape the music, modifying and adapting themselves to the other players. . . . The music that results is in a continual state of co-evolution, each agent influenced by the interpretations and improvisations of the other players. It is the job of the quintet to self-organize to create an interpretation that meaningfully expands the understanding of the piece of music" (160–161). "Creativity and efficiency emerge naturally. Some basic rules, positive contacts, and relationships among members of the organization allow solutions to emerge from the bottom up" (Olson and Eoyang 2001, xxxv).

A third example of a complex adaptive system is the Internet, as described by Pascale, Millemann, and Gioja (2000).

> Users of the Internet provide an illustration of a network in an emergent state. As icons of self-organization, they interact with no architect. No one is in charge; there are no formal rule makers or police. Users, as a community, evolve through self-organization. Emergence is evident in the growing number of the roles the Net performs and the enterprises it fosters (126).

The authors continue to explain how complex adaptive systems favor a decentralized structure. "The self-organizing potential of a system is enhanced by (1) devolving power to the nodes, (2) establishing rich connections to form networks, and (3) enriching the value of those networks with information" (130).

In complex systems, diversity, asymmetry, variety, and cross-pollination are sources of strength and adaptability. As discussed by Kiuchi and Shireman (2002), diversity enhances a system's long-term efficiency and effectiveness. "The more diverse the organisms in an ecosystem, the more types of resources are available to deal with any challenge and the greater the likelihood of success" (111).

Complex systems have limitations as well. Most important, they are not stable since they exist in a constant state of flux. Between times of stability, which is the majority of the time, systems are in a state of uncertainty and unpredictability. Further, it is difficult for a system to sustain itself at the edge of chaos. It requires maintaining a balance between the forces promoting stability and the forces creating instability.

Edge of Chaos

All complex adaptive systems can operate in one of three zones: a stable zone, an unstable zone, and at the edge of chaos, a narrow transition zone between stability and instability (Stacey 1996). In the stable zone, they tend to ossify; in the unstable zone, they disintegrate; but at the edge of chaos, they can innovate and thrive. The edge of chaos has been described as "bounded instability" (Kelly and Allison 1999, 4) and "the sweet spot for productive change" (Pascale, Millemann, and Gioja 2000, 61). It is "the place that harbors both the capacity to perform the most complex tasks and the capacity to evolve most adequately in a changing world" (Kauffman 1995, 227).

McMillan (2004) refers to the edge of chaos as "a place . . . where the parts of the system never quite lock into place, and yet never quite break up either" (22). This place, or zone, "is not an exact spot or an edge like the edge of a cliff" (94). An organization balanced at the edge of chaos has "sufficient freedom for creativity, entrepreneurship, experimentation and risk taking to emerge. There is ongoing change, but there is a dynamic balance so that the organization does not tip over into massive confusion and uncertainty" (95).

Figure 8.2 provides a visual representation of the edge of chaos. The figure shows the order-chaos continuum and the distinctions between the zone of equilibrium and

Figure 8.2   **Order, Chaos, and Complexity**

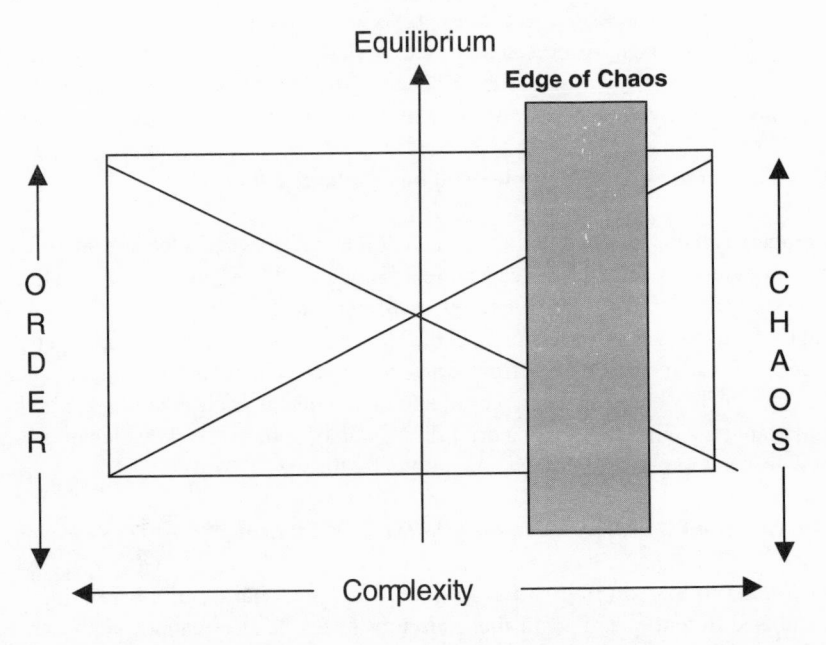

the edge of chaos. It is difficult to represent the dynamic nature of these elements on a static chart, but indeed, the elements are in a constant state of flux.

Self-organization and Emergence

Self-organization and emergence are "two sides of the same coin of life" (Pascale, Millemann, and Gioja 2000, 113). Self-organization is the ability of certain systems operating far from equilibrium to develop new types of order and to renew themselves. This concept is based on the work of Ilya Prigogine, a Russian chemist, who won the Nobel Prize in 1977 for his work on "dissipative structures." His research demonstrated a paradox—that order can arise from disorder. The implication for social systems is that systems can survive and achieve order in states far from equilibrium. Emergence is the outcome of self-organization in which complex adaptive systems develop new and more complex capabilities.

Fitness and Adaptation

In complex systems, the goal of the system is not equilibrium. According to one scholar, equilibrium is "death" (Stacey 1996, 248). Pascale, Millemann, and Gioja (2000) assert that "over time and on very large scales, equilibrium becomes hazardous. It dulls an organization's senses and saps its abilities to cope with danger" (2). The system's goal is to survive, adapt, evolve, and maximize its capabilities through ongoing realignment. A term that is used by many scholars to capture this set of goals is *evolutionary fitness*. As described by Kelly and Allison (1999), fitness "is a measure of how well a system adapts within its context and environment" (149).

Key Perspectives from Complexity Theory about Leadership

Complexity theory offers a number of valuable perspectives about leadership in complex systems. My research on leadership and complexity has involved conducting a case study of an organization operating as a complex adaptive system at the edge of chaos. It suggests that leadership in complex systems is radically different than the picture of leadership we draw from conventional organizational and management theory, which is based on principles of authority, control, centralization, hierarchy, and planning. What follows is a brief discussion of some of the key elements of a new leadership paradigm based on complexity theory.

Determinism/Control → Indeterminism/Lack of Control

According to Stacey (1996), "Far from certainty and equilibrium, leadership has a rather different meaning. In these circumstances, leaders cannot know where the organization is going" (275). Jackson (2003) asserts that "complexity theory requires a complete mind shift for managers. Managers have to accept that the long-term future of their organizations is inherently unknowable. Long-term planning is impossible" (119). Griffin (2002) writes: "It is astounding that we continue to hold fantasies that single persons or small cliques of persons can steer such complexity to achieve targets they have set in advance" (218).

As pointed out by Pascale, Millemann, and Gioja (2000), it is "extraordinarily difficult" (157) for managers to come to terms with indeterminism and the need to let go of control. "You don't have the same kind of control that traditional leadership is used to. You may have more control, but in a different fashion. You get more feedback, you learn more. But, you still need to let go of the old sense of control" (192).

Based on a series of interviews with leaders in American and British companies, Lewin and Regine (2000) found that "leading in an interconnected, dynamic system requires a different way of being a leader. Leading in a dynamical system is more like an improvisational dance with the system rather than a mechanistic imperative of doing things to the system, as if it were an object that could be fixed. This casts the meaning of leadership itself in a different light . . ." (17).

Directing → Facilitating/Enabling

Complexity scholars describe the leadership role and function in terms that differ from traditional organizations. As opposed to being an idealized notion of a person in charge who directs, controls, influences, and motivates, the leadership role in a complex system is more of a catalyst, collaborator, or facilitator (Kelly and Allison 1999).

An intriguing example is offered by Kurtz and Snowden (2003) who describe the experience of a group of West Point students who were assigned to manage the playtime of a kindergarten class as a project.

> They planned; they rationally identified objectives; they determined backup and response plans. They then tried to "order" the children's play based on rational design principles, and in consequence, achieved chaos. They then observed what the teachers do. Experienced teachers allow a degree of freedom at the start of the session, then intervene to stabilize desirable patterns and destabilize undesirable ones; and, when they are very clever, they seed the space so that the patterns they want are more likely to emerge (466).

One Leader → Many Leaders

The role of leadership in a complex adaptive system is different from a traditional system in several critical respects. First, instead of one or several leaders, there is the possibility that leadership could be exercised by virtually everyone in the organization. Leadership is not role based; it is more related to behaviors and attitudes and can shift from situation to situation. As such, leadership is a very dynamic process.

Static, Role-based Leader → Emergent Leadership

According to Griffin (2002), complexity science challenges the dominant thinking around leading and following. "Leaders would not just be individuals outside the system observing the system, forming visions for its development and making plans for strategy and change" (17). In describing his model of participative self-organization in *The Emergence of Leadership,* Griffin (2002) says:

> As groups evolve and develop a past, they begin to recognize various members in roles, one of which is leader. The "mask," the role, of leader emerges in the interaction and those participating are continuously creating and recreating the meaning of the leadership themes in the local interaction in which they are involved (217).

Implicit in this view is the notion that leadership roles evolve and are not static and role based. Another important element of this perspective is that leadership is created through interaction with others and is continually constructed.

Traditional Attributes → Complexity-based Attributes

What emerges from complexity theory is a different style of leader with a different set of attributes or competencies, and a different temperament. A discussion of these follows:

- *Process Orientation*: Leaders still need to be concerned about results, but in complex systems, their control over results is not causal and is often nonlinear. However, they can have an enduring impact on *how* work is done. Leaders in complex systems focus heavily on process, such as communication and conflict resolution.
- *Zeal and Persistence*: These attributes are especially important in a volatile and highly competitive environment where passivity and timidity are not rewarded. Zeal and persistence do not mean highly aggressive, combative, and noisy behavior. Such leadership involves emotional maturity and intellectual versus personal ambition.
- *Agility/Resiliency/Adaptability*: Without these leadership attributes, a highly complex organization will simply not survive. Since things are always in flux, the ability to regroup, change directions, modify plans, and adjust thinking is absolutely vital. Included in this is the ability to deal with paradox, be comfortable with ambiguity, and have a positive outlook on change and uncertainty.
- *High-level Communication Skills*: Effective communication in a complex system involves much more than effectively conveying information. Listening is an equally if not more important process and skill. So too are dialogue and inquiry and reflection.
- *Boundary Crossing/Collaboration*: Leaders in complex organizations consider boundaries to be permeable membranes. One of the primary roles of those exercising leadership is to keep boundaries fluid, develop and sustain connections, and promote collaboration.
- *Commitment to Diversity*: Complexity theory demonstrates how critical variety is to a system's ability to adapt and achieve higher levels of fitness. Diversity needs to be demonstrated, not just in terms of what is considered to be politically correct but in truly valuing diverse perspectives and allowing alternative perspectives to be heard.
- *Commitment to Continuous Learning*: This attribute is so fundamental to a complex system that without it, it might cease to exist. Continuous learning is not a luxury; it is essential to the vitality and survival of the organization. This attribute has best been described by Senge (1990) in terms of the learning organization.
- *Self-awareness/Maturity/Authenticity*: Operating effectively within a complex system requires a high degree of maturity. This is not necessarily a function of age; it has to do with one's emotional maturity. Individuals exercising such maturity exhibit the following kinds of key characteristics: confidence, wisdom, security, intuition, willingness to learn from others and admit mistakes, ability to see other perspectives, and humility. Authenticity is a related characteristic. As noted by Keene (2000), "Leadership [in today's complex organizations] has more to do with being than doing" (17). Griffin (2002) says that leaders in complex systems will "need to come to a new way of understanding themselves" (77).

Single-Leadership Paradigms → Multiple-Leadership Paradigms

Many complexity scholars believe that complexity leadership will not replace other types of leadership but need to coexist with them. Stacey (1996) identifies a serious dilemma with this. "These different leadership roles do not blend harmoniously with each other. Instead, they conflict with each other; directing and intentionally not directing are diametrically opposed ways of behaving and both are required of an effective leader in a complex adaptive system" (277). According to Knowles (2001), the leadership challenge is to perform the "leadership dance" (126), which involves using the right form of leadership at the right time.

Summary

I believe these perspectives are creating a new leadership paradigm. While the exact parameters of this new leadership paradigm are still emerging, it is clear that the traditional role, perspectives, behaviors, and competencies of leadership are not sufficient to achieve effectiveness in highly complex, volatile, and uncertain organizations. Leadership in complex systems will require new perspectives, behaviors, and attributes. At the same time, traditional leadership perspectives, behaviors, and attributes may be needed in certain situations. The dual challenge for leaders is to master the art of the new leadership paradigm while maintaining the ability to function in situations calling for more conventional leadership abilities and perspectives. This will require a tremendous amount of judgment, adaptability, and ability to master a variety of leadership capabilities.

Issues in the Application of Complexity Theory to Leadership

While there are many benefits to applying the principles of complexity science to leadership, it is important to assess what has been the progress to date and to recognize some of the constraints and issues involved.

First, complexity theory has had relatively little influence on mainstream management, leadership, and organizational research. What Stacey wrote in 1996 still rings true today; he wrote, "The complexity paradigm is still in the shadow system of management and organizational research; it does not govern the current research agenda" (244). References to complexity in standard business management and leadership texts are rare, and there are only a few doctoral dissertations on complexity in social systems.

Within the field of public administration, there is little scholarly work linking complexity theory to management and leadership (Kiel 1989; 1994). For the most part, this work is not recent and it has not generated enough momentum to generate substantial interest or following. Perhaps this is due to the natural chasm that exists between scientists and non-scientists (Amato 1992). Perhaps this is because "politics, business and education have managed to remain far behind in their integration of new thinking" (McMaster 1996, x). Or, perhaps, we are in the midst of a profound paradigm shift and the pioneers are relatively invisible. As Kuhn (1996) notes, "the proponents of competing paradigms practice their trades in different worlds" (150).

The second issue, related to the first, is that of transferring language and concepts. According to Cowan, Pines, and Meltzer (1994, 10),

> Interdisciplinary studies can be hampered by language problems as researchers from different disciplinary backgrounds come together and attempt to communicate in their diverse technical vocabularies. One of the consequences of this process is that words that appear useful originally can lose their meaning as they gain broader use.

As noted by Kurtz and Snowden (2003), "We are sorry to say that in our opinion too many of the books written for a popular business audience on the subject [of complexity] have been marred by misunderstandings, misapplications, and most of all misplaced zeal . . ." (464).

Third, much of the literature linking the two constructs lacks sufficient empirical research. It tends to be either theoretical or prescriptive in nature, not research based.

Implications

A new view of leadership, along the lines I have outlined in preceding sections, has significant implications for the practice of leadership, the education of current and future leaders, executive selection and succession planning, and organizational performance. These implications are discussed in turn.

For Leaders

Those exercising leadership will need to temper illusions of control, certainty, and control. According to Dotlich and Cairo (2002), they will sometimes need to adopt behaviors that counter conventional wisdom to operate effectively in today's turbulent climate. They will need to share leadership and become a different kind of leader. Lewin and Regine (2000) contend that some leaders will require "nothing short of a personal conversion" (264). The kind of self-awareness, personal development work, philosophical sophistication, emotional maturity, and positive orientation toward change required to become a truly effective complexity leader may not be possible for everyone.

For Educators

Those in the field of leadership development will need to discard outmoded leadership competency models that bear little relationship to the reality of current organizational contexts and leadership challenges. We will need to revamp our educational curricula and learning strategies and design educational models that support the kinds of developmental work described earlier. This work will not be easy.

We will need to recognize that there are no "quick fixes." Many of the leadership attributes described earlier are based on inherent personality differences and deeply held value orientations. Some people are born with a preference for order and stability and resist change; others thrive on uncertainty, are spontaneous, and operate well in highly fluid environments. Some people are born with drive; others approach life more passively. Some people are naturally collaborative; others prefer to work alone. However, such natural proclivities can be adjusted and enhanced through coaching, feedback, and transformational learning experiences.

For Research

Looking at leadership from a complexity theory perspective represents a relatively new undertaking. So, there is plenty of room for additional research and intellectual activity. The main limitation of my research is the limitation of any case study research; the findings are not directly transferable. The larger and more diverse the pool of organizations studied using complexity theory as a major conceptual framework, the more valid and credible these findings and conclusions will be. I hope that this research has also demonstrated the value of reaching beyond traditional boundaries to seek new perspectives on the theory and practice of leadership.

For Organizations

I believe that the development of a new leadership perspective based on complexity concepts will help organizations survive and thrive in this very different environment. Conventional leadership behaviors and attributes are still relevant in today's climate, but decreasingly so. Organizations need to recognize the validity of this new leadership paradigm and invest in the continuing development of their current and emerging leaders.

Conclusion

The goal of this chapter has been to probe new ways of thinking about leadership. These perspectives transcend sector; they apply to public-sector leadership as well as leadership in the business and nonprofit sectors. They also transcend national boundaries and can be viewed as truly global phenomena.

Complexity theory offers a powerful way to understand the changing nature of leadership in the highly complex, dynamic, non-linear, and uncertain organizational context we confront as public managers. It is my hope that this discussion will stimulate additional research and dialogue that will ultimately lead to the development of a new cadre of public-sector leaders who will not only survive but thrive at the edge of chaos.

References

Amato, Ivan. 1992. "Chaos Breaks Out at NIH, but Order May Come of It." *Science* 256 (5065): 1763–65.

Axelrod, Robert, and Michael D. Cohen. 1999. *Harnessing Complexity: Organizational Implications of a Scientific Frontier.* New York: Free Press.

Burns, James M. 1978. *Leadership.* New York: Harper & Row.

Cowan, George A., David Pines, and David Meltzer, eds. 1994. *Complexity: Metaphors, Models and Reality.* Reading, MA: Addison-Wesley.

Dotlich, David L., and Peter C. Cairo. 2002. *Unnatural Leadership: Going against Intuition and Experience to Develop Ten New Leadership Instincts.* San Francisco: Jossey-Bass.

Eisenhardt, Kathleen M., and Mahesh M. Bhatia. 2002. "Organizational Complexity and Computation." In *Companion to Organizations,* ed. Joel A.C. Baum, 442–66. Oxford: Blackwell Publishers.

Eoyang, Glenda. H. 1997. *Coping with Chaos: Seven Simple Tools.* Cheyenne, WY: Lagumo Corporation.

Falconer, James. 2002. "Accountability in a Complex World." *Emergence* 4 (4): 25–38.

Fulmer, William E. 2000. *Shaping the Adaptive Organization: Landscapes, Learning and Leading in Volatile Times.* New York: American Management Association.

Griffin, Douglas. 2002. *The Emergence of Leadership: Linking Self-organization and Ethics.* London: Routledge.

Gronn, Peter. 2003. "Leadership: Who Needs It?" *School Leadership and Management* 23 (3): 267–90.

Gryskiewicz, Stanley S. 1999. *Positive Turbulence: Developing Climates for Certainty, Innovation, and Renewal.* San Francisco: Jossey-Bass.

Jackson, Michael C. 2003. *Systems Thinking: Creative Holism for Managers.* West Sussex, England: John Wiley and Sons.

Kauffman, Stuart A. 1995. *At Home in the Universe: The Search for Laws of Self-Organization and Complexity.* New York: Oxford University Press.

Keene, Angelique. 2000. "Complexity Theory: The Changing Role of Leadership." *Industrial and Commercial Training* 32(1): 15–18.

Kelly, Susanne, and Mary Ann Allison. 1999. *The Complexity Advantage: How the Science of Complexity Can Help Your Business Achieve Peak Performance.* New York: Business Week Books.

Kettl, Donald F. 2002. *The Transformation of Governance: Public Administration for Twenty-First Century America.* Baltimore: Johns Hopkins University Press.

Kiel, L. Douglas. 1989. "Nonequilibrium Theory and Its Implications for Public Administration." *Public Administration Review* 49 (6): 544–51.

———. 1994. *Managing Chaos and Complexity in Government: A New Paradigm for Managing Change, Innovation and Organizational Renewal.* San Francisco: Jossey-Bass.

Kiuchi, Tachi, and William K. Shireman. 2002. *What We Learned in the Rainforest.* San Francisco: Berrett-Koehler.

Knowles, Richard N. 2001. "Self-Organizing Leadership: A Way of Seeing What Is Happening in Organizations and a Pathway to Coherence." *Emergence* 3 (4): 112–27.

———. 2002. *The Leadership Dance: Pathways to Extraordinary Organizational Effectiveness.* Niagara Falls, NY: The Center for Self-Organizing Leadership.

Kuhn, Thomas S. 1996. *The Structure of Scientific Revolution.* 3rd ed. Chicago: University of Chicago Press.

Kurtz, Cynthia F., and David J. Snowden. 2003. "The New Dynamics of Strategy: Sensemaking in a Complex and Complicated World." *IBM Systems Journal* 42 (3): 462–83.

Lewin, Roger, and Birute Regine. 2000. *The Soul at Work: Embracing Complexity Science for Business Success.* New York: Simon & Schuster.

Mainzer, Klaus. 1997. *Thinking in Complexity: The Complex Dynamics of Matter, Mind and Mankind.* Berlin: Springer-Verlag.

Marion, Russ. 1999. *The Edge of Organization: Chaos and Complexity Theories of Formal Social Systems.* Thousand Oaks, CA: Sage.

Marion, Russ, and Mary Uhl-Bien. 2001. "Leadership in Complex Organizations." *Leadership Quarterly,* 12 (1): 389–418.

McMaster, Michael D. 1996. *The Intelligence Advantage: Organizing for Complexity.* Boston: Butterworth-Heinemann.

McMillan, Elizabeth. 2004. *Complexity, Organizations and Change.* London: Routledge.

Nicolis, Gregoire, and Ilya Prigogine. 1989. *Exploring Complexity: An Introduction.* New York: W. H. Freeman and Company.

Olson, Edwin E., and Glenda H. Eoyang. 2001. *Facilitating Organizational Change: Lessons from Complexity Science.* San Francisco: Jossey-Bass/Pfeiffer.

Osborn, Richard N., James G. Hunt, and Lawrence R. Jauch. 2002. "Toward a Contextual Theory of Leadership." *Leadership Quarterly* 13 (6): 797–837.

Pagels, Heinz R. 1988. *The Dreams of Reason: The Computer and the Rise of the Sciences of Complexity.* New York: Simon & Schuster.

Pascale, Richard, Mark Millemann, and Linda Gioja. 2000. *Surfing the Edge of Chaos: The Laws of Nature and the New Laws of Business.* New York: Crown Business.

Sanders, T. Irene. 1998. *Strategic Thinking and the New Science: Planning in the Midst of Chaos, Complexity and Change.* New York: Free Press.

Senge, Peter M. 1990. *The Fifth Discipline: The Art and Practice of the Learning Organization.* New York: Doubleday.

Sherman, Howard, and Ron Schultz. 1998. *Open Boundaries: Creating Business Innovation through Complexity.* Reading, MA: Perseus Books.

Stacey, Ralph D. 1996. *Complexity and Creativity in Organizations.* San Francisco: Berrett-Koehler.

Stumpf, Stephen. A. 1995. "Applying New Science Theories in Leadership Development Activities." *Journal of Management Development* 14 (5): 39–49.

Wheatley, Margaret. 1992. *Leadership and the New Science.* San Francisco: Berrett-Koehler.

9

Transformational Stewardship

Leading Public-Sector Change

JAMES EDWIN KEE, KATHRYN NEWCOMER, AND S. MIKE DAVIS

Public-sector leadership in the twenty-first century is challenging and change oriented. Rapidly evolving global conditions and shifting political and economic influences are changing our ideas of "what" government should do. Advancements in operational technologies and methodologies and rising expectations of leadership require a similar evolution in "how" government accomplishes its mission. Unfortunately, the tragedy of the 9/11 terrorist attacks, the multiple National Aeronautics and Space Administration (NASA) disasters, and the failed Federal Emergency Management Agency (FEMA) response to Hurricane Katrina highlight the necessity for public leaders to adapt quickly to various types of events. Public leaders face rapidly changing circumstances that require them to transform their organizations.

Public-sector change is a risky business. Organizational change is inherently unsettling, demanding new approaches to traditional structures, and sometimes new paradigms altogether. Pay-for-performance, competitive sourcing, public-private partnerships, performance-based budgeting, and other initiatives often create an unsettling environment in which the public leader must satisfy a variety of constituencies while shaping new organizational norms and values.

To meet the challenge of change, public leaders in the twenty-first century must be *transformational stewards*. We contend that transformation and stewardship are reciprocal and mutually reinforcing aspects of public service, and are two vital responsibilities for tomorrow's government leaders. As transformational stewards, public leaders must pursue organizational transformation, while serving as stewards of their organization and core public administration values. We posit that public leaders of the future require heightened creativity and initiative, concern for the larger public community, and careful management and leadership of change.

In this chapter, we establish the foundation for this vision of public leadership by presenting three important aspects of transformational stewardship. First, we explore the concept of transformational stewardship as a new way to define public leadership, building on traditional thinking about leadership and public administration, while extending this thinking to address the transformational challenges of modern public service. Second, we present a specific tool to enable public leaders to better manage the risk of change, thus fulfilling their transformational stewardship responsibilities. Here, we draw on our previous work modeling change-related risk in order to provide a comprehensive backdrop for considering the transformational steward's responsibilities. Finally, we consider the specific roles and responsibilities of transformational stewards in relation to the different aspects of a particular change. Before describing the concept of transformational leadership, however, we want to briefly consider some of the major demands for change on public-sector leaders.

The Landscape for Public-Sector Leaders

The need for transformational leadership in the public sector is most evident when we examine the pressures for change felt by today's public managers. These change pressures come from many sources: an aging public-sector workforce, resource constraints, new horizontal relationships with nonprofit and private-sector organizations, globalization, technology breakthroughs, and increasingly complex public problems. In many cases, these demands for change conflict with one another and constantly compete for the public manager's time and resources. The following are a few high-visibility change drivers in the federal government (state and local governments face similar pressures):

- *The Change to Be More Performance Oriented*: Managers must meet evolving performance-management demands presented by the Government Performance and Results Act (GPRA), pay-for-performance, the application of the Office of Management and Budget's (OMB) Program Assessment Rating Tool (PART), and demands for performance measurement in a variety of other laws.
- *The Change to Become a Younger and More Diverse Workforce*: Managers must prepare for a major changeover in staff (half of all top civil service executives are over fifty), while ensuring that the institutional knowledge that resides in these existing staff members is not lost.
- *The Change to Become More Competitive and Entrepreneurial*: Managers must compete with the private sector to continue doing the public's business (for example, competitive sourcing) or must engage in new, unfamiliar public-private partnerships.
- *The Change to Restructure to Meet Evolving Mission Requirements and Stakeholder Expectations*: Managers must create and evolve new organizations to meet new national threats or needs (Homeland Security or FEMA) or increasing expectations of constituents and Congress to be more consumer friendly (IRS).

The one common element in all of the previously mentioned forces for change is the need for agencies to adapt and transform themselves. Yet, change is not easy. While potential rewards may be great, change carries risks for the agency, the manager, and other stakeholders. This is true in the private sector as well as the public sector; but there is reason to believe that change in the public sector is more "risky" than in the private sector. A private-sector CEO has to satisfy his or her board of directors and ultimately the stockholders, but can often proceed in relative secrecy, without a great deal of collaboration. In contrast, public-sector leaders have significantly more stakeholders. They include those within the organization, such as unions and senior political appointees, and those outside the organization, such as political leadership (both elected and appointed), suppliers, citizens/consumers, and others. Generally speaking, organizational change in the public sector must be transparent, requires extensive consultation, and is usually conducted in a highly visible arena. Additionally, the nature of political leadership results in a short-term horizon for many of the stakeholders, making long-term change initiatives more problematic.

While we refer to organizational change, the reality is that change is not organizational unless it is first individual change and then team change. At these levels, several change stakeholders emerge—including employees, peers, and agency leadership. For each of these stakeholders, there are distinct and often very different perceptions, expectations, and "stakes" in whatever change is being proposed. In addition, the perceptions, expectations, and stakes of the manager also influence the course of change. While local stakeholders are more prominent in the manager's daily environment, the increasing complexity and scope of the managerial role in government—with its increased emphasis on public-private partnerships, globalization, and intergovernmental arrangements—means that all stakeholders, to some degree, must be on the manager's radar. Collectively, these relationships and their influences on the change process constitute the manager's "change landscape." Becoming aware of and thinking critically about this landscape is a critical first step toward deliberately negotiating it with proficiency and skill.

Transformational Stewardship

Given the strong change influences that have emerged in the contemporary public-leadership landscape, how does the concept of transformational stewardship provide a viable path for fulfilling the responsibilities of public service? In order to answer this question, we first address the seeming paradox of public-sector leaders as both change agents and stewards of the public trust as they seek to accomplish their organizational roles and responsibilities. At the heart of this discussion is an ongoing debate about managerial discretion and the role of public managers that harkens back to the Finer (1940)–Friedrich (1940) debate—arguments that have recently been rejoined in the discussion between advocates of New Public Management (NPM) and those who see the role of public managers as conservators within a tightly controlled system of democratic accountability.

New Public Management is one of the current change drivers—an embodiment of a "tidal wave of government sector reform" that has swept the world since the 1980s (Kettl 1997). The widespread adoption of NPM ideas reflects its advocacy by a number of international organizations, including the World Bank. This reform movement largely is a reaction to a perception that government agencies have become too large and ineffective, and therefore must transform themselves. The leadership literature and adherents of NPM place a great deal of emphasis on the role of leaders in organizational change. They are the entrepreneurs (Osborne and Gaebler 1992), change agents (Kotter 1996), and creators of "new mental maps" (Black and Gregersen 2002). The term *transformational* best fits this type of leader. Burns (1978) defined transformational leadership as a process where the leader and follower engage each other in creating a shared vision that raises the level of motivation for both leader and follower, transforming the organization.

A chorus of public administration scholars, however, has raised some serious concerns about transformational leaders in the public sector who are seen as potentially unaccountable "wild-eyed entrepreneurs" (Terry 1995, 1998; Moe 1994). To this group, public managers must first and foremost be "conservators," politically and legally accountable within a vertical hierarchy. NPM processes, it is argued, with their emphases on efficiency and entrepreneurial activity of government managers, interfere with democratic governance and with other values that are highly prized—such as fairness, justice, and democratic participation.

Upon initial analysis, the concept of stewardship would seem to align with critics of NPM. A steward is "a person who manages another's property or financial affairs, or who administers anything as an agent of another" (*Random House Dictionary* 1968). A common stewardship definition is "to hold something in trust for others" (Block 1993, xv). Like Block, we view stewardship in a broad sense, which entails wisely using the resources available in a creative process that aggressively pursues the mission of the organization. This broad view envisions the leader creating a balance of power in the organization with a primary commitment to the larger community, wherein each person joins in defining purpose. Stewardship is a governance strategy designed to create a strong sense of ownership and responsibility for outcomes—including change—at all levels of the organization. It also means giving more control to citizens and creating self-reliance and partnerships among the organization's stakeholders (Block 1993; Kee 2003).

Thus, the concept of transformational envisions an active public leader, facilitating change through building organizational capacity, developing partnerships, and thoroughly analyzing the risks of change, in order to maximize potential gains while minimizing—to the extent possible—potential losses associated with change.

Attributes of Transformational Stewardship

Transformational stewardship, in the broadest sense, can be thought of as a leadership function in which those exercising leadership (those with "legitimate"

Table 9.1

Key Attributes of the Transformational Steward in the Public Sector

Innerpersonal Beliefs/Traits
- Ethical
- Empathetic
- Visionary/Foresight
- Reflective/Learning Oriented

Operational Mind-set
- Trustee/Caretaker
- Mission Driven
- Accountable
- Attention to Detail

Interpersonal/Interactions with Others
- Trust Builder
- Empowering
- Power Sharing
- Coalition Builder

Change-centric Approach
- Creative/Innovative
- Comfortable with Ambiguity
- Integrative/Systems Thinker

authority as well as others throughout the organization) have developed certain attributes that guide their actions. These attributes reflect leaders' personal outlook or beliefs (their innerpersonal beliefs or traits), how they approach a situation (their operational mind-set), how they involve others in the function (their interpersonal actions/interactions with others), and their commitment to change and innovation (their change-centric approach). While there are many leadership attributes, Table 9.1 displays a list of the fifteen attributes that we believe are most important for transformational stewardship, followed by a discussion of each attribute.

Innerpersonal Leadership Beliefs/Traits

The "trait" theory of leadership is one of the most persistent concepts about what makes a good leader. Some argue that individuals are either born with leadership traits (such as intelligence) or not. Others argue that the most important leadership traits are those that can be learned (such as understanding the job or task at hand). Trait theories of leadership attempt to develop a list of defined characteristics of leadership; common ones include intelligence, self-confidence, decisiveness, courage, empathy, determination, integrity, and sociability. Among the recent proponents of the trait theory of leadership is the "emotional IQ" or maturity approach of Goleman, McKee, and Boyatzis (2002) who believe that leadership traits can be learned through self-evaluation and mentoring.

We believe the most important personal leadership beliefs/traits are not ones that we are born with but those that develop throughout our lives and provide us continuing guidance on how to act in a particular situation—they become inner-personal guides to our actions. We believe that the most vital traits for transformational stewards are ethical conduct, a reflective and continuous learning attitude, empathy toward others, and the foresight or vision to lead an organization toward a preferred future.

Ethical. An overriding innerpersonal trait, commonly cited, is integrity or ethical values and standards. Transformational stewards must maintain a high level of standards for themselves and their organizations that allow leaders and followers to elevate the organization to a higher plane. Leadership scholar James MacGregor Burns (1978) posits that moral values lie at the heart of transformational leadership and allow the leader to seek "fundamental changes in organizations and society" (Ciulla 2004, x).

Similarly, those arguing for a servant leadership approach (often aligned with the concept of stewardship) argue for the importance of "core ethical values, including integrity, independence, freedom, justice, family and caring" (Fairholm 1997, 133). Ethics and moral standards have their roots in principles we learn throughout our lives, either from parents or mentors, or from our own inquiries into what constitutes just action.

Reflective/Continuous Learning. Wheatley suggests: "Thinking is the place where intelligent actions begin. We pause long enough to look more carefully at a situation, to see more of its character, to think about why it is happening, and to notice how it is affecting us and others" (2005, 215). Transformational stewards are willing to step back and reflect before taking action. They take the time to understand and to learn before acting. A Chinese proverb asks, "Can you remain still, while the water is turbid and cloudy, until in time it is perfectly clear again?" (Thompson 2000, 175).

Thompson argues, "Beyond a certain point, there can probably be no personal growth, no individualization, without the capacity for self-reflection" (2000, 152). While continuous learning is critical for organizations (Senge 1990), it is equally important for individuals. Self-reflection, including personal awareness and continuous learning, is not always easy or calming—just the opposite—"It is a disturber and an awakener" (Greenleaf 1977, 41). Transformational stewards must be awake to new approaches to problems, new understandings of relationships, and potential consequences of actions and impacts on others. In this manner, they can lead with confidence.

Empathetic. A transformational steward demonstrates concern for others, both within and outside the organization. Organizational change involves potential winners and losers. If leaders are seen as primarily acting in their self-interest, transformation of the organization could be derailed. However, if leaders have a genuine concern for others and address potential losses, they may find the path easier. Empathy is a trait that is a product of both our nature and how we are nurtured; but understanding its importance can provide us with an incentive to pay more attention to the needs, views, and concerns of others.

Empathy is more than just being a "good listener," though that is an important skill. Leaders must both hear and understand. Thompson explains: "If by that we mean only that we have learned certain skills and techniques that make the other person *feel* heard, we have still largely missed the point. To empathize is to both hear *and* understand, and to grasp both the thoughts the other person is trying to convey and the feelings he or she has about them" (2000, 181). Transformational stewards participate in other persons' feelings or ideas, leading to a broader understanding of the situation and potential courses of action.

Visionary/Foresight. A transformational steward is able to look beyond the current situation and see the big picture and the organization's potential. This is true throughout the organization, although as a leader progresses in an organization and has more responsibility, the vision and foresight required are greater (Graham 2003).

Mary Parker Follett refers to the need for leaders to "grasp the total situation. . . . Out of a welter of facts, experience, desires, aims, the leader must find the unifying thread . . . the higher up you go the more ability you have to have of this kind. When leadership rises to genius it has the power of transforming, transforming experience into power" (Graham 2003, 168–9). While vision is necessary to transform an organization, it is equally necessary for a good steward. Failure to fully assess potential gains and risks for an organization will lead to a waste of resources and an inability to achieve the full potential of the organization. Follett continues:

> I have said that the leader must understand the situation, must see it as a whole, must see the inter-relation of all the parts. He must do more than this. He must see the evolving situation, the developing situation. His wisdom, his judgment, is used, not on a situation that is stationary, but on one that is changing all the time. The ablest administrators do not merely draw logical conclusions from the array of facts of the past which their expert assistants bring to them, they have a *vision for the future* (169, emphasis added).

Operational Mind-set

The "Style" approach or theory of leadership focuses on how leaders interact with followers and stresses the need for leaders to balance a "concern for people" with "concern for production or results." The Blake and Mouton (1985) Managerial Grid is one of the most well-known tools reflecting this approach. We believe that the operational mind-set of a transformational leader is important but goes beyond balancing people with results to include a number of attributes of both transformational leader and steward.

Trustee/Caretaker. Transformational stewards recognize that they hold their position and use organizational resources for others, not for their own self-aggrandizement. They take responsibility for the public in general, both current and future generations, and future members of the organization. Thus the broad concept of "public interest," while not always easy to define, must be a constant touchstone for the leader. Public servants, whether elected, appointed, or part of the large civil service system, are only temporarily in charge of their resources and responsibilities. They hold them in trust for the public—hence they serve the public and must act in the public interest, not for personal self-interest. "Public managers are, after all, public servants," argues Colin Driver (1982, cited in Moe 1994). "Their acts must derive from the legitimacy, from the consent of the governed, as expressed through the Constitution and laws, not from any personal system of values, no matter how noble" (404). In NPM's rush to "steer" rather than "row," the Denhardts note, we have to remember "who owns the boat" (2003, 23).

Kass (1990) defines public stewardship as "the administrator's willingness and ability to earn the public trust by being an effective and ethical agent in carrying out the republic's business" (113). Because ethical considerations may conflict with efficiency criteria, Kass believes that stewardship requires that efficiency and effectiveness (the traditional measures of administrative success) be "informed by and subordinated to the ethical norms of justice and beneficence" (114).

Mission Driven. Transformational stewards fiercely and courageously pursue the mission of their organization. In most cases, they act as agents of those who established that mission—the legislature, the chief executive, or the courts. Sometimes, conflicting goals and agendas require the public servant to arbitrate. To the question, "What should public managers do in the face of legislative ambiguity: ask for clarification, or provide it?" Behn says that public managers must courageously define their responsibilities (1998, 215). It may be in the legislature's interest to be ambiguous; in addition, "the political process itself creates a diffusion of power and responsibility that makes articulation of central values difficult" (Kee and Black 1985, 28). Thus, the transformational steward must seek to find the common purpose, values, and aims that drive the organization.

Public managers can find this common purpose by engaging the people in their agencies, citizens, and other stakeholders who will assist the leader in defining the agency's mission or core values—in effect, determining the public interest. Follett notes that the "invisible leader" becomes the "common purpose" and that "loyalty to the invisible leader gives us the strongest possible bond of union" (Graham 2003, 172).

At other times, the organizational mission is clear, but the organization may have multiple means of achieving the mission, and its leaders must weigh how those means will affect the agency, its mission, and the larger public interest. "Legislation, public scrutiny, and constitutional checks and balances all create legitimate legal and political limitations on the freedom of public managers to act. Yet within the constraints, there is considerable room for experimentation and action" (Kee and Black 1985, 31). Unless proscribed or prescribed to act in a certain fashion, the agency leader (with the people in the agency) has considerable latitude as to how to pursue the mission.

Accountable. Transformational stewards measure their performance in a transparent fashion and share those results with those who can affect the organization and its success. This is consistent with efforts at the federal level to get agencies to articulate and measure progress toward their performance goals (for example, the Government Performance Results Act of 1993). Transformational stewards support processes such as performance-based budgeting, balanced scorecards, and other efforts to measure program results in an open fashion and subject them to periodic review and evaluation. What is important is not measurement for the sake of measurement or the creation of short-term output measures, but measurement for the sake of legitimate feedback and program revision aimed at achieving the agency mission. "Stewardship asks us to be deeply accountable for the outcomes of an institution . . ." (Block 1993, 18).

An open process ensures accountability and allows others to see how the agency and its stewards are defining and fulfilling the public interest. This, by necessity, must be a multifaceted process, as Vaill (1989a) suggests, that considers a variety of important values, not simply economic ones that might drive a single bottom-line mentality. An open process provides a natural check on how transformational stewards define and lead progress toward achievement of the organization's mission. Finally, transformational stewards, throughout the organization, take responsibility (legal, professional, and personal) for the results (Harmon 1990; 1995).

Attention to Detail. Transformational stewards know that details do matter (Addington and Graves 2002). Details are often the way in which government programs ensure important democratic values, such as equitable distribution of public benefits or access to public programs. Process "red tape" is often the means by which we ensure adherence to procedural imperatives; however, it should not be used as a cover or an excuse for lack of performance. Rather, transformational stewards need to distinguish between those processes designed to achieve certain public purposes and those designed primarily to impose excess control. With the latter, transformational stewards might seek waivers, exceptions, and so on to enable the agency to better organize itself to accomplish its mission.

Interpersonal/Interactions with Others

Leadership theories increasingly stress the importance of the leader's interaction with others. For example, the "Situational" approach characterizes the leader's role along a "supportive" and "directive" matrix, based on the development level of the followers (Hersey and Blanchard 1993). Leaders delegate, support, coach, or direct, depending upon the capacity of the followers—specifically as to the job (competence) and psychological maturity (commitment) of the followers. We see transformational stewards approaching their interactions with others differently than many other leadership theories prescribe. The chief goals for transformational stewards are empowerment and engendering trust in employees throughout the organization.

Trust Builder. Transformational stewards build program success through developing and maintaining trust—with the members of their agencies, their constituents, and their principals. Leadership is principally about developing trust, wherein leaders and agency members accomplish mutually valued goals using agreed-upon processes. "Leaders build trust or tear it down by the cumulative actions they take and the word they speak—by the culture they create for themselves and their organization members" (Fairholm 2000, 91).

Developing trust is about building community, "the creation of harmony from, often diverse, sometimes opposing, organizational, human, system and program functions" (Fairholm 2000, 140). Public stewards also must build trust with the citizens they serve and the principals (executives and legislatures) to whom they report.

Mitchell and Scott (1987) insist that stewardship "is based on the notion that administrators must display the virtue of trust and honorableness in order to be legitimate leaders" (448). Trust is an ephemeral thing, hard to gain, easy to lose. Trust leads to involvement of citizens and grants of discretion from principals.

Empowering. Closely related to trust is the concept of empowerment. Trust demands empowerment of agency employees and, where possible, decentralization of authority—real decision making—throughout the organization. Follett, writing in the 1920s, put it this way: "Many are coming to think that the job of a man higher up is not to make decisions for his subordinates but to teach them how to handle their problems themselves, teach them how to make their own decisions. The best leader does not persuade men to follow his will. He shows them what is necessary for them to do in order to meet their responsibilities . . . the best leaders try to train their followers themselves to become leaders" (Graham 2003, 173).

Developing leaders for a common purpose is a key function of transformational stewardship. Stone (1997) makes a useful distinction between the market and the "polis." In the market, economic principles and incentives are the norm. In the polis, the "development of shared values and a collective sense of the public interest is the primary aim" (Stone 1997, 34). To the extent that leaders empower others (employees and citizens), they become co-leaders and stewards in fulfillment of the public interest. This is a fundamental role, and opportunity, for transformational stewards throughout the organization.

Power Sharing. Transformational stewards rely less on positional authority for their power and more on personal power sources, persuasion, and moral leadership to affect change (Hill 1994). Beyond personal power, transformational stewards rely on "group power." Follett claims that "it is possible to develop the conception of power-with, a jointly developed power, a co-active, not a coercive power." And "the great leader tries . . . to develop power wherever he can among those who work with him, and then gathers all this power and uses it as the energizing force of a progressing enterprise" (Graham 2003, 173).

Coalition Builder. Transformational stewards recognize that they cannot fully meet their mission with their given resources (people, dollars, and so forth) without involving others. They know that horizontal relationships and coalition building with other organizations, within government, in the nonprofit sector, and in the for-profit sector, are essential for the success of their organization. Such coalitions might be critical for the organization's successful transformation or vital when the organization is faced with a crisis (such as Hurricane Katrina). Coast Guard Admiral Joel Whitehead refers to the necessity of developing "pre-need" relationships, noting that this is one of the Coast Guard's fundamental principles—a recognition that they cannot do everything and must rely on others as partners in achieving their organizational mission (Whitehead 2005).

Change-centric Approach

Building upon trust, empowerment, and power sharing, transformational stewards are able to be change-centric, focusing on the needed change itself rather than the source of the call for change (from the leader [top down] or from the followers [bottom up]). What matters is finding the proper balance of top-down and bottom-up management that leads to a successful change effort (Kee and Setzer 2006). Achieving positive change should be the focus, not assigning inflexible leadership roles. The focus of change-centric leadership is on the successful change effort itself, which is not to say leadership has no important role to play. On the contrary, the leader or leaders of an organization serve as facilitators of change. They should strive to be cognizant of when change efforts require more initiative from the top, and when the success of change efforts may hinge upon allowing more employee participation in formulation of the change vision. Dialogue among all levels of leadership is encouraged, but not to the extent of damaging the decision-making process. Sometimes the top leaders in an organization will need to make change decisions, especially when time and resource constraints do not allow for more employee involvement. However, change efforts in the public sector are often completed over a longer time frame, and thus, more participation from lower ranks can be cultivated. The concept of change-centric leadership is very consistent with Follett's "law of the situation" (Fox and Urwick 1973). In order to be change-centric, transformational stewards need to be creative, innovative, and comfortable with ambiguity and with navigating complex systems.

Creative/Innovative. Transformational stewards do not wait for a crisis to innovate and create; they attempt to build an environment that values continuous learning and in which workers constantly draw on current and past experiences to frame a new future for the organization. Vaill (1996) acknowledges that "creative learning" is seemingly a contradiction in a world of institutional learning where people who "know" transfer knowledge to people who do not know. However, in a change environment there often is no "body of knowledge" to transfer; thus it is up to the transformational steward to create the knowledge. This requires an inquiring mind willing to explore options. Just as an artist might not always know what the final product will look like, transformational stewards must be open to the unknown, willing to surprise themselves, and recognize "in that surprise *is* the learning" (Vaill 1996, 61).

Comfortable with Ambiguity. Transformational stewards recognize that conflicting organizational objectives and priorities often require a careful balancing act: continuity and change; efficiency and equity; and so on. Public managers, like their private counterparts, live in an era of "permanent white water," bombarded by pressures both from within and without the organization (Vaill 1996). Transformational stewards recognize that their "solutions" are among many plausible alternatives and must be continually reassessed and adjusted as conditions change.

Integrative/Systems Thinker. Thanks largely to Senge's pathbreaking book *The Fifth Discipline* (1990), systems thinking has become one of the most important concepts in the field of leadership. But systems thinking is not always an easy concept to grasp or apply. Vaill (1996) notes continuing evidence that demonstrates an absence of systems thinking: our tendency to think in black and white; to believe in simple linear cause-effect relationships; to ignore feedback; to ignore relationships between a phenomenon and its environment; and to ignore how our own biases frame our perceptions. Vaill sees the core idea of systems thinking in the balancing and interrelating of three levels of phenomenon: first, the "whole," or phenomenon of interest itself; second, the inner workings of the whole—the combining and interacting of the internal elements that produce the whole; and third, the world outside the whole that places the phenomenon in its context—all moving dynamically in time (1996, 108–9). Vaill argues that the key to learning systems thinking—and we believe it can be learned—is "understanding oneself in interactions with the surrounding world" (1996, 110).

A prime example of systems thinking is presented by Steven Kelman, former director of the Office of Federal Procurement Policy within the Office of Management and Budget. In his book *Unleashing Change*, Kelman recounts his firsthand experience leading procurement reform efforts during the first Clinton administration (2005). Although Kelman saw a need for reform, he did not push a change agenda down through the ranks. Instead, he sought information, attempting to understand the procurement system as a whole and its many parts that made up the whole. He found that many of the frontline procurement officers were also calling for change in the system. Kelman refers to these individuals as the "change vanguard," allowing their innovations and creativity to take the lead. Kelman utilized the power of his position to unleash the change effort that was formulating at the lowest levels. In this instance, he served as a facilitator of the change effort; he was a leader pushing for change while simultaneously helping those in the change vanguard to see their initiatives succeed.

Building the Attributes for Transformational Leadership

Transformational stewards are special leaders, combining personal traits, specific mind-sets, relations to others, and a change-centric approach that enable them to succeed in meeting the changing needs of public managers. Table 9.2 summarizes the key attributes we envision for transformational stewards and it grounds this model in existing literature.

An example of an organization that supports transformational stewardship is the U.S. Coast Guard, where leaders emphasize pushing leadership down throughout the organization and encourage a flexible approach to collaboration and decision making. According to Donald Phillips and Admiral James M. Loy (USCG, ret.) in their book *Character in Action* (2003), leadership in the Coast Guard exhibits a number of ideals that are very consistent with transformational stewardship: having a decentralized decision-making structure, stressing individual initiative along with promoting team over self, cultivating caring relationships and strong alliances, having effective communications, making change the norm, encouraging decisiveness, and empowering the young. Furthermore, although graduates of the Coast Guard Academy receive a heavy dose of the sciences, those subjects are complemented by several specific courses in leadership—more than typically exist in professional "management" degrees.

A Change Appraisal Tool for Transformational Stewards

Through our study of the mechanics and dynamics of change in individuals and organizations, we have come to believe that transformational stewardship encompasses a set of tangible, articulated skills and abilities. The concept is useful to both public and private leaders for their understanding and management of the risks of change. Awareness of the sources and nature of operational risk is rapidly becoming essential for change leaders. While the concept of "risk management" was initially applicable only to financial analysts and insurance providers, risk analysis can inject a dose of reality and anticipation into any change-planning process. Transformational stewards have a critical strategic advantage. They are skilled in assessment of the factors that are preconditions to change success and in assessing risks involved in change efforts in understanding where managers or leaders can most appropriately shape the change process.

Table 9.2

Attributes of Transformational Stewardship

Attribute	Description	Selective Supporting Authors
Innerpersonal Beliefs/Traits		
Ethical	Maintains high standards of integrity for themselves and their organization, elevating organization to a "higher plane"	Burns 1978; Ciulla 2004; Fairholm 2000; Johnson 2002; Thompson 2000
Reflective/Learning Oriented	Is able to step back from the situation and consider alternative meanings and options; learns from success and failures; is self-aware and tolerant	Senge 1990; Greenleaf 1977; Thompson 2000; Wheatley 2005
Empathetic	Demonstrates concern for others, both within and without the organization, over self-interest; takes others' views and concerns into account; is self-deprecating	Autry 1992; Coles 2000; Goleman 1998; Thompson 2000
Visionary/Foresight	Is able to look beyond the current situation and see the big picture for the mission and the organization; constantly scans the environment; is strategically aware; creates a vision for the future	Bass and Avolio 1994; Bennis and Nanus 1985; Burns 1978; Fairholm 1997; Graham 2003
Operational Mind-set		
Trustee/Caretaker	Holds position and organizational resources in trust for others—the public, in general, and future members of the organization	Block 1993; Denhardts 2003; Driver 1982; Kass 1990; Kee 2003
Mission Driven	Fiercely and courageously pursues the mission of their organization; creates "common purpose"	Block 1993; Kee and Black 1985; 2003; Matheson and Kee 1986

Accountable	Measures results in multiple ways, in a transparent fashion, and shares with those who contribute or affect the organization's success; takes responsibility (legal, professional, and personal) for the results	Behn 2001; Block 1993; Demming 1986; Harmon 1990, 1995; Moe 2001; Romzek and Dubnick 1987; Vaill 1989b
Attention to Detail	Details often affect the manner in which change is seen and felt by those within and without the organization; a *Transformational Stewardship* is able to sort out those that impact people from the "red tape" that slows change	Addington and Graves. 2002; Block 1993; Moe 1994; Terry 1995
Interpersonal/Interactions with Others		
Trust Builder	Builds program success through developing community and maintaining trust—with the members of their agencies, their constituents, and their principals (Congress and political leadership)	Fairholm 1997, 2000; Greenleaf 1977; Mitchell and Scott 1987; Phillips and Loy 2000
Empowering	Within the organization and for citizens that are served by the organization; TS is at the center of the motivation of both leaders and followers—everyone in the organization can do it	Denhardts 2003; Graham 2003
Power Sharing	Relies less on positional authority and more on persuasion, moral leadership, and group power to achieve goals	Autry and Mitchell 1998; Graham 2003; Hill 1994; Kee 2003
Coalition Builder	Recognizes the importance of building coalitions with other organizations, within government, in the nonprofit and for-profit sectors	Kelman 2005; Phillips and Loy 2003
Change-centric Approach		
Creative/Innovative	Focuses on the change needs for the organization, rather than who leads the change; encourages others to find solutions to organizational problems; is open to new ideas, intuition, inspiration; is willing to take risks	Bennis 2000; Dunphy 2000; Kee and Setzer 2006; Thompson 2000; Vaill 1996
Comfortable with Ambiguity	Conflicting organizational objectives and priorities often require a careful balancing act: continuity and change; efficiency and equity, and so on; *Transformational Stewards* recognize that their "solution" is only one of many plausible alternatives	Depree 1989; Kee and Black 1989; Thompson 2000; Vaill 1989a
Integrative/Systems Thinking	Understanding forces for change and interrelationships; ability to find integrative, rather than polarizing, solutions	Attwood et al. 2003; Graham 2003; Senge 1990; Thompson 2000; Vaill 1996

Figure 9.1   **Risk Assessment Framework**

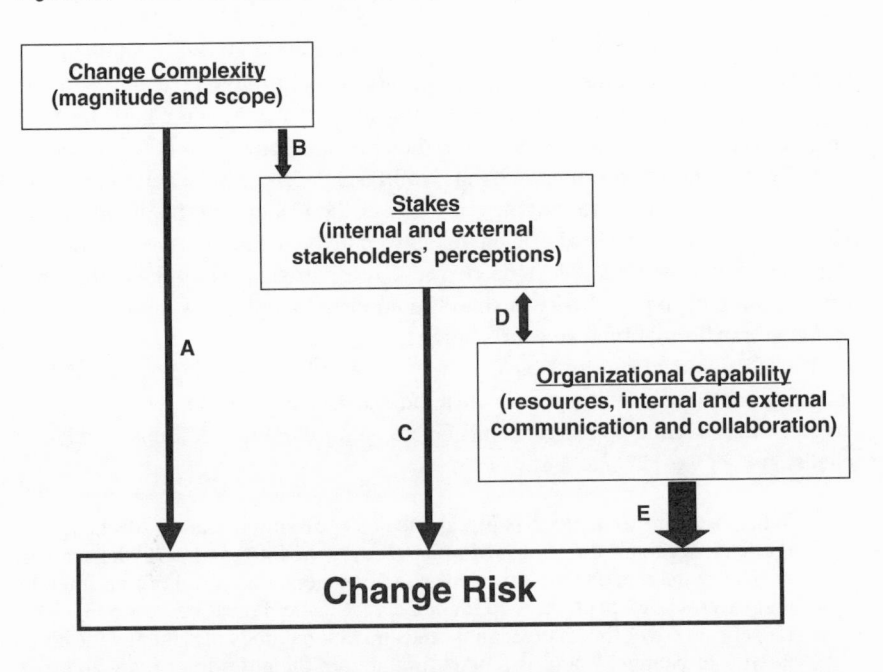

We offer a conceptual tool to assist public leaders in assessing and mitigating change-related risks. It is a function of three sets of factors: (1) the complexity of the change being undertaken, (2) the intensity of stakeholder perceptions of their stake (their potential gain or loss) in the change outcome, and (3) the change capability of the organization. Analyzing the interrelationship among these sets of factors can help leaders comprehend the level of risk involved in any given change. They can then employ appropriate strategies to empower and involve internal and external stakeholders to reduce risks.

We provide a framework for assessing the level of risk presented by change efforts in Figure 9.1. The three sets of factors represent the nature of the change, the stakes real or imagined in the outcome of the change, and organizational capability.

The magnitude and scope of the change affects the risk involved (path A), as do perceptions of both internal and external stakeholders regarding how much they gain or lose through change processes (path B). The intensity in the feelings held by either internal or external stakeholders about how they will be affected will affect every risk (path C), but may be mitigated by the organizational capability (path D). Leaders require organizational resources to reduce anxiety among stakeholders and to reduce the overall risk to the ongoing organizational performance (path E).

Viewing change risk as a function of the three sets of contributing risk factors simplifies the often ambiguous responsibility to lead change by reducing it to a more tangible charge—to act to influence change by identifying and addressing the sources of risk that stand to impede the change process. By anticipating and strategically managing relationships between complexity, stakes, and organizational capabilities, a transformational steward can control the level of risk to the organization and its network. Managing change efforts without the knowledge of change risk factors is much more unpredictable and potentially counterproductive. By pushing for too much change, too fast, the risks of unanticipated and unfavorable outcomes are heightened for both the leader and the organization. However, pushing too slowly on change also may be dangerous—organizations may miss major opportunities or be viewed as recalcitrant and inefficient. In either case, leading change is "risky business," and understanding just how risky it is can give transformational stewards much needed leverage.

Transformational stewards have an advantage in leading change because their innerpersonal traits, their operational mind-set, and the way they relate to others help them facilitate change. Coast Guard Admiral Patrick Stillman stated the challenge:

> What we want to achieve is a realistic sense of simplification of change so the leaders can do their jobs. Similar to cost schedules and performance and project management, the utility of risk management, from both an internal and external perspective, is to identify what leaders must be aware of. They must be aware of the change landscape and find methods of reducing the complexity of change. There is a need to maintain the altitude of focus in order to achieve the change outcomes. Also, we must ruthlessly measure outputs and inputs in order to achieve the desired outcomes and put accountability at the top of the priority list, or change will fail. That is the challenge and opportunity (2005).

Roles and Responsibilities of the Transformational Steward

Although public leaders continually deal with change, the responsibilities associated with transformation and stewardship need further articulation. Without a clear understanding of transformation and stewardship roles, leaders and managers may lack the skills necessary to facilitate successful change processes and to deploy necessary resources to affect successful transformation. Being technically proficient and managerially inclined is necessary but insufficient for leading effective organizational transformation. In agencies whose very mission and future depends on significant change (which we would argue is the majority), the failure of leaders to recognize and understand their transformational responsibilities means that—at best—the performance of these roles will be ad hoc, making organizational success unpredictable. Compelling examples of this occur in agencies that experienced a major institutional failure, subsequently attempted to realign their capabilities, and then experienced a second major breakdown that exposed the insufficient system change.

Two very public examples come to mind from recent history: the Federal Emergency Management Agency (FEMA), which is part of the Department of Homeland Security (DHS), and the National Aeronautics and Space Administration (NASA). In the case of FEMA, the agency's response to Hurricane Andrew in 1992 was viewed by many to have fallen well below expectations. Agency reorganization and realignment to ensure more effective responses to disasters was undertaken in the mid-1990s. In 2005, following a decade of publicly touted improvement at FEMA and its reorganization into the new Department of Homeland Security, Hurricane Katrina exposed the fact that the reforms had not sufficiently addressed basic management deficiencies. While Hurricane Katrina presented a disaster of epic proportions and many of the conditions were simply unanticipated, many of FEMA's failures were no different than those mistakes identified in previous reviews. In the case of NASA, the safety-focused reforms from one catastrophic shuttle disaster were insufficient to address management conditions that led to a second catastrophic disaster.

In both FEMA and NASA, certain technical advancements and alignments were necessary and may have been only indirectly related to subsequent breakdowns. But without a doubt, the management conditions that persisted through the episodes mentioned were critical factors in the public failures. Why? There were certainly skilled and committed managers and leaders in both organizations who were very capable public servants. We would argue, though, that when the complexity of change, stakes, and required organizational capabilities are not understood, it is unlikely that leaders and managers will act with awareness of what to do and how to do it. Most public leaders and managers receive little or no progressive training and development related to the challenge of leading and managing major organizational change. When we consider the prevalence of organizational transformation, the consequences of leaders' transformational ignorance make it clear that defining and understanding transformational stewards' roles and responsibilities is an indispensable part of building organizational change capability.

We have organized the leaders' roles and responsibilities in analyzing the major risk factors in a change or transformation (complexity, stakeholder perceptions, and organizational capability) in Table 9.3.

Complexity

While the complexity of a change may seem a given—uncontrollable and unalterable by the leader—in actuality, the transformational steward has various responsibilities that can influence how the complexity of the change interacts with stakeholders and the organization itself. Perhaps the most important leadership role is the development of strategies, processes, policies and procedures, and structures to deal with the complexity. For example, a leader should undertake an analysis of the complexity of a proposed change or transformation prior to initiating the change itself.

The existence and utilization of formal strategies aimed at identifying and

Table 9.3

Leadership Roles and Responsibilities

Roles and Responsibilities:

Transformational Steward	Strategy	Process	Structure	Culture
Change Complexity (Magnitude and scope of change)	Formal strategies to identify, measure, and adjust to the scope and magnitude of a change	Processes, policies, and procedures developed and adjusted to address the complexity of the change	Organizational and team roles, responsibilities, and reporting relationships restructured to accommodate the scope and magnitude of the change	Awareness of how change complexity will impact organizational culture and efforts to mitigate adverse impacts
Stakeholder Relations (Perceptions of gain or loss due to change)	Formal strategies to identify, measure, and adjust to perceptions of gain or loss of affected stakeholders	Processes, policies, and procedures to modified to enhance communication with and help to involve external and internal stakeholders, to receive formal feedback, and to mitigate perceptions of loss	Organizational structures modified to enhance communication with and help to involve external and internal stakeholders in the change process	Awareness of the extent to which the organization's culture supports and encourages the identification and involvement of internal and external stakeholders in the change process; efforts to strengthen cultural support and overcome cultural resistance

Organizational Capabilities

Capacity	Strategic use of resources—time, money, human capital, and infrastructure—in an efficient and effective manner during the change process	Processes, policies, and procedures to ensure the effective and efficient use of resources	Organizational structures that enhance the efficient use of resources during a change	Promotion of a culture that seeks to use resources in an innovative, flexible, and efficient fashion
Internal and External Communication and Collaboration	Genuine involvement of internal and external stakeholders in the strategic planning of any major change	Processes, policies, and procedures to promote communication and collaboration between all stakeholders and senior management	Organizational structures that facilitate communication and collaboration between stakeholders and senior management	Creating an environment in which stakeholders feel that their ideas will be heard and taken seriously during the change effort
Implementation	Development and use of a change implementation strategy	Processes, policies, and procedures to facilitate change and encourage innovation, such as transparency, rotational assignments, and feedback loops	Organizational structures—such as a designated change team—that support and facilitate the implementation of the change	Creating an implementation environment open to hearing new ideas, addressing false perceptions, and encouraging authentic communication between the change team and management

measuring the scope and magnitude of a change will provide the leader with the information necessary to move forward or to alter change strategies to accommodate the degree of change complexity and the type of change (for example, voluntary versus involuntary change). If the scope of change exceeds the current organizational ability to accommodate it, the leader might consider scaling down the scope or developing a pilot project to allow the organization to gain experience in dealing with the change.

A transformational steward will need to adjust organizational processes, policies, and procedures (the three "Ps") and the organization's structures depending upon the complexity of the change. This might involve restructuring team roles, responsibilities, and reporting relationships to accommodate the scope and magnitude of the change. Finally, a transformational steward must be aware of the change's impact on the organization's culture. Complex changes may stretch the fabric of the organization's culture. Transformational stewards must overcome or mitigate the difficulty of cultural change in relation to the change complexity. While each case is unique, Kelman's approach of using a "change vanguard" to pilot procurement reform was an effective method of obtaining the support of key actors that helped initiate a cultural change (2005).

Stakeholder Perceptions

Awareness and identification of those who have a stake in the change event is a critical task for the transformational steward. The leader must understand the possible influences stakeholders can exercise on a proposed change event and the strength and likelihood that those influences will impact the change. Learning from past change efforts and how they were impacted by various stakeholders can provide important information to the change leader. To enhance the success of a change, the transformational steward may need to tailor change strategies in order to mitigate negative stakeholder perceptions and magnify positive influences of stakeholders.

Transformational stewards should develop a formal process for identifying those who have a stake in the change and develop a method to measure their perceived gains or losses due to the change—this is similar to a "stakeholder analysis" or "social network analysis." This identification should include the types and degree of importance of various stakes (for example, resources) that stakeholders perceive to be affected by the change. Finally, leaders should develop processes to help stakeholders understand and be prepared for likely gains or losses due to the change, correcting any misperceptions of stakeholders regarding the magnitude of the gain or loss.

Proactive action can reduce resistance to change. This may require the modification of organizational structures to enhance communication with and help to involve external and internal stakeholders in the change process. Transformational stewards must be aware of the extent to which the organization's culture supports and encourages the identification and involvement of internal and external stakeholders in the change process. Leaders also must overcome or mitigate problems arising from a culture that does not support or encourage stakeholder involvement in the change process.

Organizational Capability

In general, the more "change-centric" the organization, the more capable the organization is to handle major change and transformation efforts. As with change complexity and stakeholders, the transformational steward's role (in the short run) is one of diagnosing organizational strengths and weaknesses and developing strategies to overcome weaknesses. In the long run, the transformational steward should seek to enhance the change capability of the organization.

An organization's capacity to deal with change is limited. However, a transformational leader can enhance that capacity through effective use of organizational resources—time, money, human capital, and infrastructure. This will happen only if the organization already has in place good structures, processes, policies, and procedures that support effective and efficient resource utilization. If not in place, a transformational steward should build that capacity in the long run, including promoting an organizational culture to use resources in an innovative, flexible, and efficient fashion. In the short run, the leader should focus on those areas most important to implement the change—addressing those areas that might inhibit the change effort. For example, if budgetary flexibility is crucial for a successful change, that may need to be the leader's priority. Further, the transformational steward may want to alter stakeholder roles and responsibilities and reporting relationships in order to maximize the efficient use of resources. This might include developing internal and external partnerships in the change process.

Internal and External Communication and Collaboration

We believe that effective communication and collaboration with internal and external stakeholders are critical to successful organizational change. This would include their involvement in strategic planning of the change, instituting routine processes and procedures that promote two-way communication between all stakeholders and senior management, and instituting processes to measure stakeholders' perceptions of existing communication and collaboration systems. The transformational steward must break down structural barriers to authentic communication and collaboration and attempt to encourage perceptions among all stakeholders that that their ideas will be heard and taken seriously and that their involvement is vital to the change effort. Processes and procedures might include advisory committees, membership on change teams, town hall–type meetings, and even suggestion boxes (that are acknowledged and responded to).

Implementation

Good strategies and policies will not alone ensure success. Transformational stewards should learn from the past, recognizing the causes of implementation successes and failures. Some common implementation strategies include creating a designated change team, rotating staff into and out of a change team, promoting processes that ensure transparent and accurate two-way communication between the change team and leaders external to the team, and ensuring that human resource personnel have the authority to effectively manage the change teams. Transformation, however, cannot be accomplished by a change team alone. A key to implementation is the degree to which transformational stewards can develop effective collaborations with stakeholders within and outside the organization—creating true partnerships for change.

Perhaps the most important role of a transformational steward is in helping create an organizational culture that supports change. This includes creating an openness to new ideas, creating mechanisms for authentic two-way communication, quickly addressing false perceptions and rumors, and, in general, creating "learning organizations" (Senge 1990) that encourage systems thinking, self-reflection, and periodic reviews of what is working and what can be improved.

Common Ingredients

Transformational stewards require three common ingredients in order to be successful. Effective leaders require sufficient *information* to understand and enact the change, clear and consistent *intent* that provides the purpose to change and enables willingness and commitment, and the necessary *influence* to accomplish the change or transformation. If any of these critical ingredients is missing, then the transformational steward may not be able to fully achieve his or her responsibilities. The combination of these three ingredients can ensure transformational stewards are successful in leveraging organizational capability to facilitate effective change.

Varying Roles of Transformational Stewards: Politician, Career Servant, Supervisor

The common elements and responsibilities for successful transformational stewardship noted earlier establish a foundation for discussing the specific roles of the unique public-sector leaders who guide transformation in government. These include three basic actors: (1) political appointees serving in an executive leadership role, (2) career civil servants in executive leadership roles, and (3) first-level supervisors and midmanagers assuming responsibilities for change implementation. While there is always a diverse range of actors and influences in any transformation effort, we will focus on the distinct responsibilities of these three actors. An important starting point for understanding these differences is the consideration of where each actor's influence is greatest and most useful. Once this is defined, it is possible to more clearly frame the specific roles that each transformational steward plays.

Political Appointees

For political appointees, their primary influence is with higher political leadership and outwardly with external groups and organizations involved in the transformation process. Due to the external relationships and expectations inherent in the political leadership role, these transformational stewards are generally most valuable in their ability to understand and influence the external stakeholders in the executive branch, as well as outside interest groups and interested members of the legislature. The core transformational role of the political leader is that of the "Advocate." In this capacity, political leaders are vital to establishing an integrated and compelling case for change that blends the policy and management priorities of the organization. They are also most likely to be knowledgeable about their agency's operational capacity, limitations, strengths, and obstacles. This connection hinges directly on the relationship between the political leader and the next level of career leadership in the agency. One of the frequent risks of politically driven transformation is that there is no real appreciation of what the agency is doing well and what the actual priorities are in order to improve performance. When this risk is coupled with rapid turnover of political leaders, the transformational landscape can quickly become an amalgam of fractured, disconnected initiatives and confused, paralyzed processes.

Career Executives

The second major type of transformational steward is the career executive, who is essential for the success and legitimacy of any change effort. While the political transformational steward is chiefly an "Advocate," the career leader must be both Advocate and "Architect." In this capacity, the career leader is the linchpin, responsible for assessing and synthesizing the transformational capacity of the organization and translating it upward to enable clear prioritization and realistic transformational expectations. Similarly, the career transformational steward must effectively support and engage political leaders to develop the change vision and priorities, and then translate that downward and laterally to ensure alignment of action at each level. It is in this middle ground that the career leader must craft the transformation plan, including scope, approach, objectives, and measures.

For career leaders who are peripherally involved and who are not charged with specifically acting as the transformational architect, their career role is that of "owning" the transformational agenda as a process or functional sponsor. A key to transformational stewardship is the pushing down of responsibility for the transformation to a wide spectrum of career managers. For example, in the area of e-government transformations, career executives steward the transformation process as primary "owners" of business processes or organizational functions, "architecting" the shape and nature of the transformation. The career leader must fulfill the transformational responsibility to anticipate and address change impacts, while simultaneously working to articulate and resolve issues and remove transformational obstacles. This role places the career leader in the dual capacity of both architect and broker, as the careerist stewards to the various interests represented by teams, units, functions, and higher political leadership. During implementation, the career leader's focus turns toward establishing integrated, sustained capabilities resulting from the transformation effort. Because the career leader's tenure with the organization is the stabilizing influence across rotating political leadership, the careerist stewardship role is critical and is the safeguard of the organization's longer-term transformational interests. But the stewardship role should not take a backseat to the need for career executives to be visibly and strongly in support of transformation; otherwise, the change effort is likely to be problematic.

Mid-level Manager/Supervisor

The third and final transformational steward that we have identified is that of the first-level supervisor and mid-level manager. There are approximately 125,000 first-level supervisors in the federal government alone (and perhaps another half million at the state and local level), and they are the most critical link that connects the larger idea of transformation within an organization to the existing structures and processes of the organization (NAPA 2003). These transformational stewards are likely to have predominantly technical skills—unless they have been involved in a leadership-development program that specifically addresses change and transformation. Successful first-level supervisors develop and apply transformational awareness and skills, rather than merely relying exclusively on technical knowledge to achieve transformation objectives.

Unlike more senior transformational stewards, first-level supervisors play a much more tactical role in the transformational process. It must be noted, though, that this tactical responsibility requires that supervisors understand and articulate the more strategic aspects of transformation. These leaders and managers are the connection between the action of the transformation in the people and processes of the organization and the overarching plan and vision that is stewarded primarily by career leaders. In this way, first-level supervisors' and managers' primary influence is interpersonal—all transformation success or failure begins and ends with the people in the organization.

The first-level supervisor's role involves bilateral communication—feeding information forward to employees in order to clarify and strengthen the nature and purpose of the change, while inquiring, listening, and feeding information back to higher career leaders about the organization's capacity for change at the level where the work is done. Interpersonal interaction is clearly critical to strengthening this link.

When working with teams, supervisory transformational stewards are the primary touch point with the source of resistance and angst related to the change effort. Here, the dynamic balance of "transformation" and "stewardship" is extremely important, as it is important for the transformation to move forward in implementation, but it is equally important that it be a collective, owned process. For this to occur, supervisors act as the "vent" for releasing the pressure of resistance, capturing valuable insights about what works and what doesn't and which employee needs are most important, and then transferring that energy into useful feedback and dialogue about the change process. The balance in this activity is to allow for open dialogue, yet keep it constructive. To the degree that the supervisory steward can accomplish this with awareness and deliberateness, the transformation process can be led and managed effectively. Still, it should be noted that this balance involves an acute awareness of when the risks of displaced anger and/or unproductive cynicism are occurring. As one example, junior military leaders are often taught that an important tool for accomplishing this "keep it constructive and deal with it now" kind of climate is for the leader to explicitly communicate to team members that they take ultimate responsibility for acting to resolve the issues or enforce the final decisions. Even if this may not always be completely possible in practice, the ethic of immediacy and responsibility permits transformational stewards at this level to prevent the "infection" of displaced criticism and helplessness from taking hold and growing within the team.

In sum, effective transformation requires the collective, complementary action of transformational stewards at all levels within the organization. By outlining the major transformational stewardship responsibilities for the political, career, and supervisory actors, we have presented a baseline for considering necessary characteristics and practices for successful change. Defining these aspects is a critical first step to developing more change-capable organizations.

Conclusion: Public Leadership as Transformational Stewardship

Twenty-first-century organizations—private, public, and nonprofits—according to Block, face three principal challenges (1993):

- *The Challenge of Doing More with Less*: Controlling costs and finding innovative ways to solve service demands.
- *The Challenge of Quality*: Providing higher levels of service to the consumer, client, and/or citizen.
- *The Challenge of Adaptability*: The need to respond to changing demands and outside forces.

As the twenty-first century gets under way, we would add the following to Block's list:

- *The Challenge of Globalization*: There is a need to examine the organization in a global context and analyze possible opportunities and threats.

- *The Challenge of Horizontal Relationships*: While democratic accountability continues to demand vertical reporting and performance monitoring, increasingly, public agencies are involved in a variety of horizontal relationships that will change the manner the agency does business: agency to agency; federal agency to state agency (or local); agency to nonprofit organization; agency to for-profit organization.
- *The Challenge to Understand the Nature of Change Itself*: There is a paucity of data and analysis on public-sector change, which creates a vacuum for public managers and a potential research venue for public administration scholars.

What leadership approach has the most potential to deal with these challenges? For the public sector, we believe the answer is *transformational stewardship*. Leaders at all levels in organizations can contribute to facilitating small-scale and large-scale as well as voluntary and involuntary change. Transformational stewardship provides a balance of competing interests, the need to change, and the need to be constant to core public values.

Transformational stewardship is not just the responsibility of the person at the "top" of the organization chart or the person with formal authority. The "leader" cannot do it himself or herself; but the leader can engage others in a dialogue about how they are contributing to the organization and how they are helping the organization deal with the modern challenges they face. In this fashion, public leaders can encourage transformational leadership throughout the organization, facilitating change and minimizing the risks of change.

References

Addington, Thomas, and Stephen Graves. 2002. "The Forgotten Role." *Life@Work* 1 (6): 25–33.

Attwood, Margaret, Mike Pedler, Sue Pritchard, and David Wilkinson. 2003. *Leading Change: A Guide to Whole Systems Working*. Oxon, England: Policy Press.

Autry, James. 1992. *Love and Profit: The Art of Caring Leadership*. New York: Avon Books.

Autry, James, and Stephen Mitchell. 1998. *Real Power: Business Lessons from the Tao Te Ching*. New York: Riverhead Books.

Bass, Bernard, and Bruce Avolio. 1994. *Improving Organizational Effectiveness Through Transformational Leadership*. Thousand Oaks, CA: Sage.

Behn, Robert. 1998. "What Right Do Public Managers Have to Lead?" *Public Administration Review* 58 (3): 209–24.

———. 2001. *Rethinking Democratic Accountability*. Washington, DC: Brookings.

Bennis, Warren G. 2000. "Leadership of Change." In *Breaking the Code of Change*, ed. Michael Beer and Nitin Nohria, 113–21. Boston: Harvard Business School Press.

Bennis, Warren G., and Burt Nanus. 1985. *Leaders: The Strategies for Taking Charge*. New York: Harper & Row.

Black, J. Stewart, and Hal B. Gregersen. 2002. *Leading Strategic Change: Breaking Through the Brain Barrier*. Upper Saddle River, NJ: Financial Times Prentice Hall.

Blake, Robert, and Jane Mouton. 1985. *The Managerial Grid III*. Houston, TX: Gulf.

Block, Peter. 1993. *Stewardship: Choosing Service Over Self-Interest*. San Francisco: Berrett-Koehler.

Burns, James MacGregor. 1978. *Leadership.* New York: Harper & Row.

Ciulla, Joanne B. 2004. *Ethics, the Heart of Leadership.* Westport, CT: Praeger.

Coles, Robert. 2000. *Lives of Moral Leadership.* New York: Random House.

Demming, W. Edwards. 1986. *Out of Crisis.* Cambridge, MA: MIT Center for Advanced Engineering Study.

Denhardt, Janet V., and Robert B. Denhardt. 2003. *The New Public Service.* Armonk, NY: M.E. Sharpe.

Depree, Max. 1989. *Leadership Is an Art.* New York: Doubleday.

Driver, Colin. 1982. "Engineers and Entrepreneurs: The Dilemmas of Public Management." *Journal of Policy Analysis and Management* 1 (3): 402–6.

Dunphy, Dexter. 2000. "Embracing Paradox: Top-Down versus Participative Management of Organizational Change; A Commentary on Conger and Bennis." In *Breaking the Code of Change,* ed. Michael Beer and Nitin Nohria, 123–35. Boston: Harvard Business School Press.

Fairholm, Gilbert. 1997. *Capturing the Heart of Leadership: Spirituality and Community in the New American Workplace.* Westport, CT: Praeger.

———. 2000. *Perspectives on Leadership.* Westport, CT: Quorum Books.

Finer, Herman. 1940. "Administrative Responsibility to Democratic Government." *Public Administration Review* 1 (1): 335–50. Reprinted in Francis E. Rourke. 1965. *Bureaucratic Power in National Politics.* Boston: Little Brown and Company.

Fox, Elliot M., and Lyndall. F. Urwick, eds. 1973. *Dynamic Administration—The Collected Papers of Mary Parker Follett.* New York: Pitman.

Friedrich, Carl J. 1940. "Public Policy and the Nature of Administrative Responsibility." *Public Policy* 1: 1–20. Reprinted in Francis E. Rourke.1965. *Bureaucratic Power in National Politics.* Boston: Little Brown and Company.

Goleman, Daniel. 1998. *Working with Emotional Intelligence.* New York: Bantam.

Goleman, Daniel, Annie McKee, and Richard Boyatzis. 2002. *Primal Leadership: Realizing the Power of Emotional Intelligence.* Boston: Harvard Business School Press.

Graham, Pauline, ed. 2003. *Mary Parker Follett: Prophet of Management.* Washington, DC: Beard.

Greenleaf, Robert K. 1977. *Servant Leadership: A Journal into the Nature of Legitimate Power and Greatness.* New York: Paulist Press.

Harmon, Michael M. 1990. "The Responsible Actor as 'Tortured Soul': The Case of Horatio Hornblower." In *Images and Identities in Public Administration,* eds. Henry D. Kass and Bayard L. Catron. Newberry Park, CA: Sage.

———. 1995. *Responsibility's Paradox: A Critique of Rational Discourse on Government.* Thousand Oaks: CA: Sage.

Hersey, Paul, and Kenneth H. Blanchard. 1993. *Management of Organizational Behavior: Utilizing Human Resource.* Englewood Cliffs, NJ: Prentice Hall.

Hill, Linda A. 1994. *Exercising Influence.* Note 9–494–080. Cambridge, MA: Harvard Business School.

Johnson, Craig. 2002. *Meeting the Ethical Challenges of Leadership.* Thousand Oaks, CA: Sage.

Kass, Henry D. 1990. "Stewardship as a Fundamental Image of Public Administration." In *Images and Identities in Public Administration,* eds. Henry D. Kass and Bayard L. Catron, 112–30. Newberry Park, CA: Sage.

Kee, James Edwin. 2003. Leadership as Stewardship. Unpublished manuscript. Washington, DC: George Washington University.

Kee, James Edwin, and Whitney Setzer. 2006. *Change-Centric Leadership.* Working paper. Washington, DC: Center for Innovation in the Public Service, George Washington University.

Kee, Jed, and Roger Black. 1985. "Is Excellence Possible in the Public Sector?" *Public Productivity Review* 9 (1): 25–34.

Kelman, Steven. 2005. *Unleashing Change: A Study of Organizational Renewal in Government.* Washington, DC: Brookings Institution Press.

Kettl, Donald. 1997. "The Global Revolution in Public Management: Driving Themes, Missing Links." *Journal of Policy Analysis and Management* 16 (3): 446–62.

Kotter, John P. 1996. *Leading Change.* Boston: Harvard Business School Press.

Matheson, Scott M. with James Edwin Kee. 1986. *Out of Balance.* Salt Lake City: Peregrine Smith Books.

Mitchell, Terrence R., and William G. Scott. 1987. "Leadership Failures, the Distrusting Public, and Prospects of the Administrative State." *Public Administration Review* 47 (6): 445–52.

Moe, Ronald. 1994. "The 'Reinventing Government' Exercise: Misinterpreting the Problem, Misjudging the Consequences." *Public Administration Review* 54 (2): 446–62.

———. 2001. "The Emerging Federal Quasi Government: Issues of Management and Accountability." *Public Administration Review* 61 (3): 290–312.

National Academy of Public Administration (NAPA). 2003. *Leadership for Leaders.* Washington, DC: Management Concepts.

Osborne, David, and Ted Gaebler. 1992. *Reinventing Government: How the Entrepreneurial Spirit Is Transforming the Public Sector.* Reading, MA: Addison.

Phillips, Donald T., and James M. Loy. 2003. *Character in Action: The U.S. Coast Guard on Leadership.* Annapolis, MD: The Naval Institute Press.

Random House Dictionary of the English Language. 1968. College ed. New York: Random House.

Romzek, Barbara S., and Melvin J. Dubnick. 1987. "Accountability in the Public Sector: Lessons from the Challenger Tragedy." *Public Administration Review* 47 (3): 227–38.

Senge, Peter. 1990. *The Fifth Discipline.* New York: Doubleday.

Spears, Lawrence. 2002. *Focus on Leadership.* New York: John Wiley.

Stillman, Patrick. 2005. Remarks December 9. Expert Panel on Transformation and Change, Center for Innovation in the Public Sector, George Washington University.

Stone, Deborah. 1997. *Policy Paradox: The Art of Political Decision Making.* New York: W.W. Norton.

Terry, Larry D. 1995. *Leadership of Public Bureaucracies: The Administrator as Conservator.* Thousand Oaks, CA: Sage Publishers.

———. 1998. "Administrative Leadership, Neo-Managerialism, and the New Public Management Movement." *Public Administration Review* 58 (3): 194–200.

Thompson, C. Michael. 2000. *The Congruent Life.* San Francisco: Jossey-Bass.

Vaill, Peter B. 1989a. *Managing as a Performing Art.* San Francisco: Jossey-Bass.

———. 1989b. "Spirituality in the Age of the Leveraged Buyout." Keynote address to a conference on Spirituality in Life and Work, Georgetown University, Washington, DC, July 21.

———. 1996. *Learning as a Way of Being: Strategies for Survival in a World of Permanent White Water.* San Francisco: Jossey-Bass.

Wheatley, Margaret J. 1984. *Leadership and the New Science: Learning about Organizations from an Orderly Process.* Birmingham, AL: University of Alabama Press.

———. 2005. *Finding Our Way: Leadership for an Uncertain Time.* San Francisco: Berrett-Koehler.

Whitehead, Joel. 2005. Remarks at George Washington University to PAD 203 Class, Washington, DC, October 22.

Part III

Leadership and Collaboration

Part III

Leadership and Collaboration

10

Leadership for the Common Good

Creating Regimes of Mutual Gain

JOHN M. BRYSON AND BARBARA C. CROSBY

Perhaps the most daunting challenge for leaders around the world today is how to bring people together from different backgrounds and different sectors—government, business, nonprofits, philanthropy, and media—to tackle complex public problems. Specifically, the challenge is for leaders to bring together diverse groups to create public value and achieve the common good through self-sustaining *regimes of mutual gain*. As we see it, a regime of mutual gain is a policy regime (or policy system), defined as *a set of implicit and explicit principles, norms, rules, and decision-making procedures around which people's expectations converge in a given policy area; regimes of mutual gain achieve widespread lasting benefit at reasonable cost and tap and serve people's deepest interests in, and desires for, a better world* (Crosby and Bryson 2005a).

A regime of mutual gain can also be described as a shared-power arrangement that generates network power (Booher and Innes 2002) and mobilizes bias (Schattschneider 1975) in favor of long-term public value. Logically, these regimes are more likely to occur when public leaders find ways to draw on the distinctive strengths of the different sectors and guard against failures to which each sector is prone.

Our aim is to help leaders in the various sectors better understand how each sector can contribute to a cross-sector regime of mutual gain, in issue areas as diverse as transportation, early childhood education, and vital aging. A few illustrations may be helpful. The U.S. income tax collection system represents a regime of mutual gain, although clearly a flawed one. The system generally produces beneficial results: relatively reliable revenue streams to fund public services, relatively low evasion rates, some redistribution of resources to low-income families, funding for Social Security, massive subsidies for home mortgages, promotion of charitable giving, and promotion of business development. Businesses, nonprofits, and government agencies help administer the system and also provide assistance (often for a fee) to citizens and organizations seeking to file tax returns or challenge Internal Revenue Service (IRS) findings. Individual taxpayers also help administer the system. Journalists track policy making in Congress and report on impacts and abuses of the system. The system also has many inefficiencies and harmful side effects: Average citizens are often baffled by the system's complicated regulations and forms; mortgage subsidies have contributed to urban sprawl and its attendant pressures on public services; and many would argue that the system in recent years has redistributed too much money in the wrong direction. Nonetheless, most people would agree that the system works reasonably well and that reform efforts should focus on adjusting the system, not changing it fundamentally.

Other U.S. examples of regimes of mutual gain include the policy frameworks and cross-sector partnerships around welfare reform, Social Security, and the promotion of home ownership. Indeed, Paul Light's (2002) discussion of the fifty greatest achievements of the federal government in the last half-century indicates that virtually all involved the creation of a cross-sector regime of mutual gain. The achievements included rebuilding Europe after World War II, expanding the right to vote, promoting equal access to public accommodations, reducing disease, reducing workplace discrimination, ensuring safe food and drinking water, and strengthening the nation's highway system.

Well-functioning communities also are regimes of mutual gain in which all sectors are strong, decent jobs are plentiful, transportation is adequate, recreation opportunities abound, the environment is protected, crime is low, news media are alert watchdogs, people's spirits are lifted, and the public interest is served.

In the remainder of this chapter, we draw on other scholars' conceptions of public value, the public interest, the common good, and commonwealth to construct a framework for thinking about how to take advantage of each sector's strengths while avoiding the weaknesses. We apply the framework to a current example of leadership for the common good—the vital aging movement in Minnesota.

The Different Sectors as Building Blocks for Creating Public Value

We use "creating public value"—Moore's (1995, 2000) evocative phrase—to mean the design of policies, programs, and practices that benefit a community as a whole. Another approach, taken by Stone (2001), is to identify overarching public values that frame contests over developing and allocating goods, services, and privileges to citizens. In the United States, the dominant public values, she argues, are equity, efficiency, security, and liberty.

In this section, we explore how different sectors can contribute to, or undermine, public value. Specifically, we consider the potential contributions and failings of markets, nonprofit organizations, democratic governments, the media, and communities.

Markets

When the conditions underlying perfect markets are met, they can be counted on to provide optimum amounts of goods and services in the most efficient way. Many goods and services are offered in competitive or nearly competitive markets, and U.S. citizens have grown used to the choice, productivity, innovativeness, service, and quality that markets can provide. Public value can be created by businesses operating in competitive markets in several ways, including through managing a large fraction of the economy, providing employment, paying taxes, and in general creating wealth. Businesses also can act as good corporate citizens and are often relied upon to provide leadership and funding around public issues and causes. Weimer and Vining (2005) outline the many ways in which markets can fail:

- Public goods (for example, defense, open space) are likely to be undersupplied, underinvested in, or overused.
- Goods involving positive externalities (for example, basic education) will be undersupplied, while those involving negative externalities (such as pollution) will be oversupplied.
- Natural monopolies will be undersupplied or inefficiently supplied.
- Asymmetries in information are likely to lead to over- or underconsumption.
- Thin markets (for example, cartelization) lead to undersupply.
- Problems with determining or aggregating preferences lead to over- or underconsumption or distributional inefficiency.
- Uncertainty problems (often resulting from incomplete or inaccurate information) lead to moral hazard, adverse selection, incomplete insurance, or misperception of risk.
- Intertemporal problems lead to problematic pricing and incomplete capital markets.
- Adjustment costs lead to sticky prices.

Nonprofit Organizations, Including Foundations, Churches, Educational and Service Agencies, Grassroots Organizations, and Advocacy Groups

Nonprofit organizations in the United States can create public value, provided they pass some basic requirements about their purpose, asset distribution, and nonpartisanship. The array of types of nonprofit organizations and their specific purposes is extraordinary (Bryce 2000, 684–95). Section 501(c)(3) of the Internal Revenue Code identifies the most common tax-exempt organizations. They are granted tax concessions because they create public value when they:

- express the First Amendment right of assembly;
- promote public welfare directly rather than through the market, as an environmental advocacy group might, or promote the welfare of a subgroup, as an association might;
- promote public welfare in a manner that goes beyond what government does,

as a religion might, or in a way that substitutes for government action, as an organization that provides housing or health care might;
- serve public purposes at a cost less than government would incur and therefore produce a savings in terms of taxes foregone; and
- serve public purposes in a charitable way, so that public or community welfare rather than individual welfare is served (Bryce 2000, 32, 40).

Nonprofit organizations can fail in a variety of ways, so public value can also be created by working to avoid such failures. Salamon (1995) identifies four categories of voluntary failure:

- *Philanthropic Insufficiency*: The sector's "inability to generate resources on a scale that is both adequate enough and reliable enough to cope with the human service problems of an advanced industrial society" (45).
- *Philanthropic Particularism*: "The tendency of voluntary organizations and their benefactors to focus on particular subgroups of the population. . . . As a result, serious gaps can occur in the coverage of subgroups by the existing voluntary organizations" (45–6).
- *Philanthropic Paternalism*: The "nature of the sector comes to be shaped by the preferences not of the community as a whole, but of its wealthy members" (47).
- *Philanthropic Amateurism*: Care that requires professional training and expertise is "entrusted to well-meaning amateurs" (48).

Governments

Democratic governments play a different role, including providing much of the framework necessary for markets and nonprofit organizations to operate effectively, correcting or coping with market and philanthropic failures, and even guarding against their own possible failures through checks and balances and the rule of law. Democratic governments can create public value through a number of overlapping activities, some of which are more appropriate to one level or type of government than another (Moore 1995; Weimer and Vining 2005; Bozeman 2002), and some of which might be thought of as activities for the polity as a whole:

- Providing a constitutional framework of laws and supporting the rule of law—not least by the government itself.
- Creating open, transparent government.
- Fostering and relying on the democratic process, including making sure that mechanisms for articulating and aggregating values function democratically.
- Protecting human rights, human dignity, and the core of subsistence.
- Ensuring that policy makers take a long-term, holistic view and act as stewards of public resources; inspiring and mobilizing the government itself and

other key entities and actors to undertake individual and collective action in pursuit of the common good (Crosby and Bryson 2005a and 2005b), which includes promoting both within-group social connections (or what Putnam calls "bonding social capital) and across-group social connections (what he calls "bridging social capital") (Putnam 2000; Nelson, Kaboolian, and Carver 2004); and catalyzing *active* citizenship, in which diverse groups of citizens create programs, projects, products, or services of lasting public value (Boyte and Kari 1996; Luke 1998).

- Maintaining an economy with reasonable levels of growth, employment, unemployment, inflation, debt, savings, investment, and balance of payments figures.
- Relying on markets when they can be expected to work, including correcting market imperfections and freeing, facilitating, and stimulating markets, and not relying on markets when they cannot be expected to work. Serving this purpose might include:

  - Providing needed public goods that private markets will not provide on their own or else will provide poorly (for example, defense, large infrastructure projects, common spaces, free parks) and ensuring that the benefits of publicly provided goods and services are not inappropriately captured by some subset of the population for whom they are intended (for example, unnecessarily restricting public access to public lands).
  - Subsidizing activities that have positive spillover effects for the general public (for example, K–12 and higher education, basic research, certain economic development activities, block clubs).
  - Taxing or regulating activities with actual or potential negative spillover effects for the general public (for example, food and drug production and distribution, building construction, automobile operation).
  - Addressing problems created by asymmetries in information availability, distribution, or use (for example, licensing or certification programs, product labeling requirements).
  - Addressing problems of loss and uncertainty (for example, government-organized or -subsidized insurance schemes, the national Strategic Petroleum Reserve).
  - Making sure that resources (such as oil and fossil fuels) are conserved rather than assuming substitutable resources will be found or invented.
  - Protecting a common heritage when it might otherwise be lost (for example, historic and architectural preservation programs, protection of areas of outstanding natural beauty, establishment of memorials to outstanding public service).

- Providing cost-effective public goods and services (for example, transportation infrastructure and systems, health and social services, police and criminal justice services).

- Using information and cost-benefit and cost-effectiveness analyses that are as objective as possible to inform public decisions.
- Making use of civic-minded public servants and their professional expertise (Frederickson 1997).

Like markets, government operating agencies—as opposed to government direction-setting, oversight, support (or overhead), and regulatory units—are prone to characteristic failures (Osborne and Plastrik 1997; Brandl 1998; Weimer and Vining 2005). Brandl (1998, 64) argues that government operating agencies can fail when:

- they lack an external orientation to accomplish public purposes (as a result of monopoly practices, lack of an appropriate pricing mechanism, or distracted monitoring);
- because they are not organized internally to achieve public purposes (resulting in or from bounded rationality or imperfect information); or
- because they are systematically indifferent to the fairness of the distributions of income or wealth.

Note that these failures parallel the failures of markets. Government direction setting, oversight, support, and regulatory agencies also can fail to do their job—for example, when they require many layers of authorization or become too allied with regulated industries. When direction setting fails, government's responsibility to steer policy systems has been reduced (Osborne and Plastrik 1997; Osborne and Hutchinson 2004). When oversight bodies fail, accountability has been compromised (Romzek 1996). When support agencies fail, the government itself does not get the service it deserves (Barzelay 1992). And when regulatory agencies fail, the public is not adequately served or protected (Weimer and Vining 2005).

The Media

The news media provide public value by performing a watchdog role—holding public servants to high standards of ethical practice, legality, and transparent, fair decision making. They inform the citizenry about public issues, and they gather and articulate public opinion. Of course, a particular media enterprise can usually be placed in one of the sectors described previously, but we have separated media as a separate—albeit hybrid—sector because of its infusion with the professional ethos of journalists and because of the critical importance of an independent media in sustaining democracy. Even when a newspaper or broadcast station is a business, the journalistic ethos and constitutional guarantees add a different dimension to the business.

The news media fails in its watchdog and educator roles for several reasons: Journalists may become too close to political elites and even become elites themselves; journalists may allow personal bias to strongly affect their reporting; they may wear professional blinders that keep them from seeing non-sensational, less-visible events as newsworthy. Additionally, the financial interests of news media owners can influence what is covered and how it is treated. For example, the loss of revenue from offended advertisers sometimes causes stories to be pulled from newspapers or the airways, or owners' desire to save money may lead to underfunded news departments. Alternative media, meanwhile, may simply be unable to raise enough funds to pay highly skilled staff and investigate complicated stories

Communities, or the Public in General

Communities can create public value by promoting a sense of individual and collective identity, belonging, recognition, and security; providing people a place to live, work, learn, enjoy, express themselves, and build families; building and maintaining physical, human, intellectual, social, and cultural capital of various sorts; and fostering a civically engaged, egalitarian, trusting, and tolerant democratic society (Boyte and Kari 1996; Chrislip 2002). Social capital in particular has been shown to have a broad range of positive effects on health, education, welfare, safety, and civic activism (Putnam 2000). Communities are necessary for our existence as human beings, and serving communities provides a justification for our existence as humans (see Friedmann 1982; Becker 1997; Grayling 2003). Communities provide rich local knowledge and relationships that are crucial to sustainable public policy improvements (Scott 1998). Communities fail when they exclude or isolate some groups, accept the domination of traditional elites, neglect collective identity, become parochial, ignore harm to individuals and the environment, and offer few opportunities for civic engagement.

Policy Intervention in Light of Sector Strengths and Weaknesses

The *implicit* prevailing theory of policy intervention in the United States builds on the notion of sectors with differential strengths and weaknesses. The theory is summarized in Figure 10.1.

In the United States, public policy intervention typically begins with what Schultze (1977, 44) calls the "rebuttable presumption." The presumption is that we will let markets work until they fail, and only if they fail will we seek an intervention. In other words, the presumption that markets will succeed must be rebutted before we move toward public policy intervention. Schultze and others argue that if markets fail, attention should first be directed toward fixing the market failures through whatever mechanism is appropriate, given the nature of the failures. Taxes, subsidies, regulations, information provision, and various other tools might adequately address the failure, given the nature of the failure and the public purposes to be served.

If the market failures cannot be fixed, then the case is compelling for direct

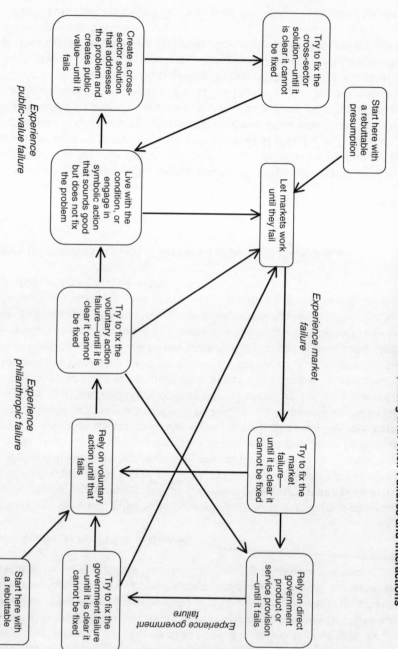

Figure 10.1 **Markets, Government, Voluntary Action, and the Public, along with Their Failures and Interactions**

government provision of products or services. For example, the rise of public schools in the United States was tied to a belief that a compelling public interest in universal, professional, non-church-based education meant markets could not be counted on to provide the education and that tax-financed public schools were the only viable alternative. The creation of the Social Security system was a response to a widely perceived failure of the private sector to provide adequate pensions for ordinary workers, their spouses, and surviving dependents.

The current school-choice movement disputes the view that public schools are working effectively. Choice advocates believe that the public schools—as government-owned and -operated monopolies—are failing and that markets or marketlike mechanisms would produce better outcomes. They advocate offering parents more choices of schools, particularly through the use of vouchers and fostering the creation of charter schools (perhaps even by allowing vouchers to be used in church-owned schools to provide yet more choice) and through allowing home schooling (Brandl 1998). Fixing the government failure may be seen in part as a move to market-based solutions but also as a move to voluntary action, since parochial schools and charter schools are nonprofit organizations. Home schooling also represents voluntary action.

Governments also make extensive use of the voluntary sector to carry out a number of government services. Indeed, approximately 37 percent of non-church nonprofit revenues come from governments (Salamon 2004, 93). For example, governments rely on nonprofit organizations to provide a wide variety of health and social services. Policy makers rely on nonprofits for a variety of reasons, but especially because they believe nonprofits are cheaper, more flexible, more innovative, and more easily terminated than government units. In others words, government often relies on nonprofits because policy makers see the sector as having strengths the government itself does not have.

But nonprofits also can fail, as noted. Attempts can be made to fix failures, through pooling and expanding resources (for example, United Way campaigns), attempting more universal solutions (for example, collaborative partnerships), overcoming paternalism (for example, developing community-based nonprofits), or increasing professionalism (for example, nonprofit educational and professional development programs or United Way vetting). When the failures cannot be fixed, three options would appear to be possible: relying on markets, if possible; relying on government service provision, if possible; or accepting that public value cannot be created.

Salamon (1995) argues that historically, the United States has relied first on voluntary action (with or without the existence of nonprofit organizations) before moving to government service provision. In other words, government service provision historically has been a product of *either* market failure *or* voluntary action failure, which means that there actually are two alternative rebuttable presumptions with which to start. For example, in the Great Depression, the federal government launched large-scale jobs programs only after business and nonprofit organizations proved incapable of providing jobs for a high proportion of the population. Congress created the food stamp program because soup kitchens run by charities simply were not covering the nutritional needs of large numbers of poor people. (Of course, the food stamp program also provided indirect support to farmers.)

If the public problems are unsolvable by any sector, then they are more accurately called *conditions* rather than problems and will remain conditions until they are turned into problems that can be solved (Wildavsky 1979). If the condition is serious but no action is undertaken by any sector to alleviate it, we might speak of a *public-value* failure. Bozeman (2002, 150) says that a "public failure occurs when neither the market nor the public sector provides goods and services required to achieve core public values." We would extend his argument to say that a public failure occurs when neither the market, nor government, nor the voluntary sector, nor the news media, nor the community provides whatever is needed (policies, goods, services, revenues) to achieve core public values. In such situations, broad-based leadership for the common good is necessary if public value is to be created.

To summarize, the implicit theory of policy intervention in the United States seems to be as follows: We will let markets or the voluntary sector work until it fails. If either fails, we will first try to fix the failures, without recourse to government intervention. This might mean relying on voluntary action to fix a market failure or vice versa. If the failures cannot be fixed, we will consider relying on government product or service delivery. If all three sectors fail and cannot be fixed, we have a public-value failure that we address in one of several ways. We can live with it; engage in some form of symbolic action that claims the problem is fixed when it is not or does not exist when it does (Edelman 2001); or seek to inspire and mobilize collective action to fashion a cross-sector solution that holds the promise of creating public value. Effective cross-sector solutions and regimes of mutual gain will build on each sector's strengths while minimizing or overcoming its weaknesses.

Leadership Tasks for Creating a Cross-sector Regime of Mutual Gain

How can leaders who want to reform an existing policy regime or build a new one use the building blocks of public value to achieve the common good? In other words, how can an understanding of the contributions and failures of markets, nonprofits, governments, media, and communities inform the main tasks of leadership? These tasks are (Crosby and Bryson 2005a):

- *Leadership in Context*: Understanding social, political, economic, and technological "givens."
- *Personal Leadership*: Understanding self and others.
- *Team Leadership*: Building effective work groups.
- *Organizational Leadership*: Nurturing humane and effective organizations.
- *Visionary Leadership*: Creating and communicating shared meaning in forums.
- *Political Leadership*: Making and implementing decisions in legislative, executive, and administrative arenas.

- *Ethical Leadership*: Adjudicating disputes in courts and sanctioning conduct.
- *Policy Entrepreneurship*: Coordinating leadership tasks over policy-change cycles.

By way of illustration, let us consider the leadership efforts of several Minnesotans to revolutionize various systems affecting older adults. In 1998, Jan Hively, a woman with a lengthy record of public service in Minnesota, became concerned about the "graying" of her state's rural communities. Young people were migrating away from small towns, just as baby boomers were nearing retirement age. At the time, Hively was working in rural Minnesota as part of her outreach job in the University of Minnesota's College of Education and Human Development. She soon joined a project sponsored by the Minnesota Board on Aging that was studying ways of helping older adults lead productive and satisfying lives.

With encouragement from an assistant commissioner in the Minnesota Department of Human Services, Hively joined Hal Freshley, from the Minnesota Board on Aging, and Darlene Schroeder, from the Elder Advocacy Network in rural Minnesota, in launching the Vital Aging Initiative, an effort to gather information about older adults' activities and interest in further education. Within a couple of years, the initiative had become the Vital Aging Network (VAN), which sponsors a variety of virtual and face-to-face forums to "promote self-sufficiency, community participation and quality of life for older adults" (see www.van.umn.edu). VAN also sponsors two projects: the Advocacy Leadership Certificate Program and Vital Force. The certificate program, offered through the University of Minnesota, provides training and field experience for people who want to become effective advocates for better policies and programs affecting older adults. Vital Force trains coaches who work with older adults to organize community projects. VAN's ultimate aim is to achieve new local to national policy regimes that make it possible for older adults to continue to contribute to their communities while receiving supports they need to stay healthy and productive.

Hively, Freshley, Schroeder, and their supporters began the change process through a combination of personal leadership and leadership in context. Personal leadership requires understanding oneself and others and using that understanding to engage in leadership work. For example, what values does the person bring to the leadership task, what does he or she care about enough to take on risky initiatives? What public problem, need, or opportunity connects with these values and cares enough to become one's "public passion?" What other leadership assets, such as professional skills and affiliations, does the person have, and how can they be used in the leadership work? Hively, Freshley, and Schroeder certainly placed high value on equity, liberty, and security for older adults. Hively, especially, developed an intense passion for creating a world in which older adults lived vibrant lives until their last breath. The three had connections or positions in government and nonprofit organizations that they could bring to the leadership work. They had expertise with aging, community change, and public policy.

Leadership in context requires understanding the social, political, economic, and technological "givens" and identifying leverage points in existing systems. We put quotations around *givens* because even political arrangements, social practices, market conditions, and technologies that seem permanent do change. An important part of the context for change efforts in the United States is the habitual reliance on market, government, nonprofit, community, and media institutions to achieve public purposes. Hively and her colleagues identified failures in all of these institutions. Some examples: Businesses were failing to develop flexible arrangements that helped older workers continue to provide expertise and service after retirement age. Government programs often made it easier for older adults to obtain expensive hospital or nursing home care than cheaper in-home assistance. Nonprofit organizations focused on serving rather than empowering older adults. Communities did not demand lifelong learning opportunities, or they permitted elderly people to become isolated in their homes. The news media depicted older adults as "greedy geezers" or frail dependents. New regimes of mutual gain would need to overcome these failures.

As they work to build new regimes, how might VAN leaders think about using the different sectors to accomplish their goals? They want to provide goods and services, obtain new laws, and open up new opportunities for work, leisure, and citizenship. To achieve these goals, they will need to take advantage of what each sector has to offer, while minimizing or overcoming its characteristic weaknesses. Table 10.1 offers examples of how business, government, nonprofit, media, and community sectors could provide public value for vital aging. If the sectors did all or most of these things, almost certainly a regime of mutual gain would be created. To make these happen, almost certainly stakeholders in each sector would have to collaborate across sector lines, thus mobilizing network power to enhance the prospects and quality of life of older adults.

We suggest that those who want to fulfill a particular need or remedy a public problem affecting their constituents (for example, older adults) should begin with a sector-by-sector stakeholder analysis. That is, within their context (a neighborhood, region, state, country, or virtual community) they should identify the specific businesses, government agencies, nonprofits, media organizations, and communities that are affected by the need or problem or that have crucial resources. Grouping the stakeholders by sectors, the advocates of change might add to standard questions about each stakeholder's expectations, interests, and power (see Bryson 2004) the following questions that should be answered using a guide like Table 10.1:

- Which of the possible sector contributions does the stakeholder make in relation to the need or problem that concerns us?
- How significant are the contributions?
- Which of the possible sectoral failures can be associated with the stakeholder in relation to the need or problem that concerns us?
- How significant are the failures?

Table 10.1

Creating Public Value for Vital Aging

Sector	Businesses	Nonprofits	Governments	Media	Communities
Possible Contributions	Develop and market a good or service that meets a need of older adults and their families and offers a possibility of profit	Convene older adults and other stakeholders	Assure all older adults a basic level of income and health care	Cover business practices and government programs affecting older adults	Informally provide goods and services for older adults
	Provide choice among goods and services	Promote advocacy by and for older adults and their supporters	Assure tax dollars are spent wisely and benefit older adults	Attend to business and government failures to support older adults	Make intergenerational connections
	Attend to the needs of older workers, including flexible schedules, pension plans, retirement planning, and assisted work spaces	Develop and provide goods and services that are not profitable	Promote dignity and rights of older adults	Attend to vital agers, avoiding stereotypes about golf-mad retirees or dotty old folks	Convene neighbors to develop ideas and strategies for supporting older residents
	Contribute a portion of corporate profits and employee time to projects benefiting older adults—for example, helping communities become more senior friendly	Provide employment and volunteer opportunities	Promote intergenerational reciprocity and equity	Engage in citizen education about trends in aging and alerting them to needs and opportunities for beneficial change	Press businesses, government, and nonprofit organizations to support older adults

Sector	Businesses	Nonprofits	Governments	Media	Communities
		Provide faith-based services	Convene diverse stakeholders to address challenges of older adults	Provide a forum for citizens to express their views about aging issues	
		Provide charitable outlets	Sponsor basic research into aging and use research to inform decisions		
		Use flexible organizational forms and practices	Provide incentives or seed funds for community, business initiatives		
		Relate well to different cultures	Provide needed services or goods not otherwise provided		
Possible Failures	Gaps in provision of services and products for older adults; Harmful effects of production		Legislative gridlock; Bureaucratic delays and mismanagement	Journalists not interested in aging issues; Journalists have little time for in-depth investigation of business practices and government and nonprofit programs and simply rely on their cozy relations with elites for their information	Isolation of older adults; Lack of civic engagement around aging issues

	Business	Faith/Community	Government	Media
Public Harms Created	Misleading advertising	Inattention to some portion of the older population	Outmoded programs	Advertiser objections squelch coverage of controversial aging issues—e.g., rights of elderly gay couples
	Poor-quality products or services	A faith or ideological perspective that excludes some older adults	Inadequate regulation of businesses and nonprofits	Journalists foster aging stereotypes
	Discrimination against older workers	Exclusion of older adults from decision making	Violation of individual rights	
			Discrimination against particular groups of older adults	
			Lack of choice	
Public Value Created	Goods, services, and employment practices that enhance quality of life for older adults	Voice for diverse older adults	Social safety net for older adults	Citizens educated about vital aging and key public issues affecting older adults	Active culture of intergenerational connection and support
	Individual and collective wealth	Paid and unpaid work	Intergenerational equity	
	Supplementary goods and services that enhance quality of life for older adults and community	Religious tolerance and respect	Democratic decision making and accountability	
			Legal frameworks that foster wealth creation and older adults' rights	
	Charitable activity	Research base		
		Innovation stimulus		

Leaders can use this analysis to build a picture of which stakeholders in which sectors are already providing some elements of a regime of mutual gain. Additionally, the analysis can highlight barriers to establishing such a regime.

Such a sector-by-sector stakeholder analysis should help leaders and their constituents develop a more comprehensive problem formulation, and it should inform their search for solutions. The sector analysis should direct attention to solutions that continue, enhance, or expand the contributions of sectoral stakeholders and that mend their failures as much as possible. If the reformers can incorporate these multisector solutions into compelling visions for change, they should be able to build and sustain cross-sector coalitions to press for new policies and oversee their implementation. The vision should show clearly how an array of solutions will serve public values and add up to a regime of mutual gain—in other words, the common good.

Conclusions

Several conclusions flow from the analysis and discussion in this chapter. First, leaders interested in creating regimes of mutual gain should begin with at least a rough framework for thinking about how to use markets, governments, the voluntary sector, the news media, communities, and the public in general in order "to create problems that can be solved and are worth solving," as the late Aaron Wildavsky (1979) said. Useful typologies of the tools that each sector provides are available (Weimer and Vining 2005; Bryce 1999; Osborne and Plastrik 2000; Salamon 2002) and provide a valuable starting point. What is missing, however, is a fully developed theory of the substance and process of tool choice and governance for the common good. In other words, there is no fully developed theory of the "new governance," as Salamon (2002) refers to it. Said differently, we surely do live in a shared-power world, but too many people do not understand that, and those who do often are in need of an effective macro framework for thinking about change that leads to creating regimes of mutual gain.

Second, part of the leadership challenge is helping assure that tool choice and governance actually serve the common good. Recent work on consensus building (see, for example, Innes 1996; Susskind, McKearnan, and Thomas-Larmer 1999), collaboration and collaborative planning (Healey 1997, 2003; Chrislip 2002; Huxham and Vangen 2005), deliberative democracy (Barber 1984), and active citizenship (Boyte and Kari 1996; Boyte 2004) indicates that it is possible to achieve the common good, at least some of the time, by engaging diverse, interdependent, knowledgeable stakeholders from different sectors in order to address important issues where goals and solution strategies are not dictated in advance.

We have offered a way of thinking about addressing important public problems or needs in a shared-power world in which cross-sector collaboration and shared-power arrangements can provide promising solutions. Regimes of mutual gain must build on the strengths of each sector while avoiding its characteristic weaknesses and failures.

Leadership for the common good clearly involves constructing, maintaining, modifying, and terminating (when necessary) these regimes. But our final conclusion is that more research is needed to more fully understand leadership and the construction of regimes of mutual gain. We can hardly imagine more important work.

Note

Portions of this chapter are drawn from the authors' paper "Leadership and Collaborative Governance for Poverty Reduction in the Northwest Area" in the report of the Rural Poverty Project sponsored by the Northwest Area Foundation and published by the Humphrey Institute of Public Affairs, University of Minnesota, August 2005.

References

Barber, Benjamin. 1984. *Strong Democracy: Participatory Politics for a New Age.* Berkeley: University of California Press.

Barzelay, Michael. 1992. *Breaking Through Bureaucracy: A New Vision for Managing in Government.* Berkeley: University of California Press.

Becker, Ernest. 1997. *The Denial of Death.* New York: Free Press.

Booher, David E., and Judith E. Innes. 2002. "Network Power in Collaborative Planning." *Journal of Planning Education and Research* 21: 221–36.

Boyte, Harry C. 2004. *Everyday Politics: The Power of Public Work.* Philadelphia: University of Pennsylvania Press.

Boyte, Harry C., and Nancy N. Kari. 1996. *Building America: The Democratic Promise of Public Work.* Philadelphia: Temple University Press.

Bozeman, Barry. 2002. "Public-Value Failure: When Efficient Markets May Not Do." *Public Administration Review* 62 (2): 145–61.

Brandl, John E. 1998. *Money and Good Intentions Are Not Enough.* Washington, DC: Brookings Institution.

Bryce, Herrington J. 1999. *Financial and Strategic Management for Nonprofit Organizations.* 3rd ed. San Francisco: Jossey-Bass.

Bryson, John M. 2004. "What to Do When Stakeholders Matter: Stakeholder Identification and Analysis Techniques." *Public Management Review* 6 (1): 21–53.

Bryson, John M., and Barbara C. Crosby. 1992. *Leadership for the Common Good: Tackling Public Problems in a Shared-Power World.* San Francisco: Jossey-Bass.

Chrislip, David. D. 2002. *The Collaborative Leadership Fieldbook: A Guide for Citizens and Civic Leaders.* San Francisco: Jossey-Bass.

Crosby, Barbara C., and John M. Bryson. 2005a. *Leadership for the Common Good: Tackling Public Problems in a Shared-Power World.* 2nd ed. San Francisco: Jossey-Bass.

———. 2005b. "A Leadership Framework for Cross-Sector Collaboration." *Public Management Review* 7 (2): 177–201.

Edelman, Murray. 2001. *The Politics of Misinformation.* Cambridge: Cambridge University Press.

Frederickson, H. George. 1997. *The Spirit of Public Administration.* San Francisco: Jossey-Bass.

Friedmann, John. 1982. *The Good Society.* Cambridge, MA: MIT Press.

Grayling, A.C. 2003. *What Is Good? The Search for the Best Way to Live.* London: Weidenfeld & Nicholson.

Healey, Patsy. 1997. *Collaborative Planning: Shaping Places in Fragmented Societies.* London: MacMillan.

———. 2003. "Collaborative Planning in Perspective." *Planning Theory* 2 (2): 101–23.

Huxham, Chris, and Siv Vangen. 2005. *Managing to Collaborate: The Theory and Practice of Collaborative Advantage.* New York: Routledge.

Innes, Judith E. 1996. "Planning Through Consensus Building: A New View of the Comprehensive Planning Ideal." *Journal of the American Planning Association* 62: 460–72.

Light, Paul L. 2002. *Government's Greatest Achievements.* Washington, DC: Brookings Institution Press.

Luke, Jeffrey S. 1998. *Catalytic Leadership: Strategies for an Interconnected World.* San Francisco: Jossey-Bass.

Moore, Mark H. 1995. *Creating Public Value.* Cambridge, MA: Harvard University Press.

———. 2000. "Managing for Value: Organizational Strategy in For-Profit, Nonprofit, and Governmental Organizations." *Nonprofit and Voluntary Sector Quarterly* 29 (1): 183–204.

Nelson, Barbara J., Linda Kaboolian, and Kathryn A. Carver. 2004. *The Concord Handbook: How to Build Social Capital across Communities.* Los Angeles: UCLA School of Planning and Social Policy Research.

Osborne, David, and Peter Hutchinson. 2004. *The Price of Government: Getting the Results We Need in an Age of Permanent Fiscal Crisis.* New York: Basic Books.

Osborne, David, and Peter Plastrik. 1997. *Banishing Bureaucracy: The Five Strategies for Reinventing Government.* Reading, MA: Addison-Wesley.

———. 2000. *The Reinventor's Fieldbook: Tools for Transforming Your Government.* San Francisco: Jossey-Bass.

Putnam, Robert D. 2000. *Bowling Alone: The Collapse and Revival of American Community.* New York: Simon & Schuster.

Romzek, Barbara S. 1996. "Enhancing Accountability." In *Handbook of Public Administration,* ed. James L. Perry, 97–114. San Francisco: Jossey-Bass.

Salamon, Lester M. 1995. *Partners in Public Service: Government-Nonprofit Relations in the Modern Welfare State.* Baltimore: Johns Hopkins University Press.

———. 2002. *The Tools of Government: A Guide to the New Governance.* New York: Oxford University Press.

———. 2004. "The Changing Context of American Nonprofit Management." In *The Jossey-Bass Handbook of Nonprofit Leadership and Management.* 2nd ed. Ed. Robert D. Herman and Associates, 81–101. San Francisco: Jossey-Bass.

Schattschneider, E.E. 1975. *The Semisovereign People: A Realist's View of Democracy in America.* Hinsdale, IL: Dryden Press.

Schultze, Charles L. 1977. *The Public Use of Private Interest.* Washington, DC: Brookings Institution.

Scott, James C. 1998. *Seeing Like a State: How Certain Schemes to Improve the Human Condition Have Failed.* New Haven, CT: Yale University Press.

Stone, Deborah. 2001. *Policy Paradox: The Art of Political Decision Making.* Rev. ed. New York: W.W. Norton.

Susskind, Lawrence, and Jeffrey L. Cruikshank. 1987. *Breaking the Impasse: Consensual Approaches to Resolving Public Disputes.* New York: Basic Books.

Susskind, Lawrence, Sarah McKearnan, and Jennifer Thomas-Larmer, eds. 1999. *The Consensus Building Handbook: A Comprehensive Guide to Reaching Agreement.* Thousand Oaks, CA: Sage.

Weimer, David L., and Aidan R. Vining. 2005. *Policy Analysis: Concepts and Practice.* 4th ed. Upper Saddle River, NJ: Pearson Prentice Hall.

Wildavsky, Aaron. 1979. *Speaking Truth to Power: The Art and Craft of Policy Analysis.* Boston: Little, Brown.

11

Creating Public Value Using Managed Networks

What is public value?

The Nature of Public Value

> If it is to build public value in the emerging digital world, the BBC must combine bold new strategies with enduring values. It must keep faith with existing audiences and their expectations yet discover a new spirit of reform and re-invention. In many ways, the new era calls for a new BBC (BBC 2004, 7).

The quest for public value is not new. The founders of modern liberal democratic thought, Adam Smith, Thomas Hobbes, John Locke,[1] as well as the sources in antiquity, Socrates, Plato, Cicero,[2] all understood that the public's acceptance of the value of government was central to its legitimacy. Despite its antiquity, recent use of the concept has cast it in the broad tradition of public administration and as a successor or companion to the New Public Management.

The BBC quote at the beginning of this chapter is an interesting recognition that reform and reinvention require a careful monitoring of the support of current "audiences" while trying to chart a course of transformation. Measuring public value is a multivariate process somewhat analogous to the measurement of shareholder value in a public company.

The shareholder cares most about the price of a share of stock and the likely trend of that share price into the future. While share price is one measure, many other measures, both objective and subjective, influence share price: the trend of earnings, market share, the composition of the balance sheet, and the opinions and expectations of analysts (Graham and Dodd 2004). In the public sector, a balanced scorecard approach might be used to highlight the creation of public value. Figure 11.1 presents categories of metrics that allow managers to demonstrate to themselves and to the public that value is being created (DeSeve 1999).

Balanced Scorecard for Government

In each of the four quadrants, the metrics represented allow managers and the public to know how the jurisdiction is doing:

Figure 11.1   **Balanced Scorecard for Government**

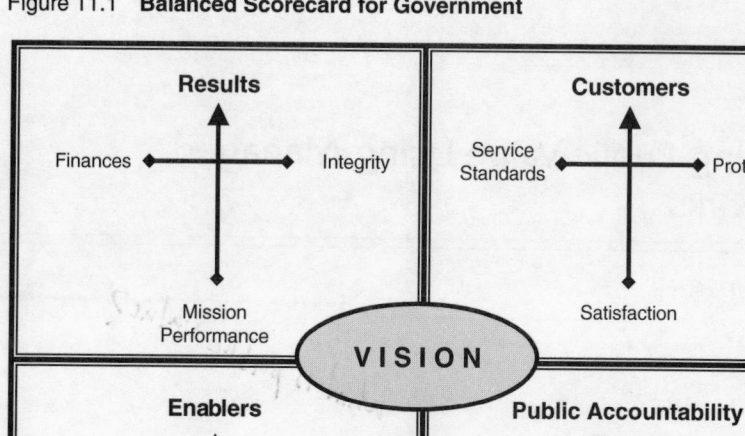

- Is government performing its mission in a cost-effective manner and without waste, fraud, and abuse?
- Are service standards being met and producing satisfied customers while protecting sometimes unwilling customers?
- Are the workforce and technological tools being used within the context of a modern learning organization that can adapt to challenges?
- Is the government able to develop and implement coherent policies and get needed legislation passed in a timely fashion? Does the public trust the government to do the right things and do them well?

While having data on all of these questions may be a demonstration of public value, the public's reaction and their assessment of the value of government is more difficult to measure. Still, this is why politicians spend enormous amounts of time assessing opinion polls.[3]

The Role of Leaders in Creating Public Value

With all the caveats regarding measurement, most political, legislative, and executive leaders would agree that creating public value is at the core of what they try to do. Further, they would agree that, in a democracy, creating public value is essential to getting elected and reelected. For example, individuals running for public office frequently go through a calculus weighing what polls tell them the public wants against the public's willingness to commit resources to achieve these ends. In crafting a campaign platform as well as in developing a legislative or executive program after election, the politician must continuously demonstrate positive public value. If the electorate does not agree that value has been produced or if the cost is too high, then the politician's continuation in office is in doubt. Newt Gingrich found this out after several government shutdowns resulted from his *Contract with America.* The public valued continuity of public services more highly than a set of abstract principles of smaller government. Finding the right balance is the essence of effective political leadership.

However, there are many different kinds of leaders, and we should describe what kind of leaders we are discussing. The answer is all kinds. The search for public value encompasses those who are "transactional" and those who are "transformational" (Burns 2004). Transactional leaders meet the needs of followers for tangible and intangible "products." They exchange public support for lower taxes or better roads or a feeling of safety. Transformational leaders have a desire to change the fundamental nature of the organization, process, service, or discussion that they are dealing with. The depth and scope of the change will transform an institution or a society. An example of a transformational leader is Mohandas Gandhi who transformed India from a backward British colony to the world's largest democracy.

For both types of leaders, the focus on public value is essential. In the case of the transactional leader, the nostrum that good government is good politics applies. In terms of good policies, good services, and good constituent service, the transactional public leader seeks to supply what the public values. We can remember the obsessive way in which former New York mayor Ed Koch would buttonhole his fellow New Yorkers and ask, "How 'm I doing?" He was seeking reassurance that he was creating public value.

A more subtle form of transactional exchange comes in the conduct of foreign affairs. George H. W. Bush dispatched Secretary of State James Baker on a tour of foreign capitals in 1991 to seek diplomatic and financial support for the Gulf War. Baker's success led, in part, to the tremendous public support that the Gulf War received. Arguably, George W. Bush's failure to "close the deal" with major European allies, such as Germany and France, helped lead to the public's ambivalence in supporting the current war in Iraq.

The role of public value in transformational efforts is less obvious. Often, transformational leaders are revolutionaries. Burns describes their efforts this way (2004, 198):

> Lacking the power of Caesar, insurgent leadership motivates followers with "symbolic and intangible inducements," addressing their grievances, appealing to transformational values, and offering prospects of deep change. The most potent

appeal to their wants and motivations is moral. Mohandas Gandhi, Martin Luther King, Jr., Nelson Mandela, Andrei Sakharov, and Vaclav Havel were all moral leaders, transforming their societies with the mobilizing powers of values.

This introduces an interesting tautology. Transformational leaders seek to change values. The reflection of their success in creating public value is the nature of the change they create and the long-term success of the government or society that has been changed.

Certainly, Mao Zedong was a transformational leader. He led the overthrow of the nationalist regime and helped create the communist state in China. Without detouring into the debate about good versus evil leaders, Chairman Mao was successful for a time, but the system he established lacked the coherence to meet public needs in a global world. His successors have focused on transactional approaches that create a stronger economy and more general prosperity.

By contrast, Nelson Mandela's South Africa continues along the transformational path that he championed. While there are difficulties in the government and the society, the nature of democracy for all is still the guidepost. The value the public places on democratic inclusion is much harder to measure. At some point, the public takes democratic principles such as universal fair elections as a given and values them only when they are taken away.

While values are clearly at the center of transformational leadership, Ronald Heifetz makes the case that all leadership is value-centric. "There is no neutral ground from which to construct notions and theories of leadership because leadership terms, loaded with emotional content, carry with them implicit norms and values" (Heifetz 1994, 14). So we make the case that leadership shapes public values even as it seeks to produce things that the public values.

Organizing to Create Public Value

Sun Tzu states, "Generally, management of many is the same as management of few. It is a matter of organization" (Sun Tzu 1988, 91). This was true in China more than 2,500 years ago, and it is true today. The question before each generation is, "What form of organization will be most successful given our circumstances and the challenges we face?"

Historic advances in both governance and management of government have come in response to challenges from the external social, economic, and political environment. From the American Revolution through the Articles of Confederation to the Constitution, the existence of external stimuli and internal struggles led the founding fathers to fight a revolution and form and reform a government, all in the space of a generation. At the turn of the century, American governments responded to increased immigration, urbanization, and corruption with an era of "Progressive" reforms featuring new regulations,[4] new tax structures,[5] and new forms of organization.[6]

In a famous quote uttered at the beginning of the New Deal, Franklin Roosevelt said, "The country needs and, unless I mistake its temper, the country demands bold, persistent experimentation. It is common sense to take a method and try it. If it fails, admit it frankly and try another" (Burns 2004, 22). The economic and social problems were clear. The need for new forms of organization from the Securities and Exchange Commission to the Social Security Administration to the Works Progress Administration was equally clear. It might be said that large bureaucracies established to carry out the programs of the New Deal, together with the military-industrial complex that grew up in response to World War II, were the defining features of government from 1932 until today.

Certainly, Thatcherism in Great Britain, privatization around the globe, the Reagan "Revolution," and the rise of the New Public Management (NPM) have all, in different ways, presented challenges to the large hierarchical public bureau as a model for government organization. However, when faced with a new challenge after 9/11, the response of Congress and ultimately of President Bush was to create a large hierarchical bureaucracy from twenty-two separate agencies. The Department of Homeland Security has become the second-largest agency in the federal government in terms of employees.

The hierarchical bureaucracy is so pervasive that to directly challenge it is probably counterproductive. Generations of public servants have grown up moving from one rung on the bureaucratic ladder to another in a continuing upward mobility toward more authority, more interesting work, and a greater ability to do the public's work.

But if the challenges facing the country during the American Revolution or the New Deal required new forms of organization, so do the challenges the nation and the world face today. The editors stated the issue well in the prospectus for this volume:

> The public sector is rapidly transforming as a result of events following September 11th and emerging trends in globalization, information technology, accountability, privatization, civil service re-engineering, politics, and governance. Our traditional notions about and effective practice of public leadership may no longer apply in an age of emergency or crisis, networked settings, or extreme politicization, conflict and polarization (Morse, Kinghorn, and Buss 2005).

These observations are buttressed by the work of the 9/11 Commission. As the Commission states, "We have been forced to think about the way our government is organized. The massive departments and agencies that prevailed in the great struggles of the twentieth century must work together in new ways, so that instruments of national power can be combined" (National Commission on Terrorist Attacks 2004, xvi). Managing the SARS outbreak around the globe and the response to Hurricane Katrina both demonstrate the need for new forms of organization to deal with the "wicked problems" we face.

There is a common thread to the response to these challenges: Leaders need to search for alternative forms of organization to meet them. The old bureaucratic structure is too rigid and slow to meet the spread of disease on a global basis or to coordinate a massive response to a natural disaster across organizational and jurisdictional boundaries. The old structure is too "stove piped" to respond to global terrorists moving across international boundaries. Hierarchical bureaucracies are organized in a way that minimizes the benefit of various technological breakthroughs. In short, "[t]he traditional, hierarchical model of government does not meet the demands of this complex and fast-changing age. Rigid bureaucratic systems, with their command and control procedures, narrow work restrictions, and siloed cultures and operational models, are particularly ill-suited to responding to problems that increasingly know no organizational boundaries" (Eggers and Goldsmith 2004, 5).

Still, there are paradoxes in adopting new forms. A recent conversation with a young upwardly mobile analyst at one of the hierarchical intelligence organizations brought home one of these paradoxes. When asked whether he would consider moving to the newly created National Counter Terrorism Center (NCTC) in the new Office of the Director of National Intelligence, he expressed concern that such a move would be a career black hole. He would lose standing in his home organization with no assurance that there would be a better job for him in the future at NCTC. Additional difficulty comes with trying to design budgetary systems for organizations that are not hierarchical. Who controls the resources and who decides how to apply them?

Despite these paradoxes, new tools for organization are being developed and deployed. It would be a mistake to think of these tools as a replacement for the hierarchical structure. Rather, they are "tools of government" that can be used by multiple hierarchies simultaneously to address the challenges that leaders face (Salamon 2002). Just as the founding fathers, the "Progressives," and the "New Dealers" invented new tools to make organizations more effective, so too must the leaders of today develop and deploy such tools.

As Heifetz suggests, the primary function of leadership is to recognize those adaptive situations that can produce true solutions to problems that are not just technical in nature, but which represent a real shift in how a nation or a culture approaches the challenge. "Over the course of history, we have successfully faced an array of adaptive challenges by developing new knowledge and organizations with new norms. Now that we have them, many of our problems have become routine" (Heifetz 1994, 72). For leaders to provide public value in meeting today's challenges, they need to find the appropriate "knowledge and organization" that will be the tools for the beginning of this century.

The Managed Public Value Network (PVN)

Governing by network represents a fundamental transformation in how governments fulfill policy goals and deliver services. While certain aspects of this phenomenon have been previously discussed, a roadmap for actually governing the networked state has yet to be crafted (Eggers and Goldsmith 2004, 9).

What would a "roadmap" look like and who would draw it? The hypothesis presented is that it would be possible to create a Managed Network to produce public value. The PVN is a tool that multiple organizations can use simultaneously to fulfill their missions, set standards, exchange information, or enhance the skills of the participants. The following sections describe work in progress to assess both the Types of PVNs that may exist and the Elements that are important to each Type. This is accomplished by developing case studies around a research tool. Work is at an early stage, and we welcome additional participants in the effort as well as constructive emendation.

Assembling the rudiments of the roadmap and suggesting a method for drawing it are presented in the following ways:

- The term *Managed Network* is defined and its relation to the creation of public value is discussed.
- A specific Type of Managed Network, the Public Value Network (PVN), is created as the central focus of this chapter.
- A Typology of PVNs is created as an analytic framework for the roadmap.
- A hypothesis is developed regarding the Elements that are critical to creating and sustaining a PVN.
- The role of leadership is described as the critical element that must orchestrate all of the other Elements.
- Three case studies are presented along with a preliminary research methodology and a tool used to validate the Typology and establish the importance of the Elements.

Defining Public Value

In our view, public value refers to the level of social and economic outcome achieved by government departments and agencies in return for monies received from the wider public in the form of taxes and charges (Accenture 2004, 3).

Public Value can be defined as the demonstrated preference of the public for a product, service, process or outcome that fills a perceived need (DeSeve 2005, 1).

These two definitions present complementary perspectives on the nature of public value. The first looks at the production of public value and the cost of production. The second looks at the public demand for a particular good or service and the acceptance of the activities taken to meet the perceived need.

In fact, there is a "third way" to think about public value by combining the two perspectives. A common definition might be:

Public Value constitutes the demonstrated level of social and economic outcome achieved by government that clearly fulfills the public's demonstrated preference for a good or service efficiently and economically.

This definition allows us to pose a series of questions that must be answered to determine if public value is being provided:

- How has the public demonstrated a preference for a particular activity?
- How has the agency defined successful accomplishment of this activity?
- How are costs measured in relationship to achievement?
- How do we know that the public agrees that the outcome has been achieved and meets their expectation?

Each of these questions leads to a measurement scheme that must be undertaken continuously with the best available information to guide program choices and the expenditure of funds. In all cases, there will be:

- uncertainty about the preferences and acceptance of the public,
- problems with allocation techniques, and
- structural issues relating to process fairness, measurement, and integrity.

Despite these uncertainties and problems, the quest for public value should be the central organizing principle of government. An old adage suggests that "perfect is the enemy of the good," and this applies in the search to create public value. Continuous improvement in measurement, cost accounting, public opinion research, and processes of budgeting and program evaluation can all contribute to the creation of public value. Critical among these is the role of leadership from the executive and legislative arms of government.

While this leadership is often exercised through single departments, agencies, or bureaus, increasingly a network that spans intra- and intergovernmental boundaries and also reaches across sectors is necessary to meet a challenge or accomplish a mission. The recent response to Hurricane Katrina highlighted the failure of government to operate in a networked fashion. The networks described here are not natural networks or social networks. Rather they are consciously constructed entities designed to function toward a common purpose. A description of the nature of these Managed Networks follows.

What Is a Managed Network?

Technicians have no trouble defining what constitutes a managed computer network. It is the result of linking hardware and software to accomplish a particular purpose, such as communication or computation. The problem gets more difficult when we realize that some Managed Networks tend to be scale free and resist boundaries that managers impose. The Internet is a classic example of a Managed Network that is open and continually growing. Still, there are elemental rules and protocols that bring order to the seeming chaos (Barabasi 2002).

When we extend the concept of a Managed Network outside the realm of pure technology, we find ourselves looking at many different kinds of networks. For example, Eggers and Goldsmith (2004) describe the diversity of networks in government management as coming "in many forms, from ad hoc networks that are activated only intermittently—often in response to a disaster—to channel partnerships in which governments use private firms and non-profits to serve as distribution channels for public services and transactions" (11).

For our purposes, we will define a Managed Network as follows:

> An integrated system of relationships that is managed across formal and informal organizational boundaries with recognized organizational principles and a clear definition of success.

Clearly excluded are social networks or natural networks that cannot be guided toward achieving a purpose (Capra 2002).[7] These networks may lack one or both of the factors examined here: purpose or conscious direction to that purpose. This is not to suggest that social networks cannot be used as part of a Managed Network. Conjoining a social network to a Managed Network can produce important results. Networks are not necessarily a replacement for traditional hierarchical organizations. They can be used as tools to achieve some or all of the purposes of traditional organizations, but experience indicates that most organizations require some form of hierarchy to reassure participants and stakeholders of their roles.

Defining Public Value Networks

The diversity of potential types and the purposes for which Managed Networks have been used are great. To narrow the scope of these networks, we have organized them around the purpose of providing "Public Value." Since Managed Networks often comprise entities inside and outside government, we call them Public Value Networks (PVN). The concept of a value network is not new. In the private sector, Verna Allee defined value networks as "a web of relationships that generates economic value and other benefits through complex dynamic exchanges between two or more individuals, groups or organizations" (2002, 9). The difference between Allee's definition and one used recently by the author lies primarily in removing the term *economic* and substituting the term *public* (DeSeve 2004).

Thus, the definition of a PVN is as follows:

> An integrated system of relationships that is managed across formal and informal organizational boundaries and sectors with recognized organizational principles and a clear definition of success in terms of Public Value realized.

The definition explicitly recognizes the role that the private sector plays as both a participant and often a leader in PVNs. In the next examples, private-sector network participants, from consulting firms to defense contractors, form important nodes in the network both as "contractors" to the public sector and as independent direct providers of goods and services.

But focusing just on the private sector or on the private sector as a provider/contractor is to miss the broader and richer context of PVNs. Often they are designed to solve the most complicated problems that societies face. Prime Minister Tony Blair observed, "Even the basic policies targeted at unemployment, poor skills, low incomes, poor housing, high crime, bad health and family breakdown will not deliver their full effect unless they are properly joined up. Joined up problems need joined up solutions" (quoted in Skidmore 2004, 92). This is the essence of PVNs: the conscious search for a solution to one or more problems across multiple boundaries.

A Partial Typology of Public Value Networks

The list of PVNs contained and described in this section is only a starting point. During our continuing research, we anticipate adding to the list or combining various types of PVNs. These groupings are a tool to determine if the critical factors discussed next are common to multiple types of PVNs.[8] Several types of PVNs have been identified previously. Eight examples follow with appropriate references:

- *Communities of Shared Mission:* "A networked collection of actors from the public, private, nonprofit, and/or civic sectors working to achieve a common purpose" (Center for Public Policy & Private Enterprise 2004).
- *Communities of Shared Practice:* Groups of individuals organized around common interests or expertise (Wenger 1999).
- *Issue Response Networks:* An example is the Laboratory Response Network of the Centers for Disease Control and Prevention whose mission is to "respond quickly to acts of chemical or biological terrorism, emerging infectious diseases, and other public health threats and emergencies."[9]
- *Strategic Alliances:* "Strategic alliances can have a variety of mandates. They can be designed to work at the operational (program delivery) level; to conduct a major research program that requires the resources, information, and expertise of more than one group; and/or to function at the advocacy (public relations) level. Under the right circumstances and when the synergies are obvious, strategic alliances in the business world, and perhaps among consumer groups in the future, could lead to more permanent arrangements such as joint ventures or a full merger."[10]
- *Joined-Up Government:* "We want to ensure that relevant citizen's services are better coordinated (joined up). Somebody with a problem should not have to visit or telephone several government offices to find a solution. Good examples of joined-up government are one-stop benefit or housing shops that are being introduced in many high-streets."[11]
- *Service Integration:* "Promote coordinated responses to persons most at risk" (Agranoff 1991, 535).
- *Customer/Vendor:* An example is the United Space Alliance (USA) whose

mission is to manage and conduct "space operations work involving the operation and maintenance of multi-purpose space systems, including systems associated with NASA's human space flight program, Space Shuttle applications beyond those of NASA, and other reusable launch and orbital systems beyond the Space Shuttle and Space Station."[12]

- *Intraorganizational:* Involves the use of Managed Networks within an organization, but including suppliers as a Critical Element in planning and execution.[13]

It is possible, as Agranoff (2003) suggests, to create a more compact Typology including four network categories: action, developmental, informational, and outreach. There are undoubtedly many more Typologies, depending on the point of view of the research being conducted. It may be possible to shrink the number even further. This research may suggest a broader framework for several of the Types described earlier. For the purposes of beginning the research, we will limit ourselves to the eight listed here. As noted earlier, this number may expand or contract as results inform our thinking (Agranoff 2003).

Critical Elements

Again for analytic purposes, the following Critical Elements[14] to the success of PVNs are proposed for examination:

- *Networked Structure:* Nodes and links that are joined together to represent the physical Elements of the PVN.
- *Commitment to a Common Purpose:* Reason for the PVN to exist; caring or commitment to achieving positive results.
- *Trust among the Participants:* Based on either professional or "social" relationships, the participants believe that they can rely on the information or effort of others in the network to achieve the common purpose.
- *Governance:*
  - *Boundary and Exclusivity:* Some definition of who is and who is not a member.
  - *Rules:* Some limits on community member behavior, with a threat of ejection for misbehavior.
  - *Self-determination:* The freedom to decide how the PVN will be operated and who will be admitted to membership.
  - *Network Management:* Resolution of disputes, allocation of resources, quality control, and organizational maintenance.
- *Access to Authority:* The availability of definitive standard-setting procedures that are broadly accepted.
- *Leadership:* Individuals or groups willing to serve as a "champion" for the PVN and guide its work toward results.

- *Distributive Accountability/Responsibility:* Sharing the governance and some decision making across members of the PVN and thus the responsibility for achieving desired results.
- *Information Sharing:* Easy access for members, privacy protection, and restricted access for non-members if appropriate.
- *Access to Resources:* Availability of financial, technical, human, and other resources needed to meet the objectives of the PVN.

The Relevance of Leadership Models to PVNs

One of the most important models in leadership studies was created and articulated by Burns. Burns (1978) distinguishes between two types of leadership as follows:

> *Transactional leadership:* When "leaders approach followers with an eye to exchanging one thing for another. . . . Such transactions comprise the bulk of the relationships among leaders and followers" (4). *Transformational leadership:* When a leader "looks for potential motives in followers, seeks to satisfy higher needs, and engages the full person of the follower. The result . . . is a relationship of mutual stimulation and elevation that converts followers into leaders and may convert leaders into moral agents" (4).

For purposes of this research, I assume that both transactional and transformational motives exist in PVNs and that the degree of these motives is informed by the type of PVN. For example, a community of shared mission may be more transformational in the nature of its leadership while a strategic alliance may be more transactional. A key question is, "What is the weight of each type of leadership in each type of PVN and what effect does the type of leadership have on the success of the PVN?"

Case Studies

One of the best ways to study the importance of the Typologies and Critical Elements described earlier is to look at case studies where networks have been successfully applied. Three case studies were developed from interviews with participants in the various efforts. There are two primary purposes for the case studies. First, they demonstrate that Managed Networks can be invoked in many different circumstances. Second, they provide a framework for managers to evaluate how they might use Managed Networks in their own work. Figure 11.2 summarizes the results of structured interviews using a research tool[15] developed by the author and his colleagues at the University of Maryland.

1. Savannah Youth Futures Authority

In the mid- to late 1980s, a grim picture on the condition of Savannah's youth was presented to city leadership: Twenty percent of all middle and high school stu-

Figure 11.2 **Summary of Case Studies: Public Value Network Summary Table**

	Savannah Youth Futures Authority	Year 2000 Computer Crisis	D.C. CASH Campaign
Type of PVN	COSM	Issue Response/COSM	COSM
Tightness	Medium	Low	High
Clear purpose	Yes	Yes	Yes
Boundary and exclusivity	High	Low	High
Self-determination	Low—now high	High	Low
Network management	Yes—YFA	Shared with sectors	Yes—CSO
Authority	Medium	Low	Low
Leadership	Effective	President	Effective
Distributed accountability/responsibility	Yes	Yes	Yes
Summary	Successful	Successful	Successful

Source: Developed by William Lucyshyn, Research Director, Center for Public Policy and Private Enterprise, University of Maryland, School of Public Policy. Used with permission.

dents failed each year; unemployment among white and black youth aged sixteen to nineteen was 15 percent and 26 percent, respectively; and teenage pregnancy was at 85 percent for black women aged ten to nineteen and 55 percent for white women of the same age.

To remedy this problem, Savannah applied for and won a grant from the Annie E. Casey Foundation. Casey's support catalyzed the new collaborative approach called the Youth Futures Authority (YFA), a networked collection of actors from the public, private, nonprofit, and civic sectors. YFA helps communities craft their own solutions to improving the effectiveness of and harmonization among entities working with communities, families, and youth.

YFA is a network of local "movers and shakers" and includes the "usual suspects," such as local businesses and public and private social service agencies. Businesses are concerned about labor shortages due to a lack of employable youth and crime and its effect on tourism revenues. Ever since the first YFA meeting, twenty-five to forty of the approximately fifty collaborative members have continued to meet every second Tuesday of the month.

2. The Year 2000 Computer Crisis (Y2K)

Leading up to the millennium, engineers and computer users realized that both hardware and software were based on a date convention that did not necessarily contemplate the existence of the year 2000. Everything from bank ATMs to air traffic control systems were at risk of failure.

President William Clinton was acutely aware of the problem, and on February 4, 1998, issued an Executive Order creating a Council on the Year 2000 to coordinate efforts to solve the problem. While the initial focus of the council was to ensure that federal agencies would be ready, it quickly became apparent that the problem was much broader in the private sector, domestically and internationally.

John Koskinen, special assistant to the president, headed the council. He structured the council to feature a very small staff component, never more than ten individuals, relying on a network of sector councils headed by individuals with great knowledge of their industries or functions. Thus, those with a critical stake in solving the problem for the financial services industry or the aviation industry or the electric power industry were in charge of developing plans for solving the problem. At the federal level, Koskinen relied on the White House Office of Management and Budget (OMB) to coordinate the plans of federal agencies and to allocate the funds necessary for the plans.

3. D.C. CASH Campaign

The D.C. CASH Campaign was established to provide low- and moderate-income residents free tax preparation assistance, taxpayer education, and access to programs and services that increase income and savings. The program was founded in 2002 by a group of nonprofit agencies in the District of Columbia's Ward 7,[16] along with a grant from the Annie E. Casey Foundation. In 2004, the D.C. CASH Campaign expanded its program to both Ward 5 and Ward 8. The D.C. CASH Campaign received continued support from the Casey Foundation, along with additional support from the CityBridge Foundation, Fannie Mae Foundation, and Kimsey Foundation.

The D.C. CASH Campaign works year-round to increase income, savings, and asset-building opportunities for low- and moderate-income workers, but their work is most visible during the tax season. In 2004, the D.C. CASH Campaign assisted 936 taxpayers with the preparation of their tax returns.

Differences among the organizations studied are much greater than their similarities. The D.C. CASH Campaign is a small neighborhood-based effort, the Youth Futures Authority (YFA) in Savannah covers a broader set of neighborhoods within a community, and Y2K is international in scope. For each, the "mission" was clearly understood and was the organizing factor for the organization. Y2K was designed to be a loose confederation of sectors reflecting the distributed nature of the challenge as well as the legal barriers to common action. By contrast, the D.C. CASH Campaign was a very tight organizational unit built around a single nonprofit.

In none of the organizations was there direct inherent authority. In the case of Y2K, the director had to leverage an Executive Order of the president to federal agencies into a platform that could create an international network. While there was appropriations legislation in support of Y2K for federal agencies, the distribution of these funds was controlled by the regular budget mechanism, not the Y2K Council.

In the case of Savannah's Youth Futures Authority, various state agencies brought their own authority to the table, but it was not vested in YFA. Effective leadership and distributed accountability were present in all of the organizations.

While three case studies do not create a base for inference, they are illustrative in viewing the use of Managed Networks to create public value. The author is happy to make available detailed results on these case studies and copies of the research tool in the hopes that the development of more case studies will yield valuable results.

Summary and Conclusions

Complicated public problems require solutions that go beyond organizational and sectoral boundaries. The conscious creation of Managed Networks designed to create public value give managers—public or private—a new set of tools in executing their responsibilities.

Managed Networks are not designed to replace hierarchies. Rather they are to assist hierarchies in linking resources with other entities in solving a problem, delivering a service, communicating information, or setting standards. However, it is important to recognize that the creation of Managed Networks can be an integral part of a manager's job, not just something that is done as a peripheral assignment.

To be able to invoke Managed Networks, it is helpful to define the Types of these networks and to describe the Elements that go into creating them. Further research is needed to determine if the Typology presented here is both comprehensive and valuable and if the Critical Elements described are essential to each type of network. For example, is the availability of authority critical in something like "joined-up" government?

The author and his colleagues at the University of Maryland recognize that this is an evolving field. We encourage researchers to develop alternative views of how networks are created and sustained. Particularly useful would be the joining of work in social networks with the ideas presented here on Managed Networks. How do we use social networks as a means of furthering government purpose? Examples such as neighborhood watch programs are clear cases in which community groups evolved a social network into an organizational structure to assist public safety officials. How can this be extended into the areas of health care, recreation, and so on in a consciously managed way? That is a key question for further research.

Networks will become more important as the speed and availability of communication increase. They will also become more important as the scope and complexity of problems increase. The Centers for Disease Control have already created a Global Public Health Information Network to track the spread of diseases such as SARS and avian flu. This model and others like it should be studied to give managers clear principles that demonstrate how networks can help them. This chapter helps provide a basis for that study.

Notes

1. John Locke's definition of political power provides a classic framing of the constitutional nature of public value: "Political Power is that power which every man having in the state of nature, has given up into the hands of society, and therein to the governors whom the society hath set over itself, with this express or tacit trust that it shall be employed for their good and the preservation of their property" (John Locke, *Of Civil Government Second Treatise,* 1689).

2. The ancient Greeks had a very direct way of expressing their view on the public value provided by those in power: "The procedure, to give a general account of it, was as follows. Each voter took an ostrakon or piece of earthenware, wrote on it the name of the citizen he wished to be banished and carried it to a part of the market-place which was fenced off with a circular paling. Then the archons first counted the total number of votes cast, for if there were less than six thousand, the ostracism was void. After this they sorted the votes and the man who had the most recorded after his name was proclaimed to be exiled for ten years, with the right, however, to receive the income from his estate" (from Plutarch's *The Rise and Fall of Athens,* commenting on the ostracizing of Aristides the Just, the chief financial officer of Athens).

3. An interesting collection of opinions on what matters to the public about government is available from Public Agenda, a New York–based nonprofit opinion research and civic engagement organization. See www.publicagenda.org. (Accessed 28 August 2006.)

4. The Sherman Antitrust Act, the Federal Trade Commission, and the Interstate Commerce Commission are all examples of regulatory frameworks enacted during this period.

5. The income tax is the most prominent of these.

6. The council-manager form of local government was born in this era.

7. For a more complete description of various kinds of networks see Fritjof Capra, *The Hidden Connections* (2002).

8. Professor Ernest Wilson suggests that research be conducted on the types of PVNs to ascertain in what situation a particular type would be used. For example, if the primary attribute required were speed, inclusiveness, or fairness, which type would be used? This is an intriguing question that we hope to address in future publications.

9. See www.bt.cdc.gov/lrn/. (Accessed 28 August 2006.)

10. See http://strategis.ic.gc.ca/epic/internet/inoca-bc.nsf/en/ca00396e.html. (Accessed 28 August 2006.)

11. See http://archive.cabinetoffice.gov.uk/moderngov/help/faqs.htm. (Accessed 28 August 2006.)

12. See www.unitedspacealliance.com/about/. (Accessed 28 August 2006.)

13. At a recent meeting with members of several directorates and centers from the National Institutes of Health, a description of the laundry allocation process within the care center appeared to be an excellent example of an intraorganizational network.

14. Drawn from work performed under the sponsorship of Booz Allen Hamilton by the Center for Public Policy and Private Enterprise at the University of Maryland School of Public Policy.

15. The very nature of public networked organizations precludes the use of publicly available databases in this study. Accordingly, it is necessary to collect the data directly from the network members. The approach taken, in this regard, was to conduct questionnaire-based interviews with representatives from the various members of three PVNs. Each of the case studies discussed was completed by a single individual using the research tool questionnaire developed by the author and his colleagues, which is available upon request. The judgments in the case studies were based on interviews or actual experience as deemed appropriate by the analyst. The majority of the questionnaire consists of questions that are answered on a

five-point Likert scale, so that quantitative analysis can be conducted on the data collected. However, the questionnaire also includes some open-ended questions so as to provide a more complete understanding of the participants' responses.

The goal is to make the research tool available to a wider audience. This can be accomplished using standard surveying techniques, or possibly a more innovative approach: making the instrument available on the Internet, to solicit many individuals involved in PVNs to perform the analysis and provide clear comments. This method, although somewhat unconventional, is similar to the creation of the *Oxford English Dictionary* (*OED*) in the late nineteenth and early twentieth centuries. In the case of the *OED*, volunteers could select a period of history from which to read books. These books would come from their own libraries or be supplied by the *OED*. The volunteers' duties are described as follows:

> They would write to the society offering their services in reading certain books; they would be asked to read and make word lists of all that they read, and would then be asked to look super-specifically for certain words that currently interested the dictionary team. Each volunteer would take a slip of paper, write at its top left-hand side the target word, and below, also on the left, the date of the details that followed: These were, in order, the title of the book or paper, its volume and page number, and then below that, the full sentence that illustrated the use of the target word (Winchester 1998, 108).

Contributions from these volunteers were then edited and compiled for review by the primary editor and finally selected for inclusion in the *OED*.

The search for Types and the importance of Elements in PVNs is in its very early stages as Eggers and Goldsmith (2004) noted earlier. The development of the research design is the next task in the process of developing the roadmap.

16. Ward 7 is predominately lower income and African American with a high rate of unemployment. See www.neighborhoodinfodc.org/wards/nbr_prof_wrd7.html. (Accessed 28 August 2006.)

References

Accenture. 2004. *The Accenture Public Sector Value Model*. White Paper. December, www. issa.int/pdf/cracow04/2Annex-Younger.pdf (Accessed 28 August 2006.)

Agranoff, Robert. 1991. "Human Services Integration: Past and Present Challenges in Public Administration." *Public Administration Review* 51 (6): 533–42.

———. 2003. "Is Managing Within Intergovernmental Networks Changing the Boundaries of Government?: A Preliminary Report." Paper presented for Second Annual Founders Forum, American Society for Public Administration 64th Annual National Conference, Washington, DC, March.

Allee, Verna. 2002. *A Value Network Approach for Modeling and Measuring Intangibles*. White Paper. Madrid: Transparent Enterprise. November. www.vernaallee.com/value_networks/A_ValueNetworkApproach_white_paper.pdf. (Accessed 28 August 2006.)

Barabasi, Albert-Lazlo. 2002. *Linked: The New Science of Networks*. Cambridge, MA: Perseus Books Group.

British Broadcasting Corporation (BBC). 2004. *Building Public Value: Renewing the BBC for a Digital World*. London. www.bbc.co.uk/thefuture/pdfs/bbc_bpv.pdf. (Accessed 28 August 2006.)

Burns, James MacGregor. 1978. *Leadership*. New York: Harper & Row.

———. 2004. *Transforming Leadership: A New Pursuit of Happiness*. New York: Grove Press.

Capra, Fritjof. 2002. *The Hidden Connections*. New York: Harper Collins.

Center for Public Policy and Private Enterprise. 2004. "Program Update and Savannah Case Study." Presentation to Booze Allen Hamilton, College Park, MD: University of Maryland, 22 December.

DeSeve, G. Edward. 1999. *Balanced Scorecard for Government.* Cambridge, MA: Harvard University, John F. Kennedy School of Government, Executive Session on Performance (November).

———. 2004. "Public Value Networks." Presentation given at National Institutes of Health, 27 October.

———. 2005. "Public Value Networks." Presentation given at Brookings Institution, 13 September.

Eggers, William D., and Stephen Goldsmith. 2004. *Governing by Network: The New Shape of Government.* Washington, DC: Brookings Institution Press.

Graham, Benjamin, and David L. Dodd. 2004. *Security Analysis: The Classic 1934 Edition.* New York: McGraw Hill.

Heifetz, Ronald A. 1994. *Leadership without Easy Answers.* Cambridge, MA: Harvard University Press.

Moore, Mark. 1995. *Creating Public Value.* Cambridge, MA: Harvard University Press.

Morse, Ricardo S., C. Morgan Kinghorn, and Terry F. Buss. 2005. Prospectus and call for papers received by author, July.

National Commission on Terrorist Attacks. 2004. *The 9/11 Commission Report: Final Report of the National Commission on Terrorist Attacks Upon the United States.* New York: W.W. Norton.

Salamon, Lester. 2002. *The Tools of Government: A Guide to the New Governance.* Oxford: Oxford University Press.

Skidmore, Paul. 2004. "Leading Between." In *Network Logic—Who Governs in an Interconnected World?* eds. Helen McCarthy, Paul Miller, and Paul Skidmore, 89–102. New York: Demos.

Sun Tzu. 1988. *The Art of War.* Trans. Samuel B. Griffith. Oxford: Oxford University Press.

Wenger, Etienne. 1999. *Communities of Practice: Learning, Meaning, and Identity.* Cambridge: Cambridge University Press.

Winchester, Simon. 1998. *The Professor and the Madman.* New York: Harper Collins.

12

Consensus Building and Leadership

John B. Stephens

There appears to be a consensus on consensus building in public administration: We are for it. Consensus building is an important skill for managers and leaders in terms of responsiveness, participation, managing in an age of diffuse power centers, and building more durable outcomes. This chapter pushes beneath this comfortable degree of agreement to critique what is known about consensus building, identifies issues on leadership from inside and outside of consensus-building processes, and proposes essential questions for leadership research to bridge the gap between practice and theory on consensus building.

Public leadership can be conceived as a process that occurs at all levels of an organization and between public-service entities. Clearly, consensus building is a decision-making process. However, my focus is primarily on leadership defined as positions of authority or power within an organization. The reason for this focus is that formal consensus building is not a legal standard or common practice in the public sector; majority rule by a board or managerial direction by an individual is practiced far more widely. Thus, this chapter examines consensus building as a choice leaders have within their discretion.

Another reason for examination of consensus building and leadership speaks to the needs of consensus-building advocates and practitioners. Whereas this audience has emphasized assessment of a situation by potential consensus-building organizers prior to starting such a process, there is value for consensus-building proponents to focus more on the role of leaders and leadership in initiating and guiding those processes. The convening dimension of leadership (Carlson and Wolf 2005) and contrasting duties of managers and leaders within consensus-building processes (Wondolleck and Ryan 1999) will be examined.

The range of books, articles, and practitioner guides about the value of and need for building consensus is prodigious.[1] Consensus decisions are promoted for resolving public issues, creating interorganizational cooperation for programs and services, and gaining team buy-in for innovation and change within an organization. There are even organizations such as the Montana Consensus Council, the Consensus Council, Inc. (serving North Dakota), and the Policy Consensus Initiative/National Policy Consensus Center.[2]

Inadequate attention has been paid to key questions about leadership in relation to seeking consensus. First, what are the trade-offs on using consensus building versus other methods for engaging stakeholders, building support, and reaching a decision that will be implemented? While advocates rightly focus on the incentives of consensus building for finding creative alternatives and gaining buy-in for easier implementation, there are concerns about negotiating away principles, compromising scientific expertise, and reaching only lowest-common-denominator outcomes.

Second, is consensus building an option among other forms of decision making and agreement seeking, or should it be embraced as a change of paradigm? Leaders must make or guide numerous decisions. Is consensus building more of a philosophical value, or simply an option that requires diagnosis for appropriate use? This question leads to the examination of assessment, design, and evaluation of consensus building: How can we distinguish between a well-designed and well-implemented consensus-building process and group think (Janis 1982)? Finally, at the extreme, consensus building can be seen as "anti-leader." If the ultimate decision depends on consensus, and every participant is equal in power to give or withhold assent, what does this mean for leaders who have authority to direct people, resources, and outcomes?

This chapter addresses consensus building and leadership in seven ways:

1. Identifies the importance of consensus building to leadership.
2. Defines consensus building and its connection to collaboration.
3. Presents criticisms of consensus building.
4. Offers guidance for consensus-building processes.
5. Probes selected difficulties in understanding and implementing consensus building in terms of leadership.
6. Proposes areas of research on consensus building and leadership.
7. Makes recommendations for consensus-building practice.

How one determines the relevant literature for consensus building and leadership is critical. I offer two notes in this regard. First, I draw from traditional public administration sources and from the field of conflict resolution. This latter field, in terms of public policy, has its own journals, professional associations, and touchstone books. There has been relatively little overlap of conflict resolution and public administration scholars and publications (Bingham, Nabatchi, and O'Leary 2005). Second, there are related works on collaborative leadership (Chrislip and Larsen 1994; Chrislip 2002), citizen participation and performance management (Epstein, Coates, and Wray 2006), and public deliberation (Roberts 1997). Some portions of these works are relevant to the narrower focus on consensus building.

My interest is analyzing models of consensus building in terms of practical "fieldwork." Thus, I draw on documents created to guide public officials in consensus-building processes. For example, *A Practical Guide to Consensus* (Arthur,

Carlson, and Moore 1999) addresses government officials contemplating consensus building and offers specific guidance on assessment, preparation, and conduct of a consensus process. On the other end of the guidebook spectrum, *The Consensus Building Handbook,* (Susskind, McKearnan, and Thomas-Larmer 1999) at over 1,100 pages, is "meant as a reference, like an encyclopedia" (xxii), and yet also for use by a wide audience, opening with a sleek fifty-page "short guide" to consensus building (3–57). My point is to draw from the interdisciplinary conflict-resolution field, as well as prominent public administration sources in addressing public leadership matters on consensus building.

Why Consensus Building?

There has been a torrent of reasons for why consensus building is becoming more important. One analysis of political power and culture sees the growing reach of government, the diffusion of power away from political parties and to many different political actors, the judicial dynamics on public policy issues, and the heightened attention to complexity and interrelatedness of social problems as leading factors for seeking more cooperative approaches to issues (Dukes 1996). These themes are shared by other authors (Booher 2004; Kelman 1992; Crosby and Bryson 2005). In the face of divided power, interconnected policy areas, and a demand for ways to promote creative and inclusive decisions, consensus building fits the bill.

Similarly, in broad brush, many entities are moving (or have moved) from hierarchical decision making to more team-oriented organizational structures that promote networked or webbed modes of decision making. Employees' views are valued, and their buy-in on decisions is even more important. Thus, seeking consensus fits the "flatter" structure and culture of many public organizations (Saint and Lawson 1994).

Turning to the public administration literature, one long-standing and several recent offerings stand out. Recently, Frederickson (2005), in his analysis of the transjurisdictional challenges that public administrators face, identifies shared power and the need for cooperation as the new model of governance for local government leaders. "Because cities and counties share their power in both horizontal and vertical directions, the ways in which they are led will be more collegial, consensual and consultative" (2005, 13–14).

A second recent contribution examines the context of new, innovative ways for civic engagement and the challenges for the roles and skills of public administrators. Bingham, Nabatchi, and O'Leary (2005) identify "collaborative policy making" as one of the areas of practice leading theory in citizen participation and the "new governance." Analogous skills that public administrators must acquire or improve include "conflict assessment, negotiation, active listening and reframing, facilitation and consensus building" (548).

Similar to Bingham, Nabatchi, and O'Leary, the "new public service" is framed, in part, in consensus-building terms. Denhardt and Denhardt (2003) first draw on John Gardner's vision of civil society where a framework of shared purpose and a collective direction and purpose contain disparate interests and needs. Then, the authors present a vision of "seeking the public interest" that relies on the creation of shared interests and shared responsibility. Moreover, they argue against simply seeking compromises among pluralist competitors, and they embrace public interests based on shared values as a consensualist framework. Finally, drawing from several sources, part of what constitutes the new public service, according to Denhardt and Denhardt, is for public servants to help citizens articulate and build a consensus on a shared public interest.

From the practitioner's level of the public administration literature, one report offers guidance on citizen engagement (and contrasts it with citizen participation). [Editors' note: Issues of citizen participation are analyzed in Buss, Redburn, and Guo (2006) in a volume in the M.E. Sharpe series.] Lukensmeyer and Torres (2006) emphasize seven values held by AmericaSpeaks, a not-for-profit organizer of dialogues to enact deliberative democracy. One of the seven values is: "Demonstrate public consensus. Produce information that clearly highlights the public's shared priorities" (10).

Turning to a long-standing public administration source on local government leadership, consensus building is identified with a particular kind of leadership: "facilitative leadership." A model and case studies on mayoral facilitative leaders are presented by Svara (1994) and contributors in his book. The authors studied cities with professional managers, meaning the mayors were most often peers with city council members. Svara argues that mayors' effectiveness as facilitative leaders rests on ten roles, two of which are relevant to consensus building. One of the "active coordinating and communicating roles" is attending to team relations and being a network builder. Those responsibilities, in turn, call for mayors to support the council internally, communicate inside and outside of government and to "unify the council" (225). An even more direct connection is leadership on goal setting. Svara says the goal-setting role depends not only on identifying problems and creating direction but also "building consensus" (225).

In terms of practical and public leadership on consensus building, a Canadian framework for consensus building is notable, and it seems absent from attention in U.S. public administration. In the 1990s, Canadian government, business, and First Nations leaders met at the provincial and national levels through the National Round Table on the Environment and the Economy (NRTEE). They focused on the importance of consensus building for addressing the balancing and sustainability of economic growth and environmental protection. NRTEE identified ten guiding principles for building consensus on sustainability issues (Government of Canada 1993) and support for initiatives recorded as part of a guide for putting principles into practice (Cormick et al. 1996). I will return to this second publication for both its clarity on consensus and consensus building and the leadership dimensions of that mode of decision making.

What Is Consensus Building?

An important aspect of leadership and consensus building is examining what consensus building is and is not. This is not as easy as the common sense meaning of the term indicates. First, "consensus building" is analyzed in relation to other leadership and decision-making terms and processes: collaboration, joint decision making, and others. Second, a simple definition becomes complicated when compared to actual standards of decision making termed *consensus*. For the present purpose, my definition centers on the decision making standard and draws limits on other elements of group management and benefits of "collaboration." Third, this analysis frames the challenges for leaders deciding to use consensus-building processes.

From a small-scale focus, consensus building, even for ardent advocates, does not extend to every decision. One guide explains that "consensus management" does not mean every decision, no matter how small, must be made by consensus. Individuals and groups can be empowered to decide on behalf of others. Thus, "consensus does not means unanimity or 100 percent agreement on everything by everybody. Consensus is not conformity" (Saint and Lawson 1994, 4).

Consensus Building: Different Terms, Focus, and Emphasis

Consensus building is one of many related words or phrases for a group seeking agreement on a question or resolving a conflict. However, "consensus building" or "consensus process" is often shorthand for "collaboration" and a family of related terms. For example, *A Practical Guide to Consensus* notes that consensus processes as an explicit way of making public decisions have been developing during the past three decades. However, the labels for the same kind of process have proliferated; the guide offers twenty-three different terms (Arthur, Carlson, and Moore 1999, 6). This list merits examination. Some can be deemed the same for all practical purposes: collaborative agreement seeking, consensus-based processes, consensus building, multiparty negotiation, for instance. However, others point to broader concepts: environmental conflict resolution, environmental mediation, negotiated processes, joint decision making, cooperative decision making. This second set of concepts does not call for full assent and can sidestep the power differences involved in "joint" or "cooperative" efforts. On a more specific level, the terms *negotiated rulemaking* and *regulatory negotiations* usually fit under a specific statutory authority (most frequently at the federal level) and thus constrain the preparation and conduct of consensus building in those settings.

The slippery slope is to equate any kind of agreement or "cooperative outcome" with consensus. The nub of consensus building is the standard of decision making. The simplest definition, from the *Consensus Building Handbook*, states consensus building as a "process of seeking unanimous agreement" (Susskind, McKearnan and Thomas-Larmer 1999, 6). Yet the unanimity also depends on a good faith effort to satisfy the interests of stakeholders, that is, the participants in the consensus-building process. Consensus is reached when "everyone agrees they can live with whatever is proposed . . . and that there has been enough time and work to satisfy stakeholder interests" (Susskind, McKearnan and Thomas-Larmer 1999, 6).

Thus, even at this early stage, sufficient time and good faith efforts are precursors to the value that can be gained from, and the authenticity of, a consensus outcome. In contrast to majority decisions, consensus advocates point to the need to attain some level of agreement from participants as critical to promote mutual respect, equalize power, and demand more creative, inclusive agreements. If there is no agreement until all agree, then attention to everyone's interests and needs are greater. Similarly, with more widespread buy-in, implementation should be more swift and sure, rather than grudging or with only partial compliance when the members of the decision-making group have power over the enactment of the agreement.

Other components, usually framed within the term *collaboration*, include mutual learning, honest inquiry into the views of others, identification of underlying interests, and satisfaction of those interests through creative alternatives (Gray 1989; Daniels and Walker 2001). Some advocates focus more on deliberation, while others frame it as collaborative learning.

Finally, some argue that even a consensus process that does not reach consensus has important value. Innes (1999) writes, "Consensus-building processes, whether or not they result in an agreement, typically produce numerous secondary consequences that are sometimes more important than any agreement. For example, consensus building can result in new relationships and trust among stakeholders who were either in conflict or simply not in communication" (635). So even taking consensus as "unanimous agreement," this standard has value only insofar as it promotes other kinds of benefits of collaboration.

Another dimension of the value of consensus depends on who is or is not in the group. The *Practical Guide* offers a definition for "consensus in public policy setting":

- The parties have reached a meeting of the minds sufficient to make a decision and carry it out.
- No one who could block or obstruct the decision or its implementation will exercise that power.
- Everyone needed to support the decision and put it into effect will do so (Arthur, Carlson, and Moore 1999, 6).

Thus, building on the need for inclusion, this definition depends on "those who could block or obstruct the decision" and "everyone needed to . . . put it into effect." Consensus is not coalition building. Coalition building involves only those of fairly similar goals and viewpoints to build agreement on how to work against other interests. Consensus calls for building bridges across coalitions or standard fault lines of "us" and "them."

Consensus Building: Beginning and End

While consensus is at heart a standard of decision making, its beginning and end is in dispute. First, the *Practical Guide* describes the "consensus process" as extending from deciding whether to initiate a process; to working to bring diverse interests to the table, organizing the process, and establishing ground rules; to holding the dialogue/negotiation itself. Moreover, the process should extend to formalizing a consensus decision, carrying it out, and monitoring the results (Arthur, Carlson, and Moore 1999, 5–6). In some ways, this is non-controversial; one could analogize to "having surgery" as involving not just the time in the operating room but the diagnosis, patient and surgeon preparation, implementation of the procedure, and immediate recovery steps. Akin to diagnosis that does not call for surgery, assessments for using consensus building can end in a determination not to proceed.

The harder question to address is when there is not unanimity. Is this consensus or something else? There is a lack of consensus by public dispute–resolution practitioners and experts on "consensus."

At a 1998 conference, a panel of public administrators, facilitators, and academics offered different views on what consensus is and its value. Susskind, a prominent researcher, writer, and practitioner on public policy consensus building, believed that consensus is a core value for public dispute resolution but is not the only standard for decision making. Holdouts who unreasonably block an agreement by the group should not have that level of power. Instead, "practitioners should 'seek unanimity' but settle for 'overwhelming agreement,' for example, a supermajority of 80 percent" (Stephens 1998). Susskind elaborates on that point:

> Most dispute resolution professionals believe that groups or assemblies should seek unanimity, but settle for overwhelming agreement that goes as far as possible toward meeting the interests of all stakeholders. The effort to meet the interests of all stakeholders should be understood to include an affirmative responsibility to ensure that those who are excluded really are holdouts and are rejecting the proposal on reasonable grounds that would seem compelling to anyone who found themselves in the holdouts' shoes. It is crucial that the definition of success be clear at the outset of any consensus building process (1999, 7).

Susskind is not alone in this view. An example of such a standard from a North Carolina government advisory body, led by a contract facilitator and seeking consensus, defined consensus as twenty-four out of twenty-eight stakeholders being in agreement. Given the diversity of views and the mix of kinds of interests represented, it was judged that this was a realistic standard for "consensus" (Stephens 2004, 15). Finally, this "less-than-unanimity" standard is also defined as consensus in federal law, under the *Negotiated Rulemaking Act* (5 USC § 561–570).

Consensus defined as "full agreement" or "unanimity" values legitimacy tied to complete assent of the stakeholders in the group. It reflects values for inclusivity, equality, and high respect for minority views. Consensus "purists" view the challenge of working with diverse viewpoints as an opportunity for learning and creativity. If the high standard of consensus is weakened, the incentives for new thinking and creating truly innovative solutions are lessened. Such a high standard can also protect against stakeholders believing that consensus building actually means abandoning principles for the sake of agreement.

Turning to consensus-building practice, it is not uncommon for a consensus agreement to specify areas of continuing disagreement. Although the details differ, the template is that stakeholders do reach consensus on most issues or topics. They also acknowledge there are points of disagreement, despite good faith efforts at resolution. Thus, the final "consensus agreement" packages the language describing the differences (sometimes labeled "minority" and "majority views") along with the areas of agreement, and the stakeholders reach consensus on the full report. The rationale is to allow the areas of agreement to be implemented, while acknowledging and explaining the remaining differences.

Criticisms of Consensus Building

Criticisms of consensus have grown along with its use in policy and program formulation. Some fears, such as giving up authority, compromising important principles, and losing face, are considered misperceptions of actual consensus practice (Susskind, McKearnan, and Thomas-Larmer 1999, xx–xxii). Other critiques come from both theoretical and experiential bases. The following summary draws from several authors, most prominently Kenney (2000), Cestero (1999), and Coglianese (1997), and almost entirely from environmental settings.[3]

A first challenge comes from the exact meaning of "consensus-based" processes. One meaning is an approach that "emphasizes cooperation, learning and accommodation of diverse interests." (Kenney 2000, 40). The other meaning, adopted by this author, is a decision rule for how individuals' views are melded into an agreement that all support; a "joint decision." Broadly, it is the difference between addressing disagreements agreeably and with an open mind, and a specific decision standard—agreement by all—even if that agreement involves some compromises and disappointments leading to an overall acceptable package.

Second, the ideas about the useful outcomes of consensus are challenged. That consensus decisions are quicker, lower cost, and more sustainable are critiqued, at least in the form of negotiated rule making (Coglianese 1997). Third, normative arguments for consensus are critiqued. There are two related normative standards on consensus decisions: the idea that there is a social value in the stability and harmony, and that such decisions are more accurate, valid, or "truthful" than other types of decisions. One danger in such "mythology" is the "bias against diversity and individualism," and the delegitimizing of confrontation and conflict (Kenney 2000, 41–43). Similarly, the ability to agree seems to rest on the assumption that the participants are reasonable people who acknowledge the interests and values of other stakeholders. Experience in actual consensus-based processes belies such an assumption. One advocate (Britell 1997) argues that past breakthroughs in justice and liberty were dependent on the refusal to seek common ground or win-win solutions. For "most turning points of history . . . in-your-face confrontation saved the day."

Another purported strength is that consensus-based processes are effective in melding differing opinions into a moderate, coherent, mutual-learning outcome. The criticism in this area is the possible confusion of consensus on opinion rather than fact. Moreover, some research indicates that in comparing consensus with other decision rules, the outcome in consensus is not a compromise or creative combination of viewpoints but an extreme position. This "group polarization" has been demonstrated in laboratory conditions (Moscovici and Zavalloni 1969).

Kenney (2000) provides a set of strategic considerations to challenge consensus, with an eye to relative power and efficacy of environmental advocates, especially local volunteers. First, there is social pressure to compromise. Second, local volunteers may not have the experience and training in negotiation when facing developers, other businesses, or government officials. Third, there can be inadequate representation of affected interests. Underrepresentation of "distant" or "general" stakeholders when focusing on a local or regional environmental matter (such as watershed management) is one representation problem. Another is explicit or subtle efforts to exclude more extreme voices in order to have a greater chance of reaching consensus. Kenney identifies one study where the supposed unanimity standard that protects minority views did not provide the maximum power for the little guy, compared to majority rule (Falk 1982).

Finally, a weakness of consensus is that general principles or statements of agreement serve to avoid the real decisions that need to be made. Such a "paper consensus" does not yield meaningful guidance for policy or programs. I add that this danger is also realized when an overall consensus agreement includes "agreement on continuing disagreements," in essence, minority reports. At the least, this critique points to questions about the form, depth, logic, and "quality" of consensus agreements crafted to reiterate continuing differences on key points.

Guidance for Consensus-Building Processes

The public policy conflict-resolution field[4] has offered guidance to government officials initiating consensus processes and for the third-party neutrals called on to design and facilitate those processes. Some of the guidance responds to the criticisms mentioned earlier. Other portions preceded some of the specific critiques but have been fine-tuned over the last two decades.

In 1992, the Society of Professionals in Dispute Resolution (SPIDR) published a list of competencies for mediators in multiparty, public disputes (Stephens 1998). This guidance grew out of both specific experience and concern about who can practice mediation or facilitation in policy areas. The experience dates back to the 1970s when mediators had been building consensus on a variety of environmental conflicts (Bingham 1986) and was an effort to synthesize the experience into specific competencies. The competencies document was, in part, designed to clarify the shared and distinct competencies for public-dispute mediators amid a burgeoning conflict-resolution field, with colleagues experienced in settings such as the courts, commercial and business matters, family, and community arenas trying their hand at public issue mediation and facilitation.

For leaders, this document serves as a useful tool in evaluating who is prepared to act as a facilitator for building consensus. Of critical importance, both to government leaders and the potential facilitator, is to analyze the situation or conflict to determine if consensus building is feasible and what kind of process arrangements make such an effort likely to succeed (SPIDR 1997, 14). A "conflict assessment," "situation assessment," or "assessment for collaboration" is a common part of most consensus efforts where the work involves more than one organization and a mix of stakeholders with competing interests.[5]

The same professional association extended their guidance to government "conveners" of consensus-building processes. Instead of competencies, eight "best practice" recommendations were identified and explained (SPIDR 1997). The terminology is *collaborative agreement-seeking processes,* but the document uses the term *consensus building* interchangeably. The assessment is one part of the "pre-process" work, along with an agency considering the appropriateness of a collaborative agreement-seeking process and the stakeholders' willingness and ability to participate (SPIDR 1997, 6–7). Moreover, the agency leaders should support the process with "sufficient resources," meaning staff time and funds (SPIDR 1997, 7–8).

The best practices call for leaders to share control in two ways: to have ground rules mutually agreed upon rather than set by the agency, and to assure the facilitator's neutrality and accountability to all participants. Finally, policy makers should resist creating overly prescriptive laws or rules because "consensus-based processes are effective because of their voluntary, informal and flexible nature" (SPIDR 1997, 9–11).

These best practices attempt to respond to criticisms of representation, stakeholder autonomy, pressure to compromise, and implementation standards to avoid paper consensus. The devil is in the details, but the practices try to provide some protection from consensus devolving into another form of power politics.

The standards outlined in these two documents produced by a professional association have been elaborated or adapted by various analysts and facilitators. Two of the most useful iterations are *Building Consensus for a Sustainable Future: Putting Principles into Practice* (Cormick et al. 1996) and *A Practical Guide to Consensus* (Arthur, Carlson, and Moore 1999).

Building Consensus for a Sustainable Future built on the dialogues of Canadian government, business, and First Nations leaders who met at the provincial and national levels through the National Round Table on the Environment and the Economy, noted earlier. Sustainable development—seeking a balance of environmental protection and economic well-being—is central to this approach to consensus. Ten principles are explained, and important questions and possible objections are addressed. Examples of Canadian consensus processes provide nice case illustrations.

The ten principles expand on the best practice recommendations: (1) the principle of self-design states that parties should design the consensus process; (2) inclusivity and voluntary participation are emphasized; (3) accountability of stakeholders' representatives to the consensus group and to their respective constituencies is enumerated; and (4) realistic deadlines are important to move things along, but not to rush the work. Of greatest utility is a clear comparison of a consensus process with other decision processes, with special attention to the overlaps and divergences between "consultation" and "consensus" (Cormick et al. 1996, 11).

The *Practical Guide to Consensus* is a product of the Policy Consensus Initiative (PCI), a nonprofit organization whose mission is to "create and support collaborative governance capacities, structures, and networks in states" and to "offer a nationally recognized source of information on collaborative governance, consensus building, and conflict resolution."[6] The "sponsor" or "convener" role is addressed, which is most relevant to leadership concerns. It is far more of a "how to" manual, from planning and organizing a consensus process, to selecting a facilitator or mediator, to writing ground rules.

In testing for consensus, but avoiding yes/no votes, "consensus scales" are commonly used. They are multipoint continuums to reflect different degrees of agreement or disagreement. Facilitators often use them to test for agreement on proposals that are then aggregated and modified to build a package of agreements.

Leaders should employ scales of consensus as a stakeholder group works on alternative proposals to gain clarity on how strong the "votes of support" need to be to have a viable consensus for implementation.

A final element in leadership and consensus building goes beyond books to education and training. While leadership development programs have employed negotiation and problem solving for a long time, the focus on consensus and its fit with management and decision making is relatively new. A leading program that has thoroughly examined its knowledge transfer model is the Natural Resources Leadership Institute, active in six states (Addor et al. 2005). Other kinds of civic education and leadership approaches are relevant as well.[7]

Difficulties in Implementing Consensus Building in Terms of Leadership

Leaders who seek to be "consensus-building leaders" face several difficulties in reaching for such broad-based support. Philosophical and practical matters are offered.

One philosophical dichotomy is between democratic norms of majority decision making and other forms of supermajority or consensus thresholds. While

Figure 12.1 **Gradients of Agreement**

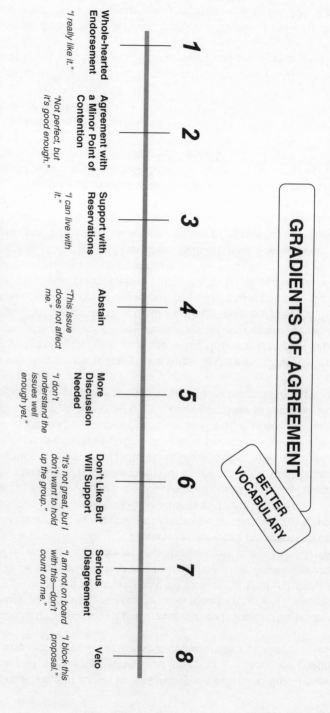

GRADIENTS OF AGREEMENT

BETTER VOCABULARY

| 1 | 2 | 3 | 4 | 5 | 6 | 7 | 8 |

Whole-hearted Endorsement
"I really like it."

Agreement with a Minor Point of Contention
"Not perfect, but it's good enough."

Support with Reservations
"I can live with it."

Abstain
"This issue does not affect me."

More Discussion Needed
"I don't understand the issues well enough yet."

Don't Like But Will Support
"It's not great, but I don't want to hold up the group."

Serious Disagreement
"I am not on board with this—don't count on me."

Veto
"I block this proposal."

This is the GRADIENTS OF AGREEMENT Scale. It enables members of a group to express their support for a proposal *in degrees, along a continuum.* Using this tool, group members are no longer trapped into expressing support in terms of *yes* and *no.*

Source: The GRADIENTS OF AGREEMENT Scale was developed in 1987 by Sam Kaner, Duane Berger, and the staff of Community at Work. Copyright © 2006 Community at Work.

a unanimous jury and a two-thirds vote requirement in a legislative body are strong examples of "more than majority" standards, they are also in the minority for the range of public decisions most representatives and executives face. Some homogenous communities (usually small scale, such as intentional communities, communes, or kibbutzim) and the Society of Friends (Quakers) are the leading examples of concerted, durable efforts to create consensus on policy matters. Thus, one conundrum is establishing the legitimacy of a consensus threshold when democratically determined majority rule is, well, the rule.

A second philosophical problem—with social science dimensions—is whether consensus decisions are truly better than other standards. As recounted earlier, consensus protects minorities; may demand more careful listening, which generates creative win-win alternatives; and can assure easier implementation. For inclusion and support, it's hard to argue against consensus conceptually. However, the demand that people adjust their judgments and preferences to come into accord with other stakeholders may yield a poor decision in two ways. First, the outcome can be a thin veil of compromises that it is minimally acceptable but lacks logic, consistency, and wisdom. As former British Prime Minister Margaret Thatcher acidly commented, "To me, consensus seems to be the process of abandoning all beliefs, principles, values and policies. So it is something in which no one believes and to which no one objects" (Thatcher 1993, 167).

In a different vein, James Surowiecki (2004) argues for the need to maintain independent judgments of stakeholders and to compile those judgments to produce outcomes that get closer to "the truth" or "a good judgment." Surowiecki's argument is that large groups of people are smarter than an expert few, no matter how brilliant the collection of experts may be. He uses examples from various settings to show the power of large numbers making independent judgments that collectively yield better results on solving problems, fostering innovation, coming to wise decisions, and even predicting the future. In most cases, the decision rule is for separate, independent judgments that are aggregated and then averaged. Thus the "group's intelligence" is better than any single member, and often better than experts in a particular field. But such intelligence is not found in changing those judgments or preferences into a single consensus agreement.

Thus, the challenge to consensus is whether the change of views—the push and pull, creativity, and compromise—yields superior, "wiser" decisions rather than those that are just more acceptable (or, at least, less objectionable). Consensus advocates can reply that durability, effectiveness, and efficiency can be achieved using consensus building far more than majority rule, compromise, or no agreement.

Turning to practical difficulties, the implementation conundrum for leaders is how to "lead" a process that demands equality of decision-making power. The first choice is for leaders to initiate and support consensus building from a distance, but not be involved in the nitty-gritty lest their power influence people's views and preferences too much. This "power to convene" is described by PCI leaders Christine Carlson and Greg Wolf (2005). Their shorthand term is *public solutions,* which refers to inclusive participation, a neutral setting, and impartiality by the powerful convener. In short, the leader can initiate and show commitment but not throw his or her weight around, trusting that a diverse set of stakeholders, working in a well-defined environment (that satisfies the leader's interests), can yield a good outcome. This approach to leadership and consensus building applies most directly to legislators, mayors, and other elected leaders.

At a level of leadership where more hands-on work is possible, or required, one analysis identified three "hats" that compete for attention in managing a consensus process. Wondolleck and Ryan (1999) reviewed studies of federal agencies' experience of collaborative resource-management processes and mediation of administrative appeals of forest plans. Their analysis yielded "three hats" (distinct roles) that agency representatives must wear: that of leader, partner, and stakeholder.

The leader encompasses responsibilities for process, issues, and decisions to be made. Process includes determining certain logistics such as hiring a facilitator and setting the timeline. Process responsibilities call on agency employees to model norms and behavior of agreement seeking and safeguard forthright discussion and accurate representation of various participants' views. Issues leadership entails preliminary analysis of the issues, setting limits of the substantive dimension of the work, and helping produce issue papers. Finally, decision leadership acknowledges the agency's additional responsibility given its position of authority. The leader of the collaboration must signal support for the consensus process and the ability to engineer final trade-offs as well as show a commitment for follow-through on the outcome.

The partner hat emphasizes the togetherness of how all participants seeking consensus should work. Demonstrations of being open-minded, flexible, and willing to listen, to teach and be taught constitute this hat. Wondolleck and Ryan (1999) believe this hat is the most challenging one because it is least consistent with traditional agency procedures and the role of technical expert. They also identify the tension between alignment as a partner in a stakeholder group and identification with the norms and expectations of one's agency. Finally, among the three hats, the authors think the roles of leader versus partner hold the greatest tension.

The stakeholder hat calls for clarity about the interests and needs for the agency's satisfaction in a consensus process. Persuasion is a key function of this hat, along with guardianship for the broad public interest, consistency with current laws and regulations, and support of organizational and professional needs. Wondolleck and Ryan (1999) emphasize the need for thorough preparation about the interests the agency must satisfy, combined with flexibility on the means of satisfying those interests.

The authors explicitly call for agency participants to *not* combine a facilitator role with the hats they must wear. Two different people from the same agency could divide responsibilities, with one being the facilitator. However, Wondolleck and Ryan (1999) see this as a risky approach.

Wondolleck and Ryan (1999) argue that the three roles are distinct. Their vision is for agency participants to balance, not merge, the roles. The only specific guidance on such balancing is for agency participants to explicitly recognize the distinct roles and to transition between them in a manner transparent to their fellow participants in the collaborative process.

Thus, the practical difficulties are:

1. How is leadership divided, or shared, among the three hats?
2. How can consensus building be supported while acknowledging the higher power roles of leader and stakeholder held by the public authority?

Consensus may not be possible or necessary in certain circumstances. When matters are trivial or routine, a managerial decision or simple majority will suffice. Consensus may not be possible when fundamental divergences of values predominate. In this case, how to engage people thoughtfully and respectfully is the key question. One approach comes from the field of pubic participation. The International Association for Public Participation offers a "spectrum of public participation" that parallels the concerns of identified stakeholders and the possibility of sharing decision power (see Figure 12.2). It is addressed to corporate or government leaders and calls for an alignment of goals and "promise to the public."

The final difficulty is in terms of a consensus standard. I have reviewed consensus scales to identify strength of support. One practical conundrum is determining the threshold for sufficient strength of agreement. Using the Gradients of Agreement (Figure 12.1), it probably falls to the leader to say if any "#4—Abstain" is acceptable for calling everyone in agreement. Moreover, where the group is tightly aligned on decision and implementation powers—those in the room are expected to work assiduously to actualize the agreement—it is doubtful that more than one person at the 5 or 6 level be considered a wise decision on implementation grounds.

Similarly, as covered in detail in Arthur, Carlson, and Moore (1999), names for consensus processes can be misleading and not be consensus. The best, shortest distinction—cooperation, coordination, and collaboration—comes from the Amherst H. Wilder Foundation (Mattessich, Murray-Close, and Monsey 2001). It offers leaders and managers a shorthand guide to distinguish the degree of shared or preserved authority, resources, and information flow for addressing different needs for working with other people and groups.

Therefore, different standards are used for reaching consensus. One leader may be a "purist" on consensus. This would mean, using the Gradients of Agreement, all participants would have to give support at levels 1, 2, or 3 for a consensus to be achieved. On the other hand, other consensus processes have operated with a consensus defined as a supermajority (per the example in Stephens 2004), or following a standard found in federal law (*Negotiated Rulemaking Act* 1990):

> "Consensus" defined as "unanimous concurrence among the interests represented" unless the committee agrees "to define such term to mean a general but not unanimous concurrence" or "agrees upon another specified definition" (5 USC § 562 (2)—Definitions).

Figure 12.2 **Increasing Level of Public Impact**

	Public Participation Goal	Promise to Public	Example Techniques to Consider
Inform	To provide the public with balanced and objective information to assist them in understanding the problem, alternatives, opportunities, and/or solutions	We will keep you informed.	• Fact sheets • Web sites • Open houses
Consult	To obtain public feedback on analysis, alternatives, and/or decisions	We will keep you informed, listen to and acknowledge concerns and aspirations, and provide feedback on how public input influenced the decision.	• Public comment • Focus groups • Surveys • Public meetings
Involve	To work directly with the public throughout the process to ensure that public concerns and aspirations are consistently understood and considered	We will work with you to ensure that your concerns and aspirations are directly reflected in the alternatives developed and provide feedback on how public input influenced the decision.	• Workshops • Deliberate polling
Collaborate	To partner with the public in each aspect of the decision including the development of alternatives and the identification of the preferred solution	We will look to you for direct advice and innovation in formulating solutions and incorporate your advice and recommendations into the decisions to the maximum extent possible.	• Citizen advisory committees • Consensus building • Participatory decision making
Empower	To place final decision making in the hands of the public	We will implement what you decide.	• Citizen juries • Ballots • Delegated decisions

Source: Copyright © 2005 International Association for Public Participation.

Areas of Research on Consensus Building and Leadership

The following are four areas for research on the leadership dimensions of consensus building. First, when is consensus building required and when is it optional? When is it more or less appropriate? The goal here is to sharpen, and possibly critique, an ideological divide between "consensualists" and "practical deciders." Consensualists emphasize the interconnectedness of people and communities and the moral obligation for affected stakeholders to have a say on actions that affect them. Consensualists focus on the power of agreement for building social capital and community learning and emphasizing gradual change and stability. The practical deciders focus on consensus as one tool for reaching decisions. Consensus is always a choice, not the Holy Grail; leaders should set a consensus standard only when conditions call for it. We see this latter strain in the "supermajority defined as consensus" examples previously.

A second question is how are short- and long-term trade-offs measured and valued? How do leaders assess the benefits and costs of pursuing and reaching consensus? Even "failed" consensus efforts can still yield benefits of greater understanding, reduced tension, and the beginnings of stronger relationships that build toward later agreements (Innes 1999). There are first- and second-order effects to be measured. Comparisons of different issues, kinds of stakeholders, and outcomes can refine our understanding of two dimensions of the benefits of consensus: agreement based and relationship based. Some may term the relationship-based dimension as the "positive externalities" of consensus building.

Third, we need to know more about role definition and analysis of leaders and supporters—who are often also the "funders"—in consensus processes. One leadership role is to serve as sponsor and/or convener for consensus building. This role is to help create the forum that "brings people to the table," but not to participate as a stakeholder at the table. A second leadership role, according to Wondolleck and Ryan (1999), is for leadership from *within* the process. The inside leadership tasks range from administrative management, to information flow assistance, to issue framing and implementing decisions. We have not had rigorous research on different kinds of "at a distance" and "in the process" leadership.

Finally, laboratory simulations and multicase analysis is needed to address the contrasting views about the "truth" or "strength" of different outcomes by different decision modes. As noted earlier, one model calls for "independent judgments compiled" but not a single face-to-face decision by consensus (that is, Surowiecki's [2004] argument). A different model emphasizes social learning and creativity as a way to induce change of the positions and viewpoints of stakeholders in order to create a consensus. Can the pluralism and diversity that is presupposed—and protected—in a majority-rule system be honored such that any consensus process truly grows out of voluntary participation, enlightened self-interest, and new insights rather than group think? In our increasingly connected and interdependent global economic and social relations, consensus may not lead to better outcomes.

We may need multiple forms of enhanced cooperation (or, at least, tolerance), but in a way that retains some independence and discretion.

Directions for Practice on Consensus Building and Leadership

In conclusion, I offer four directions for applied work on consensus building and leadership. First, there need to be better evaluation tools for understanding the conjunctions and disjunctions of consensus building and other skills, needs, and traits of leadership. Perhaps in a shared-power world every leader needs to be a facilitative, consensus-building leader. However, other conditions seem to call for individual judgment, courage and conviction, and the ability to move followers toward the leader's conclusion rather than waiting for a consensus to form.

Second, more rigorous reflection by leaders and consensus-building practitioners can deepen understanding of the degrees of consent needed for leaders' actions. Leaders often decide without consensus, that is, consensus is the exception not the rule. What are the conditions for judging the "right level" of cooperative behavior and decision making? How can we clearly distinguish the value of a "consensus" as opposed to a large or overwhelming majority?

Third, a concerted examination of the different models of collaboration and consensus building is required. Many models of collaboration and consensus building exist (for example, Chrislip 2002; Gray 1989; Linden 2002; Straus 2002; Wondolleck and Yaffee 2000). Just to name three areas of contrast: (1) different emphases on emotion and relationship; (2) various approaches to science (for example, complexity theory) and rationality; and (3) the degree of regimented or flexible steps in seeking consensus. There needs to be a better assessment of the strengths and weaknesses of different, comprehensive models on consensus building to help guide leaders.

Finally, more regular use of tools to judge the potential for consensus building is needed. One such tool is offered by the Policy Consensus Initiative (PCI). In their training manual that accompanies *A Practical Guide to Consensus,* PCI presents an assessment module for starting a consensus process and offers a ten-point screening tool as one step in that process.[8] This is but one resource for near-term, practical benefit to public-sector leaders.

Conclusion

This chapter has addressed consensus building's importance and its connections to public administration trends of new governance and collaborative management, and it has summarized the criticisms of decision making by consensus. For public-sector leaders working with a great diversity of groups within organizations and with stakeholders from different organizations or constituencies, more concerted research on the conditions, models, and evaluations of comparable cases is essential to support their effectiveness as consensus builders.

Notes

1. Collaboration is the closest fit to "consensus building" with works such as Gray (1989), Huxham (1996), Chrislip (2002), Linden (2002), and Straus (2002). As detailed later, a "public dispute resolution" field has formed, with consensus decision making being a key concept. Representative early books are Susskind and Cruikshank (1987) and Carpenter and Kennedy (1988). However, the focus on getting buy-in, assent, or "consensus" extends to works on program management and interorganizational relations; facilitation; organizational learning and change; regulatory negotiation; natural resource management and environmental conflict resolution; and deliberative democracy, citizen engagement, and governance. A sampling from those areas of interest are Crosby and Bryson 2005; Daniels and Walker 2001; Gastil and Levine 2005; Booher 2004; Hajer and Wagenaar 2003; Bingham, Nabatchi, and O'Leary 2005; Winer and Ray 1994; Langbein and Kerwin 2000; Weeks 2000; Weber and Khademian 1997; Kelman 1992; Roberts 1997; Roberts and Bradley 1991; Zhiyong 1997; Luke 1998; Schwarz 1994; Bryson and Anderson 2000; Grubbs 2000; Leach, Pelkey, and Sabatier 2002; Wondolleck and Yaffee 2000; O'Leary and Bingham 2003.

2. The respective Web sites for these three organizations are http://mcc.mt.gov/, www.agree.org/, and www.policyconsensus.org/. (Accessed 12 June 2006.)

3. A school-based critique of consensus building is offered by Erbes (2006).

4. This field is epitomized by the Environment and Public Policy section of the Association for Conflict Resolution (see www.mediate.com/acrepp/) and characterized by Dukes (1996). (Accessed 1 October 2006.)

5. See, for example, assessment reports from the U.S. Institute for Environmental Conflict Resolution at www.ecr.gov/s_publications.htm and the dialogue on the standards for, and challenges of, implementing conflict/situation assessments at www.ecr.gov/pdf/OnlineDialogue.pdf. (Both accessed 13 October 2006.)

6. From Policy Consensus Initiative Web site, www.policyconsensus.org/about/mission.html. (Accessed 13 October 2006.)

7. For example, see the Alliance for Regional Stewardship, www.regionalstewardship.org/bootcamp.html. (Accessed 13 October 2006.)

8. For details, see www.policyconsensus.org/publications/practicalguide/index.html. (Accessed 13 October 2006.)

References

Addor, Mary Lou, Tanya Denkla Cobb, E. Franklin Dukes, Mike Ellerbrock, and L. Steven Smutko. 2005. "Linking Theory to Practice: A Theory of Changes Model of the Natural Resources Leadership Institute." *Conflict Resolution Quarterly* 23 (3): 203–23.

Arthur, Jim, Christine Carlson, and Lee Moore. 1999. *A Practical Guide to Consensus.* Santa Fe, NM: Policy Consensus Initiative.

Bingham, Gail. 1986. *Resolving Environmental Disputes: A Decade of Experience.* Washington, DC: The Conservation Foundation.

Bingham, Lisa B. 2006. "The New Urban Governance: Processes for Engaging Citizens and Stakeholders." *Review of Policy Research* 23 (4): 815–26.

Bingham, Lisa B., Tina Nabatchi, and Rosemary O'Leary. 2005. "The New Governance: Practices and Processes for Stakeholder and Citizen Participation in the Work of Government." *Public Administration Review* 65 (5): 547–58.

Booher, David E. 2004. "Collaborative Governance Practice and Democracy." *National Civic Review* 93 (4): 32–46.

Britell, Jim. 1997. The Myth of "Win-Win." Unpublished Essay. www.britell.com/use/use11c.html. (Accessed 5 April 2006.)

Bryson, John M., and Sharon R. Anderson. 2000. "Applying Large-Group Interaction Methods in the Planning and Implementation of Major Change Efforts." *Public Administration Review* 60 (2): 143–62.

Buss, Terry F., Steve Redburn, and Kristina Guo. 2006. *Modernizing Democracy*. Armonk, NY: M.E. Sharpe.

Carlson, Christine, and Greg Wolf. 2005. "The Power to Convene." *State News* (November/December): 12–13, 36.

Carpenter, Susan, and W.J.D. Kennedy. 1988. *Managing Public Disputes*. San Francisco: Jossey-Bass.

Cestero, Barb. 1999. *Beyond the Hundredth Meeting: A Field Guide to Collaborative Conservation on the West's Public Lands*. Tucson, AZ: Sonoran Institute.

Chrislip, David D. 2002. *The Collaborative Leadership Fieldbook: A Guide for Citizens and Civic Leaders*. San Francisco: Jossey-Bass.

Chrislip, David D., and Carl E. Larsen. 1994. *Collaborative Leadership: How Citizens and Civic Leaders Can Make a Difference*. San Francisco: Jossey-Bass.

Coglianese, Cary. 1997. "Assessing Consensus: The Promise and Performance of Negotiated Rulemaking." *Duke Law Journal*, 46: 1255.

Cormick, Gerald, Norman Dale, Paul Edmond, S. Glenn Sigurdson, and Barry D. Stuart. 1996. *Building Consensus for a Sustainable Future: Putting Principles into Practice*. Ottawa: National Round Table on the Environment and the Economy.

Crosby, Barbara C., and John M. Bryson. 2005. *Leadership for the Common Good: Tackling Public Problems in a Shared-Power World*. 2nd ed. San Francisco: Jossey-Bass.

Daniels, Steven E., and Gregg B. Walker. 2001. *Working through Environmental Conflict: The Collaborative Learning Approach*. Westport, CT: Praeger.

Denhardt, Janet V., and Robert B. Denhardt. 2003. *The New Public Service: Serving, Not Steering*. Armonk, NY: M.E. Sharpe.

Dukes, E. Franklin. 1996. *Resolving Public Conflict: Transforming Community and Governance*. New York: Manchester University Press.

Epstein, Paul D., Paul M. Coates, and Lyle D. Wray with David Swain. 2006. *Results that Matter: Improving Communities by Engaging Citizens, Measuring Performance and Getting Things Done*. San Francisco: Jossey-Bass.

Erbes, Kristen. 2006. "The Promise and Pitfalls of Consensus Decision Making in School Management." *Review of Policy Research* 23 (4): 827–42.

Falk, Gideon. 1982. "An Empirical Study Measuring Conflicts in Problem-Solving Groups which are Assigned Different Decision Rules." *Human Relations* 35 (12): 1123–38.

Frederickson, H. George. 2005. "Transcending the Community: Local Leadership in a World of Shared Power." *Public Management* (November): 8–15.

Gastil, John, and Peter Levine, eds. 2005. *The Deliberative Democracy Handbook: Strategies for Effective Civic Engagement in the 21st Century*. San Francisco: Jossey-Bass.

Government of Canada. 1993. *Building Consensus for a Sustainable Future: Guiding Principles*. Ottawa: National Round Table on the Environment and the Economy.

Gray, Barbara. 1989. *Collaborating: Finding Common Ground for Multiparty Problems*. San Francisco: Jossey-Bass.

Grubbs, Joseph W. 2000. "Can Agencies Work Together? Collaboration in Public and Nonprofit Organizations." *Public Administration Review* 60 (3): 275–80.

Hajer, Maarten A., and Hendrik Wagenaar, eds. 2003. *Deliberative Policy Analysis: Understanding Governance in the Network Society*. Cambridge: Cambridge University Press.

Huxham, Chris, ed. 1996. *Creating Collaborative Advantage*. Thousand Oaks, CA: Sage.

Innes, Judith E. 1999. "Evaluating Consensus Building." In *The Consensus Building Handbook: A Comprehensive Guide to Reaching Agreement*, eds. Lawrence Susskind, Sarah McKearnan, and Jennifer Thomas-Larmer, 631–75. Thousand Oaks, CA: Sage.

Janis, Irving L. 1982. *Groupthink: Psychological Studies of Policy Decisions and Fiascoes.* Boston: Houghton Mifflin.

Kaner, Sam, Lenny Lind, Catherine Toldi, Sarah Fisk, and Duane Berger. 2007. *Facilitator's Guide to Participatory Decision-making.* 2nd ed. San Francisco: Jossey-Bass.

Kelman, Steven. 1992. "Adversary and Cooperationist Institutions for Conflict Resolution in Public Policymaking." *Journal of Policy Analysis and Management* 11 (2): 178–206.

Kenney, Douglas S. 2000. *Arguing About Consensus: Examining the Case Against Western Watershed Initiatives and Other Collaborative Groups Active in Natural Resource Management.* Boulder, CO: Natural Resources Law Center, University of Colorado School of Law.

Langbein, Laura I., and Cornelius M. Kerwin. 2000. "Regulatory Negotiation versus Conventional Rule Making: Claims, Counterclaims and Empirical Evidence." *Journal of Public Administration Research and Theory* 10 (3): 599–632.

Leach, William D., Neil W. Pelkey, and Paul A. Sabatier. 2002. "Stakeholder Partnerships as Collaborative Policymaking: Evaluation Criteria Applied to Watershed Management in California and Washington." *Journal of Policy Analysis and Management* 21 (4): 645–70.

Linden, Russ. 2002. *Working Across Boundaries: Making Collaboration Work in Government and Nonprofit Organizations.* San Francisco: Jossey-Bass.

Luke, Jeffrey S. 1998. *Catalytic Leadership: Strategies for an Interconnected World.* San Francisco: Jossey-Bass

Lukensmeyer, Carolyn, and Lars Hasselblad Torres. 2006. *Public Deliberation: A Manager's Guide to Citizen Engagement.* Washington, DC: IBM Center for the Business of Government.

Mattessich, Paul, Marta Murray-Close, and Barbara Monsey. 2001. *Collaboration: What Makes It Work.* 2nd ed. St. Paul, MN: Amherst H. Wilder Foundation.

Moscovici, Serge, and M. Zavalloni. 1969. "The Group as a Polarizer of Attitudes." *Journal of Personality and Social Psychology* 12:125–35.

Negotiated Rulemaking Act. U.S. Code. 1990. Title 5, § 561–570.

O'Leary, Rosemary, and Lisa B. Bingham, eds. 2003. *The Promise and Performance of Environmental Conflict Resolution.* Washington, DC: Resources for the Future.

Roberts, Nancy. 1997. "Public Deliberation: An Alternative Approach to Crafting Policy and Setting Direction." *Public Administration Review* 57 (2): 124–32.

Roberts, Nancy C., and Raymond Trevor Bradley. 1991. "Stakeholder Collaboration and Innovation: A Study of Policy Initiation at the State Level." *Journal of Applied Behavioral Science* 27 (2): 209–27.

Saint, Steven, and James R. Lawson. 1994. *Rules for Reaching Consensus: A Modern Approach to Decision Making.* San Francisco: Jossey-Bass/Pfeiffer.

Schwarz, Roger M. 1992. *Competencies for Mediators of Complex Public Disputes* (An Overview Developed by the SPIDR Environmental/Public Disputes Sector).

———. 1994. *The Skilled Facilitator: Practical Wisdom for Developing Effective Groups.* San Francisco: Jossey-Bass.

Society of Professionals in Dispute Resolution (SPIDR). 1997. *Best Practices for Government Agencies: Guidelines for Using Collaborative Agreement-Seeking Processes.* (Report and Recommendations of the SPIDR Environmental/Public Disputes Sector Critical Issues Committee).

Stephens, John B. 1998. "Public Dispute Resolvers Lack Consensus on 'Consensus.'" *SPIDR News* 22 (2): 1, 3, and 5.

———. 2004. *Guidebook to Public Dispute Resolution in North Carolina.* Chapel Hill, NC: University of North Carolina at Chapel Hill, School of Government.

Straus, David. 2002. *How to Make Collaboration Work: Powerful Ways to Build Consensus, Solve Problems, and Make Decisions.* San Francisco: Berrett-Koehler.

Surowiecki, James. 2004. *The Wisdom of Crowds: Why the Many Are Smarter Than the Few and How Collective Wisdom Shapes Business, Economies, Societies and Nations.* New York: Little, Brown.

Susskind, Lawrence. 1999. "An Alternative to Robert's Rules of Order for Groups, Organizations, and ad hoc Assemblies that Want to Operate by Consensus." In *The Consensus Building Handbook: A Comprehensive Guide to Reaching Agreement,* eds. Lawrence Susskind, Sarah McKearnan, and Jennifer Thomas-Larmer, 3–57. Thousand Oaks, CA: Sage.

Susskind, Lawrence, and Jeffrey Cruikshank. 1987. *Breaking the Impasse: Consensual Approaches to Resolving Public Disputes.* New York: Basic Books.

———. 2006. *Breaking Robert's Rules: The New Way to Run Your Meeting, Build Consensus, and Get Results.* New York: Oxford University Press.

Susskind, Lawrence, Sarah McKearnan, and Jennifer Thomas-Larmer, eds. 1999. *The Consensus Building Handbook: A Comprehensive Guide to Reaching Agreement.* Thousand Oaks, CA: Sage.

Svara, James H. 1994. *Facilitative Leadership in Local Government: Lessons from Successful Mayors and Chairpersons.* San Francisco: Jossey-Bass.

Thatcher, Margaret. 1993. *The Downing Street Years.* New York: Harper Collins.

Weber, Edward P., and Anne M. Khademian. 1997. "From Agitation to Collaboration: Clearing the Air through Negotiation." *Public Administration Review* 57 (5): 396–410.

Weeks, Edward C. 2000. "The Practice of Deliberative Democracy: Results from Four Large-Scale Trials." *Public Administration Review* 59 (3):187–97.

Winer, Michael, and Karen Ray. 1994. *Collaboration Handbook: Creating, Sustaining, and Enjoying the Journey.* St. Paul, MN: Amherst H. Wilder Foundation.

Wondolleck, Julia M., and Clare M. Ryan. 1999. "What Hat Do I Wear Now?: An Examination of Agency Roles in Collaborative Processes." *Negotiation Journal* 15 (2): 117–33.

Wondolleck, Julia M., and Steven L. Yaffee. 2000. *Making Collaboration Work: Lessons from Innovation in Natural Resource Management.* Washington, DC: Island Press.

Zhiyong, Lan. 1997. "A Conflict Resolution Approach to Public Administration." *Public Administration Review* 57 (1): 27–35.

13

The Challenge of Leading through Networks

Institutional Analysis as a Way Forward

BRENT NEVER

The increasing complexity of public problems is followed by increasingly complex governmental responses. Dynamic humanitarian disasters—Hurricane Katrina, the Southeast Asian tsunami, and even domestic terrorist attacks—test the skills of public administrators to work outside of traditional organizational boundaries. While the fact that such momentous events require unique responses is not surprising, public problems once considered to be traditional are now appreciated for their complex and dynamic nature. Issues of local economic development, education, and public safety require new tools in order to be solved. Both administrators and policy makers are increasingly turning to network forms of governance versus responses by hierarchical organization. The question that practitioners and theorists face is how to lead a networked organization specifically designed to cut across rule-bound hierarchies. How can administrators craft new rules of the game to address public problems that could not be answered by hierarchies?

The challenge for administrators facing such complex public problems is the need to create networked organizations intended to cut across the rules that bind traditional hierarchal organization. How does one create a network structure that facilitates new modes of collaboration and communication while at the same time creating an organization that can be led? Principal-agent relationships dominate hierarchies where subordinates are contractually beholden to their supervisors. Rules are intended to facilitate information flow and collaboration within the organization. Those very same rules can inhibit interaction outside of the organization.

Horizontally organized networks are designed explicitly to facilitate collaboration between organizations, that is, between sets of rules. Leaders need to devise ways for network members to move outside of their affiliations to their home organizations in order to achieve the collaboration for which networks are intended. Institutions, the formal rules and informal social norms that guide social conduct (North 1990), are tools for administrators of both hierarchy and networks. This chapter argues that in the context of networks, administrators have only their understanding of institutions and the mental models upon which those institutions rest.

Without powers inherent in a supervisor-subordinate relationship, administrators need to hone their understanding of existing institutions to design future institutions that will encourage cooperation and stability in a dynamic environment.

Institutions present both challenges and opportunities for administrators seeking to govern through networks. This chapter holds that institutions are built upon a set of mental models—understandings of how the world operates. If one were to consider the management-leadership dichotomy (Zaleznik 1977; Kotter 1990; Yukl and Lepsinger 2005), individuals fitting the manager archetype would be concerned with operating within existing institutions while those labeled as leaders would concern themselves with changing the mental models of existing institutions. An institutional perspective of organizations in general, and network organizations specifically, draws attention to the connection of the rules that administrators use to guide action and the mental models that provide the foundation for an understanding of the rules.

Public administrators face great uncertainty when working through networks and must be fluent in their understanding of both techniques typically relegated to managers and to leaders (Zaleznik 1977). The first section of this chapter considers the nature of networks in contemporary public administration. The past century has seen an unparalleled increase in the size and scope of governments throughout the world. The structural response to increasingly complex societal challenges—brought about by contextual changes such as the increase in commerce, rapid urbanization, and expanding communication—has been to create complex hierarchies. These hierarchies, though, suffer from principal-agent problems; the response of administrators has been to increase rules and regulations in order to get a better handle on what subordinates are doing. Today we have reached a point where the inefficiencies inherent in hierarchies governed by excessive rules and regulations have led policy makers and administrators to explore the use of other structures to deliver public goods and services. These structures are networks.

This chapter asserts that contemporary public administrators face complex social situations in trying to govern through networks. A way to disentangle those structures is to understand the institutional basis—formal rules and informal norms—of all social interaction. The second section explores the basic nature of institutions as the rules of the game. The third section goes one step further to state that all rules are based upon mental models. Mental models are the lenses through which humans view the world. Whether through trial and error or through socialization, members of organizations tend to make sense of their world through the use of such models. Administrators facing the task of leading through networks have the challenge of leading a set of subordinates who all have different mental models learned from their home organizations. A skilled administrator cannot lead only through the creation of new rules; he or she must also match new rules to the mental models that subordinates already possess.

Leading through networks entails interesting challenges for contemporary administrators. "Proposed goals may be vague or not provocative. Important actors may be absent, while the presence of other actors may discourage the participation of necessary actors. Crucial information about goals, means, and actors may be lacking. Discretionary power may be absent. The absence of commitment of actors to the common purpose may also be a reason for failure" (Kickert, Klijn, and Koppenjan 1997, 9). The flexibility inherent in any network also means that administrators have greater responsibility to create a framework of understandings through which participants can work. The fourth section explains how network administrators can use the logic of institutions as a means to lead under such difficult circumstances.

The Nature of Networks in Contemporary Public Administration

While conventional wisdom may hold that public-sector leaders, as well as public administration theorists, are wedded to a concept of leadership as protection of the status quo (Gabris, Golembiewski, and Ihrke 2000; Terry 1995), the recent concentration on public management networks as solutions to complex problems indicates that public administrators are increasingly interested in circumventing the staid view of leadership. The complexity of public problems has driven public administration practitioners and scholars to consider new forms of organization. The structure of the welfare state in many ways has been unable to be flexible enough to deal with the dynamism of contemporary society (Kickert, Klijn, and Koppenjan 1997). Administrators have traditionally worked through rule-bound hierarchies in order to address the pertinent issues in their community. The major thrust of administrative theory in the past century has been toward making organizational structures, as well as the individuals who inhabit them, more efficient and effective. Movements toward reinvention as well as hollowing the state indicate that practitioners and public officials are searching for different ways to address dynamic issues. Changes in the knowledge of the problems we face, as well as changes in the technology that we employ to address those problems, have made organizing outside of the formal rule-bound relationships of hierarchy a more attractive option for practitioners.

Hierarchy induces stable relationships among employers and employees. The employment contract allows administrators to remain relatively confident that their employees will pursue organizational goals. If they do not, supervisors theoretically are able to terminate employment and seek others who will fulfill the contract. Of course, practice indicates that employees may not faithfully pursue the interests of their employers, leading to a classic principal-agent problem (Miller 1992). Individuals may find it in their interest to shirk duty especially when they know that they will not be sanctioned for shirking. Supervisors have limited resources, such as time and money, to devote to monitoring workers.

While supervisors are unable to perfectly monitor their workers, they can set up rules that will both hinder the ability of workers to stray outside the interests of the supervisor as well as facilitate the transmission of information (Miller 1992). Rules can circumscribe permitted actions and permit methods of monitoring as well as regulate information flow from subordinates to supervisors. The nature of the principal-agent problem is that supervisors face resource and cognitive limitations in being able to completely monitor the actions of subordinates. Outside of designing a matrix of formal rules, administrators also can shape the informal norms and mental models that provide organization members a sense of common purpose (Kreps 1990; Schein 1992). Considered more of an art than a science (Schein 1992), leadership can manipulate both abstract mental models as well as concrete physical objects. Crafting mission statements, as well as designing the physical layout of an office, is a method for leaders to mold organizational values.

The logic of transformational versus transactional leadership (Burns 1978) fits neatly into an understanding of institutions as the formal written rules as well as the mental models upon which those rules are built (North 1990). If one were to take the traditional leadership and management dichotomy to its logical extreme, a transformational leader and a transactional manager would be two separate people. While increasingly being challenged today (Yukl and Lepsinger 2005; Kotter 1990), leading a hierarchy requires somebody focused on the big picture of where the organization is to go as well as the general organizational culture that shapes the attitudes and actions of employees (Zaleznik 1977). The specialization of hierarchical organizations can potentially lend itself to a division between management and leadership tasks, although even this contention is called into question.

Governing through networks requires an administrator to be well versed in both transformational as well as transactional leadership (O'Toole 1997; Frederickson 2005). Public administration networks, theoretically, are created in order to address complex public problems that were ineffectively addressed by more traditional hierarchies. The leader of a network faces a serious problem: Not only do new networks not have a set of formal rules or informal organizational values to guide behavior but members of the network come with rules and values from their home organizations. Leaders are tasked with the twofold challenge of understanding the current rules of the game for each participant and then creating a new set of rules that will guide future conduct. By understanding the impact of institutions on human behavior, leaders of networks are better able to face this difficult challenge.

The Nature of Institutions

As public administrators increasingly move toward using networks as tools to transcend traditional organizational boundaries, difficult challenges present themselves. Municipal executives who create a local citizens' action committee, agency directors who form interorganizational task forces, as well as the president of the United States creating an independent blue-ribbon commission—all face two related issues. First, administrators of networks draw network members from existing organizations. Individuals already work by a set of formal organizational rules as well as informal norms. In order to effectively lead through a network, administrators need to recognize that each individual brings a set of existing institutions to the bargaining table. In order to create a common purpose, administrators face having to create an atmosphere where network members can create a new set of rules and norms. Oftentimes it is not realistic to expect individuals in a new network to completely forget the parochial interests they bring from their home organizations. However, successful leaders of networks facilitate the creation of new institutions that do not conflict with existing ones, where individuals appreciate that there can be a different way to work within the network that is productive both for the network as well as for their home organizations. Administrators of networks have a heightened interest in understanding the structure of institutions.

Institutions structure long-term social interaction in a community (North 1990). These "rules of the game" are human creations, involving more craft than science in their creation even when they are knowingly created. In fact, a great number of social norms are created organically by individuals who interact with each other repeatedly over long periods of time (Knight 1992). Oftentimes individuals are not conscious of an organization's social norms but rather have internalized those norms through a process of socialization. Ironically, even the creation of the formal rules of the game, whether they are written out in bylaws or simply verbalized to all members of a community, is an organic process of pragmatic trial and error (Ostrom 1980). The difficulty for administrators of networks comes from the lack of a common socialization process.

Institutions affect the distribution of resources in a community or an organization (Knight 1992). Rules and norms set out the opportunities that individuals have in investing their own resources in various activities. They guide social interactions, whether in formal organizations such as the Department of Transportation or informal networks such as a local citizens' commission on school safety, by indicating what activities are allowed and what ones are prohibited. The strength of the rules depends on the application of sanctions to rule breakers. As rules help to determine how individuals can invest their resources, institution making and changing is a contentious process where people stand to gain or lose depending on the contours of the specific institutions. Ideally, institutions allow for long-term social exchange and would allow a community to reach some sort of social optimum, whether Pareto optimality or some other measure of social efficiency. Of course, the world is replete with cases where the rules of the game result in great inefficiencies.

Institutions are created by individuals who are "boundedly" rational (Simon 1955). Individuals do not completely understand complicated social environments; they must invest time and cognitive resources in contemplating change. The need to change rules comes about with a change in relative values in a community. Individuals perceive the fact that values have changed and then rework their existing institutions in order to take advantage of these new realities (North 1990). This is a dynamic process.

Administrators of horizontal, networked organizations inherit a set of employees who have been socialized into the formal rules and informal norms of their home organizations. The preset institutional foundations of network members cannot be swiftly erased; rather, effective network administration involves a process of cataloging existing institutions, determining the overlap of those institutions, and the molding of new institutions that take areas of convergence as the basis of moving the business of the network forward. This has been labeled as transactional in nature, that is, a management task. Leadership on the other hand involves transforming the larger mental models upon which the institutions rest.

Institutions and Mental Models

Administrators of horizontal, networked organizations face what have been called leadership and management tasks (Zaeleznik 1977). If viewed through the lens of institutions, the traditional view of management involving transactions indicates that managers are manipulators of the institutions within an organization. In order to facilitate compliance in principal-agent relationships, managers invoke formal rules and informal norms. Institutions, though, must be built on a set of ideas or understandings of a complicated world. For example, the formal rule that employees in the United States generally are to work forty hours per week, along with an informal norm that great workers will put in even more time, is based on a larger set of ideas that Weber considered to be indicative of a Protestant work ethic. There is a dialectic relationship between institutions and the mental models upon which they are based (North 2005). Leaders, traditionally interested in organization transformation, spend more effort focusing on the mental models behind the formal institutions in an organization. Network administrators face a need to understand institutions as well as mental models in order to operate in organizations where all participants arrive with different sets of priorities.

This section considers the nature of ideas as inductively created frames used to understand a complicated world. It then moves on to consider how rules are based on these particular understandings.

Social interactions are complicated. Institutions are powerful tools for individuals in that they limit the potential actions that other community members may take. The crafting of institutions is based on some common social understanding of how the world works (Denzau and North 1994). Mental models help to focus attention on the most important environmental factors that a community faces, a way of separating out what individuals feel are important events as opposed to unimportant events (Hayek 1952). Mental models serve both an organizational as well as an institutional function; common ideas about cause and effect serve to provide a common set of focal points for a community, giving individuals common ideas around which they may act collectively (Schelling 1960).

People form mental models as they interact with the world. Learning is not abstract in nature—the idea of a tabula rasa upon which humans can construct a holistic understanding of their environment—but rather an inductive process of matching patterns in the environment with an evolving model of that environment (Edelman and Tonini 2001). This inductive approach entails individuals divining cause-and-effect rules from their daily interactions (Holland et al. 1986). Individu-

Figure 13.1 **Components of Mental Models: Inductive Approach**

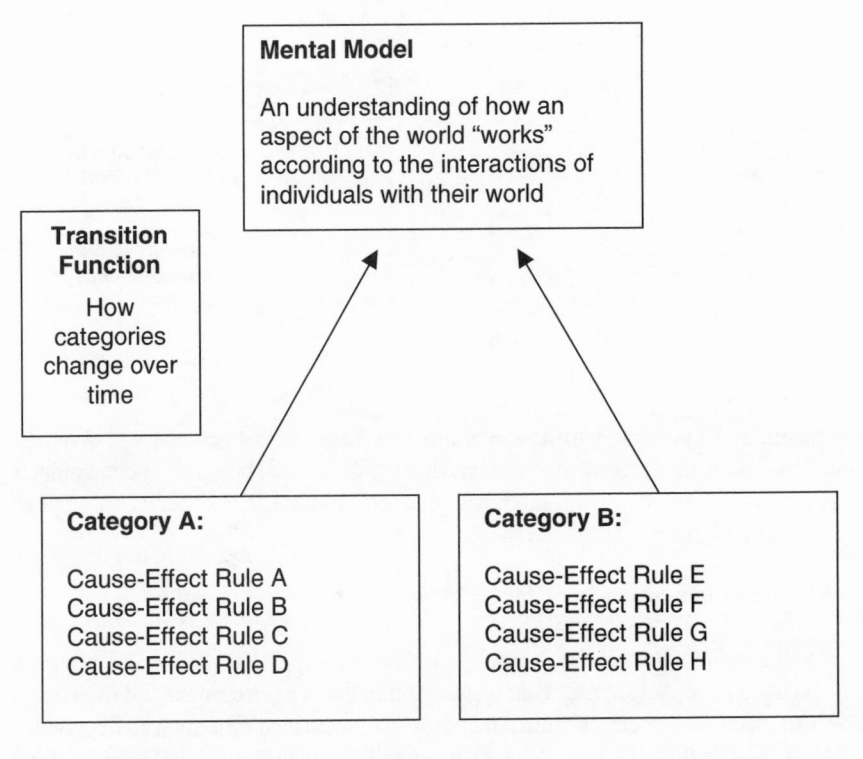

als then put these rules into larger conceptual categories. A mental model, then, is an understanding of how a set of categories interacts with one another over time (Holland et al. 1986).

Human beings have three sources of mental models: genetic endowments, personal experiences, and communicated models from others' experiences (North 1994). All animals are genetically endowed with some cause-effect rules that form mental models (flight or fight being one) (North 1994). A good number of animals also learn from their experiences in an environment, yet it is a unique quality of humans to have developed a system of communication to transmit their own personal experiences to others. Human beings, with complicated systems of oral communication, have the tools to communicate complicated empirical phenomena to others. Whereas chimpanzees are able to indicate to other chimps their ability to use sticks as crude tools to extract food from shells (a cause-effect rule), humans are able to convey whole sets of cause-effect rules, categories, and transition functions. Transferring this mental framework is costly in several different ways. Cognitive mental models can be extremely complicated, involving many different categories and perhaps hundreds of cause-effect rules.

Groups of individuals organize around mental models. With a common un-

Figure 13.2 **Interplay of Environment and Institutions**

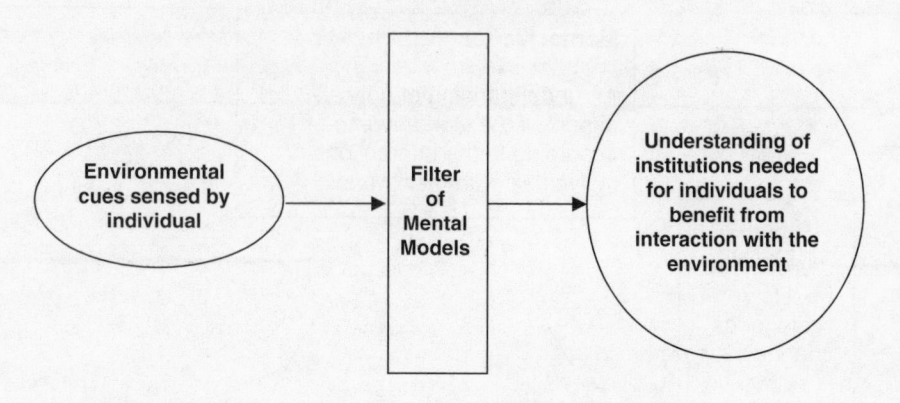

derstanding of how the world works, it is less costly to collectively act. Whereas institutions are the external mechanisms that regulate social behavior, mental models are the internal intellectual frameworks that individuals use to order a complicated world (see Figure 13.2).

The Composition and Use of Mental Models

A fundamental tension with sentient animals, and especially with human beings, is the need to actively sense what is going on in one's environment and then being able to place this experience into a memory so that the next time such an experience occurs, one does not have to reinvest the cognitive resources needed to understand what is happening (Jones 2001). At what point is it desirable to learn from an environment and at what point is it better to rely on stored information? Humans are excellent cognitive misers, in that not only are they proficient at storing information from their own experiences but also through various forms of communication they are able to draw on the similar experiences of others to make sense of their own situations (Jones 2001; Ostrom 2005). "People act in part upon the basis of myths, dogmas, ideologies, and 'half-baked' theories" (Denzau and North 1994, 3).

The objective reality of the world is less important than the subjective reality of that world. If humans were fully rational and able to see an objective reality, then it would follow that an analyst could predict the choices they make without understanding how they do it.

> If, on the other hand, we accept the proposition that both the knowledge and computational power of the decision maker is severely limited, then we must distinguish between the real world and the actor's perception of it and reasoning about it. That is to say, we must construct a theory (and test it empirically) of the processes of decision. Our theory must include not only the reasoning processes but also the processes that generate the actor's subjective representation of the decision problem, his or her frame (Simon 1986, 210–11).

Bounded rationality models assume that individuals have cognitive limitations. There is a gap between that objective reality and how people perceive reality; the greater the gap, the greater the need for cognitive shortcuts to help individuals cope with a complicated environment (Heiner 1983). Jones (2001) finds that while humans can sense many things all at once, as well as store a seemingly endless amount of data in long-term memory, the major limiting factor is short-term memory. Given this biological limitation, humans create frames, Denzau and North's "half-baked" theories," to filter all of the information bombarding them from their environment. The way that filters are constructed has profound effects on how individuals view their world (Tversky and Khaneman 1986).

Holland et al. (1986) create an inductive approach to understanding how individuals develop mental frames. Individuals develop their "half-baked" theories through experience with their environments, either their own personal experiences or the credible experiences of others whom they trust. Humans put information in categories, frameworks that help boundedly rational individuals to link similar experiences into a conceptual group.

> Models must consist of components that can be flexibly constructed and interrelated. Our most basic epistemic building block is a condition-action *rule,* which has the form "IF such-and-such, THEN so-and-so," where the IF part is the condition and the THEN part is the action (Holland et al. 1986, 14).

A young child, very early in development, learns that higher-pitched vocal patterns mean that a human is generally happy, while lower-pitched patterns indicate a problem. Humans are genetically hardwired with certain categories, such as when certain experiences will induce flight instincts while others induce fight, and create others from experience. The fundamental unit of any mental model of the environment is a rule, a single understanding of cause and effect (Holland et al. 1986). Similar cause-and-effect rules are packaged into common categories of cause and effect. Mental models are inductively created.

Not all cause-and-effect relationships are as important as others, depending on the environment in which an individual finds him- or herself. There are two elements to consider. First, rules can have different importance to the same individual depending on the individual's environment. While hiking in the deep backwoods of Alaska, the arrival of a grizzly bear with her cubs might trigger the "flight" rule; from experience one knows that the arrival of a very large animal with big teeth indicates the need to leave the area quickly. Conversely, while at the local zoo with one's small children, the arrival of the same bear with her cubs in the bear enclosure triggers the "stay" rule, where one knows that the enclosure provides good protection from the large animal with teeth.

In the case of a public organization, a subordinate may be happy to relax and share her personal feelings with the boss when she has built a long-term understanding that her boss is open to discussing issues that do not fall under the narrow scope of official work. That same worker, when facing a new supervisor in a networked situation, is unlikely to share information as freely. The challenge that the leader faces is creating a common understanding of cause and effect where the sharing of personal information is not frowned upon.

The second element to consider is that not only does a change in environment result in a different understanding of cause and effect but also a change in individuals in the same environment could result in very different cause-and-effect rules. On the Alaska backwoods adventure, the arrival of the grizzly bear would trigger in the hunter's mind the need to grab the hunting rifle, while in the nature photographer's mind it would trigger the need to grab the camera. In the case of members of a newly formed network, the addition of individuals who previously had no contact with the group is likely to create tension or lead people to remain silent. The administrator needs to discover what mental models are at work with each individual and then develop a means for individuals to recognize that they have certain commonalities in the way that they view the world. Cause-and-effect rules are contextual and inductive in nature, meaning that humans through time place disparate experiences into meaningful mental categories (Holland et al. 1986; Denzau and North 1994).

Mental categories, grouping similar cause-and effect-rules, are organized in a default hierarchy where certain categories are more fundamental than others (Holland et al. 1986). For a young child outside playing in the yard, the approach of an object triggers a search of fundamental categories. Is it an inanimate object blown by the wind or an animal moving under its own power? Once the child determines that it is an animal, the next level of specificity triggers the question, is this animal cute, cuddly, and furry and thereby friendly, or is it scaly and slimy and thereby unfriendly? If the child considers the animal to be in the friendly category, the response is to approach the animal in order to interact with it. Unfortunately, if it is the neighbor's guard dog, trained to ward off uninvited guests, its vicious barking and potential bite will make the child reconsider his default hierarchy. The experience could be only mildly traumatizing, resulting in the child reconsidering categorizing all cute animals as friendly, or it could be deeply traumatizing and cause him to feel that all moving objects in his or her yard (for the time being) need to trigger the flight response.

Higher-order rules of cause and effect, such as the idea that cute animals are friendly, are built upon lower-order rules, such as animals move under their own power. When one considers the process of creating mental rules as being inductive in nature, built upon real-world experience, it follows that individuals are more likely to change higher-order rules much more readily than lower-order rules (Holland et al. 1986, 205). As Sabatier and Jenkins-Smith (1993) indicate, ideas fundamental to one's understanding of the environment are difficult to change due to their abstract nature. Broad categories of cause and effect at lower-order, fundamental levels are created to in order to catch very broad empirical phenomena. Being broad in nature, singular empirical events that suggest that the categories are incorrect can easily be labeled as aberrant (Holland et al. 1986, 37).

Leaders of networks face the task of discovering the hierarchy of mental rules for subordinates. One must understand which rules are malleable, less fundamental to an individual's belief system, and which are untouchable. For example, a leader may be able to get a police officer to consider different tactics for arresting juvenile offenders while the officer may be completely unwilling to discuss how to change the juvenile legal code. The officer in this case has a mental hierarchy where he or she is comfortable in interpreting agency policy while unwilling to interpret law. The policy and law are the formal institutions at play, while the officer's interpretation that the role of an officer can extend to interpretation of policy but not law is the larger mental model constructed through a process of socialization. In a network situation, such as a local juvenile crime task force, the effective leader may notice that the officer is unwilling to discuss changes to law. This may seem like tacit approval, or disinterest, rather than the fact that the officer has been socialized not to discuss changes in law. The way forward for the leader, then, may be to discuss how changes in policy could affect juvenile crime.

A group of cause-and-effect rules delineate a category. The category of "cuddly animal" for the young child includes rules about what such an object will feel like, look like, and how it will react to the child's interaction. A mental model is a set of categories and a transition function (Holland et al. 1986, 37). Transition functions animate an individual's understanding of how a state of the world moves from point A to point B through time. An object that fits into the category of "cuddly animal" for a child may follow a transition function where the child approaches the cuddly animal and then the cuddly animal becomes the child's playmate. The full mental model for the child includes the individual cause-effect rules about this approaching object, the categories that encompass the several rules into the idea of a "cuddly animal," and a transition function that indicates how the category can change through stimulus either from the child or from other external impacts. In this inductive approach an individual's mental models change from the bottom up, meaning interactions with an environment that serve to question the validity of cause-effect rules that, in turn, call into question categories and transition functions.

Learning from Experience

The question then becomes, how do individuals learn from experiences? According to Denzau and North (1994) there are two different learning processes: a process of normal learning where experiences serves to strengthen the current categories, and a process of representational redescription. Mental models serve to order a complicated world, so a certain amount of rigidity in categories aids individuals in putting the many disparate experiences into common conceptual boxes. The cognitive benefits of mental models are due to the shortcuts that they produce (Jones 2001). An individual does not have to completely reconsider what is happening in the world every moment but rather can find certain cues (cause-effect rules) from any situation that can quickly and cheaply label that experience as being part of an existing category. Individuals continually have experiences with their environments, and the process of incorporating those experiences into their current mental categories is that of normal learning (Denzau and North 1994).

Normal learning is about the testing of the cause-effect rules from an individual's experience with the world. While the strength of mental models may lie in their ability to reduce cognitive costs, they must also be able to adapt to changing environmental stimuli. The second type of learning, the process of representational redescription, occurs when empirical facts begin to call into question not only the validity of the cause-effect rules but also the mental categories. Individuals generalize from their specific experiences, recombining former rule elements with newer rules derived from recent experience.

Individuals continually evaluate their experiences in the environment with their mental models.

> Rules are in competition with each other for the best description of empirical reality. Competition will favor those rules that (a) provide a description of the current situation (match), (b) have a history of past usefulness to the system (strength), (c) produce the greatest degree of completeness of description (specificity), and (d) have the greatest compatibility with other currently active information (support) (Holland et al. 1986, 49).

The assertion made here is that there is a tendency for individuals to not update their understandings of how the world works even in the face of repeated experiences that would indicate that the mental model in use no longer accurately explains what is going on in their world. The tendency to hold on to incorrect models is due to the two different types of learning. Normal learning occurs often as humans routinely interact with their environments. By contrast, representational redescription requires individuals to make a significant cognitive investment in reconsidering how their world works. Individuals face a choice as they start to sense that environmental factors have changed: They can decide to update their current mental models through either normal learning or representational redescription.

Boundedly rational individuals will choose to "satisfice" (Simon 1955), meaning that the first rule that minimally explains the reason for aberrant cues from the environment will be used (Holland et al. 1986, 78). Individuals can decide whether to broaden the applicability of their mental categories in order to fit seemingly aberrant information into the current model; or, they can view conflicting data simply as aberrant and decide that it has little impact upon their current model (Holland et al. 1986, 37). Individuals, as cognitive misers, are more likely to consider experiences that do not follow the posited cause-effect rules to be aberrant rather than an indication that their existing mental models may be faulty (Holland et al. 1986, 205–6).

Mental models are the key filter between events in an environment and the humanly devised formal rules and informal norms that structure social interaction. The design of mental models helps determine how informational cues from the

Figure 13.3   **Cues, Categories, and Institutions**

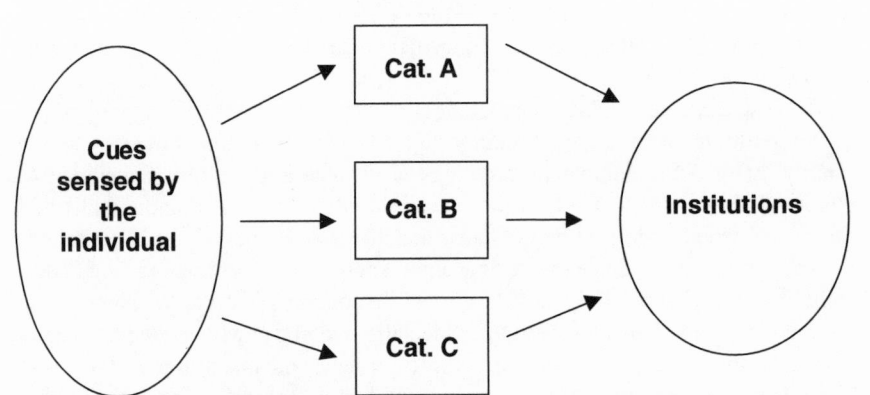

environment will be processed. The ability of individuals to tailor new institutions to a changing environment is dependent not only on what information is out there to be gleaned but also on what information individuals see fit to communicate to others. The social aspect of mental models, the fact that many models are socially created and transmitted through the use of language (Ostrom 1990), inherently means that individuals will tend to process information by using the current mental models and will in turn pass the information to other network members packaged in the existing categories of the common mental model. Such a tendency serves to limit how environmental cues impact upon current institutions (see Figure 13.3).

Individuals tend to place cues within the framework of existing categories (normal learning) rather than investing in the costly process of representational redescription. When individuals are working with their own, individually created mental models, there most likely will be a point where placing environmental cues incorrectly into preexisting categories results in suboptimal rules and norms, which would indicate the need to reconsider those categories. A different dynamic occurs when mental models are socially created and shared. Individuals no longer experience environmental cues themselves, as it is not possible to transmit direct physical cues (such as the feeling of intense sunlight on one's face); rather they rely on the communication of such cues by other individuals (the communication that the sunlight created a sunburn, which is a socially understood category resulting from the cause-effect rules for extended exposure to the sun). By only communicating how an experience fit into a category, the receiver of such information is not able to make a sound judgment as to whether that experience with the environment really warranted such a label. The result is a system where environmental cues can be consistently misinterpreted, leading to the extension of current mental models beyond their usefulness.

There also is a relationship between mental models and organization. Individuals with similar interpretations of how the world works face lower transaction costs because they do not need to invest in communicating these complicated ideas among each other. Once organizations have formed around a core of mental models, those organizations themselves provide a convenient heuristic for organization members (Simon 1998; 2000).

Because the creation of mental models is an inductive process, where individuals slowly build understandings of their world, it follows that mental models are not rapidly changed. Similar to understandings of organizational culture (Schein 1992), changing mental models occurs through an iterative process as individuals find that their current understanding of cause and effect no longer adequately explains their reality. As individuals invest time and resources into creating existing understandings of the world, they must face pressing concerns in order to change those models. The role of an administrator, especially one in a newly created horizontal organization, is not as a creator of completely new understandings of the world but rather as an interpreter of the current mental models that different organization members hold. After the period of investigation the administrator faces finding enough common understanding to make the organization functional.

Challenges for Network Leadership

Networks as forms of organization provide a necessary flexibility to address complex public problems. At the same time they also produce significant challenges for public administrators who increasingly spend more of their time trying to lead through fluid relationships. There are two interrelated issues that deserve further attention for scholars of public administration. The first is an issue of pedagogy. How do we teach current and future public administrators to be effective in both hierarchical and horizontal organizations? The second deals with constructing a theory of network productivity. That is, how do people work through networks? With that knowledge, one can begin to consider the role of the public administrator in trying to lead in this increasingly frequent type of organization.

The dominant form of public organization over the course of the past century has been hierarchy. Public administrators have been trained to be effective at bridging specialized subordinates. Master's programs in public administration almost universally create pedagogies around a core set of technical skills as well as greater understandings of the public environment. Students are instructed in how to strategically plan, budget, implement, and evaluate public programs. Sometimes courses on human resources, decision making, and administrative ethics augment these programs. Almost all courses are designed with the understanding that public administrators will be working within hierarchies, if not leading them. In fact, programs overwhelmingly teach transactional modes of administration: how students can understand current rules and mold future rules.

This chapter holds that future public administrators need to be exposed to a broader range of organizational concepts. The concept that network managers are faced both with traditional management and leadership tasks, that is, using both rules and the mental models that undergird those rules, lends itself to teaching students less concrete techniques and more about how to think situationally. As long as an organization remains complicated, whether that means hierarchically or horizontally, there will be a place for administrators to specialize in technique. At the same time, administrators will be challenged to appreciate the larger environment in which the organization occurs. Part of that environment is the matrix of institutions that guide social life. As Schein (1992) indicates, administrators would be helped by learning to recognize physical and social cues that point not only to formal rules but also mental models. That is to say, institutional analysis is a skill that should be practiced.

Discerning what mental models are at play in an organization, hierarchical or network based, is difficult. Oftentimes they are so basic or ingrained in the subconscious that people are unable to articulate that they even exist. Given that challenge, what makes successful leaders adept at understanding these underlying frameworks? There are three categories that leaders can consider. For one, successful leaders foster their own abilities to *discern patterns in what is said or not said.* Organizational stories or myths, passed down through generations of members, hint at the contours of underlying models. Stories about how an organization's founder clocked into work at 5 o'clock in the morning, every morning, points toward a model that values timeliness throughout the organization. Successful leaders will encourage existing organizational members to tell the war stories that may seem trivial at first but hint at deeper meaning.

A second strategy for successful leaders is to *identify how language frames communication.* Modern organizations have their own languages with different groups of organization members assigning specific meanings to words. On a transactional level, a manager would be best served by understanding the definitions of words and acronyms in order to communicate with his or her employees. On a transformational level, leaders endeavor to understand how a vocabulary can serve to provide meaning for a group in different circumstances. For example, a term such as *performance-based management* could have a specific textbook definition for a recent graduate of a public administration program. That same term could be packed with an entirely different meaning when it is used by a group of public-sector workers who recently faced rapid downsizing due to a process of contracting out a core service. Only through experiencing the impact of a vocabulary on social interaction can a leader understand underlying mental models.

Last, successful leaders become adept sociologists in *understanding how people physically relate to each other* (Schein 1992). Are office doors open? Do employees rapidly return telephone messages? Do people congregate in the cafeteria or do they eat alone at their desks? Each one of these aspects of social relations could provide a clue as to the underlying logic to the institution in use for an organization.

The difficulty of discerning mental models is compounded when one considers the task of leading a newly formed network. Not only are mental models at work but there is a diverse set of models coming from a myriad of different home organizations. Success in network leadership depends on creating structures that facilitate members communicating about how stories, vocabularies, and interactions work in their own organizations. Discussions of the way different member organizations work, the vocabulary they employ, and their organizations' structures could all provide a means to understand deeper mental models. Network leaders can also seek to spend one-on-one time with each new network member in order to begin the relationship on a relaxed and informal basis. The most important lesson for those leading networks is to aim to facilitate long-term communication and mutual learning between network members. Only through repeated contact can members begin to construct a common set of models that will structure future interactions.

References

Burns, James M. 1978. *Leadership*. New York: Harper & Row.
Denzau, Arthur T., and Douglass C. North. 1994. "Shared Mental Models: Ideologies and Institutions." *Kyklos* 47 (1): 3–31.
Edelman, Gerald M., and Guilio Tonini. 2001. *Consciousness: How Matter Becomes Imagination*. London: Penguin.
Frederickson, H. George. 2005. "Transcending the Community: Local Leadership in a World of Shared Power." *Public Management* 87 (10): 8–15.
Gabris, Gerald T., Robert T. Golembiewski, and Douglas M. Ihrke. 2000. "Leadership Credibility, Board Relations, and Administrative Innovation at the Local Government Level." *Journal of Public Administration Research and Theory* 11 (1): 89–108.
Hayek, Friedrich A. 1952. *The Sensory Order: An Inquiry into the Foundations of Theoretical Psychology*. Chicago: University of Chicago Press.
Heiner, Ronald. 1983. "The Origins of Predictable Behavior." *American Economic Review* 73 (4): 560–95.
Holland, John H., Keith J. Holyoak, Richard E. Nisbett, and Paul R. Thagard. 1986. *Induction: Processes of Inference, Learning, and Discovery*. Cambridge, MA: MIT Press.
Jones, Bryan D. 2001. *Politics and the Architecture of Choice*. Chicago: University of Chicago Press.
Kickert, Walter J. M., Erik-Hans Klijn, and Joop F.M. Koppenjan. 1997. "Introduction: A Management Perspective on Policy Networks." In *Managing Complex Networks: Strategies for the Public Sector*, eds. Walter J.M. Kickert, Erik-Hans Klijn, and Joop F.M. Koppenjan, 1–13. London: Sage.
Knight, Jack. 1992. *Institutions and Social Conflict*. New York: Cambridge University Press.
Kotter, John P. 1990. "What Leaders Really Do." *Harvard Business Review* 68 (3): 103–12.
Kreps, David M. 1990. "Corporate Culture and Economic Theory." In *Perspectives on Positive Political Economy*, eds. James Alt and Kenneth Shepsle, 90–143. Cambridge: Cambridge University Press.
Miller, Gary J. 1992. *Managerial Dilemmas: The Political Economy of Hierarchy*. New York: Cambridge University Press.
North, Douglass C. 1990. *Institutions, Institutional Change, and Economic Performance*. New York: Cambridge University Press.
———. 1994. "Economic Performance through Time." *American Economic Review* 84 (3): 359–68.

————. 2005. *Understanding the Process of Economic Change.* Princeton, NJ: Princeton University Press.

Ostrom, Elinor. 1990. *Governing the Commons.* New York: Cambridge University Press.

————. 2005. *Understanding Institutional Diversity.* Princeton, NJ: Princeton University Press.

Ostrom, Vincent. 1980. "Artisanship and Artifact." *Public Administration Review* 40 (4): 309–17.

O'Toole, Laurence J., Jr. 1997. "Treating Networks Seriously: Practical and Research-Based Agendas in Public Administration." *Public Administration Review* 57 (1): 45–52.

Sabatier, Paul, and Hank Jenkins-Smith. 1993. *Policy Change and Learning.* Boulder, CO: Westview Press.

Schein, Edgar H. 1992. *Organizational Culture and Leadership.* 2nd ed. San Francisco: Jossey-Bass.

Schelling, Thomas C. 1960. *The Strategy of Conflict.* Cambridge, MA: Harvard University Press.

Simon, Herbert A. 1955. "A Behavioral Model of Rational Choice." *The Quarterly Journal of Economics* 69 (1): 99–118.

————. 1959. *Models of Man: Social and Rational.* New York: John Wiley and Sons.

————. 1986. "Rationality in Psychology and Economics." *Journal of Business* 59 (Supplement): S209–24.

————. 1998. "Why Public Administration?" *Journal of Public Administration Research and Theory* 8 (1): 1–11.

————. 2000. "Public Administration in Today's World of Organizations and Markets." *PS: Political Science and Politics* 33 (4): 749–56.

Terry, Larry. 1995. *Leadership of Public Bureaucracies: The Administrator as Conservator.* Thousand Oaks, CA: Sage.

Tversky, Amos, and Daniel Khaneman. 1986. "Rational Choice and the Framing of Decisions." *Journal of Business* (Supplement), 59: S251–77.

Yukl, Gary, and Richard Lepsinger. 2005. "Why Integrating the Leading and Managing Roles Is Essential for Organizational Effectiveness." *Organizational Dynamics* 34 (4): 361–75.

Zaleznik, Abraham. 1977. "Managers and Leaders: Are They Different?" *Harvard Business Review* 55 (2): 67–78.

Part IV

Leading Change in Different Contexts

Leading Change in Different Contexts

14

Leadership and Management in Local Government

KARL NOLLENBERGER

"Leadership," notes Bernard Bass, "is one of the world's oldest preoccupations. The understanding of leadership has figured strongly in the quest for knowledge" (1990, 3). The study of leadership is the study of history. Some say history is about what leaders did and how they did it. Machiavelli's *The Prince*, published in 1513, was a study of leadership. Management, by comparison, traces its roots to the Industrial Revolution. It became necessary to organize (manage) resources for the production of an end product. This chapter focuses on leadership and management in local governments in the United States. Local government impacts the lives of its citizens directly and daily. The availability of police and fire responses, the condition of the streets, the provision of health care to the less advantaged, and even the ability to get water out of the tap and flush the toilet are the results of well-led and well-managed local governments. Thus, it is important to understand the impact of leadership and management in local government and the roles played by the elected officials and professionals in this arena.

In attempting to define leadership, Bass concludes that "the search for the one and only proper and true definition of leadership seems to be fruitless, since the appropriate choice of definition should depend upon the methodological and substantive aspects of leadership in which one is interested" (1990, 18). However, one of the better definitions is offered by John Gardner who views leadership as

> the process of persuasion or example by which an individual (or leadership team) induces a group to pursue objectives held by the leader or shared by the leader and his or her followers. . . . Leaders cannot be thought of apart from the historic context in which they arise, the setting in which they function (e.g., elective office), and the system over which they preside (e.g., a particular city or state). They are integral parts of the system, subject to the forces that affect the system (1990, 1).

Management has also been the subject of many attempts at defining the role played by executives. Chester Barnard describes the essential executive functions as "first, to provide a system of communication; second, to promote the securing of essential efforts; and third, to formulate and define purpose" (1968, 217). The boundary between leadership and management has been the subject of much discussion. While there are some clear distinctions between the two functions, Gardner concludes that "every time I come across first-class managers they turn out to have quite a lot of leader in them" (1990, 3). Local governments in the United States have the same needs for leadership and management that have prevailed throughout society over time.

City governments operate under one of five types of governmental structure —weak mayor-council, strong mayor-council, commission, town meeting, or council-manager. The weak mayor-council form tends to be found primarily in small jurisdictions with populations less than 5,000, while commission and town meeting forms are infrequently found in cities today. The two primary forms of government for cities over 5,000 are the strong mayor-council and council-manager forms. These two primary forms will be the focus of leadership and management in this chapter.

Leadership and management roles of mayors, council members, and managers have been found to differ between the forms of government. The common theme in this chapter is for mayors, council members, and managers to adapt to the situation whether it is the form of government, nature of the community, or events of the time, among others. An additional theme is the recognition of the enhanced policy role of the professional manager in forging a partnership with the elected officials regardless of the form of government. The complexity of urban issues in the twenty-first century has challenged the traditional concepts of leadership and management in local government. This chapter is organized into discussions of leadership and management in strong mayor-council government, leadership in council-manager government, managerial leadership and administration, and a summary of these topics. Leadership and management styles have a variety of descriptions, as will be discussed in this chapter. The multitude of local governments and the diverse settings that exist in American culture have a significant impact on the patterns of leadership and management that are found in these localities.

Leadership in Mayor-Council Government

The mayoral position in strong mayor-council forms of government has been the focal point of most research looking for the best practices in governing cities. The mayoral position is the most visible position in local government in most communities. Clarence Stone explains:

> There is no well developed theory of political leadership, perhaps not even a
> universally accepted definition. Office holding bestows authority, but the authority

conferred is highly limited. Particularly at the local level, governmental authority commands only modest resources. The weakness of formal authority thus gives added importance to the personal leadership of prominent urban actors, especially in the loosely structured context of local politics in America (1995, 96).

In the American political system, when difficulties arise, inevitably there is a call for leadership. Leadership is at the very heart of politics. In our fragmented federal system, local issues can be addressed by people coming together under leadership. The office of mayor is a particularly visible leadership platform.

Leadership is interactive by nature so the situation that it occurs within is important to the exercise of leadership. But leadership is also creative, so the personal factor is important as well. The question always arises as to how to measure the performance of leadership. The community power studies in the past measured it within the context of community decision making and power. But more recent research on leadership in local government looks at leadership from a multiframe perspective. It is this perspective that is the focus of this chapter.

The mayoral position, the one with the largest potential policy impact in local government, can be greatly underutilized as a leadership post. "In the furtherance of their personal and career ambitions, mayors go after quick successes, insulate themselves from citizen involvement, or indulge in posturing" (Stone 1995, 110). Holli looked at the best and worst of 782 mayors in the fifteen biggest American cities from 1820 to 1995. Leadership in Western democratic societies is conceptualized as "a mix of applying persuasion and exercising formal office authority" (1999, 127). Holli notes that while the "trait" theory of leadership held the foreground for most of the twentieth century, the identification of the right traits had mixed results. Subsequent investigation tended to focus on behavior patterns of leaders. These leader-behavior studies cluster around two poles—one that focuses on the relationship with followers and a second group that focuses on the tasks and goal achievement (1999, 133).

In the 1960s, the advent of the contingency theory of leadership took place. Contingency theory links the leader to the situation in developing an integrated theory of leadership. There is no one best style of leadership applicable to every situation; different leadership or management styles work in different situations. The task-oriented leader and the relationship-oriented leader are responding to different situations. The task structure is used to identify the city's most pressing problems and to determine their solution. Examples are uprooting crime, eliminating corruption, and parceling city services citywide. The relationship-style mayor is less effective in task-oriented roles while taskmasters excel in structures with problem situations and also in times of crisis and chaos. In justification of the contingency or situational style, "There are situations for leaders, leaders for situations—a principle that Esther Fuchs illustrates succinctly in pointing out that New York's John Lindsay would never have been elected mayor of Chicago, and Richard 'Boss' Daley would never have resided at Gracie Mansion" (Holli 1999, 151).

Pressman's (1972) research on the City of Oakland and his theoretical outline for mayoral leadership is frequently referred to by other authors as a basis for measuring mayoral leadership. Written at the time of the "urban crisis," the need for mayoral leadership was widely heralded as a means to address the crisis. While it was acknowledged that few mayors have all the resources necessary to deal with the tasks facing them, an alert mayor can use the brokerage function to accumulate influence and power. Pressman (1972, 2) outlines seven resources that would be the ideal for a mayor to possess for successful leadership:

- Sufficient financial and staff resources on the part of the city government.
- City jurisdiction in social program areas—such as education, housing, redevelopment, job training, etc.
- Mayoral jurisdiction within the city government in these policy fields.
- A salary for the mayor that would enable him to be full-time on the job.
- Sufficient staff support for the mayor—for policy planning, speech writing, intergovernmental relations, and political work.
- Ready vehicles for publicity, such as friendly newspapers or television stations.
- Politically oriented groups, which the mayor could mobilize to help him achieve particular goals.

Pressman also acknowledges that the personality of the mayor is a potential source of influence in addition to these resources.

Even with some of the resources missing, the mayor can still be an effective leader. But the style and consequences of the leadership are dependent upon the type of government and political system. Writing in 1972, Pressman recognized that the question of how alternate governmental structures affect the ability of officials to direct policy was still an open question. He leaves unanswered the question as to what personal characteristics were most successful in the ability to pyramid resources successfully. He felt that there needed to be more research to determine the kinds of leadership that are possible in political arenas with low resources as he defined them earlier.

Svara (1999b) suggests that the ideal mayor in the strong mayor-council form of government has the entrepreneur or innovator style. This mayor looks for creative solutions and accumulates resources to build coalitions and gain leverage. The approach is power oriented within this structure. The resources are both formal (appointment of department heads, development of budget, direction of departments, veto authority) and informal (political party or community-elite support, strong popular backing, private backers indebted to the mayor for various reasons). Trends in the political system have reduced many of these informal resources due to a decrease in political party influence, splintering of the community elite, increases in interest groups, diversity of council members, implementation of civil service and purchasing reform, and court actions on hiring. The mayor's personal attributes (experience, financial support, time and energy commitment to job, and media savvy) also impact the leadership role.

A study of mayoral leadership in Boston and San Francisco in the 1970s looks at three variables—political skills, political systems, and political culture (Ferman 1985). The focus on political skills was to overcome the limitations of previous studies while the focus on systems and culture was to give a context to the mayoral leadership. The political system influences the resources and strategies available and the opportunities for mayoral leadership. The use of political culture was a narrow definition relating to the public-regarding/reform ethos in San Francisco versus a private-regarding/non-reform ethos in Boston. The political systems and culture make the political skills of the mayor a necessity. The study concludes that there cannot be a single theory of executive leadership. There may be some broad conclusions that apply in every setting, but the theories of leadership have to be viewed at they relate to a specific setting. Political culture plays a role in determining leadership opportunities.

In the 1960s, attention was focused on urban issues, and the role of the mayor increasingly became a focus of these urban studies. In a study that looked at twenty city mayors in cities with populations ranging from 152,000 to 938,000 from 1971 to 1973, Kotter and Lawrence (1974) address the questions of the styles of mayoral leadership, roles played by mayors, the impact of a mayor on the city, the impact of resource constraints, and whether it is possible to make generalizations about mayors or whether every situation and city is unique. Their desired goal was to better understand the mayoral role in the urban governance process.

The authors concluded that no existing model was capable of explaining even one of the situations that they had studied. They created a new framework based on their assessment of system dynamics. The mayor's behavior is differentiated into three processes in the new model—agenda setting, network building, and task accomplishment. There are a wide variety of behavioral options in all three processes. The behavioral pattern best for the process depends upon the situation itself. The depth and breadth of the mayor's domain or areas in which the mayor behaved in light of these three processes were examined in the study. It was determined that the legal basis for the position alone was not a predictor of the domain of the mayor. While mayors in council-manager cities tended to have smaller domains legally than strong mayor cities, there were exceptions dependent upon the mayor's agenda setting process (Kotter and Lawrence 1974, 202).

For instance, the mayor of Dallas (council-manager) set a larger policy agenda than the mayor of New Orleans (strong mayor). The agenda setting of the mayor determined the domain in the greater picture. The second key process of network building and maintenance was the "votes, money, laws, human skills, and task accomplishment capacity" of the mayor (Kotter and Lawrence 1974, 65). The network that was built by a mayor was vital to the accomplishment of the tasks and his reelection. The third and final key process for mayors of task accomplishment involved how the mayor undertook the tasks on his agenda.

Using these processes and the behaviors described as background, five types of mayors are identified in the study as follows (Kotter and Lawrence 1974, 189):

- *Ceremonial*: Relies on personal appeal; has no staff, a limited network, a neutral relationship, and an individualistic process.
- *Caretaker*: Relies on personal appeal; supports a discrete exchange process for network building; makes limited modifications to the network; builds loyal staff with few resources; uses bureaucratic and individualistic task accomplishment process to moderate degrees; differs from a ceremonial mayor in that this type has resources to exchange.
- *Personality/Individualistic*: Relies on personal appeal and to some extent on purposive appeal in network building; has no staff; does not try to shape the network; supports individualistic task accomplishment and occasionally bureaucratic and entrepreneurial processes; is like a ceremonial mayor who has become more aggressive in agenda setting, purposive appeal, and increasing involvement in individualistic task accomplishment.
- *Executive*: Supports network building to a moderate degree (through discreet exchange, purposive appeals, personal appeals); modifies network members to a small degree; supports individualistic task accomplishment process moderately, bureaucratic process considerably, and entrepreneurial process in limited ways; has a staff with some limited resources; is like a caretaker who became more aggressive and enlarged his domain; has an impact that tended to be toward some change.
- *Program Entrepreneur*: Uses all network-building processes skillfully; actively tries to modify some of his network members; has a staff of important useful resources; uses all the task accomplishment processes, especially the entrepreneurial.

The type of mayor existing in each city was clearly situational. After completing the research project, Kotter and Lawrence came to the conclusion that talking about "good" or "effective" or "best" type of mayor was misleading and not useful (1974, 202). Because we all have different ways of viewing the world, putting a standard on some behaviors versus others is difficult to impossible.

Another study dealing with governing in twelve middle-sized cities was based on "two simple beliefs: that mayoral leadership is important in sustaining and revitalizing cities and that in the study of mayoral leadership, mayors of middle-sized cities have been grossly over-looked" (Bowers and Rich 2000, ix). The study noted the following significant items that impact upon the environment in which the mayor performs:

- Formal structure of city government—strong mayor versus weak mayor forms.
- Extent to which community-focused organizations are present.

- Quality and functioning operation of the city government.
- Level of intergovernmental relations and cooperation.
- Racial and economic makeup of the city.
- City's overall fiscal condition—mayors can be frustrated by lack of resources.

The study concludes that leadership is "crucial to the sustainability of middle-sized cities." Mayoral leadership occurs when mayors are change agents, when they "impact on the flow of events" in such a way that "something happens that would otherwise not take place" (Bowers and Rich 2000, 217). Both innovation and conservation (the halting of a trend that can undermine a community's sustainability) can bring about change. The environment can help or hinder the results of mayoral efforts. The individual variables specific to the mayors themselves helped to determine if they were able to provide effective leadership. Their styles and their prior experience helped to determine that success.

Rob Gurwitt suggests in 1993 in an article, "The Lure of the Strong Mayor," that the age of municipal reform as it has been known in the twentieth century was coming to an end due to the attraction of the strong mayor form of government. The reason is pure politics and the demand for more of it. The issue of responsiveness is more important today than those of economy and efficiency that were the foundation of the council-manager form of government. Gurwitt suggests that professional management is possible under the strong mayor form along with responsiveness since over one-third of the strong mayor forms have hired a professional administrator reporting to the mayor.

In a later article on Oakland, Gurwitt (2000) describes a situation where the city adopted a strong mayor form and also had a strong manager. Oakland Mayor Jerry Brown explains that "the council form, in smaller towns of great homogeneity and stability, works more or less all right, but when you have deadlock, when you have drift, when you have serious urban problems, when you have a divided constituency, there has to be a way to mobilize leadership, and that leadership can't just be rhetorical. There has to be a linking of management and the public role of the highest elected official, the mayor" (Gurwitt 2000, 18). Gurwitt suggests that cities all over the country are looking for ways to empower the weak mayors with more authority.

Leadership in Council-Manager Government

The roots of the council-manager plan in the early 1900s resulted from the growth of urbanization, the popularity of business ideals, the Progressive reform movement, and the advent of scientific management with its applicability to the public sector (Stillman 1974). The National Municipal League, a reform organization organized in the late 1800s, was a major force in the advocacy of the council-manager plan with the adoption of the Model City Charter and its support of the reform movement.

The first city to adopt the council-manager plan was Ukiah, California, in 1904

Table 14.1

Cities That Have Adopted Most Elements of the Council-Manager Plan

	Cities over 50,000	Total Reformed	Percent Reformed
Northeastern States	80	23	29
Midwestern States	137	77	56
Southern States	112	78	70
Western States	262	243	93
Total	591	421	71

Source: Adapted from International City/County Management Association and U.S. Census 2000.

(Stillman 1974, 14). The first large city to adopt the council-manager plan was Dayton, Ohio, in 1914, and the Dayton Plan soon became the most popular of the reform initiatives of the era (114). In urban government today, the council-manager plan retains recognition as the most popular form of city government, as shown in Table 14.1. Over 71 percent of the cities over 50,000 population in the United States have adopted the council-manager form, with significant differences in different regions of the country. In the Northeastern states, only 29 percent of the cities over 50,000 have adopted the reformed governmental structures compared to 93 percent in the Western states, where most of the cities were incorporated after reform had become widely accepted throughout the country.

In contrasting council-manager government from mayor-council government, Chet Newland makes three distinct contrasts:

- Council-manager government facilitates more collaborative civic authority, combined with coordinated, institutionalized administration. Mayor-council government emphasizes separation of powers with the focus on mayoral leadership, and administration is more fragmented and ad hoc.
- Transformational politics is the ideal of the council-manager form, searching for a collaborative, community-wide orientation. Transactional politics is the ideal of the mayor-council form, facilitating brokerage among different interests.
- Professionally expert administration is the ideal in council-manager government, with neutrally equal access and responsiveness. Politically sensitive administration is the ideal in the mayor-council form with non-routinization to facilitate responsiveness (1994, 278).

While some persons allege that the authority given to the manager undermines democracy, others argue that the manager's reporting to the city council without any protection of tenure is the check and balance necessary to protect democracy while enhancing the quality of local government (Svara 1995).

In order to understand the role of the mayor in council-manager forms of government, it is necessary to understand the division of roles between the mayor, city council, and manager. The politics-administration dichotomy has been the subject of much debate over the past century in its applicability to the council-manager form of government. Many today contend that the dichotomy of policy (as differentiated from politics) and administration is a myth (Ammons and Newell 1988; Montjoy and Watson 1995; Svara 1995, 1998). They suggest that although there is a degree of difference, mayors do manage and city managers do engage in policy. While mayors tend to emphasize the political role, the manager tends to emphasize the managerial and policy role.

Those questioning the dichotomy feel that there has never been any question that the manager is involved in policy making. Others have found the dichotomy to be more of a continuum in that it still serves as a guidepost for managers in their dealings with the city council and their structuring of employee-council relations. The unique competences that managers bring to the discussions and their exposure to the physical, economic, and social problems of cities have made managers a part of the debates and action plans dealing with urban policy formulation (Henry 1971). While the council-manager plan has been frequently criticized for inhibiting political leadership, there are few who question the team approach that the plan brings to resolving issues. White (1927, 226) reported that city managers felt they were a combination of administration and leadership even as far back as his 1927 study.

Local government managers identify with the models showing the separation of politics from administration, but a partnership model has strong support where public administrators see themselves as having a role in the policy arena. The separation between politics and administration has always been blurred, but city managers have always had a role in policy (Dunn and Legge 2002; Nalbandian 1994). Yet, the city management profession still is measured against the traditional view that the city manager is a politically neutral administrator. The differentiation that is significant is that between politics and policy. The city manager is politically neutral and remains out of partisan politics. However, the city manager is involved in policy formulation, policy adoption, and policy implementation. The original desire to insulate the city manager from partisan politics took the dichotomy issue into the policy sphere as well.

One of the arguments made for strong mayor-council form of government compared to council-manager government is that the former adheres to the separation of powers doctrine that dates back to the formulation of the Constitution of the United States to prevent undue influence in any one political body. William Hansell (1993), who served as the executive director of the International City/County Management Association (ICMA), suggests that there is not the same need for separation of powers in local government since local governments are creatures of the state and not autonomous. The council-manager form of government establishes a quasi-parliamentary system of governance. The executive serves under the governing body and can be changed at any time. The success of the system has been the presence of the coordinated executive capacity to facilitate quick and direct responsiveness to public interests.

The role of a mayor/chair in the council-manager plan requires a rethinking of the standard assumptions of the role of a mayor/chair. The dominant literature reviewing mayoral roles in strong mayor forms thinks of leadership as the acquisition and use of power, but the acquisition and use of power is not the dominant feature of the council-manager form of government. A facilitative style of leadership is the most effective in the council-manager form (Svara 1995). In his work on leadership in cities, Svara examines the roles of elected officials and administrators in the urban governmental process to seek ways to improve performance. In this research, Svara is careful to distinguish the governmental process from the political process. "The governmental process refers to the way that officials make public policy decisions, implement them, and manage resources and ongoing operations. . . . The governmental process may be viewed as that part of the political process that occurs within government itself" (Svara 1990, 4). The political process includes political actors such as business elites and special interests, other institutions, higher levels of government, and economic and natural resources and constraints.

In a mayor-council city, the mayor is the key initiator of action. In a council-manager form, the mayor may take on that role or it is shared with the city council and manager. The mayor takes on a facilitator role to promote communication and effective interaction in the process. They empower others and provide a sense of purpose. "In this sense, the mayor is a guiding force in city government who helps ensure that all other officials are performing as well as possible and that all are moving in the right direction" (Svara 1995, xxvii). The mayor or chairperson provides political leadership, and the manager provides professional leadership.

The governmental process described as a continuum of mission to policy to administration to management activities is a reconceptualization of what is traditionally referred to as policy and administration. Mission is the purview of the elected officials (with important contributions from the city manager). Policy and administration are shared responsibilities, with the elected officials having a greater role in policy and the appointed official having a greater role in administration. Management is the purview of the manager (who is of course appointed and reviewed by the council). These dimensions help to define the proper roles of the elected officials and administrators in the governmental process and the interaction of these players in these roles.

Svara (1995) examines the contributions of the various officials in the government process based upon these four dimensions of governance. The preeminent role of the elected officials in the mission dimension and the similar preeminent role of the manager in the management dimension are tempered by shared responsibilities in the policy and administration dimensions. The preeminent roles are not totally exclusive but, as reflected in Figure 14.1, what Svara referred to as a dichotomy-duality model. In subsequent research, Svara (1999b) dropped the terminology of *dichotomy-duality* as he identified more managerial involvement in mission and described in its place the complementarity of politicians and administrators.

Figure 14.1   **Dimensions of Governmental Process**

Council's Sphere

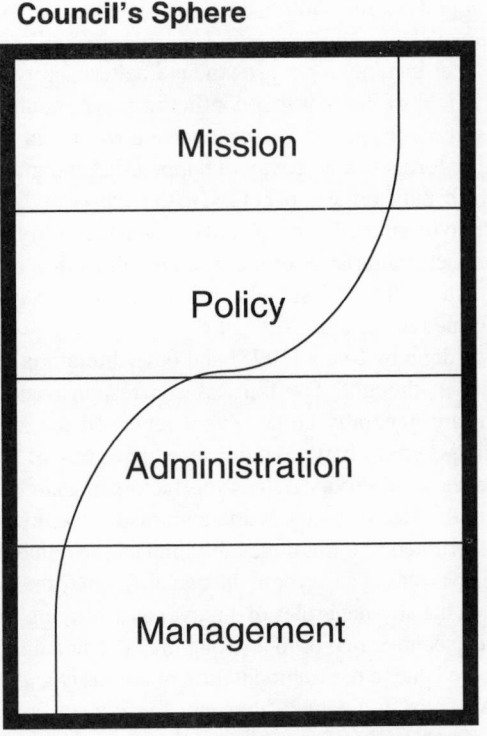

Manager's Sphere

Source: Svara 1985, 228.

In a commonly held interpretation of urban politics, Banfield and Wilson asserted that "politics arises out of conflict, and it consists of the activities . . . by which conflict is carried on" (1963, 5). The community power studies, which were based on this conflict model, measured how power was acquired and used by the players in the urban scene. Yet, Svara maintains that conflicting conditions are not the only means of dealing with the governmental process. A cooperative pattern is present in some community settings. Cooperation is the basis for the council-manager form as opposed to the power theme that is the basis for mayor-council form of government. The most important elements in a cooperative arrangement are common goals, sharing of rewards, and coordinated efforts.

The separation of powers in the strong mayor form of government "predisposes officials to conflict" (Svara 1990, 45), which raises the issue concerning the roles of the mayor and council on mission and policy. Since both represent the general polity, there may be conflict over the mission, goals, and policies as well as the boundaries of the administration dimension. In a council-manager form of government, the council possesses all authority except for what is delegated to the manager. There is no separation of powers. In addition, the types of cities that have a council-manager form of government have other characteristics that are predisposed toward cooperation such as higher income, more growth, and better quality of life.

There is a school of thought that conflict in mayor-council forms may be unpleasant but is necessary to assure responsive government, while cooperation in council-manager forms is a nice way of suppressing the interests of the poor and minorities to the benefit of the upper class. In this school of thought, the unreformed jurisdictions (mayor-council form of government) tend to be more responsive to the demographic characteristics of their communities than reformed jurisdictions (Renner and Santis 1998, 32). Social conflicts affect the decision-making process more in unreformed governments.

The research done by Svara (1995) and other literature, however, do not support this school of thought. The fairness and responsiveness of the two forms of government are generally equal. Svara reviewed the areas of elections and representativeness, group participation, responsiveness of staff, spending levels and responsiveness, and service delivery as factors in analyzing the outcomes and contributions of the elected officials and administrative staff. In each of the areas, the form of government did not noticeably impact the outcomes of policy.

In assessing the roles of a mayor in the two different forms of government, Svara (1995) describes the alternate roles of a mayor as a "driving force" versus a "guiding force." The executive mayor in a strong mayor-council form of government is the "driving force" due to the fragmentation of authority and conflictual pattern of interactions. A mayor in a council-manager form of government serves to foster communication and facilitate interaction and to provide a greater sense of purpose and thus serves as the "guiding force" in the government. The resources available to a mayor in the council-manager form do not preclude leadership initiatives by the mayor. Behavior that is effective in an executive mayor form may cause problems in a council-manager form. The mayor in this form is the single most important agent of cooperation among officials. The mayor becomes the facilitator by accomplishing objectives through enhancement of the efforts of others. The mayor is a central coordinative position to facilitate and initiate policy directions. A mayor in the strong mayor form of government would find it difficult to serve in a facilitative role due to the natural presence of conflict and distrust.

The facilitative mayor in a council-manager form of government takes on the eleven tasks shown in Figure 14.2 (Svara 1995).

The first three roles are built into the office and are "automatic." The next eight roles are the ones that differentiate the activist mayor/chair with the passive one. The roles are played concurrently and are mutually reinforcing. Effective mayors do not necessarily supplant the role of the city manager; they can have mutually beneficial roles. Mayoral leadership was shown to improve the working relation-

Figure 14.2   **Facilitative Mayor Roles and Tasks**

Traditional or "Automatic" Roles	
Ceremonial Figure	Spokesperson
Presiding Officer	
Coordinating and Communication	
Educator	Liaison with Manager
Team Builder	
Policy and Organizing Roles	
Goal Setter	Delegator/Organizer
Policy Advocator	
External Relations	
Promoting the City or County	Intergovernmental Relations

Source: Svara 1994, 14.

ship with the city manager. The performance of the mayor makes a difference and is not an imitation of the executive mayor. These mayors build effective leadership by strengthening others in the governing process.

Despite charges of weaknesses in the form, the council-manager form has proven to be adaptable over time (Hansell 2000). As compared to the original reform movement plan of a five-member council, at-large elections, and a mayor chosen from among the council, many cities have adopted larger councils, have gone to district elections (35.5 percent), and have adopted direct election of the mayor (66 percent in 2002). In addition, some cities have given the mayor in this form of government additional powers such as veto power, appointment power of council committees and advisory boards, the receiving of the budget for submission to the council, the making of an annual report to the community, and the initiation of the hiring or termination of the manager (Newland 1994; Hansell 2000). Mayors in larger, more heterogeneous communities have tended to play a larger role in managing political conflict than in smaller, more homogeneous communities (Wikstrom 1979). Yet the form remains a parliamentary system with involvement by the whole council and the manager.

Council-manager government provides for "specialization of roles but not separation of powers" (Svara 1999a, 144). There are two aspects of leadership that impact how the chief executive officer performs. The first is the function, such as political and/or executive leadership. All mayors are in the position to provide political leadership in their cities. The political leadership is the translating of the needs and demands of the citizens into goals and policies and supporting their adoption. Today's urban communities have challenges that demand strong political leadership. But looking for political leadership does not mean elimination of the council-manager plan. The needs of the city for leadership are for consensus building and facilitation rather than power wielding. Effective mayors enhance the ability of the council and the manager for top performance. "In the final analysis, what really is needed in today's urban communities are Strong mayors, Strong councils, and Strong managers" (Blodgett 1994, 11).

Svara (1995) looks at the role of the city council by comparing them as a counterweight in the strong mayor form versus a senior partner in the council-manager form. The council member serves as a representative, a governing official, a supervisor, and a judge. As a representative, the council member speaks on behalf of the constituents. In the governing role, the council member legislates and gives direction. As a supervisor, the council member is an appointer and supervisor of staff. And as a judge, the council member resolves disputes. In a strong mayor form, the council is more likely to be in the representative role and the legislative-ratification role. The council-manager form gives the role definition to the council to fulfill. There is no competition in the final authority to make that definition, as in the strong mayor form.

Managerial Leadership and Administration

City management has evolved from its beginnings in the early 1900s, but still maintains much of its roots. In 1927, White wrote one of the first publications about the new profession of city management after the reform era. He explains that "the origin of the council-manager plan is embedded in the revolution of the civic and business interests of the American city, aided and abetted by various forward-thinking groups, against the waste, extravagance, and sometimes corruption which characterized politician government of the last century" (1927, ix).

While the legal position that the charter of the community assigned to the manager and council respectively was a major factor in the success or failure of the manager plan, the relationship between the manager and council is extremely important for the success and proper operation of the plan of government (White 1927, 171). The manager's role in administration is important, but the role that he or she plays in aiding the council in their role is equally important in White's opinion. The credibility of the manager rests on his or her role in running government in a businesslike manner. Yet, their leadership skills are frequently better developed than those of the elected officials in the city. Unless the manger exercised restraint, the system could come to elevate the manager position to a level higher than the council. Even in 1927, the leadership and management role of the city manager was recognized as a potential concern.

Others have reflected that the city manager form has worked but differently than originally anticipated (Ehrenhalt 1990). The manager definitely has a role in the policy arena. While high impact and low visibility of the manager are still adhered to by most managers, in some communities, the desire to have the manager more visible is becoming more of the norm. Some communities are beginning to see the city manager as the broker in chief among competing power interests.

The debate over whether city managers are managers/administrators or leaders is an ongoing dialogue. Fairholm explains,

> Management deals with organizational complexity, transactions between leader and led, solving organizational problems, and control and prediction. . . . Leadership deals with changing organizations, transforming leader and led, setting and aligning organizational vision with group action, and ensuring individuals a voice to grow into productive, proactive, and self-led followers. . . . Both are the realm of the modem public administrator. In fact, both are the essence of public administration (2000, 6).

The public administrator must be proficient at both management and leadership in the successful organization.

Leadership is essentially a human business; 90 percent of an executive's time is spent on human interaction. This human interaction has four behaviors in leadership—visioning, communicating your vision, acting on your vision, and caring about people in the organization (Barbour and Sipel 1986). The excellent manager provides leadership through a clear vision for the organization building on the elected officials' vision for the community. In addition they are able to communicate that vision and sell it to the people in the organization. Excellent managers are risk takers and encourage others to take risk. The excellent manager has a high level of concern for people. He or she seeks involvement, celebrates successes, has clear understanding of performance, and cares about employees as human beings. The good public-sector managers have to be both managers and leaders (Ross 1986). The art of public administration differs from the science of public administration (Crewson and Fisher 1997). The art involves skills such as understanding local politics, assessing the needs of the community, handling interpersonal relations, and performing consensus building while the science of administration involves skills in finances, personnel, and other technical disciplines. The art skills are those usually associated more with leadership attributes.

The real issue seems to be what type of a leader the manager is rather than whether the manager is a leader. The situation of the local community is a major factor in that analysis. Because of the link between the profession and the community, the responsibilities of the professional manager changes as the community changes (Green 1987). At different times in a community's life, it needs a manager with different professional skills (Loble 1988, 19). In 1945, Ridley, then executive director of the International City/County Management Association, recognized that the manager needs to understand "what a city is, what kind of people live in it, what services they need and expect from their city government, and how their city government can give them those services" (259).

The role difference between administrative manager and policy leadership is one that the effective managers must navigate within the context of the community where they work. The most important issues are issues of human relationships and politics. Managers must rely on "an uncommon blend of expertise, creativity, fortitude, and political acumen to survive" (Stillman 1974, 111). The manager's role in the processing of issues so that solutions are developed, agreed to, and implemented has become more important than the technical aspects of the position. The manager spends more time (approximately 70 percent) on policy making than other issues (Blubaugh 1987, 9). The internal work of management has increasingly been performed by an assistant manager. In addition, the unionization of employees and growing minority participation have impacted that role. Because of the urban issues in large cities, managers have taken on more of a policy role. Communities with a high degree of political conflict have forced the manager to take on more of a policy role. Local government professionals have reported that the biggest difference in their work over the past ten years is the increase in degree of participation in public policy making and problem solving (Nalbandian 1999). The manager has become a facilitator to help promote problem solving and develop consensus among interests.

The manager is also a community leader. As far back as the 1940s and 1950s, there were three styles of city managers working in local governments—the administrative manager, the policy researcher and manager, and the community leader and manager (Bosworth 1958; Svara 1998). The community leader and manager role has been in the profession for a long time, but in the last decade managers are acknowledging their role in this sphere more frequently. Many managers have gained acceptance in the community power structure. Regardless of the role that they follow, the managers "must seek to be among the best politicians in town, for their work deals with the satisfaction of the wants of people who have the privilege of discussing and voting about his work" (Bosworth 1958, 220). The need to be politically astute without being political was recognized even in 1958. Community building and local government management have to be related (Nalbandian 1999). C.A. Harrell, ICMA president in 1948, identified the city manager as a "community leader." He added that the "ideal manager" is a "positive, vital force in the community' who "visualizes broad objectives, distant goals, far-sighted projects" (Svara 1998). The manager has to be able to lead the council and community to build visions while also being concerned with equity and balanced participation.

The bringing of issues to the city council, the information presented to support recommendations, and the direction to staff on the implementation of the policy decisions all involve the manager in the policy-making process (Nalbandian 1991). Fifty-six percent of managers in a 1985 survey indicated that policy making was their major role. The increase from twenty-two percent in 1965 came at the expense of other managerial roles. In a survey in 1987–1988, managers felt that the most important skills for a city manager were performing situational analysis, assessing community needs, handling interpersonal relations, and bargaining, negotiating, and consensus-building techniques. These skills are reflective of the policy role played by the manager (Nalbandian 1999, 66).

In a survey done in 1997, 79 percent of city managers in large cities over 100,000 population indicated that their most important role in local government was policy and council relations (Svara 2004, 30). Twenty-one percent identified management as the most important role. The council role in policy recommendations and relations was considered much more important than the community leadership role by city managers. The challenge is to differentiate between the policy-making process and community politics. The role of the manager can be seen as situational leadership. "The same manager acting the same way but working for two different councils, or even the same council at different times, may be perceived in one instance as acting politically and in another as acting administratively" (Nalbandian 1991, 106).

Managers must be able to read situations and create the opportunities to solve problems. Since the city council members have to deal with value-laden issues, the manager must spend more time building relationships with them. That means dealing beyond the interior of the city hall. Communication skills and focusing on a few important issues has become critical in the interjurisdictional and intra-jurisdictional setting. Managers will have to become highly sensitive to political issues in order to help the mayor and council facilitate more effectively. The partnership with the mayor and council is important to the success of dealing with these issues. In a successful council-manager form of government, all members of the governing body and the manager are part of the process of developing cohesion within the group. That means open communication and delivery of services consistent with the priorities of the community. The mayor is the spokesperson for the government and promoter of the cohesion. The manager must support the policy making and oversight by the governing body by providing information, formulating policy proposals, advising on policy proposals, and ensuring that the delivery of services is consistent with the governing body's policy direction (ICMA 1995).

Richard Child, father of the council-manager plan, stated in 1918, "The great city managers of tomorrow will be those who push beyond the old horizons and discover new worlds of service" (Newland 1994, 264). The successes of the past in city management are becoming the failures of the future due to the lack of change to keep abreast of the changes in the environment (Golembiewski and Garbs 1994). Rather than being just an administrator, the modern manager has to be a player in the development and infusion of values in the community. Unstable communities are more the norm than the exception in today's world. In addition to the old theories of economy and efficiency, management must focus on effectiveness. Doing the right things is of great importance. There is a need for a partnership between the manager and the elected officials. Mutual respect has to be in place between the mayor and the manager for the system to function well (Rattley 1990). They must work as a team to support each other's roles.

The municipal management profession is beginning to recognize that a city comprises political and social units as well as economic and physical units that have to be dealt with. The manager is the bridge between the governing body and the administrative staff. The manager must be able to translate the elected officials' pronouncements into policy, goals, objectives, and work plans. In addition, the manager must be able to foresee issues on the political horizon. At times, that means listening to what the elected officials mean even if it is not articulated well (Nalbandian 1994).

Summary

A common theme of the research on strong mayor leadership patterns is the influence of the situation on the style of the mayor. Holli (1999), Pressman (1972), Ferman (1985), Kotter and Lawrence (1974), and Bowers and Rich (2000) all comment on the impact of the local culture and situation on the success of the mayor and the utilization of a style. As was noted, John Lindsay was right for New York, Richard Daley was right for Chicago, but neither one would work in the other city due to styles. While Ferman (1985) and Pressman (1972) emphasized the need for resources for a successful mayor, Kotter and Lawrence (1974) and Bowers and Rich (2000) indicated that it depended more upon the local situation and the style of the mayor.

In addition to the situation, mayoral leadership in a council-manager form of government requires the observer to adopt a new concept of thinking about the role of leadership by a mayor. As noted by Svara, facilitative leadership based on a concept of cooperation supplants the power form of leadership based on the conflictual nature of the strong mayor–council separation of powers form. The predominant role of the mayor and elected officials in the mission sphere, the shared roles of the elected officials and manager in the policy and administration spheres, and the predominant role of the manager in the management sphere are a new way of thinking about the old politics-administration dichotomy issue. It is more reflective of the working relationships and the partnership between the mayor and manager and mayor-council and manager that is the base for the form of government.

The long-standing dimensions of leadership by the manager in the council-manager form of government have been expressed differently as circumstances have changed in the last 100 years. The manager's role in policy and community leadership is virtually undisputed today. Commentators made the same observation in the 1920s and the 1950s, but what it takes to successfully fulfill this role today has changed. Most authors recognized the importance of managers to perform their responsibilities within the context of the environment in which they worked. The role that works in one socioeconomic setting within the political culture prevalent in that environment may not work well in another setting. The role of the manager is clearly situational.

Leadership and management in local governments are crucial to the success of communities today. While the styles of leadership and management may differ between forms, the most successful of the mayors and managers have adapted to the situation they find themselves in and mobilize resources to meet the goals of the organization.

References

Ammons, David N., and Charldean Newell. 1988. "City Managers Don't Make Policy: A Lie, Let's Face It." *Public Management* 70 (12): 14–17.

Banfield, Edward C., and James Q. Wilson. 1963. *City Politics.* New York: Vintage Books.

Barbour, George P., and George A. Sipel. 1986. "Excellence in Leadership: Public Sector Model." *Public Management* 68 (9): 3–5.

Barnard, Chester I. 1968. *The Functions of the Executive.* Cambridge, MA: Harvard University Press.

Bass, Bernard M. 1990. *Bass & Stogdill's Handbook of Leadership—Theory, Research, & Managerial Applications.* 3rd ed. New York: Free Press.

Blodgett, Terrell. 1994. "Beware the Lure of the 'Strong' Mayor." *Public Management* 76 (1): 6–11.

Blubaugh, Donald A. 1987. "The Changing Role of the Public Administrator." *Public Management* 69 (6): 7–10.

Bosworth, Karl A. 1958. "The Manager Is a Politician." *Public Administration Review* 18 (3): 216–222.

Bowers, James R., and Wilbur C. Rich. 2000. *Governing Middle-Sized Cities—Studies in Mayoral Leadership.* Boulder, CO: Lynne Rienner Publishers.

Crewson, Philip E, and Bonnie S. Fisher. 1997. "Growing Older and Wiser: The Changing Skill Requirements of City Administrators." *Public Administration Review* 57 (5): 380–86.

Dunn, Delmer D., and Jerome S. Legge, Jr. 2002. "Politics and Administration in U.S. Local Governments." *Journal of Public Administration Research and Theory* 12 (3): 401–22.

Ehrenhalt, Alan. 1990. "The New City Manager Is: Invisible, Anonymous, Non-Political, None of the Above." *Governing Magazine* (September): 1–46.

Fairholm, Matthew. 2000. "Reclaiming Leadership in Public Administration." *Public Administration Times* (July): 3.

Ferman, Barbara. 1985. *Governing the Ungovernable City: Political Skill, Leadership, and the Modern Mayor.* Philadelphia: Temple University Press.

Gardner, John W. 1990. *On Leadership.* New York: Free Press.

Golembiewski, Robert L., and Gerald Garbs. 1994. "Today's City Managers: A Legacy of Success-Becoming-Failure." *Public Administration Review* 54 (6): 525–30.

Green, Roy. 1987. "Local Government Managers: Styles and Challenges." *Baseline Data Report* 19 (2).

Gurwitt, Rob. 1993. "The Lure of the Strong Mayor." *Governing Magazine* (July): 36–41.

———. 2000. "Mayor Brown & Mr. Bobb: Can a Strong Mayor and a Strong Manager Find Happiness Together on a City with Big Problems? So Far, Yes." *Governing Magazine* (January): 16–20.

———. 2001. "Council-Manager Government: Alive and Leading Today's Best-Managed Communities." *National Civic Review* 90 (1): 41–43.

Hansell, William J. 1993. "Council-Manager Government: A Form Whose Time Has Come Again." *Florida League of Cities* (August): 36–38.

———. 2000. "Evolution and Change Characterize Council-Manager Government." *Public Management* 82 (8): 17–21.

Henry, Charles T. 1971. "Urban Manager Roles in the '70s." *Public Administration Review* 31 (1): 20–27.

Holli, Melvin G. 1999. *The American Mayor: The Best & The Worst Big-City Leaders.* University Park, PA: Pennsylvania State University Press.

International City/County Management Association (ICMA). 1995. *A Look into Our Evolving Profession: 1995 Report of ICMA's Council Manager Plan Task Force.* Washington, DC: ICMA.

Kotter, John P., and Paul R. Lawrence. 1974. *Mayors in Action.* New York: Wiley.

Loble, Arlene. 1988. "Becoming a Risk Taker—and Then a City Manager." *Public Management* 70 (3): 18–20.

Montjoy, Robert S., and Douglas J. Watson. 1995. "A Case for Reinterpreted Dichotomy of Politics and Administration as a Professional Standard in Council-Manager Government." *Public Administration Review* 55 (3): 231–39.

Nalbandian, John. 1991. *Professionalism in Local Government.* San Francisco: Jossey-Bass.

———. 1994. "Reflections of a 'Pracademic' on the Logic of Politics and Administration." *Public Administration Review* 54 (6): 531–36.

———. 1999. "Facilitating Community, Enabling Democracy: New Roles for Local Government Managers." *Public Administration Review* 59 (3): 187–97.

Newland, Chester. 1994. "Managing From the Future of Council-Manager Government." In *Ideal and Practice in Council-Manager Government,* ed. H. George Frederickson, 263–83. Washington, DC: International City Management Association.

Pressman, Jeffrey L. 1972. "Preconditions of Mayoral Leadership." *American Political Science Review* 66 (2): 511–24.

Rattley, Jessie M. 1990. "Mayors & Managers—A Relationship in Evolution." *Virginia Town and City* (July): 12–14.

Renner, Tari, and Victor S. Santis. 1998. "Municipal Form of Government: Issues and Trends." In *The Municipal Year Book,* 31–41. Washington DC: International City Management Association.

Ridley, Clarence E. 1945. "The Job of the City Manager." *Public Management* 27 (9): 258–63.

Ross, Joyce D. 1986. "Integrating Management and Leadership." *Public Management* 68 (8): 14–15.

Stillman, Richard J., II. 1974. *The Rise of the City Manager—A Public Professional in Local Government.* Albuquerque: University of New Mexico Press.

———. 1977. "The City Manager: Professional Helping Hand, or Political Hired Hand?" *Public Administration Review* 37 (6): 659–70.

Stone, Clarence N. 1995. "Political Leadership in Urban Politics." In *Theories of Urban Politics,* ed. D. Judge, G. Stoker, and H. Wolman, 96–116. Thousand Oaks, CA: Sage.

Svara, James H. 1985. "Dichotomy and Duality: Reconceptualizing the Relationship between Policy and Administration in Council-Manager Cities." *Public Administration Review* 45 (1): 221–32.

———. 1990. *Official Leadership in the City: Patterns of Conflict and Cooperation.* New York: Oxford University Press.

———. 1995. "Dichotomy and Duality: Reconceptualizing the Relationship Between Policy and Administration in Council-Manager Cities." In *Ideal and Practice in Council-Manager Government,* ed. H. George Frederickson, 29–52. Washington, DC: International City/County Management Association.

———. 1998. "The Politics-Administration Dichotomy Model as Aberration." *Public Administration Review* 58 (1): 51–58.

———. 1999a. "The Embattled Mayors and Local Executives." In *American State and Local Politics: Directions for the 21st Century,* ed. Ronald E. Weber and Paul Brace, 139–65. New York: Chatham House.

———. 1999b. "The Shifting Boundary Between Elected Officials and City Managers in Large Council-Manager Cities." *Public Administration Review* 59 (1): 44–53.

————. 2004. "Achieving Effective Community Leadership." In *The Effective Local Government Manager,* ed. Charldean Newell, 21–56. Washington, DC, International City/County Management Association.

Svara, James H., and Associates. 1994. *Facilitative Leadership in Local Government: Lessons from Successful Mayors and Chairpersons.* San Francisco: Jossey-Bass.

White, Leonard, D. 1927. *The City Manager.* Chicago: University of Chicago Press.

Wikstrom, N. 1979. "The Mayor as Policy Leader in the Council-Manager Form of Government: A View from the Field." *Public Administration Review* 39 (3): 270–76.

15

Four-Frame Leadership in Authentic, Results-oriented Management Reform

Case Studies in Canada and the United States

BRENDAN F. BURKE AND BERNADETTE C. COSTELLO

The study of results-oriented management reform, under the guise of "reinventing government" (Osborne and Gaebler 1992), "New Public Management" (Barzelay 2001), "Liberation Management" (Light 1997), or other names, is fraught with the challenges of confronting and changing an entrenched paradigm. The academic community and government practitioners are at odds about the potential worth of converting management philosophies and structures from a process focus to a results orientation. In essence, the reform involves a movement from a "top-down" approach, which focuses on strengthening internal management's capacity to guide policy and administration, toward a "bottom-up" model involving the empowerment of creative, capable workers throughout the organization, held accountable to results or service outcomes. Is the movement toward a results orientation appropriate from a theoretical standpoint? Can it actually work in contemporary organizations and circumstances? Would it, or could it, amount to a sustainable new paradigm for public services into the (relatively) new century?

These questions are difficult to answer, because measuring results-oriented reform has proven complex. In particular, survey research has found that the use of results-oriented tools of performance measurement and strategic planning are commonplace within American state and local governments, so the reform would appear to be well under way (Berry 1994; Poister and Streib 1999b; Melkers and Willoughby 1998; Wang and Berman 2001). A separate pool of research, coming from various management scholars, finds "pitfalls" to the engagement of performance measurement (Behn 2002) and that strategic planning has already assumed a "rise and fall" (Mintzberg 1994). In-depth case studies may also be less encouraging about the feasibility of implementing the results orientation (Durant 1999).

This chapter's broader research base contends that academics and practitioners alike need to study reforming organizations more closely and deeply and to assess several aspects of leadership practice to understand the true engagement of the results-oriented reform tools of performance measurement and strategic planning (Burke and Costello 2005). The more targeted goal of this chapter is to address the needs of twenty-first-century public managers as they consider contemporary reforms, especially the movement toward a results orientation. We advocate that managers and other analysts are better served by scrutinizing the platform of leadership techniques on which the performance management tools reside, in addition to studying the documented qualities of the measurement and planning systems. An authentic or "holistic" results orientation includes constant and focused attention to reform among an organization's leaders and throughout the organization; a skill-building effort within the organization's human resources function to develop new abilities within the workforce and comfort with unfamiliar techniques; and the nurturing of a new type of organizational culture, where the public interest rather than organizational maintenance is encouraged, recognized, and celebrated.

The following sections elaborate on a richer model of reform leadership. First, an overview of the initial research methodology regarding the impact of performance measurement and strategic planning provides a background to the purpose and the mechanics behind both an underdeveloped and an authentic implementation approach. Second, we discuss the work of Bolman and Deal's (1997) organizational frames as a way to understand why some organizations are more authentic and successful in the development and implementation of performance measurement and strategic planning reforms. Third, to understand what makes some efforts more successful than others, we describe the findings of surveys and interviews with "performance leaders" in the United States and in Canada, in the form of frame-based cases. Last, through the lens of organizational frames, we offer implications and suggestions for twenty-first-century public managers as they lead organizational reform efforts.

The Process and Practice of the Results Orientation and Its Core Activities

During our own careers, first as government practitioners and more recently as academics, we have seen the difficulty of finding authentic models of performance measurement and strategic planning, as opposed to only rhetorical or symbolic versions of these tools. Many of America's local government "reputation leaders" for quality and efficiency have been engaging in something similar to the results orientation for decades. For example, among the jurisdictions that we studied, Phoenix, Arizona, Charlotte, North Carolina, and Dayton, Ohio, began measuring performance in a rudimentary fashion around 1970. Many jurisdictions followed the national lead in creating strategic plans under the "Managing by Objectives" (MBO) rubric.

Basic Performance Measurement and Strategic Planning Designs

The International City/County Management Association (ICMA) and the Urban Institute (Hatry 1999) have formalized performance measurement, and the Gov-

Table 15.1

Types of Performance Measurement

Inputs	Resources (worker time, expenses) related to providing a service
Outputs	The product from the use of inputs; quantity of services delivered (miles of road paved, phone calls answered)
Efficiency or unit-cost ratios	The relationship or ratio between inputs and outputs (dollars spent per mile of paved road)
Intermediate outcomes	Results of programmatic effort that lead to a desired end but are not the end itself (public hearing attendees on the transportation plan); these outcomes are within the control of the service provider, where end outcomes tend to involve other societal or environmental factors
End outcomes	The ultimate result that is sought from the production of a service, within its broader context (citizen satisfaction with the government's design and construction of its road plan)

Source: Hatry 1999.

ernment Accounting Standards Board (GASB) has supported governmental efforts on the whole of the results orientation, under the title "Managing for Results" (MFR). In 1991, GASB's Service Efforts and Accomplishments project offered a standardized measurement structure of inputs, outputs, efficiency, and effectiveness indicators. Many American local governments use this structure, with some moving into the presentation of intermediate and end outcomes in recent years (see Table 15.1 for brief descriptions of the measurement types). In 1998, GASB initiated an MFR focus on strategic, program, and activity planning as well as measuring, monitoring, analyzing, and reporting programmatic results. GASB has developed a number of helpful state and local case studies, as well as a clearinghouse of other MFR examples.

Training materials for the National Performance Review (NPR) defined strategic planning as "a continuous and systematic process where the guiding members of an organization make decisions about its future, develop the necessary procedures and operations to achieve that future, and determine how success is to be measured" (NPR 1997, 6). Most public organizations that participate in strategic planning employ one or a combination of three types of processes. Possibilities include:

- *SWOT Model*: Assessment of the strengths, weaknesses, opportunities, and threats facing a "business" unit. This technique is usually credited to the Harvard Business School and covered by Kenneth Andrews (1980).
- *Hierarchical Model*: The development of mission, strategies, corresponding budgets, and control mechanisms. The hierarchy involves the movement from

general statements of organizational purpose, down to departmental goals and strategies, with some possibility of informing individual work plans. These are powerful coordinating mechanisms, but may be inflexible in their "top-down" orientation.

- *Stakeholder Analysis*: The integration of economic, political, and social concerns as they affect different organizational participants. These place an emphasis on listening via focus groups or other mechanisms to customers, citizens, or staff when used in governments or nonprofit agencies (Bryson 2000).

Separating the Authentic from the False Reformer

While in government, we researched leaders in performance measurement and strategic planning in place in well-known innovative municipal governments. But frequently when we looked to a given "best practice," the first few examples studied proved to be weak designs, not worth emulating or adapting to our needs. Through the analysis of surveys and interviews, we found many organizations employ performance measurement and strategic planning in name only, while others operate with authentic efforts to integrate the reform techniques throughout the organization. There is evidence along these lines (Burke and Costello 2005).

The choice of jurisdictions for a broader research effort was derived from a purposive sample of "reputation leaders" (Ammons 1991) on performance measurement and Managing for Results. The starting case list came from three sources: The Government Performance Project/*Governing* magazine's Grading the Cities/Grading the Counties jurisdictions (Barrett and Greene 2000); example municipalities from the Urban Institute's effective textbook on performance measurement (Hatry 1999); and an inventory of successful cases on the development and use of performance measurement disseminated by the Government Finance Officers Association in training forums (GFOA 2002). These three sources identified twenty-four reputation leaders, many identified in all three studies. More details on the research design and the full list of "reputation leaders" can be found elsewhere (Burke and Costello 2005); but the results (see Figure 15.1) bear review, especially that many jurisdictions integrate their performance measurement systems into only a scant range of management processes.

Approximately two-thirds of the survey respondents brought performance measurement into their strategic plans and other public documents, while three-fifths of these jurisdictions use performance measures to establish a results orientation in their budget processes. Only a quarter of the respondents used performance measurement in their employee evaluations processes and in agency reorganization efforts. Even though this survey used a small number of respondents, findings were consistent with earlier research that has shown that some reinvention techniques are commonly used, and others are used more sporadically (Willoughby and Melkers 2001; Brudney and Wright 2002).

Figure 15.1 **Use of Performance Measurement in Varied Management Processes: Percentage of Jurisdiction-wide Application among Respondents**

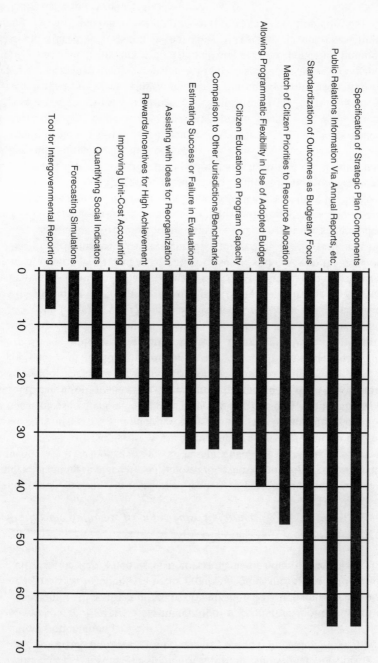

Source: Burke and Costello 2005.

Jurisdictions used the MFR tools of performance measurement and strategic planning in many ways. Table 15.2 designates limited and comprehensive implementation of these tools (contrasted as "Ritualistic" and "Holistic" effort). The table shows that one can have a basic performance measurement system and a rudimentary, documented strategic plan but with limited focus and use of these tools. We called this Ritualistic implementation. Many of the study's jurisdictions fall at various points on the spectrum; they meet with a range of success in their implementation of MFR techniques. But a number of the municipalities that we studied use an integrative model in their approach to MFR, inserting the planning and measurement tools in a wide range of management and decision-making processes. We characterize these jurisdictions as Holistic implementers of this reform (Poister and Streib 1999a originates the name).

Ritualistic Implementation: The False Start in Reform

Many of the jurisdictions that we studied had a fundamental problem with implementing a results orientation. The reform tools were designed and created, but then were brought into management decisions only in the most simplistic ways. These governments crafted basic hierarchical strategic plans, including agency missions, goals, and objectives, but the process was limited to consultation between senior agency and budget or executive staff. Performance measurement systems look strong throughout budgets and other public documents, usually using the GASB Service Efforts and Accomplishments language and recommended measures. But the plans and measures inform only internal budgetary dialogue, mostly between budget and management staff. Elected boards rarely discussed strategic plans and outcome measures in these governments, though board members might occasionally request new goals and measures as parts of their plans.

Utility of the MFR tools followed leadership and employee motivational factors; if these were not emphasized, then the tools were largely ignored. Respondents told us, "Our (line) employees don't know about our strategic plan," and "We revisit this process just at budget time." Planning and measurement tools might be a priority for budget or audit professionals but not for top management in Ritualistic organizations. We heard, "Our strategic plan is found only in our budget" as a documented but less used expression of missions, goals, and values. When power is restricted to or by top elected and administrative leaders, the plans and measures may be the center of conflict and thus will be downplayed when there is broader disagreement about planning direction. One department, especially the budget office, may fight to establish the importance of measurement, at odds with other departments that do not perceive their benefit or necessity.

Ultimately, the Ritualistic organizations prepare plans and measurement in a fashion that is insincere with regard to results-oriented policy establishment and administration. These are organizations that appear among the "reputational leaders" because they have developed comprehensive systems of performance mea-

Table 15.2

Contrasting Factors Underlying Managing for Results Implementation

Nature of Effort	Structure of Planning	Employee Involvement/ Buy-in	Leadership Focus/ Continuity	Symbolic/ Cultural Content	Structure of Measurement	Use of Measurement
Ritualistic	Highly centralized; uses some or all components of the Hierarchical model in a simplistic fashion; annual, mainly in connection with budget submission process	Minimal outside of management, highly centralized, in implementation of directives from executive and elected board; on high; little awareness of the overall planning effort	Inconsistent; highly sensitive to external stimuli; high level of reactivity; concern for positional power	Image, perception, and form of high importance; "dramaturgical"; "Consortium" wide variance in perception across the organization	Many measures, especially GASB/SEA and "Consortium" systems; more weight on input and output than outcomes	Specification of strategic plan components (goals, objectives, targets); tool to enhance internal budgetary dialogue; public relations
Holistic	Simultaneously centralized (for/ with staff) and decentralized (for/with citizens); sophisticated and varied formats used simultaneously; integration into decision making by a single clearinghouse (i.e., planning or audit agency); frequent and ongoing (quarterly or monthly efforts are possible)	Frequent and ongoing at most levels; with multiple simultaneous processes, opportunities for input abound, during development, planning, implementation, and evaluation stages	Strong, with consistent guiding tone in leaders' speeches, reports, and training components; resistant to many environmental threats; works from executive leadership, with employee considered a valuable resource; high use of team and matrix systems	Stories and symbols are centered around stories and perceptions (among management); problem solving and action oriented	Fewer well-chosen measures for central processes; emphasis on outcome and service-level indicators; choice at department level for intensity of (and quantity of) measurement structure	Most of goals, objectives, targets; budget allocation dialogue and decision making; citizen education regarding program capacity; reorganization support; rewards/incentives for achievement; activity-based accounting; comparisons/ benchmarks; standardization of budgeting away from input-output orientation

Source: Adapted from Burke and Costello 2005.

sures, probably in keeping with a standard like GASB's accepted design, but do little with them. Bolman and Deal (1997, 275) called this mind-set and approach "dramaturgical"; an organization pursues a reform or other policy change literally for show, to demonstrate that they are progressive and create reassurance among citizens and staff that the organization is consistent with the effective practices of other reputable peers.

Our research also highlighted the Holistic reform implementer, whose specifics are contrasted with the Ritualistic implementer in Table 15.2. Use of the reform tools (especially strategic planning) is widespread, as is employee and citizen involvement with the jurisdiction's management processes. Performance measurement is used in calculated and conscientious ways by a range of organizational leaders, who see measurement not as a burden but as a fundamental base for an innovative organizational culture. The next sections describe the theoretical basis for the Holistic model, Bolman and Deal's (1997) organizational study *Reframing Organizations,* and then provide American and Canadian cases corresponding to each of their four "frames."

A Framed Approach for Authentic Reform Efforts

The failure of the Ritualistic organization is a failure of creative engagement of the "human" side of the reform, encompassing the engagement of internal politics, consensus building, and persuasion of stakeholders with regard to the benefits of the techniques. Bolman and Deal (1997) offer a leadership philosophy useful for implementing Holistic reform. They posit that it is incomplete to assess only structural components of organizations while neglecting human resources, political, and symbolic frames. Real organizational leverage, which can be seen as large gains for comparatively moderate effort (Senge 1991), comes from analyzing situations through the other frames and mustering corresponding types of management tools as needed.

The Structural Frame

The structural frame helps us to understand how the relationships, roles, and responsibilities are physically organized. The organization's reporting structure, mission, goals, and policies are considered as structural components (Bolman and Deal 1997, 13). Accuracy of process and procedure on decision making is critical in this frame orientation. Technical expertise and knowledge is highly valued (272). Through appropriate rules and formal systems, advocates of this frame feel that the organization's effectiveness is optimized. GASB Service Effort and Accomplishments measures and basic hierarchical strategic plans are fine examples of stand-alone institutional structures. When organizations operate in a stable environment and employee involvement and development is less important, the structural frame is an effective starting point for reform efforts. The reform efforts begin with altering processes and procedures or reorganization to mirror the needed change. However, "structural thinking can overestimate the power of authority and underestimate the authority of power" (280). The manager cannot simply command, "make it so," and watch the results orientation fall into place.

The Human Resource Frame

The human resource frame involves mutual recognition between organizational and employee needs. "[O]rganizations need ideas, energy, and talent; people need careers, salaries, and opportunities" (Bolman and Deal 1997, 102). Appropriate and current personnel systems are part of the modern public organization, but at least one important human factor is frequently neglected: the motivation and ability of all employees in an organization to work collaboratively. To drop the process orientation in favor of an outcome focus involves the conversion to a "seamless" system, where communication and effort cross old boundaries. Some organizations may arrive at a collaborative disposition easily, but others may require training and leadership emphasis to drive the change.

The Political Frame

This frame traditionally operates in the context of power, power relationships, and competition for organizational resources (Bolman and Deal 1997, 14). The importance and relevance of self-interest is counted on to further reform movements. Pfeffer (1992) contends that organizational power is facilitated by reducing the influence of coalitions and exercising a collective self-interest. If that is the case, the results orientation faces a serious challenge, because it involves the conversion of an entire workforce toward a less parochial focus. The manager and his or her team can muster their power in some standard ways. The team controls the agenda and can keep it focused consistently on results. Leaders have position power (authority) and control of rewards to emphasize appropriate behavior. But they also may want to acknowledge the two-way flow of power. This especially comes through New Public Management techniques of empowerment, collaboration, and networking, and it may be more consistent with the ways of knowledge workers (Borins 1995).

The Symbolic Frame

The symbolic frame is concerned with culture, organizational context, and symbols that reflect the organization's vision. The higher-level mission and goals of an organization need to be salient at all times in order to maintain a focus on high achievement, innovation, and focused service. But vision can be communicated in many varied ways. Bolman and Deal discuss vision within the context of organizational "symbols" (Schein 1985). Among the important forms of organizational symbols are the rituals and ceremonies that take place; the interaction and "play" within groups; and the myths, stories, and lore told to entertain and communicate the verbal history of the organization. Within the stories and symbols are issues and problems. Stories are related in a problem-solving and action-oriented perspective. Symbolic content is not goal oriented, but instead reveals deeper meanings within organizations. Symbols of conflict and competition within the organization, such as the "fight" for resources or other rivalries, may indicate an organization will have difficulty establishing intra- or interorganizational collaboration. Malaise can turn up in the symbols and stories in one office, while in others stories of sacrifice and pride tell of an energized organizational environment.

Case Studies in Framing Reform

Based on the description of the four frames, we can elaborate on the specific nature of the results-oriented reforms that follow from a four-frame approach. Table 15.2 displayed the nature of the Holistic reformer as one who attended to all of the frames in an active and ongoing manner. Next, we discuss several Holistic municipal governments, both in Canada and the United States, and offer more detailed description of programmatic content that corresponds with each frame. We begin with the "human side" of the results-oriented reform, depicting effective human resource, political, and symbolic content. Near the outset of this chapter, we described the basic structural nature of performance measurement and strategic planning, with the caveat that a single-minded focus on the written structure was a necessary, but not sufficient, basis for reform. At the end of this section, we return to structure to offer designs that appear to be better supported by and more compatible with the other three frames.

What does the Holistic form of the results orientation look and feel like to those within the organizations? Might public managers in other organizations striving for results-oriented reform learn from these authentic models? And last, if academics want to establish a true foothold in measuring results-oriented "reinvention" or New Public Management reform, what should they measure in addition to the presence of strategic management and performance measurement systems? Surveys cannot stop with a general question of whether the results-oriented tools are "used"; researchers must track how much are they used and in what ways, and then they can begin to establish the added value of truly engaging the results orientation.

Structures and behaviors within the following eight jurisdictions may not be easy to emulate, and the dedicated professionals who nurture results-oriented systems may not be commonplace in American and Canadian governments, but these examples should help focus the search. Each of the following four sections offers case evidence from two municipalities, one American and one Canadian per section. They range across the continent and vary in size. One constant is that they are all council-manager governments, which may lower the bar a bit for the political complications of engaging reform—in essence, leadership may have a greater opportunity to endure over time in these governments than in strong mayor systems, for example.

Human Resource Frame: Develop Employees

Organizational buy-in is crucial to results-oriented reform, as workers from the top to the bottom of the organization must change their thinking from work in separate specializations, oriented toward process fulfillment, to an empowered ability to creatively fulfill high expectations from the public. The human resource function of participating organizations is necessary to train on the nature of new forms of work, as well as to reduce hesitation and fear of the needed changes. It can be frightening to be allowed to use one's own ideas instead of the procedures manual, and it can be difficult to share one's work with a team, rather than working on one's own.

The following two organizations devote themselves to the human resource dimension, by easing the transition to the new paradigm for all of the government's workers. Consistent with the Holistic design, these cities engage in positive pursuit of all four frames, but here we highlight just the focus of supporting the organization's employee base. The Austin case focuses on reform-oriented strategies; the Airdrie, Alberta, case focuses on human resource leadership.

Austin, Texas

Austin (population 656,500) has been the capital of Texas since 1846. The city manager is Toby Hammett Futrell, who has spent her entire career in Austin, working her way up from the line level. Austin initiated its focus on results-oriented reform in the latter half of the 1990s. Initially, the city focused on developing internal commitment and departmental and individual support for the reform effort. Austin's leadership understood the importance of managing the relationships between and across departmental lines. The city encouraged input from all levels of employees to bring about this cooperation. Austin reduced uncertainty in employee efforts by publishing extensive but accessible training guides relating to results-oriented techniques, in tandem with in-house training sessions. Guides are honest assessments of the complications, and the rewards, of outcome orientation.

Results-oriented reform in Austin has gone through a few changes since its inception. At the beginning of the process, pages and pages of measures were included for all areas and functions of the city, but these were met with resistance from many on the city's staff. In essence, too much measurement focus impeded the ability to do the main public service tasks. After experiencing the difficulty of managing and maintaining such a large effort, the city refocused on measures that track to the city council's priorities. Although departments can track some forms of more detailed data for internal uses, the city has aligned measures to provide a much clearer focus for managers and individual contributors. Through internal surveys and "walking around and talking to people," employee input was sought regarding measurement systems and now continues to occur throughout many aspects of organizational reform.

Austin's internal managerial planning processes rely upon a wider range of output and efficiency measures as well as intermediate outcomes to assess the impact of virtually every employee on jurisdiction-wide results. Austin uses the *Success Strategy Performance Report (SSPR)*, a tool in which the annual (or more frequent) employee evaluation uses specific performance measures that aggregate to departmental levels and are even "aligned" with cross-disciplinary service delivery. Support comes from the continuous revision and improvement of plans and measurement processes across departmental boundaries.

Austin's *SSPR* is not just about pay-for-performance. Its most important impact on the city's results orientation is that each employee knows his or her place within the service mission of the city and can help design his or her own efforts to pursue it. As should be the case in a well-integrated and innovative culture, leadership, employees, and the ongoing mission all appear to gel in a consistent yet latent fashion. One of Austin's most visible artifacts of its collective spirit is its vision statement: "We want Austin to be the most livable city in the country." Organizational leadership vocalizes this in varied ways, and the planning process ensures the idea is present in ideas and actions of employees as well.

Airdrie, Alberta

Airdrie, Alberta, (population 26,000) is located on the western North American plain, within sight of the Canadian Rockies and within commuting distance of the major city of Calgary. Airdrie benefits from a passionate human resource team, focused on the growth of every individual in the city's government. City Manager George Keen hired Bert Assen to be the director of human resources after Assen had decided to leave the private sector. Assen brought contemporary ideas from the business world, along with an unflinching desire to make the public sector and its employees better. Assen's touchstone is the growth and development of the individual worker and his or her place on the Airdrie team, which involves fluid and changing alignments of workers, depending on the challenge of the day or week.

The Airdrie human resource function operates from a rich employee orientation program and policy document, which contains both the mundane (use of city property, tracking work effort, and so on) as well as developmental topics. Airdrie has an established norm of recognizing positive effort by other members of the workforce, reinforced within the personnel manual. When a given worker serves another well, he or she may be recognized with a small "gift" of a travel mug, golf shirt, pen, wall clock, paddleboard, or other item, or be singled out with the story of their good service at team meetings. Keen, Assen, and other managers encourage and take part in recognition almost daily.

Airdrie's workers also come together to share in the reading of management texts at Keen's or Assen's recommendation, including books like Jim Collins's *Good to Great* and Gay Hendrick's *A Year of Living Consciously,* as well as articles in the employee manual covering Daniel Goleman's work on "emotional intelligence." The entire workforce takes part in training courses such as Communicating for Results. While the human resources team has strong skills in training, they recognize the benefit of an ongoing relationship with an independent trainer, Cormier Consulting Group, which participates in the development of the ongoing growth of the Airdrie work force. One of Airdrie's five "corporate scorecard" components is the measurement of the amount and quality of cross-departmental communication.

One of the most successful ongoing training efforts, and a factor central to Airdrie's successful results orientation, is the "Accountability Agreement." Airdrie ensures the linkage between individual actions and departmental "Business Plans," especially through personal work plans that, like those in Austin, link upward to the organization-wide vision. The key to the strength of the Airdrie effort is their parallel focus on developing the match between higher-level and personal goals, accompanied by the development of the personal ability to carry out individual plans. For example, an employee may recognize a need to develop both his or her own work topic, such as clerk's duties, but may also see a need to develop skills at handling the accounting procedures of enterprise funds. He or she will include the cross-training component in his or her work plan, and management will fund the growth initiative and track his or her success in the city-funded course. The personal development component is an ongoing, and appreciated, aspect of employee plans. They vary from public speaking emphases to master's degrees.

While Assen is conversant on most modern private-sector HR strategies, he does not believe in pay-for-performance and is vehement on the subject. It simply is not consistent with the public service. But that does not mean that Airdrie under Keen and Assen's guidance ignores recognition. The small acknowledgments abound; the support for personal growth is real; and the emphasis on applying for provincial awards through the Alberta Municipal Excellence Network, the Institute of Public Administration of Canada, or other outlets is ongoing.

Political Frame: Persuade and Share Authority

"Command-and-control" strategies for using power do not appear consistent with major "postmodern" reforms like the movement toward a results orientation. Because a key reform component is empowerment of lower-level employees, there is a clear philosophical disconnect with *ordering* employees to be original and creative. In addition, empowered systems offer far too many opportunities for shirking if employees feel coerced into changes that they do not support. While the human resources frame and function address some of the tracking and training of line employees, leaders in Holistic organizations can create a more authentic and sustainable path for the workforce through persuasive efforts to champion the reform. The Phoenix case, next, displays many examples of a consensus-based authority system. The more that Phoenix leaders orient the organization toward positive habits and results, the more entrenched their positive authority becomes. The Peel case discusses a leadership team's efforts to solidify its place as a Canadian government leader on reform and innovation through a recognition process.

Phoenix, Arizona

Phoenix (population 1.4 million) has a long history as a reputation leader on various management innovations, including competitive contracting and the results orientation, and it has been recognized as the "Best Run City in the World" by the Bertelsmann Foundation. The reputation did not arise overnight; but the Phoenix leadership team has had a hand in the historic development of the city's strong abilities.

The current city manager, Frank Fairbanks, has served Phoenix since 1972, starting as a management assistant and rising through the ranks. He served for many years as assistant city manager under the legendary Marvin Andrews, learning as well as developing the innovative culture of the city's government. Fairbanks is surrounded by a team of assistant and deputy city managers, as well as budget and audit managers who have been with the city for decades. Phoenix has developed an inclusive model of management, wherein several strategic planning processes take place at the citywide, government-wide, agency, and problem levels. The varied efforts involve broad swaths of citizens and staff and are coordinated into a cohesive management message facilitated by the budget and audit departments.

One of the central tenets of the Phoenix leadership team is the respect and development of line employees. Theirs is an adaptive leadership model, where the broad goals and values of the organization are expressed, and staff is given flexibility in how to fulfill the specifics of the job (Heifetz 1994). When Phoenix's workers carry out their duties, they also carry, literally, the core values of the organization:

> We are dedicated to serving our customers.
> We work as a team.
> We each do all we can.
> We learn, change, and improve.
> We focus on results.
> We work with integrity.
> We make Phoenix better!

The values are ubiquitous in the city's government, in buildings, on reports, on business cards, and in presentations. The first two are crucial to a standard attitude among Phoenix employees: that their work will be carried out on behalf of clients and service users and that it will be collaborative in its execution.

The leadership style in Phoenix is not heavy-handed. It includes recognition for solid effort and experimentation on behalf of the mission. Outside of an employee suggestion system, which rewards ideas with 10 percent of cost savings, recognition is similar to the system in Airdrie—with a personal focus at staff celebrations, between and among work teams. Fairbanks attends many of these and uses them partially as a demonstration to enforce the empowered system of individual leadership and responsibility. While workers are encouraged to innovate, they will not be punished for taking well-considered risks. The more experiments that staff engage in with innovative ideas, the better they become at constructively confronting risk.

Phoenix's performance measurement system is well developed, but work units and staff are not mandated to track measures for accountability. Instead, the measures are a resource for clarifying work situations and quality. Given the Phoenix culture of first-rate service, the majority of programs and service units voluntarily develop a focus on existing performance statistics or develop their own systems of outcome measurement tailored to their services.

Peel Regional Government, Ontario

Peel Regional Government (population 1.1 million) was a part of Ontario's establishment of a "two-tier" system of municipal governance in 1974, and it now provides housing, social welfare, and environmental services to the residents of three suburbs (Mississauga, Brampton, and Caledon) on the western border of Toronto. The regional government serves a diverse and growing population and shows many signs of strong management with its "AAA" bond rating, low taxes and debt, and continuous stream of recognitions for innovation and service excellence.

Roger Maloney was the chief administrative officer (CAO) of Peel Region from 1998 to 2005. He served with the regional government from its inception and thus was among the individuals who gave Peel its reputation for day-to-day work of a high standard. As director of social housing, he was one of the first to implement service benchmarks in Canada and started several efforts to reconfigure public-private partnerships in this function. Once he became CAO, he set about unifying the excellence of the individual departments to enhance Peel's overall organizational reputation and unity as a workforce. Along the way, he found an opportunity to highlight and solidify a strong results-oriented model.

Peel's internal auditor suggested the National Quality Institute's (NQI) Canadian Quality Criteria for the Public Sector program as a potential challenge for the organization, and Maloney recognized its merits. The NQI program could serve as a way to both recognize disparate individual and programmatic achievements throughout the Peel government, but also to shore up some of the services to a common standard of excellence. The Quality Criteria supported relatively well-developed areas of Peel's organization: engaged leadership; a functioning strategic plan that guides organizational improvements; a strong focus on citizens and clients; the development of the workforce; and attention to process and partnerships. Most, but not all, of Peel's departments supported these ideas in an unspoken and unrecognized manner. But pursuit of NQI accreditation could reinforce the understanding among Peel's workforce regarding how successful they really were. Maloney had a choice once he started the drive for NQI certification: He could either lead his best departments toward it or initiate an organization-wide effort. He chose the latter, so that all services would have buy-in to the effort and share in the pride of accomplishment.

The Excellence Initiative, as Maloney named it, has a core component designed to bring employee buy-in, recognition, and support for the NQI criteria. The BEST, or "Building Employee Satisfaction Together," survey is a comprehensive effort to gain ideas for regional "action plans," which over time have altered dozens of cross-functional work processes to enhance citizen-based service delivery. The Excellence Initiative has four staff people as well as specific budget resources to facilitate cross-functional improvement.

Maloney's quiet, secondhand leadership paid off, as Peel Regional Government achieved the third-level NQI certification, a height reached by no other Canadian government or agency. The Excellence Initiative continued in 2005 after Maloney's retirement, as David Szwarc, one of the government's team of commissioners, was promoted from within to CAO.

The Symbolic Frame: Innate Values

Administrative actions can have multiple meanings. The content of an executive's speech might tell the organization of new reforms; but if only a small percentage of the organization attends the speech, the lack of enthusiasm and support may show that the documented reform has little chance for success. Rituals like speeches and ceremonies are important to maintaining an organization's culture. The stories from Airdrie and Phoenix especially demonstrate the way that managers nurture positive feelings about reform through their enthusiasm at formal and informal meetings. In these organizations, employees have a strong desire to participate in the rituals.

There is more to the symbolic frame and study of organizational culture. Schein (1985) describes culture as unstated but powerful orienting systems for any form of group. He suggests that we look first for artifacts of organizations, such as the rituals described earlier, but also possibly stories told within the organization about successes and failures. The artifacts mask underlying values. George Keen's and Frank Fairbanks's positive reception as they recognize employees indicates that those employees support personal challenge, personal growth, and public service. The sum of the values is a "basic assumption" for the organization, which will be difficult to dislodge in favor of other administrative philosophies (Khademian 2002). The next two cases come at the symbolic frame in different ways. In Dayton, there is a long-standing philosophy of citizen interaction and service, which turns up in the ongoing actions of the organization and in individuals. The Lethbridge case describes a reform that worked well for the innovative culture, highlighted in the value-based comments of its employees.

Dayton, Ohio

Dayton (population 166,000) is a pleasant, medium-sized city with a manufacturing base in its past and a diversifying employment base currently. Dayton is known in public management circles for its strong efforts to enhance citizen and neighborhood participation. Its innovative nature usually ties back to this dynamic of enhanced stakeholder involvement. The participatory efforts define the basic culture of Dayton's city government, such that the natural expectation for the government's workforce is that the city's policies will be citizen driven.

During the past decade, there have been two major strategic planning efforts to establish a broad vision for Dayton and a number of smaller ad hoc planning efforts. In 1996, a new planning director initiated Dayton Vision 2003. This process involved the entire community and resulted in a document outlining six areas of focus for change, improvement, and development to enhance public and private infrastructure and the life of Dayton's residents. Dayton's Vision 2003 initiated the measurement of department and service success through a management by objective process. Although the system was not formally connected to the budgeting process, the community-based performance elements were used symbolically to steer the leadership and direction of Dayton as well as create a connection to city residents.

Although the initial process started as a land-use planning method, the process slowly developed a life of its own. The document created an identity and focus for Dayton. The strategic planning processes led to the development of Dayton's CitiPlan 20/20. The CitiPlan document clearly demonstrates the significance of neighborhoods and the city's history. CitiPlan is issue focused and action oriented. Construction of a minor league ballpark in the downtown area began with a great deal of pessimism. Using the CitiPlan and the vision for Dayton, the ballpark became a turning point for the city and is now a focal point and symbol of success for residents. Other spin-off processes, such as an effort to reorient public transit in a balance between service users and downtown stakeholders, are carried out in a successful manner because of the staff and citizen group familiarity with group deliberations. Collective action on Dayton's policy issues is well entrenched as "how things are done" in this city.

Lethbridge, Alberta

Lethbridge (population 77,000) is the largest city in southern Alberta and northeastern Montana. The downtown has well-preserved architectural styles from the early twentieth century. The city's government earns frequent accolades from professional associations for innovation and quality of services. One innovation, the movement of the city budget to a three-year-long appropriation, has enhanced the flexibility of city service leaders to respond to citizen demands consistent with community-wide and agency planning processes.

The policy change is quite simple in its structure and involves a rolling calendar of governance procedures. City council members in Lethbridge serve three-year terms. Immediately after an election, council participates with the city staff to establish three-year business plans, which orient the qualitative programming and goals of each agency. At the end of the council's first year, a new budget is adopted for each department, and that funding allotment will carry the department for three years. Thus, following the 2004 election and subsequent planning process, Lethbridge's departments are currently in the midst of their 2006–2008 budget. The city's current council had only one chance to adopt budget priorities consistent with the city's strategic and business plans, and from there, the public servants have leeway to operate in the manner they select on into the next city council term.

Lethbridge's three-year budget has advantages as well as challenges. This is an empowered system, where agencies are financially accountable for the long range. If a department saves monies during its first two years, it does not need to return to council to allocate the savings for some innovative service experiment in the third year. But, if a department encounters a fiscal challenge, it is on its own in resolving it. Reform was built upon strong planning and performance models, and thus it shows in the perceptions and attitudes of staff that the change was consistent with the prevailing organizational culture.

In interviews with departmental leadership, most expressed how the budget change allowed them to operate "like a business," setting their own course without political alterations. It made departmental leadership and staff feel "more mature," more competent, and trusted in their service areas. They are more inclined to test new ideas with their newly acquired flexibility. When asked, "What would you do if you overspent your appropriation through something unforeseen?" "We won't," one department head answered succinctly, and credibly. He added, "Who would want to be the one to make this grant of authority fail?"

Lethbridge's movement toward a long-term, results-driven fiscal orientation fits the capabilities of this prairie city. They moved to the three-year process incrementally, testing a two-year appropriation without problems, and completed the first three-year budget cleanly in 2005. Many Alberta cities, including Calgary, have copied Lethbridge's design.

The Structural Frame Revisited: Tools That Reflect the Human Side

The design of rules, work groups, and other formalized aspects of the organization is an appropriate starting concern for public managers. A manager must start to devise specific, visible techniques to bring about his or her goals. We leave the structure or designs of Holistic results-oriented tools until now because the other human factors inform the design features. The following examples of performance measurement and strategic planning do not display the only ways to implement the results orientation effectively, but they would appear to contain some basic compatibility with authentic reform.

As discussed in the next cases, Charlotte, North Carolina, is as parsimonious as it can be, measuring only what it needs to measure with the goal of streamlining the effort of government services and workers to account for their actions. This does not mean that Charlotte has few measures—only that they narrow measurement to the necessary areas to track overall organizational success. In the Canadian regional government of Halton, strategic planning is ubiquitous, occurring at several organizational levels with a wide range of participation from internal and external stakeholders. The results orientation is not required to have a limited set of measures and virtually unbounded planning processes, but several of the governments described up to this point create the same type of measurement scheme (see Austin, Airdrie, and Phoenix) and planning program (see Phoenix and Dayton especially).

Charlotte, North Carolina

Charlotte is a city growing in size (population 600,000) and stature during recent decades. It has learned about performance management over the past thirty years, since it was one of the early municipal experimenters with the productivity tool. Based on its history, Charlotte has adopted the Balanced Scorecard (Kaplan and Norton 1996) variant as a structure for performance measurement to accompany their two-tiered strategic planning design.

The Balanced Scorecard is so named because it is based upon separate significant measurement areas that track organizational health and success. It is not enough to measure service results or citizen satisfaction; the well-being of staff and financial viability are also necessary adjuncts to strength in a results orientation. Each Charlotte department prepares measures in the following four areas, to support the goals in their business plans:

- *"Serve the Customer"*: This area involves intermediate and end service outcomes, such as crime reduction, neighborhood qualities, and the performance of environmental protection functions. The list of services to measure comes from the citywide strategic plan, as adopted by the city council.
- *"Run the Business"*: The focus here is on the effectiveness of the internal processes on which the results orientation is based, such as the number and quality of collaborations across agencies, internal and external customer surveys, and efficiencies gained through information technology solutions.
- *"Manage Resources"*: These are financial measures, including the stability of finances (bond rating), the maintenance of infrastructure (capital budget ratios), range and intensity of competitive delivery of services, and effectiveness of other finance professionals such as the tax collector.
- *"Develop Employees"*: Efforts to recruit, retain, and develop the workforce are tracked here, including offerings to promote growth and learning and surveys that measure employee perceptions of the workplace climate.

The measures cover the entire organization, not just the direct public services. The four components of the Balanced Scorecard both specify the focus of Charlotte's results orientation and limit the need to count varied inputs simply for the sake of counting. As in Airdrie, Austin, and Phoenix, the choice of measures includes the concerns of the city's elected officials but also the needs of the organization's workers to meet their highest potential.

Halton Regional Government, Ontario

Halton Regional Government (population 495,000) was formed in 1974 at the same time as the Region of Peel, in a wave of municipal consolidations driven by the Ontario provincial government. It is located between the major Canadian cities of Toronto and Hamilton, central to Ontario's "Golden Horseshoe" of economic and population growth. Parts of Halton, especially along Lake Ontario, could be considered urban, but there are still large swaths of farmland and open space within the region's borders. The main functions of the Halton government are to serve public health needs, establish provider networks for social and community services, and provide planning and public works functions shared by the four cities of Halton—Burlington, Oakville, Halton Hills, and Milton.

The Halton government's leadership style is inclusive and empowering throughout many strategic planning processes, including coordination of plans across the four cities, business plans within each of the regional government's departments, and cross-cutting deliberations on services in transition or in need of broader stakeholder input. It is especially within the last area, of ad hoc planning processes, that participation across the region's government is expanded. A case in point is the Halton Comprehensive Housing Strategy, which took place in 2005.

Ontario went through extensive reconfigurations in its provincial-municipal mix of services over the past decade, including extensive privatization of governmental enterprises and off-loading of responsibilities from the province to localities. Public or "social" housing was one of the services given over to municipalities. At first, Halton attacked the problem from a top-down rationale, but under a growing norm of public consultation on service issues, the process of deciding upon state, local, private, and nonprofit (or "voluntary sector") responsibilities and approaches was given over to a deliberative process involving 200 participants, with approximately six months to develop a plan for political and administrative support from the regional government.

On a given day in the middle of the planning process, attendance is strong; the participants are divided between twenty tables with all stakeholder groups represented. An outside facilitator runs the overall meeting, but Halton staff present statistical information and give the charge for the day. Each table is facilitated by a Halton staff person, who received brief training in running such discussions and reporting back to the large group. In this way, Halton's line staff develop familiarity and attachment for the ad hoc planning processes while still limiting their immersion into the strategic planning profession.

Austin uses the term *alignment* for connections between planning processes. Halton has created rich "linkages" from the regionwide plan down to individual employee performance plans. The typical manager in Halton's system is involved in understanding the personal plans of his or her team members. Most supervisory employees must be familiar with the work plan of their supervisor and of all of those who they manage—down two layers in smaller units. Ed Archer, the region's former finance director, developed a unique time-tracking software application for management reporting. When employees report their time on projects, the SAP-based application converts hours to match goals and action steps within departmental business plans and government-wide strategic plans. This simplifies the linkage between the employee and the overall guiding documents of the regional government. So far, this software has been implemented only for Enterprise and Internal Funds but is available for use in the other agencies.

Summary Observations on Four-Frame Leadership

While the cases previously discussed highlight individual frames, the reader may see cross-cutting evidence of other related frames within the narrative. Are the recognition programs in Airdrie and Phoenix examples of persuasive leadership (political frame) or of human resource frame-based personal development? Certainly both; the forms of progressive leadership identified here include the value of subordinates. Are the stories in recognition forums "symbols" or positive rituals, too? Indeed they are. The organizational culture underlies all else—leadership effort, a developmental focus, and appropriate structure within reform designs.

Overlap within in how we observe the frames may impede proper measurement of results-oriented reform. Design and testing of such schemes is for a future research study. But the cases point toward succinct and relatively straightforward advice to twenty-first-century leaders. Public managers interested in pursuing an authentic version of results-oriented reform should:

- Work to establish a shared leadership style with their management teams and model and promote this style consistently.
- Invest in human resource staff and programs that train and promote teams, evaluate employees based on the mission (with or without pay-for-performance), and fund employee recognition efforts.
- Draw attention to rituals and encouraging stories that suggest positive movement within the culture.
- Constantly assess the planning and measurement designs in place within their organizations, to determine if they support all other important frame-based aspects of the results orientation.

The twenty-first century will be the time in which we will see whether the results orientation really does grow, whether or not it is a real paradigm shift. The leaders and many employees within the Holistic governments discussed herein are convinced of the benefits.

The goal may be Holistic implementation of the reforms; but how can individual leaders in different organizations and cultures use these case studies to begin to revitalize their organizations in reform efforts? What of these lessons can leaders identify with and apply in their organization? The leadership lessons learned from these case studies are twofold: one, identify the organization's strengths and begin work in the frame which will best support that strength, and two, once the reform process has begun, leaders should integrate strategies from the other frames to increase organizational commitment and sustainability.

Austin began its efforts in the human resource frame and then adopted structured processes to included measurement data in the budget and resource allocation process. The importance of ritual in the annual surveys has become part of how Austin does business. The Barton Springs Natural Swimming Hole and the South by Southwest Music Conference are examples of icons for the city's efforts at living the vision, in essence, creating a crossover between an internal and an external culture that highlights human development.

Dayton started its reform effort in the symbolic frame and, like Austin, moved to formalize the process by linking to structural processes like performance measurement, budget planning, capital facility planning, and development of legislative policy. Employees are connected to the results orientation through annual work review plans and the staffing of community committees. Through the human resource frame, Dayton was able to work together differently through consensus building and in the community with broad-based collaboration.

Sometimes leadership appears as if someone is stepping in front of a parade that is already under way; such might be the observation of Roger Maloney's guidance of the "Excellence Journey" in Peel Regional Government. The only difference is that Maloney made some strategic decisions, such as including every department on the journey rather than just the best ones, and communicated clearly and consistently what the journey was about. His may have been an easy leadership challenge; nevertheless, he worked the circumstances to perfection.

Beginning in the organization's most developed operating frame offers leaders an opportunity to work in concert with the organization's systems, process, and employees in ways that are familiar and less likely to face resistance. As the level of organizational support and acceptance grows, leaders can begin to utilize the other frames to facilitate and grow increased commitment across and outside the organization. Integrating the various strategies across the other frames enhances leadership and organizational flexibility. As leaders of the reform effort become more capable of assisting the organization to meet the various challenges of the organization's change efforts, the better chance the reform effort has to take hold and become integrated into the organization's way of operating.

There is only one caveat in starting in a single frame. The cases have demonstrated careful attention to effective structures, be they departmental alignments,

306 BRENDAN F. BURKE AND BERNADETTE C. COSTELLO

design of rules, or formal engagement of management techniques. But research contacts, as well as Bolman and Deal (1997), caution against concluding their reform development once they have found the best structure. Among the "reputation leaders," there is at least one jurisdiction whose measurement systems are the envy of metropolitan governments around the world. But admiration for the systems is not unanimous within the organization. "We are overdoing it with the measurement," says one insider. "Departments and programs really don't know what's going on within all of these measures. They are just an end in themselves." Training has fallen off, and the culture and power alignments within the organization have favored a "command and control" mentality, which has become entrenched over time. It may be harder to move from the mechanics or "structure" of reform to the human dimensions embodied in the other three of Bolman and Deal's frames, rather than in reverse, as has been seen in my cases. Awareness of all four frames and their importance is a start for contemporary leaders, or possibly for middle managers who wish to prod a conventional leadership philosophy toward progressive possibilities.

Acknowledgments

The authors wish to thank Gordon Whitaker, David Ammons, and the public servants who participated in the research for their assistance, as well as the Canadian Embassy to the United States for research funding. The findings are solely the responsibility of the authors.

References

Ammons, David N. 1991. "Reputation Leaders in Local Government Productivity and Innovation." *Public Productivity and Management Review* 15 (1): 19–43.

Andrews, Kenneth. 1980. *The Concept of Corporate Strategy*. Homewood, IL: R.D.

Barrett, Katherine, and Richard Greene. 2000. "Grading the Cities." *Governing* (February): 17–90.

Barzelay, Michael. 2001. *The New Public Management: Improving Research and Policy Dialogue*. Berkeley, CA: University of California Press.

Behn, Robert D. 2002. "The Psychological Barriers to Performance Management, or Why Isn't Everyone Jumping on the Performance Management Bandwagon?" *Public Performance and Management Review* 26 (3): 5–25.

Berry, Frances. 1994. "Innovation in Public Management: The Adoption of State Strategic Planning." *Public Administration Review* 54 (3):322–29.

Bolman, Lee G., and Terrence E. Deal. 1997. *Reframing Organizations: Artistry, Choice, and Leadership*. 2nd ed. San Francisco: Jossey-Bass.

Borins, Sandford. 1995. "The New Public Management Is Here to Stay." *Canadian Public Administration* 38 (1):122–32.

Brudney, Jeffrey L., and Deil S. Wright. 2002. "Revisiting Administrative Reform in the American States: The Status of Reinventing Government During the 1990s." *Public Administration Review* 62 (3): 353–61.

Bryson, John M. 2000. "Strategic Planning." In *Defining Public Administration: Selections from the International Encyclopedia of Public Policy and Administration*, ed. Jay M. Shafritz, 208–29. Boulder, CO: Westview Press.

Burke, Brendan F., and Bernadette C. Costello. 2005. "The Human Side of Managing for Results." *American Review of Public Administration* 35 (3): 270–86.

Durant, Robert F. 1999. "The Political Economy of Results-Oriented Management in the 'Neoadministrative State:' Lessons from the MCDHHS Experience." *American Review of Public Administration* 29 (4): 307–31.

Government Finance Officers Association (GFOA). 2002. *Performance Management and Budget Reform National Satellite Videoconference*. Chicago, IL: GFOA.

Hatry, Harry P. 1999. *Performance Measurement: Getting Results*. Washington, DC: Urban Institute.

Heifetz, Ronald A. 1994. *Leadership Without Easy Answers*. Cambridge, MA: Belknap/Harvard University Press.

Kaplan, Robert S., and David P. Norton. 1996. *The Balanced Scorecard: Translating Strategy into Action*. Boston: Harvard Business School Press.

Khademian, Anne M. 2002. *Working with Culture: How the Job Gets Done in Public Programs*. Washington, DC: CQ Press.

Light, Paul C. 1997. *The Tides of Reform: Making Government Work, 1945–1995*. New Haven, CT: Yale University Press.

Melkers, Julia, and Katherine Willoughby. 1998. "The State of the States: Performance-Based Budgeting Requirements in 47 out of 50." *Public Administration Review* 58 (1): 66–73.

Mintzberg, Henry. 1994. *The Rise and Fall of Strategic Planning: Reconceiving Roles for Planning, Plans, and Planners*. New York: Free Press.

National Performance Review (NPR). 1997. *Serving the American Public: Best Practices in Customer-Driven Strategic Planning*. Washington, DC: Federal Benchmarking Consortium.

Osborne, David, and Ted Gaebler. 1992. *Reinventing Government: How the Entrepreneurial Spirit Is Transforming the Public Sector*. Reading, MA: Addison-Wesley.

Pfeffer, Jeffrey. 1992. *Managing with Power: Politics and Influence in Organizations*. Boston: Harvard Business School Press.

Poister, Theodore H., and Gregory D. Streib. 1999a. "Strategic Management in the Public Sector." *Public Productivity and Management Review* 22 (1): 308–25.

———. 1999b. "Performance Measurement in Municipal Government: Assessing the State of the Practice." *Public Administration Review* 59 (4): 325–35.

Schein, Edgar H. 1985. *Organizational Culture and Leadership*. San Francisco: Jossey-Bass.

Senge, Peter M. 1991. *The Fifth Discipline: The Art & Practice of the Learning Organization*. New York: Doubleday Currency.

Wang, XiaoHu, and Evan Berman. 2001. "Hypotheses about Performance Measurement in Counties: Findings from a Survey." *Journal of Public Administration Research and Theory* 11 (3): 403–27.

Willoughby, Katherine G., and Julia E. Melkers. 2001. "Performance Budgeting in the States." In *Quicker, Better, Cheaper? Managing Performance in American Government*, ed. Dall Forsythe, 335–64. Ithaca, NY: State University of New York Press.

16

Leadership Strategies for Large-scale IT Implementations in Government

MARILU GOODYEAR AND MARK R. NELSON

The U.S. Internal Revenue Service (IRS) is working on a taxing problem that has very little (and yet everything) to do with taxes. That problem is a series of large-scale information technology (IT) projects focused on agency modernization. In the late 1950s and early 1960s, the IRS invested heavily in information-processing equipment to automate a variety of data-processing functions. Perhaps the most critical component of the resulting design was the IRS "Masterfile." Over time, many additional system components arose around the central Masterfile, creating an elaborate configuration of systems and processes. Since the late 1960s, the IRS has expended considerable effort and resources on modernization. Most of those efforts ended in some of the most widely cited failures in IT project management history. While the IRS improved existing tax systems through software and hardware replacements, elements of the IRS Masterfile are reportedly still in use. This creates one of the most significant and complex challenges to the agency today: how to modernize legacy systems without risking organizational failure.

The number, size, complexity, and importance of large-scale IT projects in government agencies are on the rise. Thus it is not surprising to find that the IRS is not alone among large-scale IT projects that have experienced difficulty in government agencies. The "high-risk" series of projects monitored by the U.S. Government Accountability Office (GAO) quickly yields a list of troubled projects at agencies like the Department of Defense, the Federal Aviation Administration, U.S. Customs Service, and others (GAO 2003a). The recent press on the Trinity Project within the U.S. intelligence community is a fresh example of a story we see repeated throughout the public sector, both in the United States and abroad.

These trends stem from a desire to integrate and modernize various existing systems in order to improve the efficiency and effectiveness of government operations and service to the public. Unfortunately, these large-scale integration-oriented IT projects are particularly prone to failure. Failures among these projects represent significant costs to both the organization and society. Projects of this criticality may span a number of years and cost hundreds of millions dollars or more.

When large government agencies undertake projects, their failure has critical effects on the large number of users of governmental services. Often in the public sector there are no viable substitutes for the products and services being delivered, and many of these situations affect the user of the service in life-threatening ways, as we have recently seen in the new Medicare prescription drug transition and in disaster response. The cost of failure is more critical and visible when large government agencies undertake major projects. In those cases, the project expense is ultimately paid by the taxpayer, and any disruption of service provided by these agencies may have far-reaching effects beyond just the functioning of the government.

Implementing new IT applications in public-sector organizations, as compared to private-sector organizations, is undeniably more difficult due to additional constraints (see for example, Rocheleau and Wu 2002; Bozeman and Bretschneider 1986; Mohan, Holstein, and Adams 1990). While there are technical challenges to overcome in the public sector, the greater challenges are organizational and managerial in nature. In relationship to likelihood to fail, prior research posits that the motivation to terminate or alter existing courses of action tied to poor performance or likely failure is lower in public organizations than in private organizations (Meyer and Zucker 1989). This likely increases the barriers to organizational learning following a large-scale IT project failure, despite the critical need to do so. Unfortunately, our understanding of these challenges is somewhat limited as the research on large-scale systems implementation is insufficiently broad, lacking methodological and model diversity, longitudinal views, and comprehensive system views (National Research Council 2000).

Drawing on prior research, this chapter will outline key elements of leadership responsibility in relation to public-sector large-scale IT projects. We begin with a brief conceptualization of the impact that the size and complexity of IT projects has on their management. We then focus the discussion by asking the question, "What are some of the most critical organizational and managerial challenges that surround large-scale, boundary-spanning IT projects in government agencies?" In response, using prior research in large-scale IT project failures, risk management, leadership, organizational change, and innovation, we will provide some guideposts for public-sector leaders to use in understanding the leadership challenge in relation to large-scale IT projects.

The Impact of Size and Complexity in IT Projects

There are a variety of definitions for *large-scale* in the literature, which stems from the difficulty in establishing a single variable or limited set of variables that define *largeness* in general (Brussaard 1992; Zmud 1980). We are not concerned, however, with large-scale systems simply as a reflection of size alone. We must also consider the degree of complexity involved. It is the complexity of the systems, in addition to size, that makes the design and development of large-scale systems using traditional development tools and techniques very difficult. Thus it is at the

Figure 16.1   **Size versus Complexity and the Common Information Systems Development Environment**

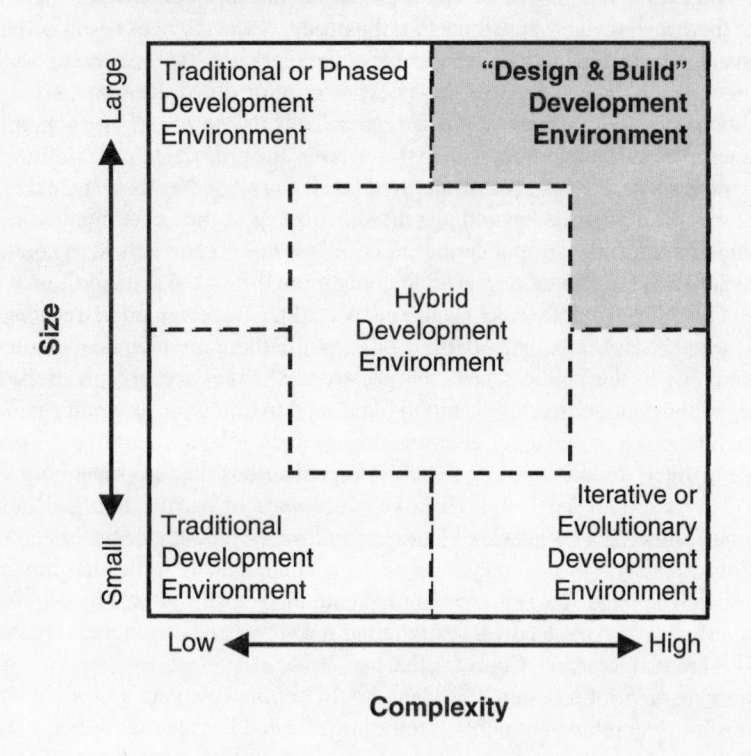

intersection of large size and great complexity that we find the class of IT projects that are most prone to failure. Unfortunately, it is this very class of IT projects that we find with increasing frequency in public-sector organizations.

Figure 16.1 illustrates the relationship of size and complexity to the information systems development environment (ISDE). We see that when project size and complexity are both low, the choice of ISDE is flexible, given that almost any developmental technique would prove effective. Traditional development techniques, such as following the systems development life cycle or waterfall model of development are common choices. If the project size remains small but the complexity is high, the ISDE calls for more iterative or evolutionary approaches to development. Examples of this ISDE include executive information systems or the development of decision support systems where prototyping and the use of spiral development models are more prevalent.

For large but fairly low complexity ISDE, such as the implementation or upgrade of an off-the-shelf transaction-processing system, the traditional waterfall approach in the form of a "big bang" implementation or a more gradual phased development approach is warranted. In the mid-range of moderate size and complexity we can find a number of hybrid approaches, such as component-based development and some agile development techniques. These hybrid techniques may be able to handle a wider range of development challenges created by size and complexity; however, they still fail to scale up to the requirements of the largest, most complex projects. Thus we conclude that most of our current development techniques are best suited for development environments that span the range from "large and simple" to "small and complex."

In the final quadrant are the largest and most complex systems. The combined size and complexity of these systems lead to ISDEs with constantly changing requirements. Examples include the baggage-handling system at the Denver International Airport, the Taurus system for the London Stock Exchange, the Trinity Project for the U.S. intelligence community, and the modernization efforts at the U.S. Internal Revenue Service. Projects in this quadrant are likely to reach a state characterized as "design and build" where developers are gathering requirements, designing, and building the final system simultaneously. Existing literature includes minimal research on design-and-build environments, despite growing case study evidence that these environments are more likely to appear as organizations attempt larger and more complex system development. Unfortunately, this lack of research means there is a lack of well-tested techniques to support developing applications within a design-and-build environment. Due to frequent changes in leadership and legislation common in the public sector, public-sector organizations engaged in large-scale IT projects can quickly find themselves in a design-and-build situation. This leads to a number of challenges for public-sector leaders, which compose the next section of this chapter.

To summarize, public-sector information systems projects are more likely to be large and complex. They are likely to experience frequent changes due to more volatility in leadership and interference from external stakeholders. Because such projects could take years to complete, with constantly changing requirements, public-sector organizations are often forced to begin development before all of the system requirements can be known—resulting in a design-and-build development environment. Such environments increase the risks present in systems development and may inhibit an organization's ability to innovate and learn.

Challenges for Public-Sector Leaders of Large-scale IT Implementations

There is no "silver bullet" able to address all of the challenges inherent in large-scale systems development, particularly in a design-and-build environment (Brooks 1987). These challenges include cost and schedule overruns during development, and user acceptance, reliability, and security vulnerabilities once implemented. The technical challenges, such as those related to data integration and migration, are significant for public-sector IT managers. However, the managerial and leadership issues have proven to be the most difficult challenges facing large-scale IT projects. Primary among the managerial and leadership challenges are:

- coordinating and integrating the constantly changing requirements as large IT projects extend over long periods of time,
- integrating the changes in technology and subsequent changes in user interaction with the system over longer periods of time,
- managing the cultural changes necessary within the agency when replacing legacy systems with new technology that forces work process changes, and
- managing a diverse set of stakeholders in a prolonged change process where functional requirements as well as end-user technology change.

Clearly, all public-sector leaders need to develop increased comfort and competency with organizational responses to the managerial and organizational challenges that accompany large-scale IT projects as well as a better understanding of the technical challenges as well.

Because large-scale IT projects are a fundamental change for the organization, success requires a wide-scale, coordinated response from all organizational units. Failure is not a failure of the technology or IT leadership alone; it is a failure of the overall organization and its leadership. This is particularly true for public-sector organizations where the additional constraints increase the likelihood that a large-scale IT project will take place in a design-and-build environment, extend over a longer period of time, and suffer from changing requirements.

Private-sector IT projects are often driven by competitive forces, where quick response is often better than no response. Public-sector IT projects, in contrast, are constrained by public accountability and visibility. Mistakes or failures can have significant negative effects on society and receive widespread media and legislative attention, thereby encouraging failure to act over acting too quickly (Bozeman and Bretschneider 1986; Margetts and Willcocks 1994). Public-sector IT projects also have greater interdependence with other organizations and require more participation from external stakeholders, each of which may have exceedingly divergent goals and expectations of IT investments (Rocheleau 2000; Kraemer and Dedrick 1997; Bretschneider 1990). Thus, public-sector organizations are subject to several distinct differences from their private-sector counterparts that complicate successful completion of large-scale IT projects.

While public-sector large-scale IT projects are prone to many challenges, we believe that important challenges can be addressed only at the organization level with the focus and attention of the organizational leader and the understanding and cooperation of managers throughout an organization. Some of the most critical challenges requiring more unified response include overcoming a failure to learn, recognizing and managing escalation of commitment, and coordinating interdependent decision making.

The research shows that in relation to large-scale government IT project failure, often the same mistakes are repeated time and again, sometimes over decades. In many cases, the errors that appear are common problems that have been well documented in both research and practitioner literature. This raises a question as to why organizations fail to learn and apply these lessons. The term *absorptive capacity* is used to describe an organization's ability to "recognize the value of new information, assimilate it, and apply it" to achieve organizational goals (Cohen and Levinthal 1990). In crisislike situations, such as the imminent failure of a large-scale IT project, organizational behaviors emerge that may decrease an organization's absorptive capacity and subsequently its ability to learn. The problem is made more difficult in situations where the environment is highly dynamic and the feedback regarding the outcomes of decisions or actions is delayed (Gibson 2000). For the design-and-build system development environment present in many large-scale government IT projects, these barriers are reinforced by rigid structural or bureaucratic elements embedded within organizational culture.

Another important aspect is the recognition and management of escalation of commitment. Escalation theory addresses the continued commitment to a previously chosen course of action in spite of negative feedback concerning the viability of that course of action (Brockner 1992; Drummond 1996; Keil 1995; Staw 1981). The result can be excessive expenditure of resources long past a point where success is feasible. Research shows that IT projects are more likely to escalate than other projects (Keil and Mann 1997), and because large-scale projects require significant long-term resource commitment and are driven by a strategic need, they are more likely to escalate than other IT projects. Evidence suggests that similar escalation behaviors exist internationally and in both government and business organizations (Keil et al. 2000; Keil, Mann, and Rai 2000; Keil et al. 1994–1995; Staw 1981; Staw 1976).

While escalation of commitment may occur in both public and private organizations, due to differences in the IT project environment it may not unfold in the same way. Due to concern over public accountability, failing projects in government agencies can evolve into situations where "failure is not an option," resulting in further escalation of commitment and resistance to corrective action. In such situations, organizations and individuals tend to restrict information processing, reduce the number of decision options and alternatives considered, and increase internal focus and reliance on established routines and procedures (Mone, McKinley, and Becker 1998; Staw, Sandelands, and Dutton 1981; Greening and Johnson 1996; Turner 1976). This can lead to inflexibility in meeting challenges and can become "an active counterforce to change" (Bowen 1987; Staw 1982), resulting in further reduction of innovation (Cameron, Whetten, and Kim 1987) and the decreased likelihood that an organization will take the actions necessary to prevent future failure. Managing escalation of commitment is critical to helping government agencies prevent large-scale IT projects from failing. This is made quite difficult by the number of individual and organizational factors promoting escalation of commitment in the public-sector systems development environment.

Another important factor is the need to coordinate interdependent decision making within the project. Two aspects of major IT projects make the coordination of decision making challenging. First, most major IT system implementations are, in fact, major work system projects. Sherer and Alter (2004) argue that many risk factors for IT projects are risk factors that relate to the changing of work processes. Decision making about major IT projects is in fact making decisions affecting fundamental work processes of the organization. This requires all the organizational managers to be fundamentally engaged in these decisions. Second, many actions and decisions made by organizations cannot be attributed to specific individuals because they result from interactions among individuals and may represent the results of established collaborative decision-making processes institutionalized or embedded in an organization. Increasingly, decisions in organizations are made by multiple individuals in order to reduce biases or risks inherent in individual decision making (Applebaum and Batt 1994; Cianni and Wnuck 1997). Top managers rarely act alone, and decisions are typically made in team structures (Hambrick and Mason 1984). This is particularly true for large-scale IT projects in public-sector organizations, where changes in functionality necessarily require the input from all internal stakeholders as well as many external stakeholders.

The presence of many stakeholders with conflicting objectives and varying levels of administrative understanding requires better methods for managing or coordinating the decision-making process. Effective decision making requires collaborative approaches including IT managers, who know the technology risks best; internal managers, who know the work processes best; and system users, both internal and external, whose acceptance is critical to success. To be effective in their roles, each of these groups needs an understanding of the technologies involved and the implications of functional administrative decisions on policy. A particular challenge for government agencies is the separation of policy decisions from understanding of the related technical and administrative decisions, which must be dealt with during an implementation (Margetts and Willcocks 1994; Derthick 1990). Due to the potentially large economic and societal implications, large-scale government IT projects that fail to meet administrative requirements are an important concern. Unfortunately, over half of all large-scale IT projects fail to meet original requirements (National Research Council 2000; Gibbs 1994; Standish Group 1994).

Despite widespread attention in the research literature and many studies providing insight and guidance for organizations, over the past decade the estimated failure rates of large-scale IT projects have seen relatively small improvement (Dalcher 2003). Because of the organization-wide implications of these projects and their interdependence, complexity, and large-scale nature, many of the underlying causes of failure are likely outside the domain or control of IT leaders and personnel. This suggests that providing guidelines for managing large-scale IT projects to IT project managers alone is not sufficient. We must focus on developing change competencies throughout an organization, and particularly among non-IT leaders and managers within an agency.

Bringing Together Organizational Approaches for Management of Large-scale IT Projects

Rather than simply repeat the conventional wisdom of the past, which appears to have had little impact on the future success of large-scale IT projects, we suggest that public-sector leaders focus on a broader set of objectives to improve future IT project outcomes. We find that the literatures of general risk management, innovation, and organizational change provide insights that could be brought into the discussion of IT project failure. We selected these literatures as examples of research bases that are currently quite distinct but where there are easy-to-identify intersections that could benefit both research and practice. We found little indication among the articles we reviewed that the research conclusions in these areas are seen as related or that collectively they may speak to managing IT projects. The purpose of this section will be to point out a few of the common leadership implications contained in these literatures. By integrating these and eventually other streams of research, we can improve understanding of the leadership elements affecting large-scale IT projects. We believe that these elements represent critical organizational competencies for adapting to and responding to wide-scale organizational change, such as what we see with many large-scale IT projects. Leaders across an organization must learn how to support and develop these competencies if current and future large-scale IT initiatives are to be successful.

Tables 16.1 and 16.2 provide an outline of areas of focus for leaders coping with major IT projects within their organizations. The focus of Table 16.1 is the individual level within the organization, including employees and major external stakeholders. Four areas of focus are recommended: (1) building trusting relationships, (2) fostering participation, (3) supporting risk taking, and (4) supporting employee learning. Table 16.2 focuses on leadership recommendations at the organization level. Three areas are recommended that relate to the successful implementation of major IT projects: (1) placing an emphasis on vision and core values, (2) improving communication, and (3) ensuring information sharing and use. In both tables, we draw from findings in the risk management, innovation, and organizational change literature to reinforce the importance of these leadership actions if large-scale IT projects are to be successful in the public sector.

Risk management literature discusses the importance of the nature of the relationships between those engaged in IT project implementation. It identifies the establishment of long-term relationships built on trust as critical to controlling risk (Keil et al. 1998; Xia and Lee 2004). Ahmed, in his review of critical organizational elements for innovation, found high-trust environments related to the generation of new ideas (1998). There is also evidence demonstrating the necessity of building trust in implementing change processes, noting that resistance to change is increased where there is distrust in those leading the change (see Rusaw 2001 and Yukl 2006). All three literatures point to the benefits of high-trust relationships in attempting organizational change processes.

Table 16.1

Leadership Actions in Large IT Projects

Leadership Recommendations	Risk Management	Innovation	Organizational Change
Leaders focus on building trusting relationships	Building strong long-term relationships is critical	High-trust environments are related to new idea generation	Resistance to change is increased where there is distrust in those leading the change
Leaders foster a culture of participation		High decentralization and employee ability originate and develop ideas critical to innovation	Substantial employee involvement is recommended to implement change
Leaders support risk taking	Scapegoating can make failure more likely; use caution with dismissing staff	Encouraging risk taking and forgiving failed risks are critical to innovation	Providing a sense of security removes a restraining force to change
Leaders support employee learning	Corrective practices can be incorporated into staff training	Personal development of employees enhances innovation	Multiple mentors support career and psychosocial development

Table 16.2

Additional Leadership Actions in Large IT Projects

Leadership Recommendations	Risk Management	Innovation	Organizational Change
Leaders focus on vision and values	Core beliefs, values, and assumptions of senior managers are important in incubating the potential for crises	Employee faith in the purpose and its possibilities is important for innovation	Underlying beliefs and espoused values need to be consistent to effect change and the vision for change that adds to the organizational vision necessary
Leaders consistently utilize communication	Communication processes may impede learning, if the complexity of language used to discuss risk excludes non-technical groups; communication needs attention throughout entire life cycle of project	Highly communicative leadership and widespread, open deliberation fosters innovation; stories of success promote innovation	Vigilant monitoring (communication toward change goal) is necessary for double-loop learning
Leaders ensure information sharing	Effective feedback is extremely important to prevent incidents escalating into crisis; decreased information processing makes organization vulnerable to systemic crisis	Reaching for information not routinely collected by the organization is a sign of increased likelihood of innovation	Actionable knowledge aimed at changing the status quo verified by valid information is needed for double-loop learning

Closely related to fostering trusting relationships during organization changes is the power of fostering employee ownership in processes. Central to innovation literature is the ability of employees to originate and develop their ideas and leadership support for diffusion of power throughout the organization (Siegel and Kaemmerer 1978). Existing research suggests that high decentralization and feelings of employee ownership are related to successful innovation (Light 1998), as is a sense of shared responsibility among work groups (Frederickson 2003). Kotter and Cohen (2002) outline a highly participatory process for effective organizational change, and Fernandez and Rainey (2006) provide an extensive summary of the participatory change process. Leaders who foster participation are likely to benefit in the implementation of IT projects, particularly when innovative solutions to unexpected problems need to be sought.

Employee involvement can have negative consequences when failure is experienced; employees can experience blame and scapegoating for the things that went wrong, providing them with a disincentive to stay involved in collaborative processes. The literature on IT failure cautions against acting too quickly to scapegoat and dismiss those perceived to be responsible for failure (Elliot, Smith, and McGuinness 2000; Iacovou and Dexter 2004). Rogers (1983) and Light (1998) both discuss the encouragement of risk taking and forgiving failed risks as essential to innovation. Lewin's (1951) observations about the importance of employee feelings of security during change processes reinforce these recommendations. Leadership support for risk taking and forgiving failed risks is a common theme in these three literatures.

Support for employee learning is also supported by all three literatures. Iacovou and Dexter (2004) provide strong arguments for corrective practices in relation to project failure to be incorporated into staff training. Support for the personal development of employees is supported in the innovation literature (Siegel and Kaemmerer 1978; Frederickson 2003). Research on mentoring as it relates to organizational effectiveness discusses the many benefits for those involved in mentoring relationships. Higgins and Kram (2001) discuss the importance of employee learning from multiple mentors who comprise a "developmental network" of individuals providing career and psychosocial support. Leaders who support employee learning by providing training and mentoring opportunities as well as learning from organizational experiences enhance their ability to effectively bring about the changes necessary for major IT projects.

Shifting to the organization level, the alignment between vision and values as they relate to organizational change and large-scale IT projects is critical to project success. Schein's (1987) work points to the importance of consistency between underlying beliefs and espoused values to be successful in change processes. The importance of focus on the "vision for change" is recommended by the organizational change literature (Holland 2000; Kotter and Cohen 2002). Ahmed (1998) and Light (1998) both note employee identification with and faith in the purposes of the organization and its philosophy as critical to innovation. Elliott and colleagues identify core beliefs, values, and assumptions of the senior managers as important in incubating the potential for crises (Elliott, Smith, and McGuinness 2000). All of these literatures point to the importance of core vision and values for organizational effectiveness during change processes and risky projects.

Recommendations for effective communication are common in organizational change processes, particularly IT projects that are large-scale and affect a number of users. Vigilant monitoring of communication is an important part of recommended organizational change processes (Kotter and Cohen 2002; Holland 2000; Yukl 2006) as well as communication aimed at double-loop learning (Argyris 1993). Innovation literature discusses the importance of a highly communicative leadership fostering widespread open deliberation as well as communication aimed at enlisting support for solving problems (Frederickson 2003; Nelson 2004). Kelley (2005) discusses the importance of "storyteller" roles within innovative organizations to build both internal morale and external awareness of capacity to innovate. Most important, the risk management literature discusses the possibility that communication processes can impede learning when it is based on the complexity of technical language (Elliott, Smith, and McGuinness 2000). The importance of communication with all stakeholders, in ways that bring understanding of the problems at the level they are capable of understanding, is needed throughout the project life cycle (Sherer and Alter 2004; Iacovou and Dexter 2004).

Closely related concepts of information sharing and use throughout the organization also appear in the literature. The need for effective feedback is important to prevent incidents from escalating into crisis (Elliott, Smith, and McGuinness 2000), and decreased information sharing makes organizations vulnerable to systemic crisis (Greening and Johnson 1996). Argyris (1993) emphasizes the importance of providing accurate information within the feedback processes needed for organizational change. This again recalls the concept of absorptive capacity, particularly within turbulent environments. The ability of public agencies to successfully recognize, share, assimilate, and apply both internal and external knowledge is critical to innovation (Tsai 2001), organizational learning (Lane, Salk, and Lyles 2001), and, we argue, successful implementation of large-scale IT projects. Increasing an organization's absorptive capacity is challenged by a potential need to sacrifice some degree of current operational performance or long-held beliefs to achieve value from uncertain longer-term performance improvements resulting from new knowledge or innovation (Cohen and Levinthal 1990). To encourage the necessary changes requires that leaders increase their own absorptive capacity in addition to ensuring improved information sharing and utilization at the organizational level.

Over the past two decades, we have learned a great deal about implementing large-scale IT projects in the public sector. This has generated much conventional wisdom, which has frequently failed to be adopted by government agencies. Changing this pattern requires leadership initiative at both organization and individual levels and coordination among leaders and managers both inside and outside of the IT area. As we have demonstrated in this section, several bodies of literature provide insight for recommendations as to how public-sector leaders can improve success and better learn from past efforts. Additional benefit could be gained by further integrating these and other bodies of literature in the future.

The Importance of the Leadership Role

It is our hope that outlining the potential roles for leaders will foster a broadening of the research in IT project management to include the role of organizational leadership as defined by other literatures. Preliminary comparisons of the literature of risk management, innovation, and organizational change point to potential roles for leaders within organizations undertaking large-scale IT projects. These comparisons point to a leadership focus on employee participation and learning, building an organizational environment based on trust and support for risk-taking behaviors. The literature also supports the leadership role of clarifying vision and core values, constant communication, and robust information sharing. These roles appear to be far more important in avoiding large-scale IT project failure than the technical challenges posed by the projects. As we noted earlier in this chapter, overcoming the failure to learn, managing escalation of commitment, and coordinating interdependent decision making are critical to large-scale IT project success. These challenges cannot be overcome without a focus on leadership within the overall organization and the roles that leaders play in encouraging and discouraging risk-taking, innovative, and positive change behaviors.

We can expect that the number, size, and complexity of large-scale IT systems in use will only increase in the years to come. As reliance of public-sector organizations on sophisticated and complex large-scale applications continues to grow, the payoff from studying the dynamics of large-scale IT projects and their management also increases. Successful resolution of the issues associated with management of large-scale systems development in the public sector will reduce future development costs, improve the predictability of outcomes, and enhance the speed of innovation. Redefining the roles of agency leaders to include new leadership capabilities and project management skills will result in more than just higher success at large-scale IT projects. These changes will contribute to developing organizational environments that can coordinate and integrate new processes and technologies more rapidly, more effectively, and at a lower cost. Over time, organizational culture may shift to become more flexible and responsive to the increasing demands of a dynamic environment. Continuing our pursuit of this line of inquiry will benefit our understanding of key elements for success at large-scale IT projects within governmental agencies.

This chapter began by introducing the challenges faced by the IRS in modernizing legacy infrastructures to better meet the current operating requirements of the agency. While noting their past failures at modernization, more recently the IRS has made significant progress in their efforts to modernize, advances attributed to improvements in project management capabilities (GAO 2003a; 2003b). Further success requires increasing the number of agency leaders skilled at managing risk, innovation, and organizational change, in addition to other leadership and management capabilities. The real challenge for the IRS and other government agencies involved in large-scale IT projects lies in how to develop the new leadership roles and capabilities rapidly enough to overcome the constantly changing demands and increasing complexity of the design-and-build development environment. We hope that this chapter, along with future research, may provide government agencies like the IRS with new tools and strategies to approach this challenge.

References

Ahmed, Pervaiz. 1998. "Culture and Climate for Innovation." *European Journal of Innovation Management* 1 (1): 30.

Applebaum, Eileen, and Rosemary Batt. 1994. *The New American Workplace: Transforming Work Systems in the United States*. Ithaca, NY: ILR Press.

Argyris, Chris. 1993. *Knowledge for Action: A Guide to Overcoming Barriers to Organization Change*. San Francisco: Jossey-Bass.

Bowen, Michael G. 1987. "The Escalation Phenomenon Reconsidered: Decision Dilemmas or Decision Errors." *Academy of Management Review* 12 (1): 52–66.

Bozeman, Barry, and Stuart Bretschneider. 1986. "Public Management Information Systems: Theory and Prescription." *Public Administration Review* 40 (Special Issue): 475–87.

Bretschneider, Stuart. 1990. "Management Information Systems in Public and Private Organizations: An Empirical Test." *Public Administration Review* 50 (5): 536–45.

Brockner, Joel. 1992. "The Escalation of Commitment to a Failing Course of Action: Toward Theoretical Progress." *Academy of Management Review* 17 (1): 39–61.

Brooks, Frederick P. 1987. "No Silver Bullet: Essence and Accidents of Software Engineering." *IEEE Computer* 20 (4): 10–19.

Brussaard, Bas K. 1992. "Large Scale Information Systems: A Comparative Analysis." In *Informatization Developments and the Public Sector*, ed. Paul H.A. Frissen, European Public Administration and Informatization Series, 2: 171–83. Amsterdam: IOS Press.

Cameron, Kim S., David A. Whetten, and Myung U. Kim. 1987. "Organizational Dysfunctions of Decline." *Academy of Management Journal* 30: 126–38.

Cianni, Mary, and Donna Wnuck. 1997. "Individual Growth and Team Enhancement: Moving Toward a New Model of Career Development." *Academy of Management Executive* 11 (1): 105–15.

Cohen, Wesley M., and Daniel A. Levinthal. 1990. "Absorptive Capacity: A New Perspective on Learning and Innovation." *Administrative Science Quarterly* 35: 128–52.

Dalcher, Darren. 2003. "Beyond Normal Failures: Dynamic Management of Software Projects." *Technology Analysis and Strategic Management* 5 (4): 421–39.

Derthick, Martha. 1990. *Agency Under Stress*. Washington, DC: Brookings Institute.

Drummond, Helga. 1996. *Escalation in Decision-Making: The Tragedy of Taurus*. New York: Oxford University Press.

Elliott, Dominic, Denis Smith, and Martina McGuinness. 2000. "Exploring the Failure To Learn: Crises and the Barriers to Learning." *Review of Business* 21 (3/4): 17–24.

Fernandez, Sergio, and Hal G. Rainey. 2006. "Managing Successful Organizational Change in the Public Sector: An Agenda for Research and Practice." *Public Administration Review* 66 (2): 1–25.

Frederickson, H. George. 2003. *Easy Innovation and the Iron Cage: Best Practice, Benchmarking, Ranking, and the Management of Organizational Creativity*. Dayton, OH: Kettering Foundation.

General Accounting Office (GAO). 2003a. *High-Risk Series: An Update.* Washington, DC: General Accounting Office. Report no. GAO-03–119.

———. 2003b. *Major Management Challenges and Program Risks: Department of the Treasury.* Washington, DC: General Accounting Office. Report no. GAO-03–109.

Gibbs, W. Wayt. 1994. "Software's Chronic Crisis." *Scientific American* 271 (3): 86–95.

Gibson, Faison P. 2000. "Feedback Delays: How Can Decision Makers Learn Not to Buy a New Car Every Time the Garage Is Empty?" *Organizational Behavior and Human Decision Processes* 83 (1): 141–66.

Greening, Daniel W., and Richard A. Johnson. 1996. "Do Managers and Strategies Matter? A Study in Crisis." *Journal of Management Studies* 33 (1): 25–51.

Hambrick, Donald C., and Phyllis A. Mason. 1984. "Upper Echelons: The Organization as a Reflection of Its Top Managers." *Academy of Management Review* 9 (2): 193–206.

Higgins, Monica C., and Kathy E. Kram. 2001. "Reconceptualizing Mentoring at Work: A Developmental Network Perspective." *Academy of Management Review* 26 (2): 264–88.

Holland, Winford E. 2000. *Change Is the Rule: Practical Actions for Change, on Target, on Time, on Budget.* Chicago: Dearborn.

Iacovou, Charalambos L., and Albert S. Dexter. 2004. "Turning Around Runaway Information Technology Projects." *California Management Review* 46 (4): 68–88.

Keil, Mark. 1995. "Pulling the Plug: Software Project Management and the Problem of Project Escalation." *MIS Quarterly* 19 (4): 421–47.

Keil, Mark, Paul E. Cule, Kalle Lyytinen, and Roy C. Schmidt. 1998. "A Framework for Identifying Software Project Risks." *Communications of the ACM* 41 (11): 80.

Keil, Mark, and Joan Mann. 1997. "The Nature and Extent of Information Technology Project Escalation: Results from a Survey of IS Audit and Control Professionals." *IS Audit and Control Journal* (1): 40–48.

Keil, Mark, Joan Mann, and Arun Rai. 2000. "Why Software Projects Escalate: An Empirical Analysis and Test of Four Theoretical Models." *MIS Quarterly* 24 (4): 631–64.

Keil, Mark, Richard Mixon, Timo Saarinen, and Virpi Tuunainen. 1994–1995. "Understanding Runaway Information Technology Projects: Results from an International Research Program Based on Escalation Theory." *Journal of Management Information Systems* 11 (3): 65–85.

Keil, Mark, Bernard C.Y. Tan, Kwok-Kee Wei, Timo Saarinen, Virpi Tuunainen, and Arjen Wassenaar. 2000. "A Cross-Cultural Study on Escalation of Commitment Behavior in Software Projects." *MIS Quarterly* 24 (2): 299–325.

Kelley, Tom. 2005. *The Ten Faces of Innovation.* New York: Doubleday.

Kotter, John P., and Dan S. Cohen. 2002. *The Heart of Change.* Boston: Harvard Business School Press.

Kraemer, Kenneth L., and Jason Dedrick. 1997. "Computing and Public Organizations." *Journal of Public Administration Research and Theory* 7 (1): 89–112.

Lane, Peter J., Jane E. Salk, and Marjorie A. Lyles. 2001. "IJV Learning and Performance." *Strategic Management Journal* 22: 1139–61.

Lewin, Kurt. 1951. *Field Theory in Social Sciences.* New York: Harper.

Light, Paul C. 1998. *Sustaining Innovation: Creating Nonprofit and Government Organizations That Innovate Naturally.* San-Francisco: Jossey-Bass.

Margetts, Helen, and Leslie Willcocks. 1994. "Informatization in Public Sector Organizations: Distinctive or Common Risks?" *Informatization and the Public Sector* 3: 1–19.

Meyer, Marshall W., and Lynne G. Zucker. 1989. *Permanently Failing Organizations.* Newbury Park, CA: Sage.

Mohan, Lakshmi, William K. Holstein, and R.B. Adams. 1990. "EIS: It Can Work in the Public Sector." *MIS Quarterly* 14 (4): 435–48.

Mone, Mark A., William McKinley, and Vincent L. Barker. 1998. "Organizational Decline and Innovation: A Contingency Framework." *Academy of Management Review* 23 (1): 115–32.

National Research Council, Computer Science and Telecommunication Board, Committee on Information Technology Research in a Competitive World. 2000. *Making IT Better: Expanding Information Technology Research to Meet Society's Needs.* Washington, DC: National Academy Press.

Nelson, Mark. 2004. *Leading Innovation: Innovation Climate and IT Unit Effectiveness.* Boulder, CO: EDUCAUSE Center for Research.

Rocheleau, Bruce. 2000. "Prescriptions for Public-sector Information Management." *American Review of Public Administration* 30 (4): 414–35.

Rocheleau, Bruce, and Liangfu Wu. 2002. "Public versus Private Information Systems: Do They Differ in Important Ways? A Review and Empirical Test." *American Review of Public Administration* 32 (4): 379–97.

Rogers, Everett. 1983. *Diffusion of Innovations.* New York: Free Press.

Rusaw, A. Carol. 2001. *Leading Public Organizations: An Interactive Approach.* New York: Harcourt.

Schein, Edgar H. 1987. *Process Consultation.* New York: Addison-Wesley.

Sherer, Susan A., and Steven Alter. 2004. "Information System Risks and Risk Factors: Are They Mostly About Information Systems?" *Communications of the Association for Information Systems* 14: 29–64.

Siegel Saul M., and William F. Kaemmerer. 1978. "Measuring the Perceived Support for Innovation in Organizations." *Journal of Applied Psychology* 63 (5): 553–62.

Standish Group. 1994. *CHAOS: A Recipe for Success.* Dennis, MA: Standish Group.

Staw, Barry M. 1976. "Knee-deep in the Big Muddy: A Study of Escalating Commitment to a Chosen Course of Action." *Organizational Behavior and Human Performance* 16: 27–44.

———. 1981. "The Escalation of Commitment to a Course of Action." *Academy of Management Review* 6: 577–87.

———. 1982. "Counterforces to Change." In *Change in Organizations,* ed. P.S. Goodman and Associates, 87–121. San Francisco: Jossey-Bass.

Staw, Barry M., Lance E. Sandelands, and Jane E. Dutton. 1981. "Threat-Rigidity Effects in Organizational Behavior: A Multilevel Analysis." *Administrative Science Quarterly* 26: 501–24.

Tsai, Wenpin. 2001. "Knowledge Transfer in Intraorganizational Networks." *Academy of Management Journal* 44: 996–1004.

Turner, Barry A. 1976. "The Organizational and Interorganizational Development of Disasters." *Administrative Science Quarterly* 21: 378–97.

Xia, Weidong, and Gwanhoo Lee. 2004. "Grasping the Complexity of IS Development Projects." *Communications of the ACM* 47 (5): 69–74.

Yukl, Gary. 2006. *Leadership in Organizations.* 6th ed. Upper Saddle River, NJ: Pearson Prentice Hall.

Zmud, Robert. 1980. "Management of Large Software Development Efforts." *MIS Quarterly* 4 (2): 45–55.

17

Government's New Breed of Change Agents

Leading the War on Terror

Daniel P. Forrester

The Urgency of Terrorism Speeds Transformational Change

World War II brought forth a generation of leaders who had scarce resources and global enemies to combat. Some of the most difficult battles in that war, such as D-day, featured political, military, and civilian leadership pushing down the decision making and authority to those closest to the enemy and the problem. This *over*authorization gave rise to decentralized decision making, innovative leadership, transformation of operations, and, most important, victory.

The War on Terror has created urgency for innovative ways to protect the American people, spawning a new breed of public manager to lead that innovation. Dramatic change is happening so quickly because the government is undergoing the largest reorganization since World War II. And just as the Greatest Generation brought forth the best and brightest to serve, a new leadership profile is emerging within the Intelligence Community (Intel), Department of Defense (DoD), and burgeoning Department of Homeland Security (DHS).

John Kotter of Harvard Business School has found that 50 percent of change initiatives fail because the urgency rate is not strong enough to get people out of their comfort zones. Based on his extensive studies, he believes that 75 percent of an organization's management must genuinely believe that business as usual is totally unacceptable in order for change to occur.

September 11, 2001, was a "forcing function," according to Linton Wells, acting assistant secretary of defense and the DoD's chief information officer. That horrific set of events triggered government executives and legislative leaders to believe that "government as usual" was no longer acceptable. It created the urgency and the budgetary freedom to pursue ideas that had been developed prior to that event, but lacked the "force" to get them off the white board and into the real world.

Seeing this renewed sense of purpose and drive for change among our government clients, we embarked on a seven-month study to better understand the profile of these emerging government leaders in the War on Terror. We call these managers *change agents*. Our goal: to pinpoint practices these leaders use in creating innovative security approaches, business processes, collaborative interagency frameworks, and, most important, organizational change.

> A change agent has a very clear focus on what he wants to get for the organization. He realizes that processes and culture have to change to achieve the objectives. He assesses the situation, sees what's at stake, finds the significant issues, and focuses.—Pete Rustan, Director, Advanced Systems and Technology, National Reconnaissance Office

We interviewed twenty-four diverse senior leaders from DoD, DHS, Intel, and academe and asked ten questions (see appendix 17.1, "Research Methodology and Protocol"). Based on these interviews, this study:

- Uncovered six management practices used by change agents in the War on Terror.
- Developed the first profile of government change agents making change happen in the War on Terror.
- Pinpointed six ways that change agents measure their success.

A New Breed of Government Leaders: Change Agents in the War on Terror

The emerging new breed of government managers leading the War on Terror are true change agents. They are in formal leadership positions as well as functional specialties; all are doing things in radically new ways toward a common vision. They are not your father's bureaucrats. Rather, they know how to enact innovative ideas by working within bureaucratic hierarchies and by injecting a sense of passion and purpose that brings along the more risk averse. "Change agents see what is and see what ought to be," said Scott Hastings, CIO for the US-VISIT program at the DHS. "You come into the senior executive service government ranks because you see a problem and are willing to take risks to fix it."

Change agents attribute their success to the following six key management practices:

- Challenge the status quo.
- Frame a clear, compelling vision.
- Focus on new outcomes versus process.
- Realign and lead within bureaucracy.
- Uncover the right talent.
- Listen intently.

Challenge the Status Quo; Frame a Vision

Change agents see new possibilities and know how to create and communicate a clear, compelling vision. "Change agents don't accept the status quo. They push the envelope for solutions," stressed John Sindelar, deputy associate administrator of the General Services Administration's (GSA) Office of Governmentwide Policy. "You must establish a vision, understand at a very core level why you are critical to that vision, assemble the right team, and then be able to articulate the vision within the group so that everyone embraces the vision and the priorities to achieve that vision," said Greg Rothwell, chief procurement officer, DHS. Retired Vice Admiral Art Cebrowski, a man who clearly had a vision for changing the underlying assumptions of the DoD when he served as the director of the Office of Force Transformation, provided the following advice to leaders stepping into positions of power:

- *Be Bold*: Don't try to do it unless it looks impossible. You have to pick up the things that look really hard. Other people will have done everything else.
- *Be Fast*: No transformational leader ever looks back and regrets moving too fast.
- *Be Specific*: If you lack specificity, your subordinates will be able to change your message to suit their own purposes.

> Stay out of the weeds. Focus on the problem and threat. Terrorists change much faster than us.—Gary Foster, Former Deputy Director for Planning & Coordination, CIA

Focus on Achieving Outcomes; Beware of Business as Usual

Government leaders often translate their visionary ideas into a blueprint, or "Concept of Operations." (CONOPS). But Charlie Allen, the CIA's assistant director of Central Intelligence for Collection, bluntly warned that "CONOPS is not easy." The change agents interviewed stressed that translating vision into strategy requires a more flexible, adaptive approach to traditional CONOPS. And, they said strategy must reach to the business-process change level.

CONOPS strategy documents can redefine everything from how an agency shares data for decision making to defining new paradigms of warfare. The documents (or their agency equivalents) are the source of endless ideas and debate around organizational change. Wary of how effective CONOPS are in DoD, Priscilla Guthrie, deputy assistant secretary of defense, advised change agents not to get bogged down in detailed CONOPS around IT, but instead take a more innovative approach.

"In IT we've learned to talk about spiral development in CONOPS because it's difficult to predict how large environments are going to behave," she explained. "We need to adopt a more adaptive approach and get away from the 'tyranny' of the predictive. This frees people to operate within broader constraints. My advice is to write as little as you can for a short horizon. We shouldn't write detailed CONOPS for what we can't predict."

Mark Forman, the Office of Management and Budget's (OMB) former administrator for e-government and information technology, looked at CONOPS from another perspective. He stressed that change has to be driven at the business-process level, where tremendous resistance often occurs. "To drive transformation and affect the business issues, you have to be able to affect business process change," he said. "Without change on that level, success is unlikely."

> Be nice to secretaries and gate guards. If you don't play by the rules, the system will come back to haunt you.—Linton Wells, Acting Assistant Secretary of Defense

Leading within a Bureaucracy

Change agents know how to engage the bureaucracy around them with care and detail. "The key to a change-management strategy is first analyzing the likely winners and losers," said the GSA's John Sindelar. "Determine the decision makers and the power holders behind the visible power symbol. Collaborate to influence both winners and losers. Align incentives as catalysts for support. Create as many win-wins as possible, and be willing to 'sacrifice' and be satisfied by getting part or most of what you want." "And remember," he added, "that a carefully thought-out communication strategy is a must. It requires overt messages as well as a more tactical, offline strategy."

Former Navy Under Secretary Jerry Hultin said that it's important to look at the bigger picture within the agency or department and recognize how much change and innovation others are capable of digesting. "You have to remember where you are in the system and you have to know your range of innovation," he explained. "Change agents focus on what should be done and figure out how to be innovative in accomplishing that goal. But pick your targets. You don't want to be innovative in everything. Apply the 80/20 rule; 20 percent should be focused on innovation." Lynn Torres, Office of Naval Research Industrial and Corporate Partners Programs, also emphasized the value of understanding where you are in the bureaucracy and the potential ramifications that policy plays in enacting a vision or agenda. "While all potential change agents have a great vision, they will eventually brush up against the infrastructure," said Torres. "A successful policy interpretation or policy/law change, with willing participants from a spectrum of disciplines, will be required to push the vision from a pilot program to long-term change."

Uncover the Right Talent

Enacting organizational change requires an astute ability to pinpoint talent, get people to buy into vision, create the right teams, and set high performance standards. "Technology and education don't make the difference. People make all the difference," said Pete Rustan of the National Reconnaissance Office. "What we are going to be able to do thirty or fifty years from now depends on the people that we have right now." Trust and diversity of in-depth skills were cited as particularly important in assembling teams. "Surround yourself with smart people you can trust, especially if you don't have the background," advised an anonymous chief technology officer from Intel. "Also, quickly understand as much as you can about the internal politics, what drives and motivates people. I'm less political and more technical. It's important to understand the outside politics. Also, you've got to learn how stakeholders view your organization. Those are the most important things."

The team skills most frequently cited by study participants include:

- Leadership skills.
- Interpersonal relationship skills.
- Science and technology background.
- Knowledge of federal processes.
- Thorough knowledge of the business and agency mission.
- Program management disciplines (e.g., risk management, earned value management).
- Acquisition and contract management skills.

Listen More

A subtle but important area that came up repeatedly was the importance of listening. "Leaders who don't listen will not lead in the long run," said Jerry Hultin, former Navy under secretary. "You have to be able to shut up and listen. You need to listen to other people's dialogues instead of creating your own," said Art Cebrowski. The Navy's Lynn Torres explained that she "listens with her ears and eyes." By listening with her eyes, Torres was referring to the ability to read people's faces and gain an understanding of what they are not saying in words but expressing or even suppressing. Scott Hastings of DHS is so keen on listening that when he's delivering a presentation he will often designate a staff member to listen with "eyes and ears" to what's going on in the room. Hastings recognizes that when he gets immersed in delivering content and messages, he may not listen as fully as possible. Hence, he assigns an active listener. Paul O'Connell, of Iona College, points to the Compstat system of police management that was used with great success by William Bratton and the New York City Police Department. He notes, "Sometimes you need to use an existing mechanism or create a new one to standardize the listening function and the ability to view and understand the entire organizational landscape."

Profiles in Leadership: The DNA of War on Terror Change Agents

While academic definitions of "change agent" vary and are difficult to pin down, almost all of the study participants viewed a change agent as a person who knows how to set a vision and achieve it. Some of the participants' definitions included:

Figure 17.1 **Character Traits and Modes of Operation**

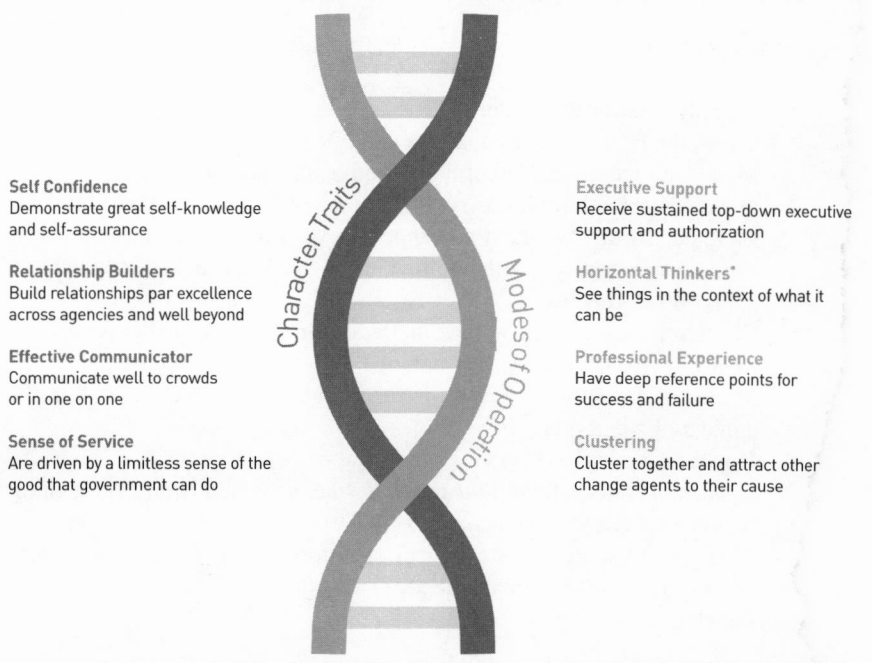

Self Confidence
Demonstrate great self-knowledge
and self-assurance

Relationship Builders
Build relationships par excellence
across agencies and well beyond

Effective Communicator
Communicate well to crowds
or in one on one

Sense of Service
Are driven by a limitless sense of the
good that government can do

Executive Support
Receive sustained top-down executive
support and authorization

Horizontal Thinkers*
See things in the context of what it
can be

Professional Experience
Have deep reference points for
success and failure

Clustering
Cluster together and attract other
change agents to their cause

- "A Change Agent is someone who is helping to either bring about a different condition (change), but more often it is someone who is leading in the transition that results from change."—Greg Rothwell
- "Someone who identifies a future state or goal and then puts the systems in place to get it done."—Jerry Hultin
- "A change agent effectively redirects the capacities of individuals or organizations to achieve either better results for a traditional mission or new outcomes based on another assignment."—Tom Ridge
- "A change agent is the person who carries the flag of a need, usually not a generally recognized need."—Gary Foster
- "A change agent is any catalyst that alters the status quo. It could be a person, group, an event, or policies."—Louis Andre

Given that there was not a single common definition of the term *change agent*, we define a *change agent* in the War on Terror as: "A forward-thinking and -acting person who is able to deliberately and tangibly impact the mission and organizational direction of a bureaucracy from its status quo into an integrated, future state capable of contemplating and ultimately thwarting security threats, including natural hazards that might befall the United States."

As with DNA, No Two Change Agents Are Exactly Alike

Digging deeper into the change-agent profile, four specific types emerged:

1. **Transformational Leaders**
   Character Traits: Bold visionaries and often senior political appointees
   Modes of Operation: Forceful, focused, tenacious, seasoned
2. **Overauthorized Senior Directors**
   Character Traits: "Make it all happen" major program managers
   Modes of Operation: Collaborative; manage up, down, and interagency
3. **Functional Mavens**
   Character Traits: Deep subject matter experts with critical cross-agency inputs to change and transformation
   Modes of Operation: Seek to innovate functional expertise within the context of a common vision
4. **Dogged Conceptualizers**
   Character Traits: The big-idea people who act patiently and know intuitively that "every good idea has its day"
   Modes of Operation: Independent operators who powerfully feed concepts to Transformational Leaders, Overauthorized Senior Directors, and Functional Mavens

Change agents are sometimes found in isolation within a bureaucracy but often cluster together in a sort of chemical interaction that can bring about profound change. Transformational Leaders, Overauthorized Senior Directors, and Functional Mavens complement one another's competencies and are more likely to cluster together and be interdependent. Dogged Conceptualizers, however, tend to be loners, big thinkers who often work with the other change agents but act as individual contributors rather than as managers or program owners.

> If you are going to be a visionary leader, then think of yourself as a drill bit. You will be used up and then thrown out, but you will make progress through the rock.—Linton Wells, Acting Assistant Secretary of Defense

Transformational Leaders: The Bold Visionaries behind Big Change

Transformational Leaders are the senior-most government leaders, often political appointees, and always the major impetus behind substantive change. "Change is not sufficiently precise to describe what change agents in the government really do," explained retired Vice Admiral Art Cebrowski. "It's about transformational leadership."

According to several other research participants, these very senior-level government executives create visions for their organizations that are fundamentally

Figure 17.2 **Types of Transformational Leaders**

different from what they inherited when they started the job. They also tend to have short tenures. "These people argue themselves out of jobs," said Thomas Barnett, author of *The Pentagon's New Map*. He explained that once these change agents' new concepts and vision are adopted, they appear less relevant for steady-state operations.

A Look at One Transformational Leader: Mark Forman

Mark Forman, the first administrator for e-government and information technology within the OMB, was a bold visionary who quickly engaged the bureaucracy around innovative technology approaches at a federal level. Forman secured his authority by enabling legislation that he sometimes helped author and by gaining the budget and people he needed to enact his vision. "Mark's vision and his tenacity in sticking to that vision was extremely strong," explained his friend and colleague John Sindelar, deputy associate administrator of the Office of Government-wide Policy at the GSA, in the magazine *Washington Technology*. Forman oversaw more than $45 billion that the executive branch spends annually on technology, including President Bush's top priority, e-government. His leadership would have implications for the War on Terror: how agencies leverage common technology assets, how agencies share data, IT security, adherence to common enterprise architecture vision, and IT acquisition.

As with other Transformational Leaders, Forman sought first to ensure that he had the requisite authority and resources to enable change. Unlike many in government, Forman questioned whether the government was spending too much money when he first landed in the job. "There wasn't a need for additional money. Do we

Table 17.1

Transformational Leaders

Character Traits	Modes of Operation
Seasoned, well-credentialed leaders	Move very quickly to attack problems
Bold visionaries who have relentless focus on alignment around a future state	Secure the authority and funding necessary to change the entire direction of the programs and people they must now manage
Forceful communicators who make their "vocal opponents non-vocal and their non-vocal proponents vocal"*	

Attract and surround themselves with other change agents
Adopt new language in order to define the future state

*Mark Forman supplied this quote during his interview.

have too much money was the question," he said. "The game was to get existing IT spending under control. In fact, there was an overinvestment in some areas." Early in his tenure, Forman also went out and established relationships with chief information officers (CIOs) and other departmental technology leadership across the federal government. This relationship building helped Forman later engage these managers in the type of massive collaboration needed to achieve his federal IT vision.

As he reflected on his tenure in government, Forman remembered that 40 percent of those he met with thought his vision was on target, although they pushed back and forced him to explain his thinking. "Another 30 percent didn't get it and had to be replaced. The other 30 percent were leading the charge, and they took ownership of the vision as it matched their views," he said. As Forman's program within OMB matured, he created a series of Quicksilver initiatives that cut horizontally across agencies and required significant business process redesign. To achieve his goals, Forman surrounded himself with other change agents. "When we did the Quicksilver Task Force we looked for change agents who wanted to be involved in major transformation, who were senior managers (GS-14 through first-level executives), and who were career appointees," he explained. "We unleashed career employees to drive the change. We didn't realize there was so much energy at the career level that wanted so much change."

Overauthorized Senior Directors—Line Managers of Transformation

Overauthorized Senior Directors (OASDs) understand not only that they must be authorized by congressional or executive orders but that they must be hyper-empowered by leadership above them. Like movie directors, these senior executives miss little in their spheres of influence and understand who they need to surround themselves with in order to enact organizational change. While change agents can exist on their own within DHS, DoD, and Intel, they are never as effective in implementing change as when they report to Transformational Leaders who give them authority and autonomy. Hence, the definition of these change agents as *over*authorized. To be most effective, Overauthorized Senior Directors need transformational leadership above them to be successful. These change agents project what Charlie Allen of the CIA calls "a force of personality" when they speak in front of audiences; they're extremely clear about the change they intend to make and the authority that is backing them to make it.

> Sustained top-down support must come with the role or it will fail.
> —John Sindelar, Deputy Associate Administrator, GSA

Overauthorized Senior Directors believe that the leadership above them is supportive even in the face of extreme criticism. They are people who have the presence and ability to speak and listen but never rely on the name of the Transformational Leader above them to command the respect of those they are trying to win over. Their authority, perceived or real, enters the room before them and leaves a few minutes after they depart. These change agents are not reckless in their use of the authority entrusted to them. Rather, they act boldly and are aggressive in enacting change and achieving a vision at a programmatic level. Thomas Barnett, whose strategic thinking has captured the imagination of the defense community, explained that "change agents are over-authorized; they do things and then ask for forgiveness later." Art Cebrowski, to whom Barnett reported at the Office of Force Transformation within DoD, said, "If Barnett did not have over-authorization from me, or if I did not have it from Rumsfeld, I would have resigned. There is no sense in doing the work if you're not over-authorized."

Almost all of the study participants shared stories that illustrated the concept of overauthorization or echoed the idea itself. Jerry Hultin said it best when he described change agents as "people who act as though there is no one above them."

Overauthorized Senior Directors are much closer to the day-to-day operations of large programs, and they work at a lower level of detail than the Transformational Leaders above them. If Transformational Leaders supply vision, then Overauthorized Senior Directors supply the steady day-to-day management to move the vision forward. Without the authority they yield, their impact and ability to change people's behavior would be severely compromised.

Overauthorized Senior Directors in the War on Terror see that interagency collaboration and integration is more important than fighting for turf within their agency. When not going deep on the portfolio they are entrusted to manage within their program areas, they consider the inter- and cross-agency implications of their actions, plans, and programs. In fact, because War on Terror government

Table 17.2

Over-authorized Senior Directors

Character Traits	Modes of Operation
Forceful personalities	Interact with and manage up to Transformational Leaders
Refined listening skills	Push decision making down within their programs
Skilled interagency champions	Seek out subject matter experts to enact change
	Manage a portfolio of change often in context of major programs

programs within DHS, DoD, and Intel do not exist in vacuums, Overauthorized Senior Directors often lead programs where multiple constituencies have vested interests in their success and potential failures. "These people see value in enterprise-wide thinking versus stove pipes," explained Keith Herrington of the Defense Intelligence Agency.

Meet Bob Stephan, an Overauthorized Senior Director

In the post-Katrina environment, the following example may seem misplaced. What Secretary Ridge calls out through this minicase is how he overauthorized Bob Stephan to drive consensus around the initial National Incident Response Plan. The plan itself was clearly not adopted during Hurricane Katrina, but that has little to do with how Stephan worked in interagency settings to arrive at a plan that could scale over time. In the post–September 11, 2001, federal environment, not all of the new rules, technologies, plans, and concepts proposed by change agents will be embraced on their first iteration. Thus, Stephan's example remains one for other change agents to consider as they will often find themselves proposing solutions to complex interagency (horizontal) problems.

Then Secretary of Homeland Security Tom Ridge tasked Bob Stephan, a former special assistant, to assemble a unified all-threats National Response Plan. "We needed someone whose vision included the development of a prototype that the state and locals would use in response to a terrorist event or a natural disaster or a horrible accident," explained Ridge. "Bob had operational experience in the Air Force and drove the consensus needed to create the National Incident Management System that now exists in this country. This system could be embedded down at the county level, with everybody singing off the same sheet, preparing and responding in a similar way with some variations. This is a huge sea change.

"Several national response plans pre-existed our effort to have just one that everyone bought into. Bob had the foresight, the energy, and the vision to amalgamate them, bring everybody in, and build a consensus around those documents. This was huge change below the radar screen. It wasn't sexy; it wasn't going to be written about much, but it was exciting to the emergency management professionals who recognized that this change would materially and positively affect our ability to respond and recover from a natural disaster or terrorist event."

In explaining the management competencies that made Stephan successful in leading change, Ridge further reinforced the profile of an Overauthorized Senior Director. "Bob had a sense of urgency that was reflected in a work ethic. He has a huge intellect and could effect change because of the clarity of his vision, the inclusiveness of his approach, and the constant pressure he put on the system to get results. Everybody embraced his vision because he was so inclusive. Ideas weren't mandated top-down, like many departments do." What Bob Stephan was able to achieve through interagency collaboration and in pushing inside and outside DHS speaks to the tenacity of Overauthorized Senior Directors.

The Functional Mavens: Innovative Subject Matter Experts

The DHS, DoD, and Intel are filled with a third type of change agent: Functional Mavens, the subject matter experts (SMEs) in areas ranging from weapons systems (technology) to human resource policy development.

Functional Mavens play a horizontal role within their organizations and usually need the cooperation of Overauthorized Senior Directors in order to be successful. Similarly, Overauthorized Senior Directors can't be successful unless Functional Mavens integrate well with them and help to accelerate process and functional change.

When Overauthorized Senior Directors are surrounded by Transformational Leaders, the Functional Mavens can have even greater impact. Mavens bring a passion to their functional areas and understand that they own and operate key parts of the portfolio upon which Overauthorized Senior Directors and Transformational Leaders rely.

Mavens can and do exist in organizations as change agents in the absence of Overauthorized Senior Directors and Transformational Leaders. When they are not in the presence of these other leaders, the change that they can enact is incremental versus transformational. In many ways, the ability of a Functional Maven to be successful is akin to a chemical compound linking with other compounds to form new things. In the presence of just other functional experts, Mavens are just Mavens. Yet in the presence of Overauthorized Senior Directors and Transformational Leaders, Functional Mavens are energized and excited to align their functional skills with the broad vision proposed by the other change agents.

"Policy Subject Matter Experts (SME) can help you steer clear of land mines," explained the GSA's John Sindelar. "They provide you the inventory of the current landscape by which you can evaluate the proposed policy change. They help anchor your vision to reality and help determine implementation strategy and timing. There

0

Table 17.3

Functional Mavens

Character Traits	Modes of Operation
Experts in specific functional areas (e.g., policy, people, IT)	Understand that they own and operate key parts of the portfolio upon which their leaders rely
Passionate about their area of expertise and their impact on programs	See their functional area in the context of the vision their leaders are putting forth
	Accelerate programmatic success

is nothing better then to have a recognized SME become your policy advocate, proactively supporting your change."

Functional Mavens tend to build relationships with other mavens (if they are present) and push the boundaries of their function to optimize for the better of the organization. It is rarely about them; it is about the success of the Overauthorized Senior Directors and the role that Functional Mavens play in accelerating that programmatic success.

Functional Mavens Live throughout Program Portfolios

Figure 17.3 depicts a typical program portfolio that exists within the Intel, DHS, and DoD communities. Programs within the War on Terror are complex entities where change takes root. The portfolio gives rise to Functional Mavens who have deep knowledge of their functional area (such as technology or policy) and understand their unique role and how they complement other Mavens within the portfolio. The entire portfolio is managed by Overauthorized Senior Directors.

The Dogged Conceptualizers: The Big-Idea Horizontal Thinkers

Dogged Conceptualizers don't own, lead, fund, or lobby to keep programs. They generate concepts that, under the right circumstances, can become the basis for startling programmatic and government-wide change. Their ideas fuel Transformational Leaders and Overauthorized Senior Directors. If enacted, their ideas will ultimately have major implications for Functional Mavens. In fact, when Transformational Leaders, Overauthorized Senior Directors, and Functional Mavens are clustered together, you usually find Dogged Conceptualizers. Several study participants noted that when multiple Dogged Conceptualizers are found in an agency, it's often a sign that a particularly massive change initiative is in the making at that agency.

Figure 17.3   **A Typical Program Portfolio**

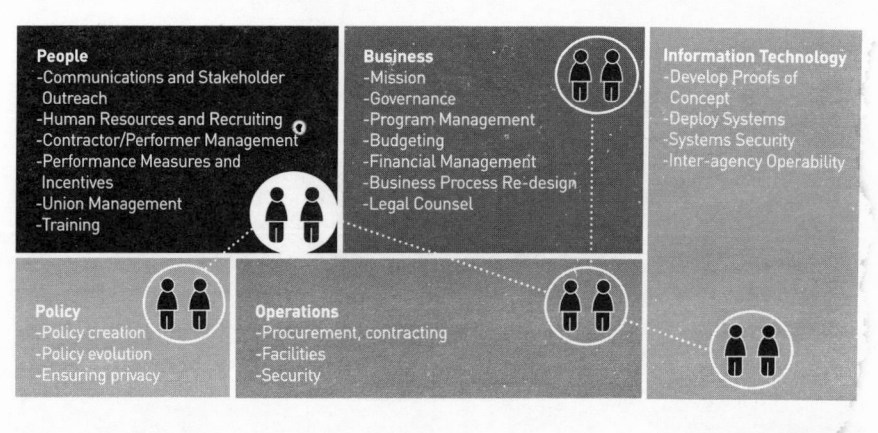

The Dogged Conceptualizers' concepts can range from recommending the reorganization of an agency to developing paradigm-shifting ways for their organizations to consider the problem set posed by the war. While Dogged Conceptualizers don't question everything, they ask the most questions and challenge the status quo. They help people and organizations frame situations in new contexts, which opens up innovative thinking and problem solving. They develop concepts for new models and methods. They eschew small problems.

The word *dogged* aptly describes these change agents because while they are never at a loss for a new idea; they also realize that major shifts in thinking within DHS, DoD, and Intel take time to set in and be acted on. Several research participants noted that ideas with major horizontal and interagency implications can take two to four years or more to develop. Tenacity and persistence are the hallmarks of these change agents. They brief in front of small and large audiences over and over, until the concept is rejected or hopefully absorbed.

A common Dogged Conceptualizer competence is the ability to succinctly describe a concept that they want to sell. Many are visual thinkers who recognize that a picture can tell a thousand words when selling new ideas. "The best way to convince someone of a new concept is with a visual pitch on an 8.5×11 piece of paper. If you can't convey it in that form, you don't have it right," explained a Dogged Conceptualizer from Intel who wished to remain anonymous. However, when presenting their ideas, Dogged Conceptualizers rarely presuppose a specific solution based on their concept. Keith Herrington, senior IT specialist in the DoD's Defense Intelligence Agency, noted that when he's in multi- and cross-agency settings, as Dogged Conceptualizers often are, he is careful not to talk about a solution too early, even if he knows intuitively that his concept may be right. Rather, he lets conversations unfold and allows consensus to build around a desired end state (or concept).

Figure 17.4 **Dogged Conceptualizers**

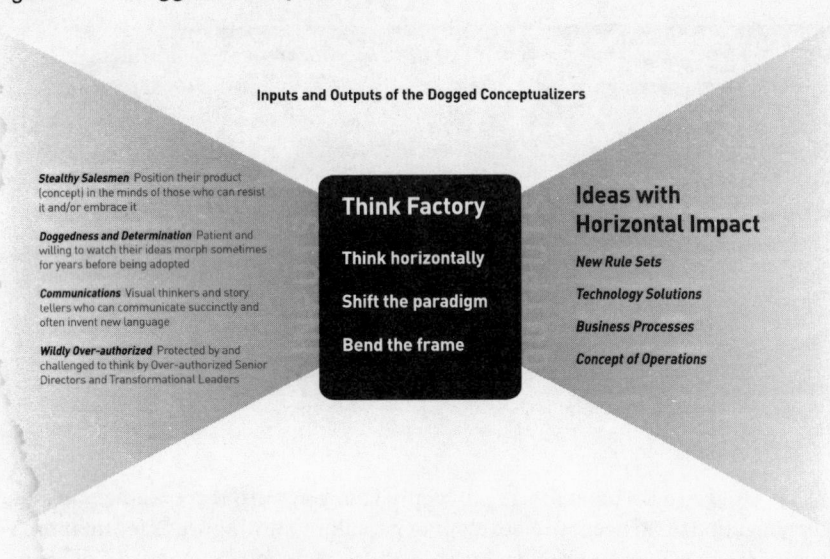

Inputs and Outputs of the Dogged Conceptualizers

Stealthy Salesmen Position their product (concept) in the minds of those who can resist it and/or embrace it

Doggedness and Determination Patient and willing to watch their ideas morph sometimes for years before being adopted

Communications Visual thinkers and story tellers who can communicate succinctly and often invent new language

Wildly Over-authorized Protected by and challenged to think by Over-authorized Senior Directors and Transformational Leaders

Think Factory

Think horizontally

Shift the paradigm

Bend the frame

Ideas with Horizontal Impact

New Rule Sets

Technology Solutions

Business Processes

Concept of Operations

How Gary Foster, a Dogged Conceptualizer, Changed the CIA's Mind-set

At the end of the cold war, then CIA Director Webster tasked Gary Foster with refocusing the mission and activities of the entire CIA. The problem Foster helped to solve is one of the most strategic and pressing that agencies within the War on Terror may face today. The way Foster approached the problem, and the organizational design and reorganization concepts that emerged from his vision, constitute a great example of a Dogged Conceptualizer in action.

In the early 1990s, the CIA was struggling with its relevancy in a post–cold war setting and how it would manage the significant budget cuts from Congress, cuts that were referred to as "end-of-the-cold-war savings." With a very small staff and the full authority of director William H. Webster, Foster pulled together a Strategic Planning Working Group comprising the second-in-command senior officers of the CIA's four directorates. He devised a program to rapidly assess the future of the CIA through the lens of twenty-two studies commissioned by his office and the working group. The forward-looking recommendations for mission realignment resulting from these studies were given to senior leadership. Reaction to the studies was mixed, with some of the CIA's four deputy directors easily aligned with the need for change and others protesting that Foster and his team—comprising their own deputies—were attempting to meddle in "their business."

To gain broader leadership acceptance of the urgent need for the CIA to change, Foster conceived a series of innovative workshops with the agency's top three tiers of leaders. An early, critical three-day workshop was held off-site in a conference room from which Foster's team had removed all tables and chairs. The eighty-five most senior managers entered and had to mill around, unable to seat themselves in natural affinity groupings. They were issued sticky notes and pens and were asked to deal with issues of change posed by titles taped to the walls. Participants discussed their ideas during the first hour of the conference, with everyone standing together as a group. Foster then gave them a coffee break, during which he and his team set up the room for an exercise that would get these senior officials to see the need for change throughout the CIA. When people came back into the conference room, Foster directed them, including Judge Webster and his principal deputy, to line up on the large oval line he had taped on the perimeter of the room's floor, positioning themselves between five numbered signs set around half of the oval.

Sign one indicated a belief that little organizational change was warranted. Sign five stood for belief in significant and immediate change. Spaces between any two signs indicated plus or minus the closest value. Using the oval shape meant that those in favor of greatest change ended up standing directly opposite those who saw the least need for change. The initial alignment was mainly between signs two and three and a half. Interestingly, there were more above three than below two, though all numbers had stalwarts.

A member of Foster's staff then asked if anyone on the line wished to say why he or she had picked his or her spot. Nobody would speak. They were fairly belligerent in their silence. Foster signaled for a junior member of his staff to approach someone in the group he knew and discuss their thinking right at the line denoted in the room. The junior member adroitly stretched out his hand to someone he knew trusted him and, as though they were in private conversation, talked about their views on change. That small act made it safe for others to talk, and one by one people began to explain their views about change until nearly all had spoken. There was much intragroup chatter and good-natured haranguing across group boundaries.

After about forty-five minutes, Foster invited people to relocate to a new number if they wished to do so, and within minutes a significant majority was standing from three and a half to five, the sign for the strongest belief in change. The "least change" advocates barely budged but came to see themselves as out of step and at risk of being isolated. Foster described this as "a powerful moment." Those likely to be most affected by change were selling themselves and their colleagues. There was little need for Foster to oversell his concepts for change. After this exercise, the next two days' discussions took on new meaning and intensity. There was a recognition and consensus for change. Foster, the Dogged Conceptualizer, had helped many to see the need for horizontal change.

Measuring Success: The Change Agents' Perspective

All study participants were asked how they assess their success as change agents. Four intuitive success metrics emerged, as did two interesting and atypical views of success.

Intuitive Measures of Success

- Deploying functionality and capability—deploying systems on time and on budget with functionality that will be adopted by end users: "Every three months, push out a product set. If you're not doing that then you will be left behind."—Deborah Diaz
- Maintaining or increasing funding and resources: "Vision without resources is a hallucination."—Louis Andre
- Revamping business processes with deeper interagency connectivity: "You have to affect business process change to drive transformation."—Mark Forman
- Securing policy changes: While it is rare that change agents actually write policy, their actions, energy, and concepts inform policy in meaningful ways: "Every change agent will either have policy on their side or know how to change it."—Lynn Torres

> The last thing we do is sit around and ask, What if we will fail?—Charlie Allen, Assistant Director of Central Intelligence for Collection

Atypical Measures of Success

- Generating complaints throughout the bureaucracy you are attempting to change: "You have to drive enough change to drive complaints."—Mark Forman
- New language is adopted with the agency: Change agents often invent new language to define a future-state concept or vision. Therefore, they know they are successful when their language is adopted, both inside and outside their agencies, and especially by those who dislike their ideas. "Language conveys culture. In order to change the culture you must change language. You cannot expect old language to carry new ideas."—Art Cebrowski

The Future of Transformational Change in Government

While 9/11 sounded the alarm for government change, subsequent events like Hurricane Katrina have underscored the dire need to further transform government processes, systems, and organizational frameworks to better protect the American people. This chapter has addressed only one of the many challenges heaped on our government through the dawn of the War on Terror. From rethinking performance evaluation across the federal government to helping private-sector executives successfully transition into key roles within the federal government in the War on Terror, there is much more left to discuss and act upon.

At the outset, we recalled the decentralized management approach employed during World War II and how it led to victory. Juxtapose World War II and the over-authorization felt throughout government at that time with the layers of bureaucracy that change agents often have to address in the War on Terror. Given this new style of enemy who are prepared to enact their agenda, the question becomes, "What are we doing to enable and 'overauthorize' change agents to enact the government-wide transformation that is required to defeat this enemy?"

As this study uncovered, there are many types of change agents in this new style of war, and they are most effective when they think and act in the presence of other change agents; it is a chemical interaction of people that can bring about transformation. As further discussed, change agents must have the *over*authorization from leadership for change if substantive progress is to be made. Aspiring change agents should also carefully consider how they assemble their teams, measure success, and adopt the best practices presented by their peers within this chapter.

The trust of the American people is vested in the change agents in the War on Terror. Their decisions, actions, and thinking will impact all of us for generations to come. In short, we need them to be wildly successful in their roles and in growing other change agents who will see this war through to the end.

To current and aspiring change agents, we say:

- Cities are relying on you to engage them in the dialogue and ensure that state, local, and municipal preparedness is met with excellence.
- Soldiers are relying on you to ensure that they have the tools, technologies, and training to succeed on the front line of this atypical war.
- The country is relying on you to execute your missions and intuitively cooperate with interagency partners.
- Families are relying on you to quickly envision a successful end state for the War on Terror and ultimately ensure that a lasting peace takes root.

Appendix 17.1. Research Methodology and Protocol

Background and Context

Since September 11, 2001, there has been massive criticism leveled at the government for the "stove piped" decision making and analysis that preceded the attacks on America that day. Yet prior to 9/11, and long after the last day of the War on Terror, Americans will find a group of dedicated, diligent, action-oriented federal government executives who strive to be the antithesis of all their critics. These high-performing senior federal leaders earn the title *change agents*. They have spent thousands of days of their lives working to rethink how our government can better protect its people, and they have spent countless hours sometimes lobbying but often forcing their peers, teams, colleagues, and opposition to understand the benefits of the interagency and cross-agency future state that they know will aid in winning this war. In many instances, these executives existed within our government before 9/11. But, now perhaps more than ever, our country needs these and future generations of change agents.

We conducted twenty-four interviews with senior leadership from throughout the DoD, DHS, and the Intelligence Community. Our efforts in interviewing leaders were to understand the profile of change agents, describe how they behave within their organizations, and decipher lessons that managers inside and outside of the federal government can learn from.

Study Methodology

We interviewed twenty-four senior officials from throughout the DoD, DHS, and the Intelligence Community and analysts and academics over the course of seven months, February through August 2005. The sample of interviewees came after creation of an abstract followed by conversations with industry analysts, Catholic University of America, peers, and research and review of secondary sources of content around the War on Terror. All of these sources were inputs to defining the target list of change agents to interview. Change agents are known to cluster together, and thus several of the research participants led us to interview other colleagues or even more senior management as the project evolved.

A questionnaire protocol was employed to guide interviewers and to ensure that a common data set could emerge. The interview setting was intimate, with each of the participants speaking with us either alone or with an aide to monitor the conversation given the security sensitivities of the research participants. All participants but two agreed to be quoted "on the record." For the off-the-record interviews, the authors agreed not to name the interviewees, but we could quote them and restate their insights within a broader context.

Expertise among study participants spans from research and development roles to IT and large-scale program leadership. Yet there are clear commonalities among the study participants in that each has served in the government (through political appointment or working their way up to senior positions) for long periods of time (here defined as fifteen years or more).

Study participants are, as one change agent described, "well credentialed" in terms of projects and programs that they have been associated with throughout their careers. The majority of the study participants are currently serving in the government, and for balance we interviewed several participants who had recently left the government after having served for long periods of time. We engaged academics and industry analysts to share initial findings and help to validate our approach. By design, all of the participants are playing or recently played roles within the government that frequently intersected with execution of the War on Terror.

Study Interview Protocol

1. Please give us your definition of the term *change agent*.
2. What are the levers within government that change agents must be familiar with in order to be successful?

3. Who has shown the most agility in enacting significant change within DoD, DHS, and the Intelligence Community? Why have they been successful?

4. What management approaches have been employed within DoD, DHS, and the Intelligence Community to help align stakeholders and get them to change behavior organizationally?

5. What advice would you give to other potential "change agents" who are entering jobs within Intel, DoD, and DHS?

6. What are some of your lessons learned about change management in the context of information technology initiatives within DoD, DHS, and the Intelligence Community?

7. Can you discuss how you give briefings? What formats and tools do you use and why? What communications skills are most important?

8. Can you discuss the idea of being well credentialed and overauthorized, and what that means to enact change?

9. What do you believe has been your impact on the government's efforts at winning the War on Terror?

10. How do you know you have been successful enacting change?

Acknowledgments

The Catholic University of America (CUA) played a unique role in enabling this research to take root. Dr. John Kromkowski assembled a group of professors and graduate students from the Department of Politics and the Life Cycle Institute to review the target list of participants, preview the interview protocol, and vet and sharpen some of the key findings within this paper. We are thankful to CUA for supporting our efforts in creating knowledge that should be useful to students considering roles within our government in the War on Terror and beyond.

We are indebted to the study participants for giving us their precious time to share their insights and lessons learned. Well over thirty hours of interviews (face to face or via conference call) were supplied by past and current senior executives from throughout the government. Without their seeking organizational approval to participate in this study and giving so generously of their time, the content and insights from this paper could not have been derived.

18

Leadership and Ethics in Decision Making by Public Managers

Christine Gibbs Springer

We know now that leadership is not a person or a position. It is a complex moral relationship between people based on trust, obligation, commitment, emotion, and a shared vision of the good. Ethics is about how we distinguish between right and wrong, good and evil, in relation to actions, volitions, and the character of human beings. Ethics lies at the heart of all human relationships and, therefore, at the heart of the relationship between leaders and followers.

We also know that leadership has become an organizational necessity given the fact that jobs are no longer traditional in terms of the how, where, what is being done, and by whom, and that personal integrity is critical to effective leadership. As an example, the fixed bundle of tasks performed by an individual worker has been replaced by a process involving a flexible team in a networked world with diverse skills, interests, and attitudes. Increasingly, authors like Stewart and Sprinthall (1993) conclude that moral decision making occurs in public organizations not due to extensive codes of ethics but rather through dynamic discussions and in-service education.

More recently, authors like Bass and Stedlmeier (2004) find that authentic leadership expands the domain of effective freedom, the horizon of conscience, and the scope of altruistic intention so as to share mutually rewarding visions of success and enable and empower employees to convert visions into realities. Likewise, leadership-based strategies are increasingly used in organizations to manage ethics. Berman, West, and Cava (1994) found that the demonstration of exemplary moral leadership by senior management and the establishment of employee-based strategies such as ethics training, the protection of whistle-blowers for valid disclosures, and the solicitation of employee opinions about ethics were actually more effective than regulatory or code-based strategies in enabling the cities that they surveyed to achieve ethics management objectives such as avoidance of conflicts of interest, reduction in the need for whistle-blowers, and improved fairness in job assignments.

This chapter explores the relationship in public management between ethics—often referred to in the literature as *moral* or *personal integrity*—and leadership. I

Table 18.1

Respondents to Leadership and Decision-Making Survey (N = 250)

Years in the Organization		Age	
2 or less	10%	20–35	10%
5–9 years	40%	35–50	30%
10+ years	50%	50–60	50%
		60+	10%

Level of Government		Sex	
City	25%	Female	35%
County	25%	Male	65%
Federal	50%		

attempt to determine who the leaders are, what kind of behavior they exhibit so as to be defined by colleagues as leaders, where they work in the organization, and how they influence decision making in their organizations. In many ways, the leaders identified by this study practice what Berman, West, and Cava (1994) identify as informal ethics management strategies based in role models, positive reinforcement, and behavior—not regulatory-based approaches. These leaders make a difference and bring about changes in individual and organizational behavior that would not occur otherwise. Leadership most often means being able to make a decision when it needs to be made and taking responsibility for having made that decision. Leadership behavior is most often demonstrated informally through such things as open communication without the prompting of formal requirements or authority. Leadership tends to be expressed collaboratively in that it occurs within the organization's context, building trust, respect, and responsibility among coworkers.

This chapter's conclusions are based on surveys[1] completed by public administrators in city, county, and federal agencies regarding their ability to make difficult decisions and the degree to which that decision-making process is influenced by organizational context and leadership within the organization. The questions were developed by a leadership class in Clark County, Nevada, during fall 2005, and those questions were administered prior to year-end to 423 public managers in Clark County, Nevada; Maricopa County, Arizona; the Bureau of Land Management; the Bureau of Reclamation; and city managers participating in the annual International City/Council Management Association (ICMA) conference. Two hundred fifty of the surveys were returned.[2] Table 18.1 offers descriptive statistics of the valid surveys.

Follow-up interviews were conducted with twenty-five managers (ten federal, ten county, and five municipal) in early 2006. Questions sought to determine where public managers look for guidance when faced with distinguishing between right and wrong in making a decision at work, what is most important to managers in making those decisions, how leaders influence managers as they make decisions,

Table 18.2

Where Leaders Look for Guidance

Where Do You Look for Guidance?	N = 250	What Is Most Important to You in Making Right vs. Wrong Decisions?	N = 250
Own personal values	1.5	Protecting the public interest	1.5
Statutory regulations	2.0	Professional code of conduct	1.7
Organization policy	2.3	Keeping agency legitimacy	1.9
Leader in organization	3.0	Consistency with vision of a leader	3.5
Colleagues	3.5	Potential for praise or reward	4.5
Organizational culture and conduct	3.7	Organizational goals	6.5

*Likert scale from high (1.0) to low (7.0).

who are the leaders that most make a difference in resolving decision dilemmas, and what characteristics in leaders make the most difference to managers today.

Summary of Findings

Respondents indicated that there are leaders in their organizations and that those leaders assist them in making ethical choices (85 percent). However, when asked where they look for guidance when making difficult decisions that involve ethical choices, public managers tend to look to their own values, then to statutory regulations, and then to organizational policy, *before* they look to leaders in the organization (Table 18.2). The reliance on values as opposed to organizational policy and statutory guidelines tended to be greater with female respondents than with male respondents (.543 correlation), and the reliance on organizational policy and statutory guidelines tended to be greater the longer a manager had been in the organization (.687 correlation) and the older in age he or she was (.564). Federal agency managers tend to more often look to consistency with a leader's vision in the organization (.59 versus .48), while city and county managers tend to value protecting the public interest more than the federal agency managers who we surveyed (.72 versus .66).

When asked how leaders influence them, managers felt that open communication and respect for their views were much more compelling than either sanctions or rewards. A vision articulated by an organizational leader tended to be more important to county managers than to city or federal managers (.49 compared to .20 and .25, respectively). Federal managers offered more often than local managers the degree to which they see executive team leaders as "role models" (65 percent) while local managers offered that first-line supervisors often are the leaders and role models (52 percent).

For example, one federal employee who was interviewed described how in 2005 a new manager for a field office found that the office was not running as efficiently as it needed to be and that the most fundamental problem was that none of his predecessors had ever articulated to the staff what the organizational culture or priorities should be. In addition, some of the divisions in the office were too large to effectively manage processes, and as a result relationships with external entities had deteriorated. The new manager first sat down with those he was working with and listened to what they had to say about the situation. He then proceeded with an officewide reorganization using an employee team to evaluate what needed to be done and to oversee transition. The manager delegated to the team the authority and responsibility to define the organization's guiding principles. The following is what the team came up with:

- The Office is committed to upholding all that we do and the principles for which we are to be held accountable, not only among ourselves, but also by the public. Now and in the future, it is our honor and pleasure to serve as steward of the lands that we manage.
- *We Believe In*: The joy of stewardship of the incredible public lands, participative management and collaboration, recognizing and celebrating accomplishments, and individuality, diversity, and creativity.
- *We Are*: Devoted to our mission, professional and focused on our goals, proactive in thought and action, and supportive and understanding.
- *We Act With*: Integrity and fairness, open and direct communication, and respect and expect the same in return.
- *We Promote*: Safety first, a positive outlook, motivation to go above and beyond, and an enthusiastic and friendly environment.

Less than one year after his arrival, the reorganization continues after having overcome two principal barriers: money and interpersonal relationships. Staff roles and authorities have been clarified, and the organizational culture is more open with staff communicating not only with one another but also with the manager and external entities about what is working and what needs to be done. The manager is viewed by both his employees and his superiors as a leader who was open to suggestions but decisive about what needed to be done and willing to take responsibility for transforming the office into a more effective entity.

Characteristics of Leaders

Survey results indicate that there are seven characteristics[3] exhibited by leaders who often are members of the executive team but also can be first-tier supervisors (Table 18.3). The seven characteristics identified are integrity, competence, vision, commitment, affinity, duty, and accountability. Interviewees were asked to define the characteristics in their own terms. By *integrity*, they mean that the individual both trusts and is trusted. By *competence*, they mean that the individual knows his

Table 18.3

Characteristics of Leaders in Public Organizations

Characteristics of Leaders in Public Organizations	N = 250	Leaders Who Most Make a Difference in Resolving Dilemmas	N = 250	How Do Leaders Influence You?	N = 250
Integrity	1.5	Executive team	1.3	Open communication	1.5
Commitment	1.5	Colleague	1.7	Respect for my views and input	1.7
Competence	1.7	Department heads	2.0	Motivation and empowerment	1.9
Accountability	1.8	Citizen	4.8	Articulating a vision	2.0
Affinity	1.8	First-line supervisor	5.2	Rewards	4.8
Duty	2.0	Elected official	5.5	Sanctions	5.6
Vision	2.0	Political appointee	6.2	Other	5.8

*Likert scale from high (1.0) to low (7.0).

or her stuff. One federal manager used Steven Spielberg as an example. While not quite thirty years of age, Spielberg directed the movie *Jaws* in an abandoned trailer at Universal Studios so as to earn a seven-year contract with the studio after he was rejected by the University of Southern California's film school. So, too, do these leaders know their stuff well enough to get the job done right.

By *vision*, those interviewed indicated that the person knows where he or she is going and why and can tell anyone who wants to know in twenty-five words or fewer. In so doing, that person is able to test ideas and proposals time and time again. Visionary leaders were described as capable of articulating where a group is going in a way that resonates with others. They then set people free to innovate, experiment, and take calculated risks within a defined structure so as to get there. Respondents indicated that vision alone does not define a leader; rather it is one characteristic that, along with the six others, defines leadership.

By *commitment*, respondents mean total focus and dogged persistence to achieving specific outcomes within a defined time frame. As an example, one city manager described how a director of a social service agency addressed the problems left by her predecessor when she was moved up to become acting director by meeting one-on-one with staff and found out that they shared her vision for the overburdened agency and its mission. She got people talking about their hopes for the future and tapped into their compassion and dedication. She voiced their shared values whenever she could. She guided them in looking at whether how they did things furthered the organization's mission, and together they eliminated rules that made no sense. Meanwhile, she modeled the principles of the new organization she wanted to create, one that was transparent and honest and focused on rigor and results. She and her team tackled the changes. The agency's work climate changed within the year from one of grudging compliance to one that reflected shared passion and commitment with a budget that then doubled within a span of eighteen months.

By *affinity*, they mean collaboration, the promotion of harmony, and the fostering of mutually respectful relationships. To manage these relationships takes time and energy as well as leadership. It requires persuasion, the bolstering of others' abilities through feedback and guidance, the initiating and managing of change, the building and reinforcing of bonds between people and stakeholders as well as cooperation and team building. Affinity was sometimes (10 percent) defined as being articulated by coworkers as someone who "takes care of his people." As an example, one county manager described a director of operations who oversaw five managers, of which four held college degrees. The one who didn't became the director's "go-to man" because he could always be counted on to do the best possible job even though he earned less than the other four because of the agency's bias toward degreed employees. The director eventually wound up pleading the go-to man's case to management and won for him both a raise and the go-to man's loyalty.

By *duty*, they mean personal and organizational realism about current conditions and responsibilities as well as what is possible should change actually begin. Duty was sometimes described as context—whether it be legal, social, emotional, or political. It amounts to an understanding of the rules that apply now and whether and when those rules can be changed. Sometimes leaders use a process of dynamic inquiry to discover the organization's condition by asking people what they care about, what is helping them get the job done and the organization to succeed, as well as what is getting in the way. Usually, these focused conversations and open-ended questions help determine what is right and what is not right so that collective concerns can be addressed successfully.

By *accountability*, they mean being willing to accept responsibility for one's own conduct. In its most narrow interpretation, accountability involves answering to a higher authority in the bureaucratic or interorganizational chain of command. This formal definition draws a very clear distinction between two fundamental questions: *"To whom is the organization accountable?" "For what activities and performance standards am I personally responsible?"* Accountability was used interchangeably by most respondents with ethics. When asked, respondents indicated that they did so because both concepts involve the means by which an organization or an individual chooses a course of action and subsequently defends it. Leaders were described as individuals who know what the legal or regulatory standards are, what the informal or implicit standards are, who the opinion leaders are, what the experience of comparable organizations facing similar decisions has been, and what strategies or tactics are available to help ensure prudent action in a changing environment.

Many times, a visible demonstration of accountability is a necessary part of the process. Such a demonstration was described by one county manager as Peter Ueberroth agreeing to run the 1984 Olympic Games in Los Angeles and promising to make $15 million in profit. Ueberroth then personally negotiated sponsorship contracts worth millions and during the actual games wore the uniform of a different Olympic worker each day. The profit at the conclusion of the games was determined to be $215 million.

When looking for leaders to be future public managers, respondents suggested that we should focus on and build upon these seven core competencies. We should encourage and support self-directed learning so as to set goals that are specific to the individual and that focus on improvements that they are passionate about, building on their strengths while filling in where there are gaps of experience, skill, or knowledge. Leadership training must be a strategic priority that is supported at the highest level. Commitment to this must come from the top, because new leadership means a new mind-set and new behaviors. In order for these to resonate, the organization's culture, systems, and processes all will probably need to change.

Operationalizing Ethical Decision Making

Follow-up interviews with public managers attempted to get them to describe and define how ethical decision making actually works in their agencies. All organizations are being evaluated today by different and higher standards. New yardsticks are being pulled out to assess performance in terms of both moral and financial standards. These yardsticks will affect voters' acceptance of governors' tax and program proposals in a short-revenue year, donors giving to nonprofits, and community support for service delivery fees and tax increases. High-performance organizations that compete unfairly, mistreat employees, or neglect civic responsibilities are rapidly becoming oxymorons. This is reflected in the growing number of annual survey responses about who is most admired and most respected by voters, employees, and customers.

Whether people are deciding where to work, buy, invest, or donate, they want to know what financial imperatives apply and what moral considerations are observed when making decisions. Respondents provided us with four perspectives critical to this assessment:

- *Employees*: Want to be respected, treated fairly, and recognized for their contributions.
- *Customers*: Want to know that the organization is reliable, fair, and honest about any risks associated with buying their product or service.
- *Communities*: Want organizations to clean up their messes, minimize the negative impacts of their activities, and obey the law.
- *Donors/Investors*: Want transparency, timely information, reliable forecasting, fair treatment, and opportunities to be heard.

Measuring Ethical Performance

This new value proposition that measures performance in terms of both financial and moral standards places managers in a more difficult role as they are increasingly judged with an "ethico-nomic" ruler.

I suggest that one way of thinking about such a measurement of performance is by using levels of assessment:

- *First Level (Acceptable)*: Organizations adhere to the law and avoid gross wrongdoing and offenses against basic justice.
- *Second Level (Good)*: Organizations comply with the law, observe norms of fairness and responsibility, and seek mutual gain in dealings with others.
- *Third Level (Excellent)*: Organizations comply with the law, observe norms of fairness, and seek opportunities to make additional contributions over and above what is required of them.

When preparing to live up to this new expectation, respondents find it helpful to have the team—the managers and employees—become comfortable with asking questions and considering what could be called the "Four Ps":

- *Purpose*: Will this action serve a worthwhile purpose?
- *Principle*: Is this action consistent with relevant principles?
- *People*: Does this action respect the legitimate claims of people likely to be affected (stakeholders)?
- *Power*: Do we have the power to take this action?

Systematic moral analyses enable managers not only to inject an important point of view into deliberations but also to help decision makers take a check of reality and avoid making mistakes. Doing so requires that:

- information and guidance systems be aligned with financial and non-financial accountabilities,
- people use decision frameworks to integrate social and financial considerations,
- performance assessments are made along both moral and financial dimensions, and
- competencies are developed in both moral and financial management.

According to the respondents of this study, organizations that learn to do this find that they become more centered and are more capable of both creative innovation and change. They also find it possible to be committed to moral and financial excellence, and in doing so, employee turnover is reduced and customer loyalty is increased.

The shift to this values-based measurement of success is not without stress. Avoiding a high-profile scandal and being able to demonstrate reliability, fairness, and respect more than compensate for the effort. In the final analysis, a good reputation attracts customers, employees, and investors. Decisions based upon both values and financial rewards also lead to increased revenue, market share, access to talent, and sustained success.

It is one thing to talk about ethical behavior and quite another to make it happen organization-wide. Regardless of the professional, statutory, or organizational code of ethics that applies, the degree to which standards are operationalized depends upon the degree to which an individual employee and leader in the organization are free of a fear and a preoccupation that they will be held responsible for harmful behaviors—often making failure the inevitable outcome.

More often than not, public managers take on more responsibility than they can handle due to a conviction that those below them cannot handle it. Passive followers sense that responsibility by them is taken away, so they withdraw from being accountable for their actions. According to the managers interviewed in this study, it is only through the redefinition of this responsibility to one of collaborative accountability for agreed-upon behavior that true ethical decision making in public service occurs. This idea is illustrated by a federal manager interviewed as part of this study who observed that for elected officials, often the most effective short-term implementation of an ethical code depends on an understanding of their leadership role and also peer enforcement.

Fear of failure was also identified by those interviewed as both personal and universal. Individuals want to win and lose in interactions, maintain control, avoid embarrassment, and stay rational. Over time, managers become skilled in designing their interactions to avoid violating these governing values, even if the cost may be outcomes they don't like. Those governing values, according to managers, are really fears—fears of losing, not being in control, being humiliated, and becoming irrational or overly emotional. These fears drive individuals toward primitive responses of "flight or fight." If managers choose *flight,* they reject responsibility. If they choose *fight,* they seize total control for the situation and shut out everyone else. The costs of making individuals fear failure when contemplating ethical behavior is a diminished capacity for genuine, productive collaboration, the development of mistrust and misunderstanding, and the atrophy of choice making.

In order to turn around such organizational inclinations, it is important, in my opinion and from my experience, to first set out some values that are important for all to follow, such as accountability, excellence, innovation, integrity, transparency, and respect. It is then important to generate robust and compelling choices and to do so without violating governing values and codes of ethics. There are several tools to do so.

Structuring Decision Making

The first tool is to structure choices. First and foremost, elected and appointed leaders must fully declare their personal allegiances and potential conflicts of interests. They must be willing to convey the message that the decision will be the group's within the operational context of codes and applicable statutes. Often, many members will not believe that—yet. From there, coming to decisions involves:

1. *Framing the Choice*: Seeing it in terms of not simply the problem at hand but also in terms of organizational and cultural values and codes.
2. *Brainstorming Possible Options*: Identifying the subset of options within the framework of choices.
3. *Specifying Conditions*: Ensuring the conditions that the group agrees on must be adhered to in order for the group to commit to supporting the option.
4. *Identifying Barriers to the Choices*: Preventing them from getting in the way of making the decision.
5. *Designing Due-Diligence Tests*: Enabling every member to commit to making and supporting the choice and taking action if the test confirms that the condition is valid.
6. *Conducting an Analysis*: Testing the condition least likely to hold up, and if it proves wrong, then moving to the next one.
7. *Making the Choice*: Deciding after all conditions, tests, and analyses are in.

Sometimes this choice process is not possible due to misunderstandings and mistrust, which undermine collaboration. Then it is necessary to ask key decision makers to reframe. We all frame reality as a way to make sense of the world. As conditions grow worse, our frames grow more extreme. Reframing asks participants to understand what assumptions they are operating under and to adjust them from knowing the answer to having data and experience but not seeing and understanding everything so that the door is open for movement, given others' input and intelligence, so as to make a better choice.

Sometimes it is necessary to structure conversations that will yield a better distribution of responsibilities and a better decision. This option is usually pursued because it is recognized that there is a fundamental lack of communication and productive conversations about decision responsibility distribution. The purpose of responsibility conversations is to divide tasks so that the responsibility assigned matches capabilities and maximizes individual choice making as well as builds internal commitment and accountability. These conversations also create a sense of collaboration and feeling of mutual support. Typically these discussions move up a responsibility ladder—from having no responsibility, to being willing to watch and learn, to generating options and asking for decisions, to considering options, making the decision, and informing stakeholders. The goals of group members should be to move up the responsibility ladder over time while helping others to do the same and to create a common language for future conversations. When entering into these conversations, I find it helpful to remember six Key Cs and to be:

- *Concise*: People appreciate it when they know that you respect their time and they pay more attention when the end is in sight.
- *Conversational*: Practice first dropping your mention into a conversation easily and naturally, without overdoing it, and then follow up.
- *Careful*: Good or bad, sound bites seem to live forever. So sum up your point of view or proposal with a sound bite that can be delivered in a seven-second phrase.
- *Candid*: Tactful candor and simple honesty are always refreshing and compelling to other people.
- *Cogent*: Begin by deciding what opinion you want changed or action taken, and go for it without shutting others off.
- *Convincing*: Show respect for whoever you are speaking with and remember that the most compelling conversation is one that makes sense.

Sometimes it is necessary to reframe structures of leadership and followership by restating or splitting responsibility through dialogue. Such a dialogue should apportion responsibility in keeping with capabilities rather than allowing the leaders to be tempted to take on more than a proportionate share of responsibility or rejecting responsibility outright, thus making the apportionment discussable. Performance should also be subjected to public testing rather than a private assessment.

For every manager in an organization who feels mired in underresponsibility and underaccountability, there is someone who also feels trapped in and burdened by overresponsibility. Sometimes this means taking on harder and trickier tasks than one feels capable of, but more often, it means loading oneself up with everyone else's responsibilities until one collapses under the weight. All of this can be resolved through choice structuring, collaborative decision making, analysis, and focus. For example, too often chief appointed officials look to their elected boards as just another constituency to be satisfied and from whom control is to be seized. Today, given the concern of the public regarding transparency and accountability and their concern about ethical dilemmas, there is a greater need to develop relationships based on collaboration and partnerships as well as the organization-wide understanding that there is no single level of responsibility that is right for all choices. Everyone is accountable. Levels of responsibility and accountability can be set collaboratively based upon organizational principles and each individual's responsibilities and abilities and can be followed with less fear on everyone's part.

Conclusion

In this chapter, we have explored the relationship between leadership and ethics in public management and the degree to which a manager's ability to make difficult decisions effectively is most influenced by organizational context, leadership, or their own personal values. We found that organizational context and where the organization is located in the federal system are predictors of the role leadership plays in making difficult decisions as well as where those leaders can be found in the organization.

We also found that there is a difference between management and leadership. Management is about coping with complexity. Its practices and procedures are largely a response to one of the most significant developments of the twenty-first century: large and decentralized organizations. Good management brings a degree of order and consistency to key dimensions like the quality and reliability of services. Leadership, on the other hand, is about coping with change and making the decision to change. Part of the reason that leadership has become so important in recent years is that the public management environment has become more volatile. Faster technological change, greater internationalization, and changing demographics of the workforce and in the community dictate that doing what was done yesterday no longer is a formula for success. Successful leaders in this context tend to exhibit seven principle characteristics: integrity, competence, vision, commitment, affinity, duty, and accountability.

Organizations are also are using new yardsticks to assess organizational performance in terms of both ethical and financial standards. These standards have been developed due to the increased understanding that employees need to be respected, customers need to know that the organization is reliable and honest, communities need to know that they can trust the organization to minimize negative impacts of their operations, and donors need to know how decisions are made.

The organizational shift to values-based measurement occurs most often when leaders in the organization, both at the top and at the bottom, agree upon values, set standards, and operationalize them using open communication. Leaders are seen as critical to this process because they are capable of first making a decision that needs to be made, articulating why the decision has been made, identifying and overcoming barriers to moving ahead, gaining commitment, and taking responsibility for guiding the process. Leaders possess the ability to structure conversations that create a sense of collaboration and a feeling of mutual support by their ability to communicate openly about what may be achieved in the future and what can be achieved through each individual's purposeful actions so that those involved believe in themselves. These leaders are able to affect the changes that are more and more necessary for the organization to survive and thrive. To use a military analogy: A peacetime army can usually survive with good administration and management up and down the organizational hierarchy along with good leadership at the very top. A wartime army, however, needs competent leadership at all levels (as Reed and

Sorenson describe in chapter 7). No one has yet determined how to manage people effectively into battle, for they must be led. So, too, it is true in public management at every level of government in the United States.

Notes

1. A copy of the survey instrument is available from the author.

2. The 250 represents a so-called convenience sample as most of the questionnaires were distributed in meetings (for example, classes, regional meetings, and conferences) where respondents had already agreed to take time to complete them. Effort was made to have a diverse sample as indicated in Table 18.1.

3. The seven characteristics are drawn from a larger set of characteristics, all receiving an average of two or lower (a one being the highest score and seven the lowest).

References

Bass, Bernard M., and Paul Stedlmeier. 2004. "Ethics, Character and Authentic Transformational Leadership Behavior." In *Ethics, the Heart of Leadership,* 2nd ed., ed. Joanne B. Ciulla, 175–205. Westport, CT: Praeger.

Berman, Evan, Jonathan West, and Anita Cava. 1994. "Ethics Management in Municipal Governments and Large Firms: Exploring Similarities and Differences." *Administration and Society* 26 (2): 185–203.

Stewart, Debra W., and Norman A. Sprinthall. 1993. "The Impact of Demographic, Professional, and Organizational Variables and Domain on the Moral Reasoning of Public Administrators." In *Ethics and Public Administration*, ed. H. George Frederickson, 205–19. Armonk, NY: M.E. Sharpe.

About the Editors and Contributors

Nanette M. Blandin is president of the Nexus Institute, a global executive education and leadership development company. The Institute designs and facilitates customized executive education programs and works with organizations to design and implement initiatives related to leadership, human capital development, and public policy. She is also an adjunct professor in American University's School of Public Affairs where she teaches graduate seminars on ethics and leadership. Previously, she worked at The Brookings Institution, the U.S. Department of Labor, the Office of Management and Budget/Executive Office of the President, and the State of California. Blandin is currently a doctoral candidate at George Washington University and holds a master's degree in public administration from the University of Southern California and a bachelor's degree in political science and French from the University of California. She is a Fellow of the National Academy of Public Administration and serves on the national selection committee for the Harry S. Truman Scholarship Foundation.

John M. Bryson is a professor of planning and public affairs and associate dean for research and centers at the Hubert H. Humphrey Institute of Public Affairs at the University of Minnesota. His expertise is in leadership, strategic management, and the design of participation processes. He is the author of *Strategic Planning for Public and Nonprofit Organizations* (3rd ed., Jossey-Bass, 2004) and coauthor with Barbara C. Crosby of *Leadership for the Common Good* (2nd ed., Jossey-Bass, 2005). He is a Fellow of the National Academy of Public Administration. He holds a doctorate and a master of science degree in urban and regional planning and a master of arts degree in public policy and administration, all from the University of Wisconsin.

Brendan F. Burke is an assistant professor in the Public Management Department at Suffolk University, in Boston, Massachusetts. Prior to his academic career, he worked for the chief executives of Prince William County, Virginia, and Wake County, North Carolina. His teaching and research focuses are leadership, organizational effectiveness, and subnational administrative reform in Canada and the

United States. Burke received an A.B. from Georgetown University and an M.P.A. and Ph.D. from University of North Carolina–Chapel Hill.

Terry F. Buss is a program director at the National Academy of Public Administration. He earned a doctorate in political science from Ohio State University. He has managed public administration programs and research centers at Ohio State University, Youngstown State University, University of Akron, Suffolk University, and Florida International University and has served as a senior policy advisor at the Council of Governors' Policy Advisors, Congressional Research Service, U.S. Department of Housing and Urban Development, and World Bank. He has published ten books and several hundred papers.

Bernadette C. Costello is a doctoral candidate at George Mason University's Higher Education Program specializing in public administration and received a master in public administration from the University of North Carolina at Chapel Hill. Her experience includes twenty years of public-sector work and consulting. Research interests include performance measurement, civic and citizen engagement, and the use of deliberative process to engage communities and citizens.

Barbara C. Crosby is associate professor at the Hubert H. Humphrey Institute of Public Affairs and a member of the Institute's Public and Nonprofit Leadership Center at the University of Minnesota. During 2002–2003, she was a visiting fellow at the University of Strathclyde, Glasgow, Scotland. She has taught and written extensively about leadership and public policy, women in leadership, media and public policy, and strategic planning. She is the author of *Leadership for Global Citizenship* (Sage, 1999) and coauthor with John M. Bryson of *Leadership for the Common Good* (2nd ed., Jossey-Bass, 2005). A frequent speaker at conferences and workshops, she has conducted training for senior managers of nonprofit, business, and government organizations in the United States, U.K., Poland, and Ukraine. She has an M.A. in journalism and mass communication from the University of Wisconsin–Madison and a Ph.D. in leadership studies from the Union Institute.

S. Mike Davis is a senior analyst at the U.S. Government Accountability Office. He has worked with and studied public organizations' involved in transformation and change while serving in various leadership positions in government, the private sector, and academic and not-for-profit organizations. He previously served as the executive director for the Center for Innovation in Public Service at the George Washington University School of Public Policy and Public Administration.

Edward DeSeve is a senior lecturer at the University of Pennsylvania's Fels Institute for Government. He has held senior management posts in all three levels of government, the most recent being deputy director for management of the federal Office of Management and Budget. In the private sector, he was founder and president of

Public Financial Management, Inc., managing director of Merrill Lynch Capital Markets, and national industry director of KPMG. He also served as a professor at the University of Maryland where he directed the Management, Finance, and Leadership Program. He earned a B.S. in Cornell's School of Industrial and Labor Relations in 1967 and an M.G.A. at the University of Pennsylvania's Wharton School in 1971. He is a Fellow of the National Academy of Public Administration where he currently serves as vice chair.

Matthew R. Fairholm is an assistant professor with a joint appointment in the Department of Political Science and the W. O. Farber Center for Civic Leadership at the University of South Dakota. He was the director of leadership studies and development at the Center for Excellence in Municipal Management and instructor of public administration at George Washington University, where he continues to serve as a senior fellow. He worked in the U.S. Department of Energy (DOE), entering the federal service as a presidential management intern. His academic and professional interests focus on public administration, leadership theory and practice, and organizational dynamics, and he has published in a number of academic and professional journals. He received his B.A. and M.A. in public policy from Brigham Young University and his doctorate in public administration from George Washington University.

Daniel P. Forrester is a director within Sapient Corporation's Government Services practice. Sapient is an innovative information technology and business consultancy. He leads Sapient's efforts with the Department of Homeland Security (DHS) as a client executive. Forrester has over twelve years of consulting experience with clients including DHS, United States Marine Corps, the Library of Congress, Sallie Mae, Verizon, Nextel/Sprint, Xerox, FMC, and Dow Chemical. His expertise is in helping large organizations to change and transform while embracing technology and navigating complex political landscapes. He is an authority on helping change agents to get to a clear vision and have success within a bureaucracy. He holds a B.A. from the Catholic University of America, where he studied English literature, and an M.B.A. from the University of Rochester's William E. Simon School of Business Administration.

H. George Frederickson is the Edwin O. Stene Distinguished Professor of Public Administration at the University of Kansas. He is president emeritus of Eastern Washington University. In 2002–2003, he was the Winant Visiting Professor of American Government at the University of Oxford, and a Fellow of Balliol College, Oxford. He is a coauthor of *Measuring the Performance of the Hollow State* and *The Public Administration Theory Primer.* Frederickson has received the John Gaus Award, the Charles Levine Award, the Dwight Waldo Award, the ASPA/NASPAA Distinguished Research Award, and the University of Kansas Irvin Youngberg Award for Research Achievement. In 2007, he will deliver the Donald Stone Lecture at the annual conference of the American Society for Public Administration. He is a Fellow of the National Academy of Public Administration.

Newt Gingrich was first elected to Congress in 1978 where he served the Sixth District of Georgia for twenty years. In 1995, he was elected Speaker of the U.S. House of Representatives where he served until 1999. Newt has published nine books including the best-sellers *Contract with America* and *To Renew America*, and his most recent book, *Winning the Future: A 21st Century Contract with America*. *Time* magazine, in naming him Man of the Year for 1995, said, "Leaders make things possible. Exceptional leaders make them inevitable. Newt Gingrich belongs in the category of the exceptional." Gingrich received a bachelor's degree from Emory University and a master's and doctorate in modern European history from Tulane University. Before his election to Congress, he taught history and environmental studies at West Georgia College for eight years.

Marilu Goodyear is associate professor of public administration at the University of Kansas, with a specialty in organizational change and information policy. From 1999 to 2005, she served as the vice provost for information services and the chief information officer for the University of Kansas. In this role, she led all campus-wide software, hardware, and networking technology services, printing services, and the KU libraries; the units that serve these functions include 350 full-time employees and spend $37 million a year. Goodyear holds master's degrees in library and information science and public administration from the University of Missouri, as well as a doctorate in public administration from the University of Colorado. Goodyear is a Fellow of the National Academy of Public Administration and serves as a Fellow of the EDUCAUSE Center for Applied Research.

Dwight Ink first served in local government, then moved through the ranks of federal service from the entry level to subcabinet positions with policy assignments for seven presidents in both domestic and national security areas. They included community development, antipoverty programs, education, atomic energy weapons and power development, energy conservation, and foreign economic and technical assistance. He headed the president's government-wide management agenda in both the Bureau of the Budget and the Office of Management and Budget, and was in charge of developing the recommendations for President Carter's Civil Service Reform Act, the most comprehensive set of changes in the history of the federal civil service. He was director of the Office of Continuing Education and Research at American University and president of the New York Institute for Public Administration. He served on the board of directors of many public-service organizations, such as the National Academy of Public Administration, and was president of the American Society of Public Administration.

James Edwin (Jed) Kee is a professor in the School of Public Policy and Public Administration, George Washington University (GW). Before joining GW in

1985, he had a twenty-year career in government. He was a legal assistant to Senator Robert F. Kennedy, a legal counsel to the New York State Assembly, and executive director of a New York legislative commission. From 1976 to 1985, he served in several executive-level positions in the State of Utah, as state planning coordinator, state budget director, and from 1981–1985 as executive director of the Department of Administrative Services, the umbrella management agency of the state. At GW, Kee has been a department chair and the senior associate dean and interim dean of the GW School of Business and Public Management. His teaching and research interests include leadership, public management, public-private partnerships, and administrative reform. Kee is the principal investigator of the Public Sector Change and Transformation project in the GW Center for Innovation in Public Service. He published the book *Out of Balance* with former Utah Governor Scott M. Matheson and has numerous book chapters and articles in such journals as the *Harvard Law Review, Public Administration Review,* and *Public Budgeting and Finance.*

C. Morgan Kinghorn is chief operating officer at Grant Thornton's Global Public Sector practice. Before joining Grant Thornton, Kinghorn served as president of the National Academy of Public Administration. Kinghorn has enjoyed a distinguished thirty-year career in senior financial management positions in the public sector at the Environmental Protection Agency and Office of Management and Budget, and in the private sector at IBM Consulting. He holds an MPA from the Maxwell School at Syracuse University.

David S. T. Matkin is a doctoral candidate at the University of Kansas in the Department of Public Administration. He will soon complete his Ph.D. and join the faculty of the Reubin O'D. Askew School of Public Administration and Policy at Florida State University. His research interests include public budgeting and financial management, public management, local government administration, and accountability and ethics. Matkin has over six years of experience in the practice of public leadership at the federal, state, and local levels of government.

Ricardo S. Morse is assistant professor of public administration and government at the University of North Carolina at Chapel Hill School of Government. His teaching and consulting work focuses on public leadership and community and regional collaboration. His publications include several articles and book chapters on collaboration and public participation. Morse received bachelor's and master's degrees in public policy from Brigham Young University and a Ph.D. in public administration from Virginia Tech.

Mark R. Nelson, Ph.D., is the digital content strategist for the National Association of College Stores, where he serves as a key strategy leader for one of the largest trade associations in higher education. He also holds a position as a research fellow with the EDUCAUSE Center for Applied Research. He has served higher education in the capacity of assistant professor, quasi-CIO, and senior higher education consultant, in addition to other roles. His areas of research interest include IT management in higher education and public-sector organizations, with particular interest in IT failures in large-scale government IT projects. In addition to fifteen years of industry work experience, he has produced dozens of papers and presentations and received multiple awards for his work. Nelson earned both his M.B.A. (marketing) and Ph.D. (information science) from the University at Albany, State University of New York, and his B.S. (computer science) from St. Michael's College in Vermont.

Brent Never is assistant professor in the Department of Public Administration, University of Illinois at Springfield. His work considers how leaders formulate change in networked environments such as commissions and task forces. He is empirically testing models of network leadership by surveying Illinois municipal executives in collaboration with the Illinois Municipal League. He holds a Ph.D. in public policy from Indiana University–Bloomington.

Kathryn Newcomer is the director of the School of Public Policy and Public Administration at George Washington University where she teaches public and nonprofit program evaluation, research design, and applied statistics. She conducts research and training for federal and local government agencies on performance measurement and program evaluation. Newcomer has published five books and numerous journal articles. She is a Fellow of the National Academy of Public Administration and president of the National Association of Schools of Public Affairs and Administration (NASPAA) for 2006–2007. She earned a B.S. in education and an M.A. in political science from the University of Kansas and a Ph.D. in political science from the University of Iowa.

Karl Nollenberger is the academic director of the Graduate Program in Public Administration at the Illinois Institute of Technology and an accomplished practitioner in public administration. His prior experience includes thirty years in local government management positions in five states. He served as president of the International City/County Management Association (ICMA) in 1994–1995, representing the association in thirty-two countries with over 8,300 members. In addition, he is a Fellow of the National Academy of Public Administration. Nollenberger received his M.P.A. from the University of Colorado and is working on his dissertation research for his Ph.D. from the University of Illinois at Chicago.

George Reed is an associate professor of leadership studies at the University of San Diego in the School of Leadership and Education Sciences. He holds a B.S. in criminal justice administration from Central Missouri State University, an M.F.S. in forensic science from George Washington University, and a Ph.D. in public policy analysis and administration from Saint Louis University. He served for twenty-seven years on active duty as an Army officer including six as the director of Command and Leadership Studies at the United States Army War College.

Georgia Sorenson, Ph.D., was the inaugural chair and professor of transformation at the U.S. Army War College in 2005–2006. She is now a research professor at the James MacGregor Burns Academy of Leadership at the School of Public Policy at the University of Maryland. An architect of the leadership studies field, she is coeditor (with George Goethals and James MacGregor Burns) of the four-volume *Encyclopedia of Leadership* (Sage Publications, 2004). Her most recent work (with Goethals) is *The Quest for a General Theory of Leadership* (Elgar, 2006). Sorenson serves on the editorial board of numerous journals including *Leadership* (U.S. editor), *Leadership Quarterly* (associate editor), and *Leadership Review.* Before joining academia, Sorenson was a senior policy analyst in the Carter White House and served on the President's Productivity Council. Sorenson is a frequent commentator on leadership and presidential politics in the popular media.

Christine Gibbs Springer is the founder and principal of Red Tape Limited, a strategic management and communications firm with offices in Nevada and Arizona. She is currently director of the Executive Master's Degree in Emergency and Crisis Management at the University of Nevada–Las Vegas. A recognized expert in facilitation, marketing, communications, and management processes, she has authored ten books and numerous articles on those subjects. She is recognized as a top woman business owner (1995–1999); Who's Who in America (2001–2003); Who's Who in Professional Business Women (2001–2003); Who's Who—Great Minds of the 21st Century 2002; and International Who's Who of Professional and Business Women (since 2000). She is a Fellow of the National Academy of Public Administration and past president of the American Society of Public Administration. She is a graduate of the University of Arizona (B.A.), Arizona State University (M.P.A.), and Indiana University (Ph.D.).

John B. Stephens is associate professor of public administration and government and coordinates the Public Dispute Resolution Program at the University of North Carolina at Chapel Hill School of Government. He is author of the *Guidebook to Public Dispute Resolution in North Carolina* (School of Government, UNC–Chapel Hill, 2004) and is coauthor of *Reaching for Higher Ground in Conflict Resolution* (Jossey-Bass, 2000). His expertise includes interagency and public policy dispute resolution, citizen participation, and group collaboration and facilitation. He has a Ph.D. from George Mason University's Institute for Conflict Analysis and Resolution and an M.Phil. from the City University, London. Before coming to the School of Government, he was research director of the Ohio Commission on Dispute Resolution and Conflict Management and managed a campaign for the U.S. Congress in Iowa.

He was co-chair of the Environment and Public Policy Section of the Association for Conflict Resolution, 2004–2006, and was a Harry S. Truman Scholar and George C. Marshall Scholar.

James H. Svara is a professor in the School of Public Affairs at Arizona State University and director of the Center for Urban Innovation. He is a Fellow of the National Academy of Public Administration and a board member of the Alliance for Innovation. He recently published *The Ethics Primer for Public Administrators in Government and Nonprofit Organizations* and edited an issue of the *International Journal of Public Administration* on Political-Administrative Relations (September 2006). He is currently coordinating a project to update and revise *The Facilitative Leader in Local Government.*

David M. Walker became the seventh comptroller general of the United States and began his fifteen-year term when he took his oath of office on November 9, 1998. As comptroller general, Walker is the nation's chief accountability officer and head of the U.S. Government Accountability Office (GAO). Prior to his appointment, Mr. Walker had extensive executive-level experience in both government and private industry. He served as a public trustee for Social Security and Medicare from 1990 to 1995 and was assistant secretary of labor for pension and welfare benefit programs from 1987 to 1989. Walker is the author of *Retirement Security: Understanding and Planning Your Financial Future* (John Wiley & Sons, 1996) and a coauthor of *Delivering on the Promise: How to Attract, Manage and Retain Human Capital* (Free Press, 1998). He is a certified public accountant with a B.S. degree in accounting from Jacksonville University and a Senior Management in Government Certificate in public policy from the John F. Kennedy School of Government at Harvard University. He has received honorary doctorate degrees from several colleges and universities, including his alma mater. He is a Fellow of the National Academy of Public Administration.

Index

Absorptive capacity, 313, 319, 327
Accountability
  balanced scorecard as tool for, 162, 203–4,
    204*f*, 302–3
  in consensus building, 230, 231
  as distributed, 214, 215–17, 215*f*, 354
  ethical behavior, as influence on, 344, 346–47,
    346*t*, 352, 353–54
  ethical leadership, as quality of, 345, 348*t*,
    349–50
  in hierarchical model, 156–57, 180
  in local governments, 80–81
  of military commanders, 127
  in network governance, 43, 84–85
  of political appointees, 50, 51, 55
  professional commitment to, xi, 43, 89, 94
  in public administration approaches, 115,
    116*f*, 117
  public sector as constrained by, 31–32, 55–58,
    82, 312, 313
  reforms, as focus of, 92–93, 95
  in results-oriented approaches, 284, 296,
    298, 301
  in transformational stewardship, 162, 168*t*, 170
  See also Ethical leadership
Administrative leadership
  in complex adaptive systems, 146–49, 150–51
  consensus building, role in, 230, 234–35
  crisis management, role in, 47, 60–62, 171
  historical perspectives on, 48–49, 69–73, 95
  military leadership, compared to, 125, 135–36
  in networks, 84–86, 88, 92, 95–96
  political leadership, interactions with
    complementarity between, 75–76, 77,
      86–89, 94
    complementarity in values, 76, 88–92, 94

Administrative leadership
  political leadership, interactions with *(continued)*
    historical perspectives on, 70–73, 95
    management/leadership, compared to,
      120–22, 121*f*
    models for, 73–77, 83, 92, 114–17, 116*f*
    teamwork, 53–55, 61, 87–88, 91–92, 327
  presidential management of, 58, 59–60
  in presidential transitions, 62, 63–64, 65
  private-sector practices applied to, 55–58, 82
  as process-driven, 29, 30, 31–32, 55
  as self-serving, 31–32, 82, 84
  as transformational stewards, 177–78
  upward mobility of, 57, 207, 208
  as weakened, 49–52, 78–81, 82–84, 85,
    95–96
  See also City managers; Management;
    Supervisors
Agendas. *See entries under Mission*
Aging of society, xii, 9, 155, 195–96, 197–99*t*

Balanced scorecard
  accountability, as tool for, 162, 204*f*
  and organizational health, 302–3
  and public value, 203–4, 204*f*
Blair administration, 78–79
BOB (Bureau of the Budget), 49, 58–59, 64
British administrators
  challenges to, 77, 78–79, 83, 207
  historical legitimacy of, 70, 73
  at local level, 80, 86
  ministers, as complementary to, 76, 89
  in network governance, 85–86
Bureau of the Budget (BOB), 49, 58–59, 64
Bureaucracy. *See* Administrative leadership;
  Hierarchical model

Bush administration
administrators, use of, 79, 80
management agenda of, 29, 64, 331
organizational reforms under, 207
public ambivalence toward, 205
Business practices. *See* Private-sector practices

Career leadership. *See* Administrative leadership
Carter administration, 50, 78, 79
Central Intelligence Agency (CIA), 338–39
Centralization of government, 52, 53, 73, 95, 290*t*
Change agent leadership
culture as viewed by, 37, 44*t*, 45, 325, 340
definition of, 34, 325, 328–29, 329*f*
as dogged conceptualizers, 330, 331*f*, 336–39, 338*f*
as functional mavens, 330, 331*f*, 335–36, 336*t*, 337*f*
management principles of, 34–36, 41, 44–45, 44*t*, 325–28
as over-authorized senior directors, 330, 331*f*, 332–35, 334*t*
performance measurement of, 339–40
study methodology for, 342–43
terrorism, as response to, 324–25, 340–41
as transformational leaders, 330–32, 331*f*, 332*t*
transformational stewards, as related to, 156–57
universal principles, as based on, 39, 44–45, 44*t*
See also Transformational leadership
Change capacity
administrators, as determined by, 177, 327
decrease in, 313, 319
as risk factor, 169, 169*f*
strategies for enhancing, 173*t*, 175–76
supervisory role, as related to, 178
CIA (Central Intelligence Agency), 338–39
Citizen engagement
administrative approaches to, 115, 116*f*, 117, 118*f*
case studies
managed networks, 215, 216–17
public value, 196, 197–99*t*, 200
results-oriented political frame, 297, 298, 299
results-oriented structural frame, 302
results-oriented symbolic frame, 300–301
in consensus building, 223, 224, 235, 236*f*
in ethical decision making, 350, 351, 355

Citizen engagement *(continued)*
at local level, 80, 81, 84
in networks, 84, 89–90, 92, 95
as performance measurement, 286*t*, 288*f*, 290*t*, 291
politicians, as secondary to, 77
as public value, 189, 191
shift towards, 9, 73, 84, 95
in strategic planning, 287
transformational stewardship approach to, 157, 161, 163–64, 167–68*t*
See also Public interest; Public value; Stakeholders
City councils. *See* Council-manager government
City governments. *See* Local governments
City managers
ethical decision making by, 345–46, 345*t*
in facilitative model, 274–75, 275*f*, 280
policy-administrative role of, 73, 81–82, 271–72, 273*f*, 276–80
in results-oriented reform case studies, 294, 295, 297
Civil servants. *See* Administrative leadership
Clinton, Hillary, 54
Clinton administration, 64, 79–80, 165–66, 216
Collaboration
administrative approaches to, 115, 116*f*, 117, 118*f*
in change agent leadership, 327, 333–35, 334*t*
change capacity as indicated by, 169*f*, 173*t*, 175, 176
in complex adaptive systems, 148
in consensus building, 225–26, 230, 234–35, 236*f*, 238
in council-manager government, 270, 271, 275*f*
in crisis management, 16, 60–61, 164, 334–35
in ethical leadership, 345, 348*t*, 349, 352, 353–54
gardener approach to, 42, 43–44
as global trend, 7, 10
in hierarchical model, 16, 211, 243–44
in large-scale IT projects, 312, 314, 316*t*, 318
as leadership approach, xii, 93–94, 327–28, 329*f*
in local governments, 223, 271, 273–74, 279, 280
in mutual gain regimes, 194, 196, 200
in network model, 223, 224, 243–44, 344
between political/administrative leadership, 53–55, 61, 87–88, 91–92, 327
presidential leadership for, 58

Collaboration *(continued)*
  in results-oriented reform, 292, 293, 302, 305
  in transformational stewardship, 164, 168t,
    179
  in transforming leadership, 107, 109, 112, 113
  See also Consensus building; Network
    governance
Command and control model
  as entrenched, 306
  in military leadership, 126
  as outdated, 208, 296
  shift away from, 7, 10, 12, 17–18
  See also Hierarchical model
Commitment, escalation of, 312, 313, 320
  See also Loyalty; *entries under Mission*
Common good. *See* Mutual gain; Public interest;
    Public value
Common purpose
  as invisible leader, 18, 161
  in managed networks, 210, 212, 213
  mental models as framework for, 245, 246–47,
    252
  in transformational stewardship, 161, 163, 167t
  in transforming leadership, 107
  See also Vision, organizational; *entries under
    Mission*
Communication
  in change agent leadership, 327, 328, 329f,
    332t, 334t
  change capacity as indicated by, 169f, 173t,
    175, 176
  in complex adaptive systems, 143, 148
  in ethical decision making, 345, 346, 348t,
    353–54
  during implementation, 173t, 176
  information technology as facilitating, 81,
    84, 90
  in large-scale IT projects, 315, 317t, 319, 320
  as management function, xi–xii, 94, 264, 277,
    279
  in mayoral leadership, 272, 274, 275f
  mental models as conveyed through, 249, 250,
    255
  mental models, as means of discerning, 257, 258
  and networks, 217, 243, 244
  and organizational understanding, xi–xii, ·
    40–41, 160, 328
  between political/administrative leaders,
    91–92, 94, 279–80
  and stakeholder involvement, 172t, 173t, 174,
    175, 287
  in supervisory role, 178–79

Complementarity
  in facilitative model, 91
  in interactions, 75–76, 77, 86–89, 94
  in value commitments, 76, 88–92, 94
Complex adaptive systems. *See* Complexity
    theory
Complexity
  gardener approach to, 39, 40, 41, 43
  in large-scale IT projects, 309–11, 310f, 320
  management as focusing on, 106, 156, 277,
    355
  networks as response to, 223, 243, 244, 245,
    246
  in relationship models, 33, 84, 211
  as risk factor in change, 169–70, 169f, 171,
    172t, 174
  and transformational leadership, 111, 170,
    172t, 174
Complexity theory
  complex adaptive systems, 143–46, 145f
  constraints on, 149–50, 151
  definition of, 139–40
  leadership, perspectives on, 146–49, 150–51
  paradigm shifts suggested by, 141–42, 141t,
    142f
Consensus building
  in change agent leadership, 334–35, 337,
    338–39
  criticisms of, 222, 228–29
  definition of, 225–26, 235
  evaluation of, 222, 238
  guidance for process, 229–31, 238
  importance of, 221, 223–24
  in local governments, 224, 233–34, 275–76
  philosophical difficulties of, 231, 233
  practical difficulties of, 232f, 233–35, 236f
  research areas for, 237–38
  theoretical basis for, 222–23
  unanimity in, 225–26, 227–29, 233
  See also Collaboration; Stakeholders
Conservator leadership. *See* Gardener leadership
Contingency theory, 265
Cooperative relationships. *See* Collaboration;
    Facilitative model
Council-manager government
  cooperation as basis for, 273, 274, 280
  domain size, as related to, 71, 264, 267, 270,
    270t
  facilitative model in, 91, 224, 272, 274–76,
    275f, 280
  political/administrative dichotomy in, 73,
    81–82, 271–72, 273f, 276–80

Council-manager government *(continued)*
  roots of, 71, 269–70, 276
  shifts in, 73, 80, 81–82
  See also City managers
County governments. *See* Local governments
Creativity
  in complex adaptive systems, 143, 144, 146
  in consensus building, 222, 226, 228, 233
  and empowerment, 294, 296
  as leadership skill, 93, 158*t*, 164–65, 166, 168*t*
  ritualistic reform as failure of, 291
  in stewardship, 157
  in transforming leadership, 113
Crisis management
  ad hoc approach to, 60, 61, 211
  administrative leadership in, 47, 60–62, 171
  barriers to, 16, 171, 207–8, 313
  collaboration in, 16, 60–61, 164, 334–35
  as driving changes, 9, 62–63, 154, 155, 243
  information sharing in, 317*t*, 319
  innovation resulting from, 49
  military leadership in, 125
  as public value network, 212
Culture, organizational
  biological principle for, 24
  change agent views on, 37, 44*t*, 45, 325, 340
  in ethical decision making, 345–47, 346*t*, 353, 355
  in gardener approach, 37, 42, 44*t*, 45
  for innovative ideas, 315, 316*t*, 320
  leader-centric, 127
  in leadership/management dichotomy, 120, 121*f*
  mental models, compared to, 256
  in public sector, 223
  as symbolic factor in reform, 290*t*, 292–93, 299–301, 304
  and systems development, 310–11, 310*f*, 312, 313
  in transformational leadership, 110–11, 114*f*, 118*f*, 119
  in transformational stewardship, 172–73*t*, 174–75, 176

Decentralization. *See* Empowerment/ decentralization
Democratic practices
  change agent vs conservator views on, 35, 44*t*, 45, 156–57
  consensus-building contrasted with, 226–27, 229, 233, 235, 237–38
  constraints on, 77, 162
  hierarchical model as linked to, 156–57, 180

Democratic practices *(continued)*
  information technology as facilitating, 84, 90
  and local government, 81, 265, 270
  and political responsiveness, 89, 265
  private-sector emphasis as undermining, 8, 55, 57, 156–57
  in public administration approaches, 115, 116*f*, 117
  public leadership as linked to, 10, 17, 35, 70, 81
  and public value, 188–90, 191, 203, 205–6
  shifts in, 72, 89–90, 96
  spread of, 25, 33
Demographic shifts. *See* Aging of society
Department of Homeland Security (DHS)
  as hierarchical bureaucracy, 207
  ineffectiveness of, 60, 61, 171
  as structural reform, 8, 155, 171
Department of Housing and Urban Development (HUD), 52–53
Department of Transportation (DOT), 52–53
DHS. *See* Department of Homeland Security (DHS)
Direct-level leadership
  emerging view on, 130, 132–34, 132*f*, 134*f*, 135
  supervisors as, 178
  traditional perspectives on, 128–29, 128*f*
DOT (Department of Transportation), 52–53

Edge of chaos, 143, 144–45, 145*f*
Education
  of citizens, 288*f*, 290*t*
  as common good, 189, 193
  mayoral role in, 266, 275*f*
  media role in, 190–91
  military commitment to, 126–27
  revamping of, 30–31, 32–33, 150–51, 256–57
  stability in, 35
  as strategic priority, 350
  See also Learning
Elected representatives. *See* Political leadership
Emergence/Self-organization, 143, 144, 145, 147
Empathy/caring
  in gardener approach, 37
  as leadership behavior, 277
  in transformational stewardship, 158*t*, 159–60, 167*t*
Empowerment/decentralization
  administrative shift towards, 73, 84, 93–94, 95
  change agents as resulting from, 324, 340–41
  in complex adaptive systems, 147
  in consensus-building, 225, 236*f*
  in ethical decision making, 344, 348*t*

Empowerment/decentralization *(continued)*
in facilitative model, 272
in innovative organizations, 93, 316*t*, 318
during Johnson administration, 52–53
management as response to, 355
in military context, 133
for over-authorized senior directors, 332–33
public administration approaches to, 116*f*, 117, 118*f*
in results-oriented reform, 284, 290*t*, 294, 296, 298
and self-organization, 144
in transformational stewardship, 158*t*, 163, 166, 168*t*, 179
See also Stakeholders
English administrators. *See* British administrators
Entrepreneurial leadership. *See* Change agent leadership; Transformational leadership
Environmental factors
city managers, impact on, 277, 278, 279–80
in complex adaptive systems, 143, 146, 148
in complexity theory, 140–41, 142, 142*f*, 151
as driving changes, 5–6, 7, 9–10, 154, 206–8
in educational programs, 256, 257
in ethical decision making, 345–46, 345*t*, 355
in gardener approach, 35, 39–41, 42, 44*t*, 45
in mayoral leadership, 263, 267–69, 275, 280
mental models as changed by, 253–56, 255*f*
mental models as filter for, 248, 250, 250*f*, 251
mental models as representation of, 250–53
in mutual gain regimes, 194, 195–96
networks as response to, 16, 84–85, 243
political leadership as shaping, 58–59, 64
in systems development, 310–11, 310*f*, 312, 313
in traditional organizational theories, 138, 139, 142, 142*f*
in transformational leadership, 108, 110–12
in transforming leadership, 112, 113
uncertainty of, 69–70, 92, 95
See also Aging of society; Globalization; Information technology; Terrorism, war on
Ethical leadership
characteristics of, 347–50, 348*t*, 355
decision making, as influence on, 344, 345–47, 346*t*, 355
media role in, 190
in mutual gain regimes, 195
performance measurements for, 350, 351–52, 355
professional commitment to, xi, 26, 43, 72, 90
public sector standards for, 31–32, 40, 56, 57

Ethical leadership *(continued)*
vs responsiveness, 79, 90, 94
vs self-interest, 31–32, 82, 84
structuring choices in, 353–54, 355
study methodology for, 345–46, 345*t*, 346*t*
transformational leadership as, 111, 159, 167*t*, 206
transforming leadership as, 107, 109, 112
See also Accountability
European administrators
autonomy of, 71–72, 73
increased control over, 78, 85, 89, 93
in shared leadership approach, 94
See also British administrators
Evolutionary fitness, 145–46

Facilitative model
in complexity theory, 146–47
in council-manager government, 91, 224, 272, 274–76, 275*f*, 280
vs individual leadership, 238
in local governments, 223
FEMA (Federal Emergency Management Agency), 60–61, 154, 155, 171

GAO (General Accounting Office), x–xii, 31, 308
Gardener leadership
change as viewed by, 36–39, 41–42, 44*t*, 45
collaborative approach by, 42, 43–44
context as critical to, 35, 39–41, 42, 44*t*, 45
overview, 34
transformational stewards, as compared to, 156–57
General Accounting Office (GAO), x–xii, 31, 308
Globalization
of communications, 25, 29, 130
contextual trends related to, 9–10
military leadership, impact on, 127, 130
as transformational trend, 7–9, 135–36, 179, 208
See also Information technology; Terrorism, war on
Goals. *See entries under Mission*
Graying of society, xii, 9, 155, 195–96, 197–99*t*
Great Society programs, 49, 52–53, 61

Hierarchical model
accountability in, 156–57, 180
in military context, 127, 130, 132
networks in, 16, 211, 217, 243–44

Hierarchical model *(continued)*
  pedagogy as focused on, 256–57
  political/administrative relationships in,
    74–75, 243, 244, 245–46
  as rule-bound, 243, 244, 245–46, 248
  shift away from, 17–18, 42, 207–8, 223
  strategic planning in, 286–87, 289
  See also Command and control model
Homeland Security Act, 80
  See also Department of Homeland Security
    (DHS)
Horizontal model. *See* Network governance
HUD (Department of Housing and Urban
  Development), 52–53

Information technology
  in balanced scorecard, 302
  citizen engagement, as facilitating, 81, 84, 90
  as driver of change, 7, 8, 26, 29, 135
  See also IT project implementation
Innovation. *See* Change agent leadership;
    Creativity; Transformational leadership
IRS (Internal Revenue Service), 308, 311,
  320–21
IT project implementation
  approaches towards, 315, 316–17*t*, 318–20
  challenges of, 311–14, 320, 321
  size/complexity of, 309–11, 310*f*, 320
  as trend in public sector, 308–9, 310, 320
  See also Information technology

Johnson administration, 49, 52–53, 61

Lateral relationships. *See* Network governance
Leadership/management dichotomy
  in ethical decision making, 355
  in leadership theories, 106–8, 110
  in local governments, 263, 264, 269, 276–80
  and mental models, 244, 246, 248, 256–57
  in military context, 355–56
  politics/administration dichotomy compared
    to, 120–22, 121*f*
Learning
  as 24/7 convenience system, 30–31, 32–33
  barriers to, 309, 311, 313, 317*t*
  in complex adaptive systems, 141*t*, 143, 148
  consensus building, role in, 226, 227–28, 229,
    237
  gardener approach to, 40, 41
  and mental models, 248–49, 251–52, 253–56
  military commitment to, 126–27
  promotion of, 316*t*, 317*t*, 318, 319

Learning *(continued)*
  in transformational stewardship, 158*t*, 159,
    165, 167*t*, 176
  See also Education
Local governments
  case studies
    managed networks, 214–15, 215*f*
    results-oriented human resources, 294–96
    results-oriented political frame, 296–99
    results-oriented structural frame, 301–4
    results-oriented symbolic frame, 299–301
  citizen engagement in, 80, 81, 84
  consensus building in, 224, 233–34, 275–76
  in England, 80, 86
  ethical decision making in, 345–46, 345*t*
  historical shifts in, 71, 73, 80–82
  management in, 263, 264, 269, 276–80
  performance measurement for, 80–82, 265–66,
    284, 285–86, 286*t*
  in public value networks case studies, 214–15,
    215*f*
  separation model in, 270, 271, 273–74, 280
  shared-power model in, 91, 223, 272, 280
  See also Council-manager government;
    Mayoral leadership
Loyalty
  American emphasis on, 70, 79–80
  as constraint, 87, 90, 93
  of political appointees, 52
  political demands for, 79–80, 89, 90, 96
  to public mission, 76, 79, 90, 93, 161

Management
  complexity as focus of, 106, 156, 277, 355
  ethical decision making by, 344, 345–47, 346*t*,
    355
  in local governments, 263, 264, 269, 276–80
  and mental models, 244, 246, 248, 256–57
  in military context, 355–56
  military influence on, 126
  principal-agent relationship in, 243, 244,
    245–46, 248
  technologies in, 120–22, 121*f*
  transactional leadership as linked to, 107–8,
    110, 117, 246, 248
  See also Administrative leadership; City
    managers; Supervisors
Managing for Results. *See* Performance
    measurement; Strategic planning
Markets, private
  as driving changes, 7, 8, 25, 135, 155
  government corrections of, 26, 189

Markets, private *(continued)*
   public administration, as offsetting, 82
   and public value, 8, 186–87, 191, 192*f*,
      193–94
   and public value networks, 211–13
   See also Private-sector practices
Marshall, George, 48, 49, 129–30
Mayoral leadership
   in consensus building, 224, 233–34
   in council-manager form, 73, 267, 271–72,
      274, 279
   environment as critical to, 263, 267–69, 275,
      280
   facilitative model for, 91, 224, 272, 274–76,
      275*f*, 280
   in mayor-council form, 264–69, 270, 272,
      273–74
   shifts in role of, 71, 73, 80–81
Mayor-council government
   administrative leadership in, 73, 269, 270
   council, role of, 276
   domain size, as related to, 264, 267
   mayoral role in, 264–69, 270, 272, 273–74
   separation of powers in, 270, 271, 273–74,
      280
Media
   communication as facilitated by, 81, 94, 266
   as constraint, 312
   failures of, 190–91, 194
   military, impact on, 130, 131, 132
   political management of, 89
   in public value case study, 196, 197–99*t*, 200
   public value created by, 186, 190, 200
Mental models
   composition of, 249*f*, 250–53
   definition of, 244, 248–50, 250*f*
   networks, as tools in, 243–46, 252, 253,
      256–58
   rigidity of, 253–56, 255*f*
   transforming, 245, 246–48, 251–52
Military leadership
   administrators, compared to, 62, 355–56
   leadership/management dichotomy in, 355–56
   levels as overlapping in, 130, 132–34, 132*f*,
      134*f*, 135
   levels in traditional view, 127–30, 128*f*, 132*f*
   mission of, 31, 125–26
   public/private-sectors, compared to, 125, 126,
      135–36
   Steel Tigers example of, 131–32
   as transformational stewards, 164, 166, 170,
      179

Mission-driven
   change agents as, 329
   ethical decision making as, 348–49, 348*t*
   and innovation, 93
   performance measurements, 204*f*, 304
   vs political responsiveness, 79, 90
   public value networks as, 209, 210, 211–13
   vs self-interest, 31–32, 82, 84
   transformational leadership as, 110–11, 139
   transformational stewardship as, 157, 158*t*,
      161–62, 167*t*
   as value commitment, 55–56, 57–58, 76, 90
   See also Common purpose; Vision,
      organizational
Mission-setting
   in consensus building, 224
   in council-manager form, 73, 272, 273*f*
   as evolving process, 125–26, 155, 161–62
   in hierarchical model, 286–87, 289
   in mayoral leadership, 267, 268, 273–74, 280
Moral leadership. *See* Accountability; Ethical
      leadership
Mutual gain
   definition of, 185
   as driver of change, 25
   in ethical decision making, 351
   examples of, 185–86
   leadership tasks for, 194–96, 200–201
   transformational stewardship approach to,
      172*t*, 174–75
   in vital aging case study, 196, 197–99*t*, 200

NASA (National Aeronautics and Space
      Administration), 154, 171, 213
Natural disasters. *See* Crisis management
Network governance
   administrators in, 84–86, 88, 92, 95–96
   case studies on, 214–17, 215*f*
   citizen engagement, as linked to, 84, 89–90,
      92, 95
   and consensus building, 223, 224
   contextual factors, as response to, 7–10, 16,
      84–85, 243
   and ethical decision making, 344
   gardener approach to, 42, 43–44
   in hierarchies, 16, 211, 217, 243–44
   mayoral leadership for, 224, 267, 268
   mental models as tools for, 243–46, 252, 253,
      256–58
   in military context, 127, 134
   in mutual gain regimes, 196
   and public value, 16, 18, 208–12, 213–14, 217

Network governance *(continued)*
 shift towards, 7, 9–10, 17–18, 180, 245
 types of, 210–11, 213
 See also Collaboration
New Federalism, 49, 53, 64
New governance concept, 3, 6, 17, 72, 200
New Public Administration, 72, 115, 116*f*, 118*f*
New Public Management (NPM)
 conservator view contrasted with, 117, 156, 157
 correctives to, 10, 161
 factors contributing to, 72, 83
 features of, 115, 116*f*, 117, 118*f*, 292
 performance measurement in, 8, 83–84, 87, 115
 as reform movement, 8–9, 72, 157, 207
New Public Service, 17, 116*f*, 117, 118*f*, 223–24
Nixon administration
 administrators, use of, 53, 61, 64, 79
 innovations under, 49, 53
Nonprofit organizations
 challenges for, 179–80
 consensus building by, 231
 government sector as compared to, 115, 119–20
 in horizontal relationships, 155, 164, 168*t*, 180
 in presidential transitions, 63, 64–65
 public value, contributions to, 187–88, 192*f*, 193–94, 196
 in public value networks, 211, 212, 215, 216
 in vital aging case study, 196, 197–99*t*, 200
Norms. *See* Mental models; Values/norms
NPM. *See* New Public Management (NPM)

Office of Management and Budget (OMB), 53, 58, 59, 61
Organizational leadership
 definition of, 4
 in military context, 128*f*, 129, 132*f*, 134, 134*f*
 in mutual gain regimes, 194
 as public leadership, 5

Partnerships. *See* Collaboration; Facilitative model
Performance measurement
 authentic vs false implementation of, 284–85, 287–91, 288*f*, 290*t*
 balanced scorecard as, 162, 203–4, 204*f*, 302–3
 for change agent leadership, 339–40
 for ethical decision making, 350, 351–52, 355
 four-framed approach for, 291–93, 304, 305–6
 in local governments, 80–82, 265–66, 284, 285–86, 286*t*
 New Public Management, as focus of, 8, 83–84, 87, 115
 political responsiveness, as linked to, 79, 87

Performance measurement *(continued)*
 reform-oriented case studies
  human resources frame, 294–96
  political frame, 296–99
  structural frame, 301–4
  symbolic frame, 299–301
 reforms, as focus of, 8, 92–93, 95, 155
 in transformational leadership, 110–11, 162, 168*t*, 170
 types of, x, 285–86, 286*t*
Planning. *See* Strategic planning
Political leadership
 accountability of, 50, 51, 55
 administrators, interactions with
  complementarity between, 75–76, 77, 86–89, 94
  complementarity in values, 76, 88–92, 94
  historical perspectives on, 70–73, 95
  management/leadership, compared to, 120–22, 121*f*
  models for, 73–77, 83, 92, 114–17, 116*f*
  teamwork, 53–55, 61, 87–88, 91–92, 327
 assertion of control by, 49–52, 78–81, 82–84, 85, 95–96
 consensus-building role of, 233–34
 in mutual gain regimes, 194
 and presidential management, 50, 59, 60, 79–80
 as public leadership, 3, 4, 5
 review needed for, 64–65
 short-term horizon of, 129, 156, 177
 as visionary, 88, 91, 330
 See also Mayoral leadership; Presidential leadership
Power
 of administrators, 71–73, 76–77, 85–86, 96
 in consensus building, 225–27, 229, 230, 233–35, 237–38
 gardener approach to, 39, 42
 in leadership concept, 4, 5, 17–18
 in local governments
  separation model, 270, 271, 273–74, 280
  shared model, 91, 223, 272, 280
 in mutual gain regimes, 185, 200–201
 political assertion of, 49–52, 78–81, 82–84, 85, 95–96
 in results-oriented reform, 289, 292, 296–99
 in transactional leadership, 107, 108, 109
 in transformational stewardship, 158*t*, 163–64, 168*t*
Presidential leadership
 administrators as facilitating, 48–49, 53–54, 55, 58–60

Presidential leadership *(continued)*
  British politicians compared to, 78
  for natural disasters, 60–62
  political appointees under, 50, 59, 60, 79–80
  transitions in, 62, 63–65
  See also individual presidents
Private-sector practices
  career leadership, as undermining, 55–58, 82
  change agents as linked to, 34, 35, 36
  gardener approach to, 42–43
  military compared to, 125, 126, 135–36
  New Public Management, as focus of, 115,
    116*f*, 118*f*, 157
  reforms, as focus of, 8, 10, 155, 157
  risk, perception of, 156, 309, 312, 313
  See also Markets, private
Public, the. *See* Citizen engagement
Public interest
  and administrative autonomy, 43, 77, 90, 94
  in ethical decision making, 90, 94, 346, 346*t*
  in holistic reform, 285
  in New Public Service, 117, 118*f*, 224
  open process for, 162
  as professional commitment, 72, 90, 161
  public schools as serving, 193
  vs self-interest, 82, 84
  stakeholders in, 161, 163, 234
  See also Citizen engagement; Consensus
    building; Public value
Public Law/traditional approach, 115, 116*f*, 117,
  118*f*
Public value
  balanced scorecard approach to, 203–4, 204*f*
  case studies
    managed networks, 214–17, 215*f*
    mutual gain regimes, 196, 197–99*t*, 200
  and communities, 191, 192*f*, 193–94
  definition of, 186, 209–12
  and governments, 188–90, 192*f*, 193–94
  leadership as creating, 5, 185, 204–6, 207–8, 214
  and markets, 8, 186–87, 191, 192*f*, 193–94
  and media, 186, 190–91, 194, 200
  and network governance, 16, 18, 208–12,
    213–14, 217
  and nonprofit organizations, 187–88, 192*f*,
    193–94, 196
Public-sector leadership. *See* Administrative
  leadership

Reagan administration
  administrators, use of, 78, 79, 207
  leadership vision under, 27–28

Reagan administration *(continued)*
  transition team for, 63
Results-oriented management. *See* Performance
  measurement; Strategic planning
Rules. *See* Mental models

Self-awareness
  in change agent leadership, 29, 93
  in complex adaptive systems, 148, 150
  in gardener approach, 38–39
  in mutual gain regimes, 194, 195
  in transformational stewardship, 159, 167*t*
Self-organization/Emergence, 143, 144, 145, 147
SMEs. *See* Subject matter experts (SMEs)
Stakeholders
  autonomy of, 228, 229, 230–31, 233–34
  change agent approach to, 35–36, 44*t*, 45,
    328, 334
  as driving changes, 155, 156
  in ethical decision making, 349, 350, 351, 355
  gardener approach to, 40, 41–42, 43–44, 44*t*,
    45
  in large-scale IT projects, 311, 312, 314, 319
  leaders as, 234–35, 237
  in mutual gain regimes, 196, 197–99*t*, 200
  public interest, as representing, 161, 163, 234
  public sector as constrained by, 55–58, 156,
    312
  as risk factor in change, 169, 169*f*
  strategic planning, involvement in, xi, 173*t*,
    175, 287
  transformational stewardship approach to,
    157, 161, 172–73*t*, 174–76
  unanimity standard for, 225–26, 227–29, 233
  See also Citizen engagement
Strategic leadership
  emerging views on, 132–34, 132*f*, 134*f*
  traditional perspectives on, 128*f*, 129–30, 132*f*
Strategic planning
  authentic vs false implementation of, 284–85,
    287–91, 288*f*, 290*t*
  case studies
    human resources frame, 294–96
    political frame, 296–99
    public value, 196, 197–99*t*, 200
    structural frame, 301–4
    symbolic frame, 299–301
  by change agent leadership, 44*t*, 45, 326–27
  complexity theory on, 146
  four-framed approach for, 291–93, 304, 305–6
  gardener approach to, 37, 39, 44*t*, 45
  by military leadership, 129

Strategic planning *(continued)*
  stakeholder involvement in, xi, 173*t*, 175, 287
  by transformational stewards, 157, 172–73*t*,
    174–76
  types of, x, 286–87
Subject matter experts (SMEs), 330, 331*f*,
  335–36, 336*t*, 337*f*
Supervisors
  council members as, 276
  ethical decision making by, 346, 348*t*
  in hierarchical model, 243, 244, 245–46
  transformational stewards as, 176, 178–79
Systems thinking, 165–66, 168*t*

Tactical-level leadership. *See* Direct-level
  leadership
Teamwork. *See* Collaboration
Terrorism, war on
  administrative leadership in, 61–62
  change agent leadership in, 324–25, 340–41
  as global trend, 9, 208
  military leadership in, 127, 130
  and organizational reforms, 26–27, 31–32,
    154, 207, 208
  public value networks in, 212
Thatcher administration, 78, 207
Trait theory of leadership, 158, 265
Transactional leadership
  and administrative approaches, 110, 117, 118,
    118*f*
  features of, 109–10, 114*f*
  management, as linked to, 107–8, 110, 117,
    246, 248
  mayor-council form as, 270
  mental models, use of, 246, 248, 257
  pedagogy as focused on, 256
  public value of, 205, 206
  transformational leadership, compared to, 108,
    109, 139, 214
  transforming leadership, compared to, 109, 113
Transformational leadership
  and administrative approaches, 17, 111–12,
    118*f*, 119, 177–79
  change agents types, interactions with, 331*f*,
    333, 334*t*, 335, 336
  as change-centric, 28–32, 158*t*, 164–66, 168*t*,
    170
  council-manager form as, 270
  features of, 110–12, 114*f*
  innerpersonal beliefs/traits, 158–60, 158*t*, 167*t*
  interpersonal abilities, 158*t*, 162–64, 168*t*,
    178–79

Transformational leadership *(continued)*
  mayoral leadership as, 266, 268, 269
  mental models, use of, 246, 248, 257
  need for, 154, 155–56, 179–80
  operational mind-set, 27–28, 158*t*, 160–62,
    167–68*t*
  public value of, 205–6
  risk management approach for, 166, 169–71,
    169*f*, 172–73*t*, 174–76
  and stewardship, 154, 156–58, 180
  transactional leadership, compared to, 108,
    109, 139, 214
  transforming leadership, compared to, 107,
    108, 109, 113
  in war on terror, 330–32, 331*f*, 332*t*
  See also Change agent leadership
Transforming leadership
  and administrative approaches, 113–14, 118*f*,
    119
  features of, 112–14, 114*f*
  transformational leadership, compared to, 107,
    108, 109, 113
Transparency. *See* Accountability

United Kingdom. *See* British administrators
United States
  challenges for, 25, 26–27, 30–31, 32–33
  policy intervention theory in, 191, 192*f*,
    193–94
  post-1950s trends in, 78, 79–81, 82–83
  preoccupation with innovation, 48
  public administration formation in, 70, 71–72,
    73
U.S. Coast Guard, 164, 166, 170

Value networks. *See* Public value
Values/norms
  and administrative autonomy, 43, 77, 86, 90,
    94
  change agent approach to, 34–35, 37, 44*t*, 45
  complementarity model for, 76, 88–92, 94
  in consensus building, 231, 234
  in ethical decision making, 346, 346*t*, 351,
    352, 355
  gardener approach to, 37, 40–42, 44*t*, 45
  in hierarchical relationships, 74–75, 243, 244,
    245–46
  mental models as framework for, 243, 244,
    246–48, 254–55
  professional commitment to, xi, 26, 43, 72, 90
  in results-oriented reform, 292–93, 297,
    299–301

Values/norms *(continued)*
  in transactional leadership, 108, 109–10, 118*f*
  in transformational leadership, 110, 111, 118*f*,
    206
  in transforming leadership, 109, 112, 113,
    118*f*
  vision, alignment with, 317*t*, 318–19
Vertical model. *See* Command and control
    model; Hierarchical model
Vision, organizational
  balanced scorecard as measurement of, 204*f*
  in change agent leadership, 36, 44*t*, 45,
    325–26, 340
  decision making, as guidance for, 346, 346*t*,
    347
  in ethical leadership, 344, 348, 348*t*

functional mavens, role of, 335–36, 336*f*
  in gardener approach, 40–41, 44*t*, 45
  in large-scale IT projects, 317*t*, 318–19
  in local governments, 91, 277, 278
  in military leadership, 129
  in mutual gain regimes, 194
  and political leadership, 50, 88, 91, 330
  in results-oriented reform, 292–93, 295, 296,
    299–301
  in transformational leadership, 27–28, 110–11,
    330–32, 332*t*
  in transformational stewardship, 160, 167*t*, 177
  See also Common purpose; *entries under
    Mission*

War on Terror. *See* Terrorism, war on